Dear Juliette

Letters of May Sarton to Juliette Huxley

Poetry

Encounter in April
Inner Landscape
The Lion and the Rose
The Leaves of the Tree
The Land of Silence
In Time Like Air
Cloud, Stone, Sun, Vine
A Private Mythology
As Does New Hampshire
A Grain of Mustard Seed
A Durable Fire
Collected Poems, 1930–1973
Selected Poems of May Sarton
(edited by Serena Sue Hilsinger and Lois Brynes)
Halfway to Silence
Letters from Maine
The Silence Now
Collected Poems, 1930–1993
Coming into Eighty

Novels

The Single Hound
The Bridge of Years
Shadow of a Man
A Shower of Summer Days
Faithful Are the Wounds
The Birth of a Grandfather
The Fur Person
The Small Room
Joanna and Ulysses
Mrs. Stevens Hears the Mermaids Singing
Miss Pickthorn and Mr. Hare
The Poet and the Donkey
Kinds of Love
As We Are Now
Crucial Conversations

A Reckoning
Anger
The Magnificent Spinster
The Education of Harriet Hatfield

Nonfiction

I Knew a Phoenix
Plant Dreaming Deep
Journal of a Solitude
A World of Light
The House by the Sea
Recovering: A Journal
At Seventy: A Journal
After the Stroke: A Journal
Writings on Writing
May Sarton: A Self-Portrait
(script of "World of Light," film by
Martha Wheelock and Marita Simpson)
Letters to May by Eleanor Mabel Sarton
(selected, edited, and with an introduction by May Sarton)
Honey in the Hive
Endgame: A Journal of the Seventy-Ninth Year
Among the Usual Days: A Portrait
(edited by Susan Sherman)
Encore: A Journal of the Eightieth Year
At Eighty-Two: A Journal
May Sarton: Selected Letters 1916–1954
(edited and introduced by Susan Sherman)

For Children

Punch's Secret
A Walk Through the Woods

Selected, Edited, and Introduced by

Susan Sherman

Foreword by

Francis Huxley

Drafts of Introductions by

May Sarton

Dear Juliette

Letters of May Sarton to Juliette Huxley

W. W. Norton & Company

New York / London

For information about permission to reproduce selections from this book,
write to Permissions, W. W. Norton & Company, Inc.,
500 Fifth Avenue, New York, NY 10110

The text of this book is composed in Bembo
with the display set in Bembo
Desktop composition by Gina Webster
Manufacturing by The Maple-Vail Book Manufacturing Group
Book design by JAM Design

Library of Congress Cataloging-in-Publication Data

Sarton, May, 1912–1995
Dear Juliette : letters of May Sarton to Juliette Huxley /
selected, edited, and introduced by Susan Sherman ; foreword by
Francis Huxley ; drafts of introductions by May Sarton.
        p.   cm.
Includes bibliographical references and index.
ISBN 0-393-04733-4
1. Sarton, May, 1912–95—Correspondence. 2. Women authors,
American—20th century—Correspondence. 3. Huxley, Juliette, 1896–
—Correspondence. I. Huxley, Juliette, 1896– . II. Sherman,
Susan. III. Title.
PS3537.A832Z483   1999
811'.52—dc21
[b]   98-49482
                        CIP

W. W. Norton & Company, Inc., 500 Fifth Avenue, New York, N.Y. 10110
www.wwnorton.com

W. W. Norton & Company Ltd., 10 Coptic Street, London WC1A 1PU

1 2 3 4 5 6 7 8 9 0

for
MAY SARTON
in memoriam, world without end

for
MY MOTHER
in memoriam
and MY FATHER,
valiant survivor

and for
POLLY THAYER STARR
and
BILL BROWN

who have loved and understood May longer and better than anyone else now alive. Their steadfast and brilliant friendships, woven into the years and atmosphere surrounding every letter in this volume, are as indispensable to me now as they were to her then.

You have made me experience, dear Juliette, something that is quite new to me: a friendship which fills my imagination and spreads over my life an interest which one other sentiment alone has inspired in me. This year especially there was something angelic about you; that charm which deigned to concentrate on me moved my soul, and I felt cut off from some heavenly influence when you disappeared.

> —Mme. de Staël to Mme. Récamier
> October 1807

Please, in all this muddle of life, continue to be a bright and constant star. Just a few things remain as beacons: poetry, and you, and solitude.

> —Vita Sackville-West to Virginia Woolf
> 8 January 1926

You really became poetry to me and that was your greatest gift. As I tried to tell you once, this has happened to me before, perhaps twice before, but never where there was any fulfillment. What such a fulfillment might be came as a complete revelation. Whatever you do in your life you did this for me and I can never never tell you what it meant.

> —May Sarton to Juliette Huxley
> 15 August 1948

Your letters are there to cull, and they are gold treasures.

> —Juliette Huxley to May Sarton
> 9 September 1986

Contents

Foreword by Francis Huxley

I am looking at this not very good photograph of May Sarton and my father, Julian Huxley, taken by my mother, Juliette, sometime in the thirties. I don't remember the occasion—very likely I was at school—but May's hairdo is unforgettable. I remember it—I was a little shy of her—from the lively weekends she spent with the family at Whipsnade. In these letters I read what was afoot between her and my parents at the time, and here too I find that May was to praise one of my young poems—what a compliment.

What more can I say? I recognise the scene of the photo well enough. Julian was then the Secretary of the London Zoo, and the family lived in a flat over the offices: he and May are on the balcony of this flat, where my brother Anthony raised cacti. (Some of them are in that dish on the windowsill.) I also recognise the settee May and Julian are sitting on—Juliette had got it, she once told me, from Lady Ottoline Morrell, in whose house at Garsington she had lived, some twenty years earlier, as governess to Lady Ottoline's daughter.

There, at Garsington, Juliette learnt to admire Lady Ottoline with all her heart, and met that strange and wonderful assortment of people known as the Bloomsbury set, whose behaviour she sometimes thought question-

May's hairdo . . . unforgettable: See photo in this volume. Sarton was often uncomfortable with her European permanents; see letter of 16 April 1948.

Whipsnade: An open zoo on the Bedfordshire Downs where the Julian Huxleys kept an apartment in a building eight hundred feet above the downs overlooking its five hundred acres and where they spent most weekends.

Lady Ottoline Morrell: Lady Ottoline Violet Anne Morrell (1873–1938) *née* Cavendish-Bentinck, flamboyant literary and political hostess known for championing the unconventional in music, art, politics, and books; known also for her affairs with Axel Munthe, Augustus John, Henry Lamb, and Bertrand Russell. In 1913 she and her husband, Philip Edward Morrell (1870–1943), bought Garsington Manor, which became a liberal, cultural retreat house for every prominent figure in the worlds of politics and the arts: her guests included Winston Churchill, Prime Minister Herbert Asquith, Clive and Vanessa Bell, Duncan Grant, David Garnett, Virginia and Leonard Woolf, T. S. Eliot, D. H. Lawrence, Lytton Strachey, W. B. Yeats, Katherine Mansfield, Siegfried Sassoon, and Julian and Aldous Huxley.

able. One summer evening, for instance, the house-guests had taken the gramophone outside and were dancing on the lawn. Soon Juliette returned to the drawing room with its silken Chinese-yellow curtains, where she told Lady Ottoline she would retire for the night. Why? Because *les messieurs* have taken off their jackets and are dancing in their shirt-sleeves and braces; *ce n'est pas convenable*, it's not proper.

Juliette came from Switzerland, and her mother, who ran a pension for girls in Neuchâtel, would have been the first to agree—the more so in that Juliette was later to be plunged into situations seriously inappropriate for a girl of her upbringing, as a consequence of being at Garsington at all. For in that dream of a house she was befriended by both Aldous and Julian Huxley, and while Aldous contented himself with talking to her about poetry, her own included (I think he had already been smitten by Maria Nys, whom he later married: she had left Belgium—this was in the days of the Great War—to find shelter at Garsington), his older brother Julian was shortly to present her with a copy of his first book, *The Individual in the Animal Kingdom,* inscribed: "To JB, to improve her mind." (He wrote poems too, of course.) Not much later, he insisted she marry him. JB—B is for Baillot, her maiden name—put up some resistance because, in the words of Katherine Fordham, to whom he had once been engaged, he was really unmarriageable; Julian, however, wouldn't take no for an answer: Anthony was born in 1920, and I in 1923. By 1929 Julian had found that married life did nothing to inspire his genius, and following the example of H. G. Wells, with whom he was writing *The Science of Life,* he sought to rekindle it by pursuing a young American girl to the United States ("I shall conquer you with my mind," he had promised her) and very nearly did not return.

Juliette took this infidelity very hard, and though Julian did return—he realised how much he needed her as a home base—he announced that he also needed further affairs to keep going, and encouraged her to find lovers of her own. She eventually followed this improper advice in spite of her Swiss nature, but when he wrote to her about May Sarton, who inspired his next passion, her answer contained the agonised cry "Must I be made miserable so that you can be happy?"

So it often seemed: and yet the photograph she took of Julian and

young American girl: Viola Ilma. See footnote to letter of 8 August 1987.
her answer contained: See footnote to letter of 8 August 1987.

May, who has her hand on his thigh while he, slouched in his corner of the settee, looks wonderfully pleased with himself as he looks at the camera, shows that she had accommodated herself to the situation. But the situation was to change, for May—whose genius required even more passions to keep going than Julian's—then found that it was Juliette she loved more than Julian, much more, in the end, than anyone else.

Some of this Juliette told me of, and here are May's letters to give life to the rest. May, I see, was as prolific a letter-writer as Julian, but where his could read like contributions to the *Guide Bleu* of his life—the phrase is Juliette's, when she told him what she thought of his memoirs—May's are full of spirit and endearments, subtly intelligent and laded with poems by others as well as herself. Some of her best are inspired by Juliette, and May takes her criticisms gladly—how unlike Julian—and tells her how love informs her mind when she is writing poetry, what it is to write poetry and to love. Here she is wonderful and wise. But in the course of their friendship her letters, once lyrical, become turbulent and excessive, as she does herself. Juliette takes alarm and, when May responds unwisely, cuts her out of her life.

This happens in 1948. Julian dies in 1975, and May sends a letter of condolence, which Juliette promptly answers. More letters come and go: May's are wise again. Juliette has a great deal on her mind now she is a widow, such as why she had to be made miserable so often—though, she would hasten to add, what marvelous travels she had, what people she met!—and she is about to write her autobiography, *Leaves of the Tulip Tree,* to make sense of things. May doesn't figure in it at all—why not? she asks, when at last the book is published.

It's a long story, as you can see, and if May had written it as a novel she would surely have dedicated it to Juliette with a message that at first glance is similar to the one Julian wrote in his first book. I have a good idea of how it would have run, for I was around on May's last visit to Juliette, then ninety-seven years old. Juliette telephoned me one morning: "May's coming to tea this afternoon, will you come too? She *frightens* me." (Her emphasis was mock-heroic.) I went to tea that afternoon, and the next. May telephoned me and told me not to appear on her third visit, because she had much to say to Juliette in private. Two days later she invited me to

---

This happens in 1948: The final letters span the last weeks of 1948 and into 1949.
May doesn't figure in it at all: For Juliette's explanation see footnote to letter of 16 February 1986.

lunch at her hotel, and told me of her joy in having opened Juliette's heart to her once more. Surely, then, her dedication to the novel she never wrote would have run "To Juliette, to open her heart."

There are many ways of improving minds and opening hearts, and I very much wonder how it was that Juliette Baillot, whose fresh mind and heart speak for themselves as clearly in her books and letters as in her sculpture, attracted two such demanding suitors as Julian Huxley and May Sarton. That was Juliette's question, too, and sometimes it looked to her as if her life had been prearranged, had been her fate. Why? What was it all about?

Well she might ask! I confess things often look like that to me also, but while I understand something of her fate and Julian's—I've been a privileged witness, after all—I have known very little about May's till now. Reading these letters gives me a vivid sense of its imaginative charge and, at one remove, of Juliette's emotions when May cast a spell over her in person. What a powerful instrument it must have been, to have Juliette break it and yet for it to be still alive, to both of them, twenty-seven years later! Such a fate is poetic, what more can I say.

Francis Huxley
Santa Fe, New Mexico
November 1997

May Sarton's love for Juliette Huxley, ignited that first moment she saw her in 1936, transcended sixty years of friendship, passion, silence, and reconciliation.

In the extraordinary breadth and variation of these letters, we see Sarton in all her complexities; we are privy to her incisive, critical mind, and to those fascinating questions, unanswerable yet necessary to raise and think about, concerning the tangled relationships between passion, love, physical intimacy, and the creative impulse.

Yet, while Juliette Huxley was the preeminent love of Sarton's life, it is not the insatiable predator in sexual pursuit that we see, but rather a lover, indeed intense, unremitting, and passionate, but a lover pursuing her muse, pursuing poetry. Hers was, I believe, always an impulse toward the muse, toward the larger life of poetry itself, toward a fulfillment which had very little to do with sex. Sarton speaks of this to Louise Bogan: "The drive which is back of two women . . . is . . . an exchange of souls."

It is said that two lovers are incomplete without God as the third, the apex of the triangle. With Sarton it was poetry which became that third element, creating the ultimate communion toward which she yearned; poetry, making the unfulfilled fulfilled. In this, the most seminal love of her life, the most creative and enduring of her passions, there was perhaps one week only of physical intimacy; the love, however, lasted until death.

As muse and "princesse lointaine," Juliette Huxley focused the world for May; she was that unassailable fortress which May could storm but not

"The drive . . . an exchange of souls": For the complete letter of 21 March 1954 to Louise Bogan see *May Sarton: Selected Letters 1916–1954.*

"princesse lointaine": Inaccessible or faraway princess, from the play by Edmond Rostand (1868–1918), *La Princesse Lointaine*, a role made famous by Sarah Bernhardt. In listing her muses, lovers, and influences, Sarton used the term "mal-aimé" for those who had been unloved; "princesse lointaine" she applied to Juliette Huxley, Margaret Clapp, and, with a question mark, Edith Forbes Kennedy.

really possess; rather, May remained, as Rilke said, a bird "circling around the pure refusal of the peaks."

The letters are remarkable for her towering passions for life in all its forms—animals and nature, people and causes, theater and politics, music and art, books of every kind, knowledge itself—remarkable for her ability to respond, giving to every person and every thing in its turn her absolute attention. In that way she was extravagant, although her passions and intensities were often difficult to bear.

Among those passions, certainly, was May's anger, which could be searing; she spoke of it as "soupe au lait," that sudden explosion of boiling milk, and its instant subsiding. For May that is what it was; once expressed, it entirely vanished, and she moved on into a clearer air—until the next time. And it was her hope that the other would move on with her. But that did not always occur; too often May's rages killed something essential in the other she had never intended to touch. For her, anger was a chastener, a purifier, a way toward growth and understanding. Increasingly, however, the truth came home to her that that was not the way it was experienced by others.

Pain in any form, particularly injustice or rejection, served only to rekindle that anger. "Try to imagine just for a second, that bad behavior on my part is always the signal of acute pain—a person who swears when his finger is caught in a door." And so it must have been. The final letters from Juliette before the break in 1949, and later in the seventies, reveal what was clearly May's fierce tenacity when faced with the possibility of losing what she most loved. For it was then, as with her anger, that the threat she never intended to carry out burst forth. Juliette perceived the threat as the ultimate breaking of faith and withdrew.

"pure refusal of the peaks": From Rilke's poem beginning "Abandoned on the mountains of the heart . . ."

absolute attention: Sarton often cited and felt affinities with Simone Weil, who said that "absolute attention is prayer."

"finger is caught in a door": Written to Marion Hamilton, 5 June 1970.

threat she never intended to carry our: In 1976, after the twenty-seven-year silence, Juliette writes: "You see, what happened in Paris left its mark on me—and the last thing I want is to harp back on the final disaster of our relationship. That it was a disaster is not in doubt—for when you threatened to 'tell all to Julian' I really felt betrayed in so absolutely unexpected a way. It is a great pity that memory of this remains so clear in my mind—as I have always felt so much admiration for your courage and your great gifts. And let me add that of course, should you now wonder, I have of course forgiven everything. And understand how you must have been yourself in a sort of no-man's land, where it was impossible to realize reasonably what was happening. But there is memory, which I cannot get rid of."

Sarton suffered profound remorse for her outbursts and demons, as she called them. But "letting feelings out" and "remaining open to the end" was a critical part of what it meant to keep the child alive in her; without those natural instincts open and unguarded, there would have been no poetry. Her anger, untethered and primal, was part of the same passion that, in other forms, let her see what others only looked at and transform all of it into poetry.

I have often imagined May during those twenty-seven years of silence, and wondered what it is that enables some of us to be faithful to love in its absence. Part of the answer, I think, lies in what she said just after we had watched *Les Enfants du Paradis*; after a parturient silence, she declared definitively: "The only pure love is unrequited love." As an indirect gift from the muse, there was something in the absence of resolution, the yearning toward it, that impelled her toward poetry; it is what she means when she says, "What we are not drives us to consummation."

Although as poet she could write "I grow rich on these despairs," nevertheless Juliette's silence had left a hole that nothing else could fill. And that this silence of twenty-seven years was mended in the end speaks not only for Sarton's willing it so, but for Juliette's magnanimity and ultimate capacity of understanding, an understanding which remained among May's truest blessings. Because as brutal as her rages and threats could feel, and as final as some indeed proved to be, the truth is that they really *were* cries of pain, cries for love and acceptance, and for those who knew that, and could move on with her, May was the richest, most grateful and nourishing of friends.

To the end of her life, Juliette never lost her hold on May's love and imagination. After the reconciliation and throughout the last years of illness, planning her next trip to London to see Juliette for tea, even while

Les Enfants du Paradise: Marcel Carné's *Children of Paradise,* considered "the finest work . . . ever composed for the screen," is set in the theater world of early-nineteenth-century Paris. Sarton is referring to the mime Baptiste, in love with poetry and with the courtesan Garance, his failed suicide, and the final scene where he runs, hopelessly crying her name, as her carriage melts into the crowd.

"What we are not . . . consummation": From "Mud Season" in *Cloud, Stone, Sun, Vine.*

"I grow rich on these despairs": See sonnet #18 in "A Divorce of Lovers" in *Cloud, Stone, Sun, Vine.*

Sarton's willing it so: Sarton's tenacity was, in part, a fierce loyalty; she never gave up on friendship or love, no matter what strains or changes it had endured.

cries for love and acceptance: She was often haunted by a phrase of Rilke's: "Perhaps everything terrible in us is in its deepest being something helpless that needs help."

she was aware she might possibly not be well enough to go, was certain balm for May; just as was planning to call Juliette "one of these days," meaning at six in the morning, the best time, lunchtime, for Juliette. But six in the morning was the worst moment of the day for May, and more often than not, at breakfast later, she would admit that despite her intentions, she had not felt up to making the call. "But never mind," she would say, "it's been wonderful *thinking* of doing it."

As for the history of this volume, sometime during the 1980s, May decided to publish her letters to Juliette Huxley; her selection ended with the letter of 1 November 1948. Nancy Hartley, Sarton's longtime secretary and archivist, typed that manuscript and did an exemplary job of footnoting it. Then followed a period of indecision; Juliette had said, "You should publish these," when she had earlier returned them to Sarton, and yet, while roughing out the 1989 notes for her preface, Sarton was struck by the lightning realization that they simply could not be published during Juliette's lifetime. "The problem is partly Julian's fame," she wrote to her editor Eric Swenson. "If this was an obscure married couple with whom I became involved fifty years ago, it would be all right to go ahead. . . . But I am quite sure that it would be wrong to publish now. . . . I am sending them to you because perhaps we could come to some agreement (no money involved) that if you think they are publishable, Norton would agree to publish them later. Juliette is 92."

In 1993 Norton did pay Sarton an advance, and the decision was made to hold the manuscript until Juliette's death. But when news of that death came in the fall of 1994, May was too ill for the sustained effort involved, and her grief once again brought back the old uncertainties; the manuscript, therefore, sat on the couch in her study and we did not discuss it.

In the spring of 1995, having cleaned out the house at 31 Pond Street, Francis Huxley returned to May all the letters she had written to his mother in the years following Julian's death, together with a number from the earlier years which had come to light. He sent them with his hope that she

---

"it's been wonderful thinking of doing it": In the last years when more and more often "thinking of doing" became her way of doing, it was a comfort for her to remember the lines she had written in 1944: "The thinking man will never be alone—He travels where he sits, his heart alight." From "Innumerable Friend" in *The Lion and the Rose*.

Eric Swenson: Eric P. Swenson was Sarton's longtime editor at W. W. Norton; this letter to him is dated 15 August 1989.

would now publish. His encouragement resolved the dilemma for May; I would select and edit the letters and she no longer would worry or be plagued by indecision.

This volume, then, is more comprehensive than the manuscript May and Nancy Hartley had worked on together in the 1980s, including, as it does, many of the letters May had not had access to at that time, and taking the correspondence to its true end; the footnotes draw on other of Sarton's correspondences, as well as letters from Juliette and Julian, all of which had been sent to the Berg Collection in the 1970s and were no longer available in the files at Wild Knoll.

As we see from the fragments of various introductions to this volume she attempted over a period of six years, it was May's intention to let the letters speak for themselves. But by the time she turned the materials over to me in the spring of 1995, she knew this volume merited fuller scope than she had originally intended.

May remained a poet to the end; the year before her death, in 1994, and in the tradition of Yeats, who also changed his form radically in old age, she published an astounding collection of poems in *Coming into Eighty,* a volume which won her the Levinson Prize. In it, as a final gift from the muse who had touched so much of her life for sixty years, is "Lunch in the Garden," the lunch being one she had had the year before in the garden at Pond Street; it ends with "Miracles do happen when you are old."

In September 1994, news of Juliette's death profoundly changed the atmosphere of May's life. Something of its light was extinguished; she who had come to symbolize the archetypical muse, and all that poetry meant, was dead. May lived ten months longer, surrounded by love and care; but with Juliette's death, poetry, and miracles, had ended, and poetry, after all, had been, as she always said, "what God intended me to do."

Susan Sherman
Riverdale, New York
January 1998

Wild Knoll: Sarton's home in York, Maine.
tradition of Yeats: See footnote to letter of 12 March 1939.

Chronology

It was Sarton's custom to set out on lecture tours in the fall and spring of each year; I have recorded only the first such tour, in 1940.

1912 Born 3 May, Wondelgem, Belgium, daughter of George and Eleanor Mabel (Elwes) Sarton.

1915 Immigrates, via England 1914, to Washington, D.C., and later moves to Cambridge, Massachusetts.

1924 Becomes naturalized U.S. citizen. Attends Jean Dominique's Institut Belge de Culture Français, Winter 1924–1925.

1926-29 Graduates from Shady Hill School; enters Cambridge High and Latin School, graduating in 1929. First poems published in *Poetry*. Joins Eva Le Gallienne's Civic Repertory Theatre in NYC.

1929-33 Member of Civic Repertory Theatre as actor, director of Apprentice Theatre.

1933-35 Forms Associated Actors Theatre, which fails in 1935.

1936 Decides to pursue writing career. Spends April–August in England and Europe, meeting the Huxleys for the first time.

1937 *Encounter in April* (poems). Spends April–September in Europe, meeting V. Woolf, Elizabeth Bowen, S. S. Koteliansky.

1938 *The Single Hound*, her first novel. Spends April–July in Europe meeting Grace Dudley and Lugné-Poë. Begins teaching at the Stuart School (leaves in 1942).

1939 *Inner Landscape* (poems). Spends June–August in Europe; meets Bill Brown.

1940-41 Begins first lecture tour through South and Southwest, wintering in Santa Fe, New Mexico, and continuing through Midwest the following spring. Virginia Woolf's suicide. Death of Lugné-Poë.

1942 Teaches at the Stuart School. Difficulty finding jobs; suffers nervous exhaustion. Extensive lecture trip in fall. Takes first aid course and works for Red Cross. Writes "Book of Martyrs," poems, unpublished. Death of Edith Forbes Kennedy.

1943 Various residences in NYC, including Muriel Rukeyser's apartment. Works for Pearl Buck's East & West and Office of War Information

(OWI). Launches New York Public Library's "The Poet Speaks" readings.

1944 Returns to Channing Place, Cambridge, which parents have bought after years of renting.

1945 Spends April–July in Santa Fe; meets Judith Matlack. Resides with her at 39 Oxford Street, Cambridge, from November on.

1946 *The Bridge of Years* (novel). Poet-in-Residence, State Teachers College of Southern Illinois at Carbondale. Sells first story to *Collier's*.

1947 *The Underground River* (play). Spends April–July in Europe and meets Brancusi, Malraux, and Spender while staying with the Huxleys in Paris; meets Ruth Pitter while in England.

1948 *The Lion and the Rose* (poems). Spends April–September in Europe meeting Sitwells, Auden, Freya Stark.

1949 Spends March–August in Europe meeting Eugénie DuBois.

1950 *The Leaves of the Trees* (poems) and *Shadow of a Man* (novel). Moves to Maynard Place with Judith Matlack; Elizabeth Bowen visits them. Bread Loaf Writers' Conference. Teaches at Radcliffe (until 1953). Deaths of Grace Eliot Dudley and Eleanor Mabel Sarton.

1951 Spends June–August in Europe; lives with Meta Budry and Mark Turian in Switzerland in July.

1952 *A Shower of Summer Days* (novel). Moves to 14 Wright Street with Judith Matlack (September). Death of Jean Dominique.

1953 *The Land of Silence* (poems). Meets Louise Bogan. CBS interview. Bread Loaf Writers' Conference.

1954 Spends August–November in Europe; meets Janet Flanner, Leonard Woolf. Travels in Italy with Eugénie DuBois.

1955 *Faithful Are the Wounds* (novel). Elizabeth Bowen visits from England. Guggenheim Fellowship. Lyric's Tidewater Prize. Death of S. S. Koteliansky.

1956 *The Fur Person* (novella). Lamont Poetry Contest judge. Lyric Prize for "Lady with a Falcon." Teaches at Radcliffe College (until 1958). Deaths of George Sarton; Dorothy Wellesley, Duchess of Wellington; Alice and Haniel Long. Sale of 5 Channing Place.

1957 *The Birth of a Grandfather* (novel). In Europe sees Elizabeth Bowen, Eddie Sackville-West, Michael Campbell, Anthony Huxley, Sybille Bedford, etc. Judith Matlack enters analysis. Deaths of Francesca Greene and "Tom Jones."

1958 *In Time Like Air* (poems). Finds Nelson house in May; signs papers in June; moves in in October. Nominated for National Book Award in two categories, poetry and novels. Teaches at Radcliffe College. Céline Limbosch visits Nelson. Lyric Prize for "Minting Time." Phi Beta Kappa visiting scholar.

1959 *I Knew a Phoenix* (memoir) and *The Writing of a Poem* (monograph). Consults analysts Volta Hall and Kitty de Forest. Death of Meta Budry Turian.

1960 PEN Writers Congress in Brazil; visits Elizabeth Bishop. Teaches at Wellesley College (through 1964).

1961 *The Small Room* (novel), *Cloud, Sun, Stone, Vine* (poems). Begins *The Music Box Bird* (play). Signs with W. W. Norton for *The Small Room*. Death of Albert "Quig" Quigley.

1962 *The School of Babylon* (monograph). Finishes play *The Music Box Bird*. Death of Dr. Volta Hall. Fiftieth-birthday trip around the world.

1963 *Joanna and Ulysses* (fable) and *The Design of a Novel* (monograph).

1964 Wellesley College contract not renewed. Judith Matlack retires.

1965 *Mrs. Stevens Hears the Mermaids Singing* (novel). September–December, Poet-in-Residence, Lindenwood College, St. Charles, Missouri. Eleanor Blair's first trip to Nelson.

1966 *A Private Mythology* (poems), *Miss Pickthorn and Mr. Hare* (fable), series of articles for *Woman's Day* and *Christian Science Monitor*. The Shipley School in Bryn Mawr cancels lectureship. Cuts hair extremely short. Since 1958 has been dividing time between Nelson and 14 Wright Street; as of June, moves permanently to Nelson. Deaths of Katharine Davis, Katrine Greene, Basil de Sélincourt, Mary Bouton.

1967 *As Does New Hampshire* (poems). Death of Mark Howe.

1968 *Plant Dreaming Deep* (memoir). Borrows donkey, Esmeralda, in June. Writes series of articles for *Family Circle*. Perley Cole in nursing home, genesis of *As We Are Now*.

1969 *The Poet and the Donkey* (fable). Articles for *Family Circle*. Bill Brown buys house in nearby Dublin, New Hampshire. Begins *Kinds of Love*. Death of Jay de Sélincourt.

1970 *Kinds of Love* (novel). First correspondence with Carolyn G. Heilbrun. Begins *Journal of a Solitude*. Deaths of Perley Cole and Louise Bogan.

1971 *A Grain of Mustard Seed* (poems). Death of Punch, the parrot. First visit of Carolyn G. Heilbrun. Hears of Wild Knoll, the house in York, Maine, from Mary-Leigh Smart and Beverly Hallam; visits it in April, and twice in August. Judith Matlack's memory begins to fail. Litter of kittens including Bramble and Bel-Gazou born.

1972 *A Durable Fire* (poems). Nelson house goes on the market. Tamas, the Shetland sheepdog, arrives. Judith Matlack, after an operation for a ruptured appendix, enters a nursing home.

1973 *Journal of a Solitude* (journal), *As We Are Now* (novel). Moves from Nelson to York, Maine. Interviewed by Barbara Walters on *The Today Show*. Deaths of Elizabeth Bowen and Conrad Aiken.

1974 *Collected Poems (1930–1973)*, *Punch's Secret* (children's book). In Europe sees the Huxleys. Scrabble, the cat, put to sleep.

1975 *Crucial Conversations* (novel). Working on *A World of Light*. Juliette Huxley comes to New York. Deaths of Helen Howe Allen, Céline Limbosch, Julian Huxley, Rosalind Greene.

1976 *A World of Light* (memoirs), *A Walk Through the Woods* (children's book). Closing of the Wright Street house.

1977 *The House by the Sea* (journal). Appears on *Good Morning America*. In Europe sees Juliette Huxley alone for the first time since 1948. Death of Anne Thorp.

1978 *A Reckoning* (novel). *Selected Poems*, ed. by Hilsinger and Brynes.

1979 Filmings of *World of Light,* made by Martha Wheelock and Marita Simpson, and *She Knew a Phoenix,* made by Karen Saum. Mastectomy in June. Deaths of Marynia Farnham and Katharine Taylor.

1980 *Halfway to Silence* (poems), *Recovering* (journal), and *World of Light* (film). Karen Saum lives at Wild Knoll for part of the year. Death of Muriel Rukeyser.

1981 *Writings on Writing* (collection of monographs).

1982 *A Winter Garland* (poems), first collaboration with William B. Ewert. *Anger* (novel). *May Sarton: Woman and Poet*, ed. Constance Hunting. Deaths of Judith Matlack, Eugénie DuBois, and Archibald MacLeish.

1983 Begins work on *The Magnificent Spinster*. Death of Mildred Quigley.

1984 *At Seventy* (journal), *Letters from Maine* (poems).

1985 *The Magnficent Spinster* (novel). Death of Bramble, the cat. Christmas-tree fire. Extraction of all teeth.

1986 *Letters to May* (from Eleanor Mabel Sarton, edited by May Sarton). Stroke in February; spring lecture tour canceled. Pierrot, the cat, arrives. Deaths of Peggy Pond Church and Tamas, the Shetland sheep-dog.

1987 *The Phoenix Again* (poems, Ewert). Arrival of Grizzle, the dachshund.

1988 *After the Stroke* (journal), *The Silence Now* (poems), *Honey in the Hive* (celebration of Judith Matlack).

1989 *The Education of Harriet Hatfield* (novel). Lambda Rising Award for *The Silence Now*. *May Sarton Revisited,* Twayne U.S. Authors Series, Elizabeth Evans. Car explodes into flames. Grizzle leaves. Death of Camille Mayran.

1990 New England Booksellers' Award as Outstanding New England Writer for 1990. Acutely ill; loses fifty pounds. Deaths of Sylvie Pasche, Evelyn Ames, Lotte Jacobi, Lola Szladits.

1991 *Sarton Selected*, ed. Bradford Dudley Daziel (anthology); *Writing in the Upward Years*, film by Stephen Robataille; *Conversations with May Sarton,* ed. Ingersoll. Day-long conference held in the Sarton Reading and Reference Room, Westbrook College, in celebration of her seventy-ninth birthday.

1992 *Endgame* (journal); *Forward into the Past*, ed. Sherman (festschrift honoring her eightieth birthday); *That Great Sanity: Critical Essays on May Sarton*, ed. Swartzlander and Mumford. "A Celebration for May Sarton," three-day national conference, Westbrook College. Two trips to London to see Juliette; small stroke. Deaths of Charles Barber, Anthony Huxley, John Summerson, Leslie Hotson.

1993 *Encore* (journal); *Among the Usual Days* (portrait in unpublished letters, poems and journals), ed. Sherman; *Collected Poems 1930–1993*; *A House of Gathering: Poets on May Sarton's Poetry*, ed. Kallet. *Live Reading, 1987*, Ishtar Films. World premier of *The Music Box Bird* produced by the Chamber Theatre of Maine. Trip to London to see Juliette. Pneumonia. Shooting of Ishtar film on aging and poetry.

1994 *Coming into Eighty* (poems), for which she wins the Levinson Prize. *A Celebration for May Sarton*, ed. Constance Hunting; *From May Sarton's Well* (selected writings/photographs), Edith Royce Schade. The Women's Press publishes her poetry in London for the first time since the 1930s—*Halfway to Silence*, containing works from the last three volumes of poems. Stroke on April 2. Chairlift installed. Deaths of Bradford Dudley Daziel and Juliette Huxley.

1995 Eighteenth honorary degree, from the University of New England,

May. *May Sarton: Woman of Letters*, New Hampshire Public Television interview by David Bradt, filmed in May and aired in June. Sends off completed manuscript for *At Eighty-Two* (journal). Dies at 5:15 on Sunday, July 16, at York Hospital.

Key to Addresses

Abbreviations and Short Forms
Used in Source Notes

139 Oxford Street
Cambridge, Massachusetts. Home of May Sarton and Judith Matlack.

22 East 10th Street
An apartment of Sarton's in New York City.

239 East 17th Street
An apartment of Sarton's in New York City.

34 High Street
Ipswich, England. Home of Eleanor Cole Elwes, mother of Eleanor Mabel Sarton.

5 Acacia Road
London. Home of S. S. Koteliansky, where Katherine Mansfield had lived in 1915.

5 Channing Place
Cambridge, Massachusetts. Home of the Sartons.

940 Acequia Madre
Santa Fe, New Mexico. Home of Edith Ricketson, where Sarton was a paying guest.

Austria
Sommerheim Seeblick Am Grundlsee, 700 Meereshohe, Salzkammergut, Steier, Austria. The summer home of Hermann Schwartzwald, Austrian director of finance in the 1930s, and his wife, Dr. Eugenie Schwartzwald, teacher and social worker; during the first four decades of this century it served as an inn for writers, intellectuals, and musicians, including Thomas Mann, Rilke, Brecht, Sinclair Lewis, Dorothy Thompson, Rudolf Serkin, the Huxleys, and May Sarton.

Bowen's Court

> Kildorrery, County Kirk, Cork, Ireland. The family home of Elizabeth Bowen, and the model for Dene's Court in *A Shower of Summer Days*.

Charlottesville, Va.

> Home of Nancy Hale.

Chez Limbosch

> The Limbosches lived in Le Pignon Rouge, 16 Avenue Lequime, Rhôdes St. Genèse, Brussels, Belgium.

Garland's Hotel

> Suffolk Street, Pall Mall, London S.W.1.

Grundlesse

> See *Austria*.

Hanswert, Zeeland

> A stop on the boat ride through Holland in June 1947.

Hotel Bristol

> Where Sarton stayed with her parents in Montreux, Switzerland.

Ipswich

> 34 High Street, Ipswich, England. Home of Eleanor Cole Elwes, mother of Eleanor Mabel Sarton.

Kingham

> Far End, Kingham, Oxfordshire, England. Home of Basil and Jay de Sélincourt.

London [JS]

> 12 Ormonde Mansions, 106 Southampton Row, W.C.1, London. Home of Jane Stockwood.

Montreux

> See *Hotel Bristol*.

New Haven

> Sarton stayed here only briefly. Specific address unknown.

Rathfarnham

> Rockbrook House, Rathfarnham, County Dublin, Ireland. Home of Lady Beatrice Glenavy.

Rockport

> Straitsmouth Inn, Rockport, Massachusetts, where the Sartons spent many summers.

Rye

Samuel Jeakes House, Mermaid Street, Rye, Sussex, England. Home of Conrad Aiken, which Sarton and four friends rented in the spring of 1937.

Samuel Jeakes House

See *Rye.*

Santa Fe [AS]

724 Canyon Road, Santa Fe, New Mexico. Home of Agnes Sims, painter and sculptor, where Sarton was a paying guest.

Vouvray

Le Petit Bois, home of Grace Eliot Dudley, in the Vallée Coquette, deep in the Touraine, three miles from Vouvray, France.

York

Wild Knoll, York, Maine, where Sarton lived from 1973 until her death.

Works Referred To

WORKS BY MAY SARTON

Anger W. W. Norton, 1982

As Does New Hampshire William L. Bauhan Publishers, 1967

"The Astounding Air" Unpublished

At Eighty-Two: A Journal W. W. Norton, 1995

The Bridge of Years Doubleday, 1946

A Celebration for May Sarton Puckerbrush Press, 1994

Cloud, Stone, Sun, Vine W. W. Norton, 1961

Coming into Eighty W. W. Norton, 1995

Collected Poems 1930–1973 W. W. Norton, 1974

Collected Poems 1930–1993 W. W. Norton, 1993

The Education of Harriet Hatfield W. W. Norton, 1989

Encounter in April Houghton Mifflin, 1937

Endgame: A Journal of the Seventy-ninth Year W. W. Norton, 1992

"Fire in a Mirror" Unpublished

Forward into the Past (ed. Susan Sherman) William B. Ewert Publisher,
    1992

A Grain of Mustard Seed W. W. Norton, 1971

Halfway to Silence W. W. Norton, 1980

Honey in the Hive Warren Publishing Company, 1988

I Knew a Phoenix: Sketches for an Autobiography Rinehart, 1959

Inner Landscape Houghton Mifflin, 1939

In Time Like Air Rinehart, 1958

Land of Silence and Other Poems Rinehart, 1953

The Leaves of the Tree Cornell College Chapbooks, 1950

Letters from Maine W. W. Norton, 1984

Letters to May by Eleanor Mabel Sarton (ed. May Sarton) Puckerbrush
    Press, 1986

The Lion and the Rose Rinehart, 1948

May Sarton: Among the Usual Days (ed. Susan Sherman) W. W. Norton,
    1993

May Sarton: Selected Letters 1916–1954 (ed. and introduced by Susan
    Sherman) W. W. Norton, 1997
A Private Mythology W. W. Norton, 1966
The Poet and the Donkey W. W. Norton, 1969
A Reckoning W. W. Norton, 1978
The Silence Now W. W. Norton, 1988
The Single Hound Houghton Mifflin, 1938
"Three Stages" Unpublished
The Underground River The Play Club, 1947
"The Waterfall" Unpublished
"We Aren't Getting Anywhere" Unpublished
A World of Light: Portraits and Celebrations W. W. Norton, 1976

FILM

World of Light: A Portrait of May Sarton Ishtar Films, 1979

WORKS BY THE HUXLEYS

Leaves of the Tulip Tree Juliette Huxley; John Murray, London, 1986
Memories Julian Huxley; Harper & Row, 1970

Dear Juliette

Letters of May Sarton to Juliette Huxley

A NOTE ON THE TEXT OF THE LETTERS

French was May Sarton's first language, basic to her nature, intrinsic to her thought and work. To the end of her life she instinctively turned to it for words and phrases, entire conversations, letters; she used it for titles and epigraphs to poems, epigraphs and prologues to books, passages in journals. French, its literature and poetry, so much at the heart of her own life, was essential to the very atmosphere between Sarton and Juliette Huxley, herself born in French Switzerland. Unless otherwise indicated, translations from the French are by this editor. I have left her French as she wrote it except where the meaning was obscured or in cases of typos or misspellings; in translating I have tried to approximate as closely as possible her own voice and locutions, even when that somewhat departs from the literal meaning of her French.

It was Sarton's custom in the early years to sign letters with a hieroglyph. Usually it was a lily of the valley; sometimes, to her parents, she used a mouse or bird; to Lugné-Poë it was often an elephant. In all her letters to Juliette Huxley, however, she used only a lily of the valley; I have indicated such hieroglyphs with brackets.

I have almost always retained Sarton's idiosyncrasies: her British variants in spelling, her underlinings, her errant capitalizations, and her casual punctuation.

S.S.

O Juliette, I have just come home from standing in Max Gordon's office in a <u>herd</u> of actresses only to be told, "you're not the type," and found a nice fat letter from Julian. How wonderful letters are, how unexpected—especially across an ocean. One has no idea what time of day, what mood, what event they are going to meet. And this was a perfect spar to a drowning man!

It is curious how often in this idiotic N.Y. life my mind goes back to certain images of last spring, as if in the green underwater spaces of your room it might rest. What are you doing? Are you doing any sculpture? It was tantalizing to see only one thing and to be dragged away from that. Though I guess that you are so busy <u>maintaining</u> peace and the very special atmosphere you have that it must be difficult to catch time enough for anything else. Women are always being torn between their <u>human</u> responsibilities and other things, aren't they? It is comparatively simple, I have an idea, to be simply embarked on a career! Still I should love to know that you are one of the magical people who can do both—if you are well. Are you well? Are you really better as well as carnivorous?

I have been trying to see Dora Clarke for weeks but first I had grippe and then she had migraine. I'm hoping that if this <u>champagne</u> weather continues we'll finally manage both to be well next week. Autumn here is unbelievable really. It makes one think anything is possible. The air is like glass—everything sparkles. I have by a miracle found a room on a little park so there are trees instead of walls to look out on. They are very thin and sad but nice. And my room is big and gray and rather Chinese, intense and peaceful all at once. It is freedom after the claustrophobia this city gives me. What else? This afternoon I went to see a small exhibition which contained the Toulouse-Lautrec of Avril leaving the Moulin Rouge—a little self-contained sober figure slipping along and it looks cold—the very <u>essence</u> of the theatre—this strange fabrication of glory by strange little people who possess it so little once they have taken off their make-up. Being in the theatre is like having an endless devouring affair with a second-rate person. Ah well. Meanwhile I try to write. Here are some poems. I can't remember what I sent Julian. Tell him I'll answer his letter in a day or so and he is an angel.

It is good to think of you and to span for a minute the huge waste of ocean between us. Be well and happy—and stay exactly as you are. I'm hoping to come back in the spring and it would be awful to find anything changed!

Love to you
May

Max Gordon's office: Max Gordon (1891–1989), theatrical and film producer, owner of the Village Vanguard nightclub from 1934 on.

a drowning man: At this time Sarton was tirelessly engaged in looking for a job, trying every possible theatrical office while also hoping to persuade *Paris-Soir* to let her do a series of American "Letters" similar to Gênet's "Paris Letters" in *The New Yorker.*

last spring: Having sailed to England on the SS *Manhattan,* Sarton disembarked in England on 26 March 1936 and spent her first night in Cornwall at the home of Dr. Charles Singer (1876–1960) and his wife Dorothea (Waley) Cohen Singer (1882–1964), historians of science and old friends of the Sartons. Julian Huxley, then secretary of the Zoological Society, was there as a guest, looking for a place to grow eucalyptus trees en masse for the koala bears at the London Zoo. On 7 May, Sarton dined at the Huxleys' London apartment, meeting Juliette for the first time. The following day she wrote to her parents: "The most exquisite atmosphere—his wife is one of the most charming people I have ever seen, like one of K.M.'s [Katherine Mansfield's] women—the apartment all pale green and she is like that—she has a slight accent— I don't know what nationality she is." Marie Juliette Baillot was born in Auvenier on Lake Neuchâtel, Switzerland, 6 December 1896.

any sculpture: Juliette had been studying sculpture at the Central School with John Skeaping, a well-known British painter and sculptor.

Dora Clarke: sculptor, friend of the Huxleys; her bronze of a Kikuyu girl was reproduced as the frontispiece for Julian Huxley's *Africa View* (1931).

Avril: Jane Avril was a dancer and figured in several of the famous posters by Henri de Toulouse-Lautrec (1864–1901), French painter who became the supreme portrayer of Montmartre nightlife, with its dancers, actresses, singers, and women of the demimonde.

what I sent Julian: Sarton had sent Julian "Out of a Desolate Source," published in *Time and Tide* (1936); "You who ask peace" (see *Inner Landscape*); and "Apologia," unpublished; see Appendix.

In response to this letter Juliette wrote: "Thank you for writing and for being so alive. I expect you make a definite impression on most people, but I feel the impression you made on us is a very true one, and that you couldn't possibly be different to what we think you are."

NEW HAVEN   December 5th, 1936

O Juliette, here I am in New Haven for a gay weekend with your letter like a secret treasure in my purse. It is going to snow (it is always just going to snow these days) and really the excitement of a snowstorm is one of the reasons for living in N.Y.—though for that matter Switzerland is superior I guess! To quote from Noel Coward who is making us all madly senti-mental, "the gods must find it entrancing." This afternoon I am thinking of writing a series of poems on snow—of which the enclosed is the first.

Your letter is like a painting. I have a sort of <u>sur-réalist</u> photograph of it—the scarlet thread on Julian's face from the chin cut, yellow chrysan-themums, little cactuses, and the frog of coral wood—with Bernard Shaw's beard somewhere. What a darling you are to write me. I am freshly startled with surprise every time I wake up and think that there you and Julian are <u>suddenly</u> upon my horizon. It still seems preposterous. But it is true don't you think that one knows—<u>definitely</u> knows almost at once whether peo-ple are going to be of one's island or not? I fell in love with you both at first sight—Julian in a storm in Cornwall and you in a little white jacket in a green room where I was so frightened by being early that I would have read you the whole of "Testament of Beauty" rather than have to talk! I sometimes wonder whether the anguish of meeting is worth any possibil-ity of further acquaintance. When I was having to raise money all the time for the theatre I had to overcome every impulse to run away so that I am able to stay rooted to the spot now but that is the most that can be said.

It is wonderful that you are working, and that you are better. I am glad!

Noel Coward . . . madly sentimental: Nine short plays by Noël Coward (1899–1973), English composer, playwright, and actor, known for his witty, sophisticated comedies about the British leisure class, under the title *Tonight at 8:30,* had opened in 1936.

"Testament of Beauty": the most ambitious work by English poet Robert Bridges (1844–1930), Britain's Poet Laureate 1913–1930, embodying his life's philosophy.

NEW YORK   December 7th, 1936

I am sitting up in bed with sun streaming in and a feeling of convalescence. Last night despair came down on me. Does it ever on you? For no <u>great</u> reason but just the <u>longness</u> of living. Sometimes I feel like a dog that someone is making jump for a bone. One gets so tired of jumping. But now it is over. Now I am full of resolutions. You know, it is the day after

Saint Nicholas. In Belgium all the children are sick from eating marzipan pigs and chocolate violins. I wish I had one to eat and one to send you!

In Cambridge I started on a short novel about three old ladies in Belgium. It could sum up more or less what is clear to me now in living without being autobiographical at all (which I want to avoid) but God knows when I'll do it. It seems to be impossible to look for a job and have any blank stretches to write in. One is in a state of continual suspense. So I've given up for two weeks trying to pull words out unless they come by themselves. I want to write a poem for Chopin beginning

> the crystal tears
> of chandeliers

a bit Sitwellian, but it could be fun. I've been reading a charming book on Chinese painting called The Chinese Eye, by a painter called Chiang Yee. Chinese painting is painting for poets I think. Have you seen it? And a perfectly wonderful book on the Greek poets by Browda (he's just at Harvard for a half-year). I never quite believed that Sappho was all she is cracked up to be until I read this—the translations are usually so bad.

Blessings on you for writing and do soon again.

Yours to command

M—

My room is gray with many white curtains—an almost emerald linen couch cover with yellow cushions (almost chartreuse) and a modern carpet in bands of thin greens, creams, gray and buff. I can't explain it but against gray walls it takes on style as a color scheme I think.

---

novel about three old ladies in Belgium: The Single Hound, Sarton's first novel, published in 1938, is based on Marie Gaspar, Blanche Rousseau, and Marie Closset (Jean Dominique, 1874–1952), a seminal influence in her life; the Belgian poet was founder of the Institut Belge de Culture Français, where Sarton went to school for a winter when she was twelve; see pp. 120–135 in *I Knew a Phoenix* and Ch. 12 in *A World of Light.*

Sitwellian: reference to Dame Edith Sitwell (1887–1964), English poet and critic known for her patterns in sound.

Chiang Yee: (1903–?), a Chinese writer who lived in England and often illustrated his own books. *The Chinese Eye* was published in 1935; he is perhaps better known for his *The Silent Traveler* series.

book on the Greek poets by Browda: Greek Lyric Poetry from Alcman to Simonides (1936) by Sir
  Cecil Maurice Bowra (1898–1971), English classical scholar.
Sappho: (b. 612 B.C.), a native of the Aegean island Lesbos; one of the most famous lyric
  poets of all time, known as "the tenth muse."
color scheme I think: Enclosed with this letter: "Invocation" appears elsewhere as "Snow";
  "At This Time"; "Out of the Torn Sky"; and "The Diviner," written for Polly
  Thayer Starr and first published in *May Sarton: Among the Usual Days* (Norton, 1993);
  see Appendix.

[5 CHANNING PLACE]   Sunday, January 31st, 1937

Dear Juliette—

Julian writes that you have been engaged in this battle of flu (it must have
been carried back and forth on the <u>Queen Mary</u>). I hope you and yours
are out of it now and somewhere high up on a dazzling snow-plain. I suppose you are expert on skis. I used to go up into the hills around here when
I was a little girl at Christmas—knowing nothing about it—but oh how
exciting! It is sheer magic, isn't it? We used to ski a lot by moonlight,
singing the Brahms <u>Requiem</u> in parts (in case of sudden death!), but I was
never any good. Do you jump? It must be the nearest thing to flying.

   The minute 1936 was over I felt as if a mountain had dropped off my
shoulders! But this year I am sure is going to be extraordinary. I feel it in
my bones. Already I have embarked on a novel which I have an awful feeling that only you and I will like (perhaps even you won't like it, but I do
count on you a little). It is about three old ladies in Brussels, particularly
<u>one</u> whom I adore and to whom the poems are dedicated (she is a poet,
Jean Dominique). It is all the things I care about and <u>feel</u> most about now.
For instance, the possibility of depth and adventure in an apparently <u>tiny</u>
scope of living. We (in America particularly) have overestimated the value
of <u>actual</u> experience, I think. I see imaginations dulled all around me by an
excess of actual physical excitement whether it be making love or driving
a motor car fast—or acting every night of the year. This sounds very silly
written down. Oh dear! It is more than that. It is going to be called <u>The
Single Hound</u> with that poem of Emily Dickinson's to head it:

                    Adventure most unto itself
                    The Soul condemned to be—

Attended by a Single Hound
Its own identity.

It is more and <u>less</u> than that, for of course it can turn out to be merely pretty and whimsical and sentimental and <u>dreadful</u>! But I find myself deep in
at the moment with no perspective at all. I hope to finish 100 by March
26th (when I sail for Port of London) and extract an advance from my
publisher. You know I am taking Conrad Aiken's house in Rye with two
friends of mine and am hoping you and Julian will come down for a weekend with Dora Clarke. The house seems to be enormous (I've never seen
it).

You haven't of course been able to do any work with all this flu. How
are you really? Is the frog finished? I can't say you are mean not to have
written you must be so busy—but your letter is a treasure and I feel like a
bird with its mouth open asking for more!

Love to you from
May

You can't imagine how I am looking forward to seeing you again!

<hr/>

on the Queen Mary: The HMS *Queen Mary,* the largest liner afloat, had made its maiden
voyage to New York City from England at the end of 1936 in 3 days, 23 hours, and
57 minutes.

mountain had dropped off my shoulders: As 1936 ended, Sarton, discouraged, had given up
going to theatrical offices and hoped instead to find a job through friends; she was
having personal difficulties with her friend Theodora Pleadwell; her room on East
17th Street was infested with bedbugs; she had just finished correcting galleys of
Encounter in April, and, as the Sartons were on a cruise to Spain and Trinidad, she
had gone to Anne Thorp's until their return.

(she is a poet, Jean Dominique): Encounter in April, Sarton's first book of poems, published in
1937, was dedicated to Jean Dominique.

Adventure most unto itself . . . : last verse of #822 in *The Complete Poems of Emily Dickinson*
(1830–1886), ed. Thomas H. Johnson (Little, Brown, 1960).

deep in: a favorite allusion of Sarton's to the dormouse in the treacle in *Alice's Adventures in
Wonderland* by Lewis Carroll (pen name of Charles Lutwidge Dodgson, 1832–1898),
English author, mathematician, and photographer.

Aiken's house in Rye with two friends of mine: The American poet Conrad Aiken (1889–1973)
and his wife, Mary, lived for a time at Jeakes House, built in 1698, on Mermaid
Street in Rye, which Sarton, together with Margaret English and Kappo Phelan,
friends from the Apprentice Theatre, rented for April and May 1937. They were
joined by Liz Johnson and Elena Flohr, who shared expenses.

5 CHANNING PLACE   March 3rd 1937
CAMBRIDGE, MASS.

Oh Juliette, you deserve no letters as you never answer them but Julian says
you have sprained your ankle and I hope that enforced quiet will bore you
sufficiently to result in an answer to my two? three? neglected children that
have lain unanswered for months. The tyranny of letters is frightful   sometimes I, who write a great many, think it more of a strain than it is worth!
My dearest friends are all in places like Prague or California so that one
mood never matches another. But it has been precious to have Julian's letters
with their picture of a fantastically busy full life and their glimpses of you.

It is quite terrifying to think of seeing you both so soon—I always
suffer unreasonably from the "mal du départ"—and the horrible cheerful-
ness of tenderness that <u>hides</u>, has already descended on Mummy and me. I
hate leaving her. It makes me feel that I am getting old that I am now constantly somewhere deep down preparing myself for the time when she will
die. It is absurd of course. The things one prepares oneself for and are
armed against never happen, do they? It's always the unexpected things.

I wonder if my book has come yet and if you like it, or which ones
you like best, or don't like at all.

Please send me a word. The only fun of a book of poems is to give it
to one's friends. It has been quite thrilling to feel it going out in different
corners of the earth. Today I <u>just</u> heard from Jean Dominique who didn't
know the dedication of course. If you ever come to Brussels you must
meet her and her two friends: Blanche Rousseau, the writer, and Gaspari,
a <u>very</u> Belgian, eccentric, humourous school teacher. The novel is about
them. Tomorrow I am going to the country for the day to work at it again.
I have been thrown off by a job of raising money for Erika Mann and a
group of German refugees—and the suspense of not knowing if the publisher would like it, but now I have the contract in my pocket I feel full of
peace and longing to get to work. The trouble is that these departures
always involve seeing so many people, I am quite exhausted.

I have a new French blue jacket like a soldier that you will like I hope.
I thought of you when I got it. Otherwise there is simply no news. I have

been reading Auden's new book Look Stranger. He is Erika's husband. Over and over again a single line touches me. "To settle in this village of the heart,/ My darling, can you bear it?" for instance, but the poem never leaps out of the page whole. I do admire him though. But on the whole I think he finds complicated ways of saying rather simple things and the great virtue of poetry—one of its virtues—is that power to say an apparently unsayable thing quite simply, don't you think? Which makes me decide that I must write you a poem—or wait to see you. I wouldn't want the enchantment that you and Julian together first of all, and then each by yourself, cast over me to be changed into anything less or more. And yet I suppose it must and nothing stays where it is. Anyway it is good to think of seeing you soon—and please save some time for me in the three days following April 6th when I think I shall be sailing up the Thames—I want to see the frog and you, peacefully!

Love

M

[   ]

---

mal du départ: pain of departure, a phrase often used by Eleanor Mabel Sarton.
my book: Encounter in April.
Gasparri: Marie Gaspar, known as Gaspari or Titi to the younger students; see "Titi" in *The New Yorker,* 11 September 1954; also footnote to letter of 5 December 1936.
the country: Sudbury, Massachusetts, home of Anne Thorp.
Mann and a group of German refugees: Erika Julia Hedwig Mann-Auden (1905–1969), daughter of Thomas Mann (1875–1955, German novelist, Nobel Prize, 1929), had just brought over her own anti-Nazi theater company, banned throughout Europe for their political satire; later she became a journalist and commentator on culture and politics. Her marriage to English poet and dramatist W. H. Auden (1907–1973) in June 1935 was undertaken to provide Mann with a British passport and escape from Nazi persecution; the marriage was never dissolved.
"To settle in this village . . .": opening of poem xxiii in Auden's *Look Stranger* (1936); U.S. title *On This Island* (1937).

GARLAND'S HOTEL, LONDON   [probably 8 April 1937]
10:30 THURSDAY MORNING

I am here wrapped up in a quilt thinking how incommensurate I am to the glories that crowd me. Dear Juliette, I wish I were coming to Cornwall to find a camellia tree with you and make petals drop on your head and walk in the wet grass—and perhaps finally talk, say something that somehow is not possible—words are terrifying. One realizes suddenly how <u>flamboyant</u> they are, how apt for exaggeration when one is dealing with the closed stern particles of the heart.

> Could mortal lip divine
> The undeveloped Freight
> Of a delivered syllable
> 'Twould crumble with the weight

There has been too much all at once. And I haven't had <u>time</u> to reach any certainty except that I would do anything in the world for you—and for <u>you</u> I could sing hosannahs and praise God. Can you guess—have you ever—how <u>entirely</u> you seem complete and beautiful, how humble you make one feel? How I would like to cover you with roses. And what a terrifying two days this has been. I think I love Julian enough and not too much to build and not to destroy. God, Juliette, I wish you weren't going away. Or that I could write you a poem—and say something completely instead of these sentences finishing in tears because of one's feelings that <u>blur</u> the cool mind senselessly.

The last thing my father said to me (which was extraordinary as he never says anything) was "Be as wise as a serpent and as gentle as a dove"— I'll try to be gentle and wise.

I'm sending you some poems with the novel—it is good to think that you will be reading them. They are the best of me, though it is not much— and they are what I would like to give you.

Couvre-toi de roses—

[   ]

[*probably 8 April 1937*]: On 5 April 1937, Sarton arrived in London on the SS *Trader* and was met by Julian, who took her for dinner with Juliette and Dora Clarke. On the afternoon of 8 April, during a long talk with Julian, Sarton recognized that they were in love, and that his marriage was indestructible. Her ensuing affair with Julian was a matter shared openly with Juliette, and with Sarton's parents.

Could mortal lip divine . . . : #1409 in *The Complete Poems of Emily Dickinson*.

to build and not to destroy: In a letter dated 10 April to Julian, Sarton writes: "Last night I thought and thought. In spite of the gallant armour we both wore it was pretty awful

bringing the emotion and thought shared of the last few days down to the <u>details</u> of an affair suddenly, like any other, wasn't it? O my darling, be very sure, won't you? I think I might be almost relieved if you wrote to say it was all over."
"Be as wise as a serpent . . .": Matthew 10:16.
Couvre-toi de roses: Cover yourself with roses.

FRIDAY MORNING   [9 April 1937]
[GARLAND'S HOTEL, LONDON]

Dear Juliette, such a soft quiet day with thin rain—Liz is muttering German beside me—there are lilies of the valley and long pink tulips and wide-open summery roses—suitcases packed and piled up around us like the last act of a Tchekov play. Tomorrow I go down to Rye to begin a new life, to work, to be silent—a wonderful man on the boat is sending us a case of Scotch and a case of burgundy which should make us glow like little stoves (I'm afraid it is going to be rather cold at first until the fires have been going awhile)—you had better come down before it is all gone.

Long ago when I first met you and Julian I was deeply struck by what a rare delicious pair you are. It sent a rather shattered faith in marriage <u>soaring</u>. Now I feel it even more—the something indestructible and delicate there is between you. That is all I can find to say—I hope it is not raining in Cornwall. I am so grateful that I know you both—

Dearest love,

[   ]

Liz: Elizabeth Johnson, recently graduated from Bennington College.
last act of a Tchekov play: The plays of the Russian playwright and short story writer Anton Pavlovich Chekhov (1860–1904), infused with the transitoriness of life, are designed around the principle of an arrival, a sojourn, and finally a last-act departure.
I first met you and Julian: Precisely one year earlier in 1936, Sarton had met Julian on 1 April at the Singers' in Cornwall and Juliette on 7 May at the Huxleys' London home.

TUESDAY EVE—   [probably 13 April 1937]
SAMUEL JEAKES HOUSE

I have just been out into the garden in the dark to pick you some flowers from <u>our</u> garden (how unbelievable it is!). It is raining and I wish I were writing to you in French instead of English.

> Je metterai dans tes mains la rose et la verveine
> Qui porteront les couleurs de ma joie et de ma peine.

Your letter filled the whole day. I would have so understood that you didn't want to write—but that you have and that your door hasn't slammed in my face is such a blessing, you can't imagine. No, you can't! Even though you think you can—because, you can't imagine how rare it is to discover someone who lives in the same private world as I (not that it is good or bad but it is <u>special</u>—it is the sense of the <u>colour</u> of the air, and the <u>edges</u> of words, and the horizons of feeling—I suppose it is feminine). The minute I saw you I knew that you did. It has nothing to do with love (it is rare that one <u>loves</u> people who understand one at all) though I do love you, it is obvious enough. But it is just I suppose like a solitary strange bird with a red crest suddenly meeting another. Oh my dear, you would think I was quite mad if you didn't have Juliette for a name and say Beefalò Beel (now that I have started to write it phonetically I can't). The truth is that I am light-headed from having swung so many mattresses into the garden to be aired, and fought with the geyser, and made beds and laughed and worked so hard that you will have to forgive me.

Julian says you want to do a head of me—you <u>must</u>, yes, if it will be any fun (I have such a funny sharp face)—couldn't you come down here for a week or two—or three—the studio is yours—it is big and light and sunny and I'll sit and think about the novel which I am in a deep woe about at present. I would come up but the trouble is that I can't afford to live in London and I'm afraid I couldn't work there, and I <u>must</u> work. When can you come? Julian would be lonely of course but you can write him letters (anyone could live on your letters).

About Julian I am very happy—it is curious, I feel it is <u>outside</u> my life like some present from the jealous gods to be accepted gladly but with trembling—I do tremble. But I trust him and I know that I am "outside" his life—and as far as unhappiness goes—there seems to be such a necessary bit of it in living—it's rather like the weather in England—a Turner-esque sky. Oh Juliette, be happy (though that is a strange thing to say).

[   ]

Je metterai . . . : I will put in your hands the rose and the verbena, which will show the hues of my joy and my pain. From *L'Anémone des Mers* by Jean Dominique (Mercure de France, 1906).

slammed in my face: Juliette had thought at first that she could never write or see Sarton again. But she did not want that, as she did "like [her] so very much." "You see dear I can really give you nothing except what is mine to give—my friendship—what you take will depend on your wisdom—what you give on your gentleness. Enough & not too much is the divine equipoise. Enough happiness—so that the sorrow be gentle & bearable. Perhaps I am mostly afraid of <u>un</u>happiness—for him & for you." Saturday [April 1937].

such a funny sharp face: This work of Juliette's was never completed but Sarton sat for other artists. In 1936 Polly Thayer Starr did a drawing which appears as the frontispiece in *Encounter in April* and now hangs in the Sarton Room at Westbrook College, Portland, Maine; Starr's 1938 portrait of Sarton hangs in the Fogg Museum in Cambridge; during the Nelson years Starr did a further drawing, now in this editor's possession; in 1948 Belgian painter Georges Baltus did a pencil drawing, also now at Westbrook. A lesser work in oil by Agnes Sims done in Sante Fe in 1945 and which Sarton never liked was sold at the estate auction in Portland, Maine, in 1996 and now hangs in a private guesthouse overlooking Sabbathday Harbor at Islesboro, Maine. Four of these appear in this volume.

I do tremble: On 11 April 1937 Sarton wrote to Julian: "I so want <u>not</u> to be an added strain because I know you are tired inside—but I guess for a little while until we have really found each other and are quite comfortable and unfrightened, there is <u>bound</u> to be strain. If you are frightened of me—what do you think <u>I</u> am? I am sometimes <u>terrified</u>—all my sophistication is simply armour that one has to wear to be fit for this world—you must think of me as not very wise, but quite simply warm and in love with you. . . ." And on 15 April Julian wrote to Juliette: "I know that both May & I are 'safe' and know it very definitely today for, my dearest, I spent the night with her last night at a hotel. It was very beautiful and happy: & so much the assurance that this was a private thing which need not interfere with anything or anyone else—& more than that, which we neither of us <u>wished</u> to make more, for we each have our own lives which we most definitely wish to live for ourselves."

But I trust him: Juliette answered that only by trusting <u>herself</u> could May bring this to a safe anchorage. "I know you can do this and that I can trust you—I know it isn't easy—Three-cornered love never is. but then we are, by some mischief of destiny, all three suddenly bound together in this way. . . . Although I've tried quite hard to turn you out of my heart, I do care for you—you are a very real person & lovely."

Turner-esque: Joseph Mallord William Turner (1775–1851), English painter of romantic landscapes, known for his play of light through fog and mist.

MON. 5:30 P.M.   [April or May 1937]
[RYE]

I am sitting in the garden in the sun (!) eating strawberry jam and tea—
our square kitten whom none of us like is bouncing from one flagstone to
another while old Squidge, Conrad's cat, rolls over to have his tummy
scratched. I have realized in the last weeks that I prefer cats to kittens. Have
realized also in the light of the sun and the peace of the afternoon that it
is a long time since I have had a word from you and that your letters have
been until now like signposts along a road—I am not sure now whether I
have lost my way. The other day at tea—(Margaret [English] was enchanted—and I was terrified as one always is when two people one loves meet
for the first time!) I felt curiously frozen out—nothing one could put a finger on but, whatever you call it, atmospheric pressure or something—and
it is true I suppose that our only reality to each other must be by letter, so
that having had none, I would have liked to run away. Forgive me if I have
said something or done something,—a _false_ step could send anyone of us
falling off the tight-rope. I am almost boundlessly yours to command, you
know. And I feel so much a beggar at your door—how can I explain it? I
know how easily things in this brilliantly illuminated world of the emotions get out of proportion. It is just, I suppose, that I have believed so
utterly that it was possible to be your friend—and to feel for a second that
it might not be fills me with an ache.

On the other hand God knows why you should be asked to do the
impossible to comfort me. Only don't think I take things for granted or
don't see them. Christ, how one hates _words_ when one is trying to speak
the simple truth.

Well, my dear, the point is that I have been thinking about staying
with you that week in June—I want to very much because it is my only
chance to see anything of you quietly—and I expect J[ulian] will be there
very little which is a good thing (our à-trois-ness is a feat but exhausting)—if you want me really I shall be very happy. But please _do_ say if for
any reason you dread it too much—or are tired—(I know how even a
mouse in the house is agony sometimes). I would be glad anyway to feel
you could be honest with me.

If all is well I shall be up for lunch _Friday_—to spend the zoo-dinner
night. Is that all right? I have to have my hair washed etc. and the simplest

would be to come straight to you and drop my bag. Shall take the 11:15 A.M. back here on Saturday. It sounds very exciting.

I have said nothing I wanted to and said it badly. But perhaps you will see anyway. There are no poems. There is nothing to send you but my love.

[   ]

Forgive me if I have said something or done something: Juliette assured her she had done nothing wrong: "It is possible and real that we are friends, only we must learn this new language—and not mind if it is sometimes a little embarrassing."

zoo-dinner night: On Saturday, 8 May, the Huxleys picked up Sarton, picnicked on the way, and brought her for the first time to Whipsnade, the open country branch of the London Zoo on the Bedfordshire Downs where the Huxleys kept an apartment 800 feet over the downs overlooking its 500 acres and where they spent most weekends. On 12 May, Sarton joined the Huxleys at the zoo for a formal dinner with maharajas and prime ministers to celebrate the coronation of King George VI.

SAT. EVE—7:00 P.M.   [29 May 1937]
[RYE]

Dear Juliette—the sudden stillness of evening is on us, the fields lit up after rain with the sudden grace of sunlight. O my dear, I wrote you a very cruel light letter—it is not because I didn't know in my heart what I am doing— I have measured it, and even this temporary parting (which I feel so <u>sure</u> doesn't touch your deep togetherness) must feel like a wound. I don't dare think of it—and I can't talk about it. (You are right—words become gestures, melodrama so easily) and just because of that I can only surround you in a fantastic cloud of my own special feeling for you—as if I were blind and deaf. I am not—and I can only say over and over like a prayer the faith I have in you both that in the end sets every fear at rest like this very peaceful hour.

I am coming to London on Wednesday morning—I would love to see you for tea that day or Thursday morning (I must go back that afternoon) and if you still want to do the head let us plan. I'll be c/o Mrs. Alan Cameron 2 Clarence Terrace, Regent's Park. Send me a note or I'll telephone. And of course don't feel you must see me at all now or ever. It fills me with terror to think that you may not. O Juliette, there are so many things—poems and flowers and all of myself that I want to bring you. It is

strange how very simple and <u>luminous</u> very complicated things can be—
what we are doing, we three, is impossible—but it <u>measures</u> the grace of
the heart, it makes me proud of being a man. O bless you.

[   ]

Wednesday morning: "Your room is yours whenever you choose to come," Juliette
    responded.
do the head: It was not until 12 June 1938 that Juliette Huxley began sculpting the head of
    May Sarton; the work was never completed.
Mrs. Alan Cameron: Elizabeth Bowen (1899-1973), Anglo-Irish novelist and short story
    writer. Shortly after Sarton's ship the SS *American Trader* docked on 4 April, she met
    Bowen for the first time; a few weeks later Bowen came as guest to Samuel Jeakes
    House, and subsequently invited Sarton to spend the weekend of 4 June in London
    with her before Bowen's departure for France and Ireland.

[AUSTRIA]   August 1st [1937]

Juliette, everything you say is true. Your letters light little fires on the tops
of the mountains. The poem is not good—nothing I am doing now is. It
speaks of confusion, of the abrupt quick spirits of the imagination and not
its deep stream.

One side of me is so happy with Julian, playing tennis in a
Thurberesque way, reading Shakespeare and Ibsen together, walking and
sleeping—the whole shape of life is good and I am so grateful to you both.
Everyone here loves him—he was delicious at a costume party, taking infinite trouble with his costume (much more than I did with mine) and being
really perfect as Malvolio. This place has a very special quality. O my darling, I simply <u>fix</u> my mind on your eventually sooner or later coming here.
You must.

The other side of me feels imminent revolution—the need for
silence. The last months have been too full. Nothing is deep and clear. I am
living on top of unexpected excitement, like sitting on a firecracker. And
besides I am haunted by the novel though beating the donkey will do no
good and the carrot to hold in front of his nose is silence, infinite <u>time</u>. I
have written 60 pages here which is not too bad but it is not soaring as it
should. Well, on the 16th I go to Belgium for 10 days.

I am anxious to hear what you have decided. I love to think of you in a boat—I love to think of you with Anthony and Francis in a boat (how they will remember it afterwards much later—how it is little seeds of sweetness you are sowing in them).

Today it is raining—soft clouds creeping down the valleys—the boats leaving thin black lines behind them on the silver of the lake. I would like to cry but it is so inapropos to cry here. It is made for gaiety, for gaiety made of paper hats and flowers. Only Dr. Schwarzwald is sad and sits reading the paper in his red-and-black checked jacket. I love him because he is silent and because I think he is sad in the same way I am for a self-defeated reason.

I am thinking already of the 26th when we shall meet again. Je t'aime comme tous les jours.

[   ]

Austria: On 15 July 1937, Sarton arrived at Sommerheim Seeblick Am Grundlsee, the summer home of Dr. Hermann Schwarzwald, Austrian director of finance in the 1930s, and his wife, Dr. Eugenie Schwarzwald, a teacher and social worker; their home served as an inn for writers, intellectuals, and musicians during the first four decades of this century. On 24 July, Julian arrived at Seeblick to spend ten days with Sarton while Juliette was on a boat trip with sons Anthony Julian Huxley (1920–1992) and Francis John Heathorn Huxley (1923–).

Thurberesque way: reference to James Thurber (1894–1962), American essayist, humorist, author, and prolific contributor to *The New Yorker* whose stories and drawings depicted people behaving rather clumsily and foolishly.

Malvolio: the smug, pompous fool in Shakespeare's *Twelfth Night* known for his absurd conduct.

to Belgium for 10 days: It was in her room on the top floor at the Limbosches' in Belgium that Sarton would always "come home to her work"; see *World of Light,* Ch. 3.

Only Dr. Schwarzwald is sad: Like Dr. Hermann Schwarzwald himself, his wife, Eugenie Nussbaum, was born in Galicia in 1872 to Jewish parents and grew up in Chernovtsy (Czernowitz), the capital of Bukovina, then part of the Austro-Hungarian Empire, now in Ukraine; her childhood was painful. In 1900 they were married. Long-suffering and melancholy, they were together honored by pre– and post–World War I Austrian society, yet were constantly trying to change it.

Je t'aime comme tous les jours: I love you as always.

FRIDAY   [probably 6 August 1937]
GRUNDLSEE

Juliette, petit pigeon aimé—your letter in pencil is here and I only want to cry too. Everything seems wrong now that was so right. But one must pretend that there is some reason and some curious pattern in such things—perhaps if you had come there would have been war or you would have hated it all—or me.

The lake is just silver now. I have been absolutely light-headed for two days like the birds qui n'ont pas de cerveau qui n'ont que de l'âme—except that I also had no stomach. I can't write properly but I wanted to send you some poems—some later ones of J.D. which I must read to you—one bad one of mine. Now I have decided to make you a book of poems so you must wait.

My darling, there are mountains and mountains. I think you have peaks of your own and a little blue lake somewhere in your heart. Find it and be happy there. I shall try to make Julian rest and be happy (how we shall miss you—it is true, you know, strange as it seems—strange as our three lives are, joined, disjoined)—and we'll meet soon.

My love tenderly,

[   ]

---

petit pigeon aimé: beloved little pigeon.
Everything seems wrong now that was so right: Juliette, sorely disappointed and extremely lonely, was unable after all to join May and Julian at Seeblick.
qui n'ont pas de cerveau . . . . : like the birds who have no brain but only soul.
J.D.: Jean Dominique
book of poems: Sarton occasionally made small handwritten illustrated anthologies of her own and other poets' poems for friends. This book of which Juliette wrote "Je lis et relis ton petit livre brun [I read and reread your little brown book]. . . . You were adorable to think of [it]," is not extant, but a number of such books which she made for Grace Dudley, Judith Matlack, and others are in Sarton's archive at the Berg Collection.

FRIDAY   [probably 13 August 1937]
[AUSTRIA]

My darlings, I am writing to you both because it is about my mother. She has sailed on the Pennland Aug. 7th on a rather sad and difficult errand. My grandmother's housekeeper is dying of cancer and my grandmother must be démenagé and the poor woman told she is dying (she doesn't know it). Mummy is not well and I am worried about her for various reasons. She may spend <u>one</u> night in London on the way and I wish you could send her some messages to the boat. Perhaps she could sup with you or something. I'm afraid she will be a little lonely and sad. Altogether it is a miserable affair. She is like a bird and a child and a poet and you will love her <u>at once</u> I know. I am sending this air mail hoping you can get the enclosed to the boat (I don't even know when it is due—<u>Southampton</u>).

I think I must go to Belgium as planned as I can't go back and also for Jean Dominique's sake. I'll go to Ipswich to see Mummy when I come to London. I don't think I can be of any help as one person already agitates my Grannie so much and she will be in a dreadful state at moving. (My dears, how <u>funny</u> all this sounds and it is not at all really—I am only happy to think you will perhaps see my Mummy.)

I finished the novel this morning in floods of tears because I think it is so bad—and I think <u>no one</u> will take it. But took a picnic lunch off to a meadow and lay in the sun—and this is such a beautiful place one can only be happy. Anyway it is done. I am looking forward to working over it now and trying to make it better.

Juliette's letter came at the zero-hour—and Julian's card (such a <u>nice</u> surprise!)—I am dying to know how the jackets fit—

love and love
M—

It is possible that because of Mummy I'll only stay in Brussels a week. I now see that this can't reach you before Monday and unless it is a very slow boat I'm afraid it will be too late. In which case forward my letter to

c/o Mrs. R.G. Elwes

34 High St.

Ipswich, Suffolk

Would you also send the poems enclosed to Mummy?—the photos are for you.

----

my grandmother: Eleanor Mabel Sarton's mother, Eleanor Cole Elwes.
démenagé: moved.
(she doesn't know it): For a full explanation of this situation see *Letters to May* by Eleanor Mabel Sarton, edited by May Sarton (Puckerbrush Press, 1986), pp. 20–24.
for Jean Dominique's sake: In a birthday card to George Sarton dated 21 August, Jean Do, as Sarton called her, writes of that visit: "May est ici, chez nous, pour nous comme un

miracle dont nous sommes comblés. Je suis eblouie de son cher génie—heureuse de sa jeune gloire—que nous aurions aimé de partager avec vous et Mabel quelques heures de ces jours qui passent—trop vite—Elles sont la fleur de la Peacockerie vieillessante." ("May is here with us, an overwhelming miracle. I am dazzled by her brilliance, rejoice in her youthful radiance—if only we could share a few of these fleeting hours with you and Mabel—they are the flower of the aging Peacockerie.") "Peacock" is the term Sarton gave to Marie Gaspar, Blanche Rousseau, and Jean Dominique. "Peacockerie" is a playful term of Jean Do's.

perhaps see my Mummy: Sarton had immediately shared the situation with her mother and from Channing Place on 5 May 1937 Eleanor Mabel Sarton writes: ". . . perhaps you'll understand enough if I tell you that I was deeply troubled by your little note saying J[ulian]'s feeling for you was so strong, it frightened you a little. . . . Then came a dear letter where you seemed to have come to a place of understanding & peace & great happiness—If I came to you with fears and warnings, I might uselessly break in upon it?—Yet I could not write and hide what I was feeling. You said "it is good because it is living & so will bear fruit"—but I feared that the fruit might be bitter for all three—& there was an ache down to the very roots of my being. (It has not quite gone)—But I am a rank sentimentalist & I believe that love can work miracles and mysteries:—apparently you three are to prove it. So long as there is peace in your heart, I think they too are safe. For I am not wholly selfish in my fears—I feel so drawn to those two people by so many different threads that I could not bear to have pain & confusion come upon them through you." On 7 July 1937, Eleanor Mabel Sarton wrote to Julian: "You two with May are certainly an astonishing trio;—I was deeply troubled about it for a time—not merely about May but because I felt instinctively that you and your wife are rare people & who have built a happy marriage—I could not bear that May should risk to bring pain or sorrow to one or both. However, by some miracle of sincerity you have arrived at this 'happy & peaceful relation'—I think too you must have a well of tenderness, of kindness in you & Juliette also & I believe that this does 'work miracles.' May has it too, growing deeper, I believe, as she grows older. Yes, I do feel her to be 'one of the most charming creatures in the world'—& constantly I discover new and lovely things in her with the same joy and little secret thrill that one discovers a new flower, unexpected & rare, in familiar woods or garden. ¶ We are indeed grateful to you & your wife for the many kind & generous things you have done for May. You have helped her to work at her novel by giving her a quiet refuge at Whipsnade, as nothing else could have done & you have given her too many real pleasures for me to think of trying to thank you."

[CHEZ LIMBOSCH?]   [August ? 1937]
MONDAY

Something so terrible though somehow expected has happened that I must tell you now so that I won't have to do it when we meet. I read most of the novel to Jean Dominique and some of it to Blanchette [Blanche

Rousseau] who reads English and read it to herself. This morning came two letters from them asking me to re-write completely so that they are unrecognizable. I had spoken in the despair of finishing of taking another six months and re-doing it but this was because living in the house I realized how much I had left out of just what they want me now to change. They are quite right and all this is my fault, the fault of a young artist who has not properly assimilated and refashioned his material. But just now it is hard. I am afraid I shall cry if I go on. Please send me a word.

[Unsigned]

WEDNESDAY   [September? 1937]
34 HIGH ST.

Juliette, my darling, thanks for writing. Things here are not so bad. Mummy really sent for me to comfort <u>me</u> (that is so typical of her) but now I am here there are things I can do. My Grannie looked so adorable in her purple silk jacket waving from the window—and is so happy to have us both—and Mummy and I "tired the sun with talking"—you <u>must</u> meet her.

I know there was something up like a wall between you and people—and me—the night I arrived. Perhaps that was what depressed me, a very final <u>click</u> of a door shutting. But I, how I understand that <u>not</u> wanting to see people—the agonies of intercourse when one feels like an anemone someone has put a finger on. But you must believe that we are friends—that I can be quite owlish with wisdom. It is all much more than a <u>dorure</u> or not a <u>dorure</u> however.

The things I want to tell you are literally <u>infinite</u>—the poems to be read, the ideas to be discussed—but they can <u>all</u> wait. They have nothing to do with the moon or the season and this is not the season. And there is no time—think of me as a good friend and true—and then sometimes, O lady, as your troubadour bound to sing sad songs.

As for my novel, my mind feels like Laocoön—I am waiting for Kot to read it before making a decision. Perhaps I will just put it aside and begin a new novel. In my room in Cambridge I have a big window that looks on poplar trees—when I see the wind making them look like waterfalls of leaves I think everything will be all right. It is strange that under-neath everything I have so much <u>faith</u>—I do believe the things that hap-pen to one <u>must</u> happen, that they are always a challenge, that in the end they are all good.

That doesn't mean of course that one doesn't have to weep a hell of a lot, and <u>ache</u>, and curse and wish oneself dead rather than having to make a fresh effort—without bitterness (that's the thing that could shrivel up a talent like hot fire).

My darling, be happy. Let us be simply happy and still when we meet—and you must say anything you want to—or say nothing. How lovely!

[   ]

I have two poems in the <u>Mercury</u> this month. I shall be back at 59 Acacia, going to Rye for the weekend.

I think this is a very pompous silly letter—

Je n'en reviens pas de la beauté, la gentillesse de tes deux fils—

———

to comfort me: concerning the changes Jean Do had requested.

tired the sun with talking: "How often you and I/Had tired the sun with talking and sent him down the sky," from "Heraclitus" by English poet and classicist William Johnson Cory (1823–1892).

a dorure or not a dorure: a gilding or not a gilding.

Laocoön: in Greek mythology, son of Priam and priest of Apollo, known particularly for his final agony when together with his two sons he was choked to death by serpents.

Kot: S(amuel) S(olomonovitch) Koteliansky (1880–1955). A Russian émigré born in the Ukraine, came to London in 1911; Sarton first met him at the Huxley's Coronation Day party on 12 May. Translator; reader for the Cresset Press, to which he intro-duced Sarton, staunch friend and supporter, of whose friendship Sarton wrote: "For Kot true friends 'happened like great and rare events,' and on these events he staked his life." Loyal friend also of D. H. Lawrence, Katherine Mansfield, Leonard Woolf, Mark Gertler, Dorothy Brett, James Stephens, Ralph Hodgson, Dorothy Richardson, Lady Ottoline Morrell, Beatrice Glenavy, the Julian Huxleys, and many others. See Ch. 9 in A World of Light.

before making a decision: regarding Jean Do's request for changes. On 1 September 1937 Kot wrote counseling her to have patience: "Whatever happens, remember that you have tremendous obligations to your talent," and "when you feel rested in yourself, and when you take yourself in hand, you will realize that what is of importance is to go on working, without troubling very much about publication." On 20 September he wrote to say that Dennis Cohen of the Cresset Press was willing to publish the novel and would pay £50, and that she should "consider all our talks about the novel very seriously" and then do exactly as she liked without paying any attention to what he called "practical" and "extraneous" matters. "It is now a question only of artistic conscience and integrity—the rest is of no importance at all."

two poems in the Mercury this month: "The Vanquished" and "Image," *London Mercury,* September 1937.

59 Acacia: Because the Huxleys had no room for her, Sarton found herself a room at 59 Acacia Road, St. John's Wood, London, close to Koteliansky's home at 5 Acacia Road, the house in which Katherine Mansfield had stayed and from whose window she saw the pear tree she immortalized in her story "Bliss."

Je n'en reviens pas . . . . : I can't get over the beauty and grace of your two sons.

---

5 CHANNING PLACE   October 17th, 1937

Juliette, nothing is quite right in my world since you haven't written. Why? I imagine many things—a feeling of unreality, no sense of touch or urgency to communicate across such vast spaces. But please do put a little bridge across. I write often to Julian of the things that happen to me because he writes to me and it is like a conversation. But with you it is a matter of essences and abstraction. So I am writing to you more in collecting a little autumn anthology than in writing a letter.

There are too few good poems about autumn and now if I don't send it off it will be winter when you get it! Hence the meagreness. The autumn here is just beyond words—you must see it someday. One clear gold day after another—with the trees flowering into flame. All its sadness is a triumphant sadness. It is full of glory. Last night there was frost. I got up very early to get breakfast and it was absolutely still outside and gold except for the continual short broken sound of leaves falling one by one (no wind). Like music, it was.

What is your life just now? Is it strange to be in a son-less world again? Are you working? Julian sounds happy and settled except about the Lubetkin business and after the headache-depression. I hope he is going to have a good satisfying winter full of happiness and work—and that you will too. Oh Juliette, how sweetly I think of you.

I am just marking time until I hear definitely and finally from J.D. who now has most of the novel in a literal translation I have just sent over. Until this is settled I shan't begin to live again. But it is lovely to be home, to be in my long room which I have just had painted the most entrancing gray. It gives one a sense of peace and balance to be surrounded by one's possessions. To be living in a place one has created for oneself.

Otherwise I am studying German hard—it is like an awful Pilgrim's Progress, isn't it, beginning a new language. But I have a very nice tutor who enjoys Andersen's fairy tales almost as much as I do. Give Alan my love and tell him that I hope someday he will write to me. Oh yes, you must give him the enclosed—I hope his falcons behave better than these!

My darling, please write. I hate being so out of your light.

love and love

[   ]

Lubetkin business: Berthold Lubetkin (1902–1990), born in Georgia, lived in Moscow, Berlin, Warsaw, and Paris; in 1931 went to England; avant-garde architect for the London Zoo's penguin pool; at the time of this letter his design for a new elephant house was objected to by the Zoo Council; he stunned the British art world when he abandoned his thriving practice in disgust over bureaucratic pressures and moved with his wife to a desolate farmhouse in rural England he named World's End.

Pilgrim's Progress: reference to English preacher John Bunyan's 1675 allegory of Christian's pilgrimage beset with trials and temptations.

Alan: Alan Best, Canadian natural historian, friend of the Huxleys, sculptor who taught Juliette rudiments of sculpting; later he became a zoo director; Juliette's lover.

---

5 CHANNING PLACE   October 30th [1937]

Juliette, my erstwhile blue flame, I can only say that because your letter sounded so stiff and unlike you, a making conversation letter, which, without the glance, the presence of you makes me draw my head and paws in like a turtle. No, I expect you wrote in a hurry and after all why should one write—never feel you must write to me unless you feel just like it. And perhaps on third thoughts your letter was really very nice (I was so glad to see your writing on the envelope; in itself it was an event). This has been a spring day with poplar trees, all gold now, waving and waving restlessly in a violent warm wind. Now it is night and it is howling around the windows. I hate seeing the leaves go—I am almost superstitious about this autumn. I don't want it to go. I would like to be frozen here, with the world stopped for awhile around me to taste it slowly, not to feel always that something is just going to happen—snow tomorrow or god knows what. But I am ashamed of this feeling, a little Peter Pannish, a little "I don't want to grow up"—is it? I think I am dreading having to settle down to a new piece of sustained work. This month has been a limbo of suspense (I still have to potter around for two weeks making changes in the first part of the old novel)—bad for the morale. And I have been writing poetry furiously, a strange story, another adventure of the mind, another hopeless love but so good and so challenging I can only bless it.

When did I write to you? Did I tell you that I am deep in the Goncourt journals which you surely read long ago but which I have just discovered—the other night I felt as if I were finding a spell when I came across these 18th century colors "Pluie de roses, Fleur de souffre, Gorge de pigeon, déséspoir d'opale"—I see scarfs and evening dresses—I see you in a pluie de roses, in a déséspoir d'opale. And this which I believe so much which I always think I am going to attain and never never do (but perhaps one must have these impossible-to-attain beliefs to keep the spirit athletic). "On ne conçoit que dans le repos et comme dans le sommeil de l'activité morale. Les émotions sont contraires à la gestation des livres. Ceux qui imaginent ne doivent pas vivre. Il faut des jours réguliers, calmes, apaisés, un état bourgeois de tout l'être, un recueillement bonnet (?) de côtes pour mettre au jour de grand, du torments, du dramatique"—

I wonder if you will like my new poems. I think they are sterner stuff and deeper than any until now. But Ah God, how tired I am of my own youngness.

I carried the photos of you and Kot about with me in my hand for days I love them so. I am so glad at last to have a photo of you and I think they are both ravishing; witty discriminating adorable face. It is on my desk. Thank you so much.

Did I tell you also that thanks to you I went through a delicious Mallarmé fever—why is it that one is suddenly prepared for a thing. There is moment [sic] when one must <u>meet</u> a certain poet, a certain painter.

I think of you so much, please write to me sometimes. What of Paris? What are you seeing? What are you working on? How are the trees outside the balcony?

Your enfant terrible
M—
[ ]

I forgot to enclose the New Yorker joke of the falcons for Alan in my last—

but perhaps he saw it anyway—6 falcons bringing down a weather-cock in triumph.

---

a making conversation letter: Alan Best, Juliette explained, had a "powerful and ridiculous suspicion" of Sarton; he had surrounded Juliette with "sentinels," inhibiting her while writing. "I have no hope to make him see sense or reason but I want us," Juliette wrote, "you & I—to remain as good friends as we can possibly be—so please take me as I am, if you can bear it."

I can only bless it: reference to her Boston friend Edith Forbes Kennedy, whom she had met as a child of eleven, and whose small shabby house on Shepard Street in Cambridge remained a mecca of wisdom and solace for Sarton. Two weeks before this letter, on 17 October 1937, Sarton wrote to Kot: "One night by a series of circumstances (how marvelous life can seem) I found myself looking right down into her heart. An old story that links Sean O'Faolain, Elizabeth, Edith and I into a knot. For the rest it has become one of those consuming inner adventures which one lives through, cursing and blessing." Edith Kennedy had told Sarton of her affair with and betrayal by Sean O'Faolain, also the lover of Elizabeth Bowen. After that, perhaps for feeling exposed, Kennedy withdrew.

Goncourt journals: Edmond (1822–1896) and Jules (1830–1870) de Goncourt, French novelists, historians, art critics, known as the Brothers Goncourt, collaborated in their work. Their famous *Journal* was eventually made fully available in 1956–58 in twenty-two volumes. Sarton read an English translation by Lewis Galantiére, *The Goncourt Journals: 1851–1870* (Doubleday, 1937).

Pluie de roses . . . : Shower of roses, Flower of saffron, Throat of pigeon (or iridescence), despair of opal; the last probably an allusion to the belief that one must never wear an opal unless it is one's birthstone, lest it bring misfortune.

"On ne conçoit . . .": "One only creates while at rest and while moral activity is dormant. Emotions work against the gestation or preparation needed for writing books. Those who create with their imaginations should not have to deal with ordinary living. One needs routine, calm, peace, a comfortable state of one's entire being, a centering down in order to illuminate the great, its torments and drama." Juliette answered: "Your Goncourt is right—up to this point, that also there must be seeds— Francis knows it and it frightens him a little. He seems to me to be bravely holding something which hurts but which he has faith in. I have too—am I right?"

like my new poems: Enclosed with this letter were the following published poems, some with minor changes: "Conversation on the Telephone," "Invocation," "Landscape" (under title "Les Brûlures de la Neige Paul Fort"), "Record," "Understatement," "Granted This World," and sonnets 4, 5, and 12, all in *Inner Landscape*. Also "Do you for an instant think these words"; see Appendix of Unpublished Poems. To these Juliette responded: "I am full of wonder at your astounding power of spanning the subtlest emotion."

Mallarmé: Stéphane Mallarmé (1842–1898), French esoteric symbolist poet, essayist, and translator known for his daring and integrity. Juliette was glad Sarton had "found" him; "He has something crystalline and inhuman."

enfant terrible: a precocious young person who says and does rash things to the annoyance of her more conservative elders.

[5 Channing Place]   Sunday, Nov. 28th [1937]

Oh Juliette, it is raining, unbearable this soft rain when it is the season for a snow-silence and for that gasp in the chest as the frosty air touches it. I have lemon yellow large single chrysanthemums like daisies on my desk. This is <u>just</u> the yellow I love, clear with a little green in it, a yellow that is the <u>essence</u> of yellow. Sunday morning—Daddy has been bringing up bottles of wine from the cellar and some French people called Beldensberger are coming for lunch.

I loved your letter from Paris with Volpone in it (one of the really brilliant pieces of theatre in the last ten years—I saw it the year I spent in Paris). Barsacq who did the sets is in N.Y. now with a French company. But first to answer. H.D. was Richard Aldington's wife, divorced I think, one of the pure "Imagists"—very much influenced by Greek. She has made translations of the plays. After a while her poetry seems over-intense, color laid on color, something a little <u>strained</u> (she is a Lesbian)—a little artificial. But I'll copy one or two for you to taste. It is a little like clover. One only wants to <u>taste</u> its savour. It is true that she stands alone in a style so marked it is unmistakable.

I am taking the ocelot to a furrier next week and think of a hat and a waistcoat edged with it. I can't wait! In it I shall be your leopard—but of course one should have gold eyes.

The week in Paris sounds good—with the echoes of Watteau and that delicious card of the sisters from Julian; thought of you going to "Volpone" and choosing dresses. And I felt as if I were looking into the enchanted world of an Easter egg (you know the sugared ones with a hole at one end and a little glass one looks through? I <u>adore</u> them!)

Of course Alan [Best] is right but it is upsetting to feel that I have to reach you through a screen—one doesn't change very much. You must not expect me ever to change as far as you are concerned but in this disembodied meeting by letter I hate to think you are "en garde." The excitement, the delight of the mind is one thing—passion is another. And in letters one is so free of the <u>mortal</u> part.

Francis' school and all you say of him touched me. To have faith in one's school, to <u>believe</u> is so rare these days and so precious I think if he does it is worth anything. But it must be a little frightening—Scotland is so far away, to me so mysterious and dark because I have never been there. You told me very little about the school—I'd like to know more. Is there a theory behind it? Or just a group of like-minded teachers? I often think of Francis and Anthony and you never give me news of them so I was glad of this.

The friend to whom I wrote the poems fainted two weeks ago and in falling hit her head—concussion—hospital—complete silence and rest. It has been a very strange experience to be so completely cut off—and a kind of limbo—an ache to be able to do something and there is nothing to do but keep away. She has been overworked for ten years, has three sons to support alone (she is divorced).

How difficult it is to love well—to know when it is better to be silent, that even joy can strain the heart so frightfully—though in general everything that denies life seems false to me.

So I have been depressed this last week—and, the reaction of writing so much—30 poems in 60 days—very tired. I went to N.Y. and just wanted to creep away and sleep instead of doing anything. But I did snatch some moments of pure joy seeing pictures. Tchelichew's portraits which I like extremely—classic almost academic painting of great purity with a poetic imagination. A wonderful Toulouse-Lautrec exhibition. I didn't realize what a great painter he was—the daring composition, the personal colour, the sense again of a created world—the Toulouse-Lautrec world—so that when one comes out everything takes on his colour, his personality and for awhile one sees with a fresh, a violent eye. A Picasso exhibition which disappointed me—where is the core in his progression? I'm afraid I am an infidel in this.

Darling, I must stop. Write to me soon. I have started the new novel in trembling and with a sense of total inadequacy—but work is good—a raison d'être—the only one for me.

love and love

[ ]

Have only sent one poem—but this poem sums up her talent and her point of view I think.

Beldensberger: Fernand Baldensperger and his wife, of 13 Rue d'Odessa, Paris 14me; friends of George Sarton.

letter from Paris with Volpone: In Paris Juliette had seen *Volpone,* based on *Volpone, or the Fox,* 1606, a comedy by English dramatist and poet Ben Jonson (1572–1637) dealing with the prolonged death of a wily miser and his avaricious friends. "My dear, how superb good acting & good staging can be. This was both—a feast—How superb Ch. Dullin is as Volpone, with a rare pointed head, & a slight stoop & a superb control & restraint—& the clothes were so good—oh you should almost take the next boat to Paris just for that! Julian was so sad to think it was going on when you were there & you could have seen it!"

Barsacq: a Russian set designer who was only twenty when he did the sets for *Volpone.* Sarton met him in 1932 in Florence, where he designed a vast pageant that the French actor and director Jacques Copeau (1879–1949) directed of the life of the fifteenth-century monk Savonarola.

H.D: Hilda Doolittle (1886–1961), an American Imagist poet, a movement adopted c. 1910 by English and American poets who followed T. E. Hulme and Ezra Pound; it demanded absolute precision in presenting a particular image or radically original metaphor rather than description. In 1913 she married the English poet and novelist Richard Aldington (1892–1962); in 1918 she met Bryher (Winifred Ellerman), the most enduring love of her life, and in 1919 divorced Aldington.

(she is a Lesbian): Sarton considered herself neither a lesbian poet nor a lesbian writer; she wanted her work to be seen as universal. Her critical mind railed against what she found to be affected or narrow in scope.

Watteau: Jean-Antoine Watteau (1684–1721), French Rococo painter in whose ethereal scenes exquisitely dressed young people idle away their time in dreamy settings.

Francis' school: Gordonstoun, famous public school founded in Scotland by Kurt Hahn, an exiled German; it moved to Wales during the war and many of its students have been royalty.

The friend to whom I wrote the poems: Sarton was now writing a great many poems for Edith Forbes Kennedy, among them "Invocation," "A Letter," "Landscape," and "*Answer.*" See footnote to letter of 30 October 1937, and Ch. 4 in *A World of Light.*

Tchelichew's portraits: Pavel Tchelitchew (1898–1957), exiled Russian painter, stage designer, prophet, best known for his famous *Hide and Seek* in New York's Museum of Modern Art; among the subjects of his portraits are Alice B. Toklas, Natalie Paley, Mrs. James W. Fosburgh, Constance Askew, Lincoln Kirstein, Edith Sitwell, Allen Tanner, Charles Henri Ford, and Ruth Ford.

A Picasso exhibition: At this time in 1937, Spanish artist Pablo Picasso (1881–1973), the most influential painter of the twentieth century, had exhibitions at both Jacques Seligmann & Company and the Valentine Gallery in New York.

started the new novel: probably "The Waterfall," unpublished.

[5 CHANNING PLACE]   13 janvier '38

It's snowing—this snow that seems to open a silence in the soul. Everything in the room seems violent with color—the green, the blue, the yellow—

it's like a festival enclosed in a veil, in a tent of snow. There is only one thing
that I have a wild desire to do—that is to put on my boots and cross the
world to see you. Suddenly for some weeks now you have become again
one of those people I write to across oceans—think that you are only a
mile from here and that I am waiting for just <u>one word</u> which does not
come—it's inconceivable. I put you on the moon—I look at you from far
away—And dear God, I long for <u>age</u> which comes so slowly. It is true that
youth is an illness. Perhaps one should shut oneself in a library to learn
everything, to <u>know</u> everything and <u>feel</u> nothing and not begin to live
until one is thirty years old. So make a sign across the distance. Isn't anything possible? Even perhaps wisdom? I wonder—

M—

This letter, written in French, found in Sarton's journal, was never sent; see Appendix for
the French.

[5 CHANNING PLACE]   le 13 janvier [1938]

This [drawing] is my hat and waistcoat of ocelot that I <u>adore.</u>

Little flame, I write to you on this hideous paper because it has so
much room on which I can send out all my thoughts—my love—my tenderness—if only it does not begin to consume itself. Above all, my "boy,"
you are young <u>and</u> wise, what a miracle. How do you manage to be <u>so</u>
young and <u>so</u> prudent at the same time. Tomorrow I will go out in the
snow to buy "the despair of the opal." It has snowed all night—we are both
of us in a white world—impossible, a veiled world, magical   our feet don't
touch <u>the earth</u>. Here after the swells and waves of snow during the night,
it is falling softly like a promise—from time to time the trees move a cen-
timetre and drop down a silent eiderdown of snow feathers.

I wish you could see me someday in this room which is my shell
where I retreat, where like a snail I withdraw my little sensitive horns,
where I work. <u>Glory?</u> But my dear don't you see that this imaginary glory
takes the place of real happiness—human joy—at moments young and
fierce and desperate I say to myself, "I am born to love unhappily and to

immortalize this unhappiness!" It is an armor, a style [panache]—and that's all.

> Glory is that bright tragic thing,
> That for an instant
> Means Dominion,
> Warms some poor name
> That never felt the Sun,
> Gently replacing
> In oblivion—

I envy you this true and profound attachment, this creature love that binds you to your children. I think of Anthony and all that he must suffer with a kind of anguish—and how difficult it is not to touch the wound if one is a mother. But it is a great joy that you enter into the very heart of life with your children. Everything has its season and its time. Oh my God, I know that one is always in peril, that to live at one's simplest (and children are life at its least simple) is tantamount to walking on water—an act of faith and love and hope constantly renewed, recreated in oneself. But you (never doubt it) you have a genius for walking on water—and you are in yourself this love and this hope. When I read your letter I cried a little. And then I worked.

I am writing a novel with all created characters (you'll be happy to know) but it means writing with one's marrow—I have to think so much before I write.

Edith [Forbes Kennedy] has returned to her daily life but she is still tired—I feel, guess rather, that she has little emotion left, that she wants to reenter into the hard but absolute pattern of a life of work for her children, and of the thousand friendships, without letting a single one of any intensity or piercingness fatally touch her heart. All that without any explanations, without clarity. I mean that I understand completely but I would love it if she would speak of it to me gently instead of closing herself up in a cruel silence. Perhaps one day we will speak of it. Sadly, I do not change. These last two months have been a long transition in a vacuum but I'm coming out of it.

One of the things that helps bring me out are these poems of Jeanne Plateau—a spinster painter—and friend (only by letter) of Jean Dominique,

who has had a sad life, almost always sick, but from whose troubles rises this
fountain of poetry.

I think with a pang at the heart of seeing you again—the first of April.
Oh, please don't close yourself off. I know it's easier to have an open heart
with an ocean between us which washes away the problems. Anyway, I love
you so much—and darling I shall try to be wise also—to love you so gently that even Alan won't guess it—and only you will know it.

Here comes the sun. I'm going to make a snowman with the children
next door. I kiss you.

M—

The book will be out in England the 10th of March—be kind to the
poor solitary Marc.

See Appendix for original French.
ocelot: Given to her by Juliette.
Glory is that bright tragic thing . . . . : #1660 in *The Complete Poems of Emily Dickinson.*
touch the wound if one is a mother: Juliette had written: "I am a little worried about Anthony
 who is moody with a love-affair with a boy he won't produce. He goes to Ballet
 with him and won't ask him to our party—he waits for letters from him like a prisoner waits for a reprieve. He is long & thin & lanky & gave me his School essays to
 read—they are astounding. He speaks of love like a grown man—the different kinds
 of—the pain of—the value of—Oh my god—why bother to have a mother! And I
 spend my nights thinking of two babies I had once, centuries ago, & didn't know
 <u>how</u> to bring up—"
I am writing a novel: "Fire in a Mirror," unpublished.
these poems of Jeanne Plateau: Poésie (Les Imprimés du Limbourg, 1938), published posthumously.
the children next door: Binks, Sally, and Elizabeth Barrett.
poor solitary Marc: the protagonist in *The Single Hound.*

[VOUVRAY]   July 19th [1938]

O Juliette, how sad about Kot and that he <u>would</u> be the Lion of Judah, but
I think perhaps under his rage it will have made him feel safe, cherished by
his friends—and even though he would always refuse <u>money,</u> still know
that people feel he is of great worth—that it was never, <u>could</u> never be

"charity" but only a kind of homage. Of course I'll be as secret as a stone. But, O my darling, what a sad thing for you. I am sorry. But when dealing with such dear bears, one must be prepared for a swift slap as well as the hug that kills!

The house is empty. G. has gone to Poitiers with her husband for the evening. It is very warm and sultry with the birds even a little overpowered, conversing in chirps instead of singing. All is well, although I am so tired that I just sit and "ne fait que regarder le bleu du temps." This is limbo. No work I fear for awhile and I am going to Belgium at the end of the week—coming to London Aug. first instead of later—and then perhaps Ireland for a month. It is necessary to set distance between torture and me to be able to work. I feel all this may be a good turning point in my life. At least one can make a pattern of events even when they seem chaotic.

The hard thing to accept is that there is no happiness with G. and her man—only endless suspense (he comes rarely) and occasional moments. But to witness the constancy and purity of that passion—through such ordeals and sordidness shining—is enough to make life seem a grand adventure. It has taught me something.

I'm glad you like the poem. Today I bought French translations of Rilke (I think Supervielle must have been influenced by him)—here are one or two.

I sent the book of poems off to Cresset—I do think it is good—it is dedicated to you and Julian

For Julian and Juliette Huxley

It should be a secret but I have to tell you! My dear one, be happy—take care of your Julian. Tender love from

May

Devance tous les adieux, comme s'ils étaient
derrière toi, ainsi que l'hiver qui justement s'éloigne.
Car parmi les hivers il en est un si long
qu'en hivernant ton coeur aura surmonté tout.

Sois toujours mort en Eurydice—en chantant de plus en plus monte,
remonte en célébrant dans le rapport put.

Ici, parmi ceux qui s'en vont, sois, dans l'empire des fruites,
sois un verre qui vibre et qui dans son chant déjà s'est brisé.

Chanson

Toi, à qui je ne confie pas
mes longues nuits sans repos,
Toi qui me rends si tendrement las,
me berçant comme un berceau;
Toi qui me caches tes insomnies,
dis, si nous supportions
cette soif qui nous magnifie,
sans abandon?

Car rappelles-toi les amants,
comme le mensonge les surprend
à l'heure des confessions.
Toi seule, tu fais partie de ma solitude pure.
Tu te transformes en tout: tu es ce murmure
ou ce parfum aérien.
Entre mes bras: quel abîme qui s'abreuve de pertes.
Ils ne t'ont point retenue, et c'st grâce à cela, certes,
qu'à jamais je te tiens.

Ma Vie N'est Pas . . .

Ma vie n'est pas cette heure abrupte
où tu me vois précipité.
Je suis un arbre devant mon décor,
je ne suis qu'une de mes bouches,
celle de toutes qui se clora la première.

Je suis l'intervalle entre les deux notes
qui ne s'accordent l'une et l'autre qu'à grand'peine,
car celle de la mort voudrait monter plus haut . . .
Mais toutes deux, vibrant durant l'obscure pause,
se sont réconciliées.
Et le chant reste beau.

––––––

Sarton had written to Julian some weeks earlier, on 29 May 1938: "A whole all embrac-
ing love is impossible for us (and in the end might not be so lovely, who knows?)
That is a great need in me—as it is in any sensitive person—the desire to belong

somewhere, to have a spiritual home. After our excursions into space you come back to Juliette, to a certainty—'This is my life.' And for four years or more I have gone from one person to another like a homing-pigeon looking for a heart where I could <u>rest</u>, to whom I could be given <u>entirely</u> and who could give themselves to me. I have felt that for us passion was like revelation, was like a <u>seal</u> on our love—but couldn't, <u>mustn't</u> become the daily bread and wine which one needs as well. I can't tell you what a relief, what a blessing it is now to have completion, the perhaps <u>narrow</u> but enclosed feeling of a world apart that two wholly free people make together. I know that it won't last forever—four or five years at most. I do so deeply want marriage but I have always thought it would come late—as it did for mother. [Eleanor Mabel Sarton was married at thirty-three.] And darling, how complicated it all is: there is a part of me, perhaps the <u>writing</u> part that needs a woman as a man needs a woman." And on 8 June 1939 she wrote: "However much one loves there are things one can't do against one's own spirit—all the tenderness, all the deep <u>loving</u> side of me goes out to you and wants you in my arms and to be in yours, but I can't sleep with you now, just now, my dear. I just can't. . . . And I believe the physical part of our love was necessary to the finding of each other but it was <u>never</u> a passion in the ordinary sense. It was more and less than that, more and less than love if you like."

a kind of homage: Because of Kot's financial problems, Juliette had had funds deposited to his account; Kot was furious and insisted the money be returned.

G: Grace Eliot Dudley. Sarton met her while crossing on the *Normandie* in April 1938; granddaughter of Charles William Eliot, president of Harvard University 1869–1909, she became a central person in Sarton's life until her death in 1950, and her home, Le Petit Bois in Vouvray, France, one of Sarton's havens; on 29 May 1938 Sarton wrote to Julian: "I love G. because I feel an extraordinarily innocent deep purity of soul—this is the most difficult thing to write about but in the end it <u>is</u> my thing." See "Grace Eliot Dudley: Le Petit Bois" in *A World of Light.*

with her husband: Grace Dudley was divorced from her husband, William, who lived nearby at Mon Bazon. On 13 July 1938 Sarton writes to Elizabeth Bowen: "Nothing is settled between G. and her husband and I think perhaps never will be but perhaps he will come over sometimes and stay. I see her carefully guarded and built up emotional stability going to pieces and there is nothing to do. Really passion is a frightful thing." In 1940 he married a Greek girl; Grace Dudley remained in love with him.

ne fait que regarder le bleu du temps: do nothing but gaze at the blueness of the weather.

glad you like the poem: "On a Dark Night," written on 10 July 1938 at Vouvray; published in *Inner Landscape* as "The Pride of Trees." Juliette writes: "[Julian] also showed me your <u>most</u> beautiful poem. I think I liked it more than anything I have seen of yours. Kot also liked it so much. This is a <u>lasting</u> poem, & I hope you will write more things as beautiful & fine."

Rilke: Rainer Maria Rilke (1875–1926), German lyric poet whose imagery greatly moved and influenced Sarton, and who, like Sarton, was also influenced by Valéry; see "At Muzot" in *In Time Like Air,* and "Proteus" in *A Grain of Mustard Seed.* In her plenary speech " 'That Great Sanity, That Sun, the Feminine Power:' May Sarton and the (New) Female Poetic Tradition," at the National Conference "May Sarton at 80: A Celebration of Her Work" at Westbrook Conference in 1992, Sandra Gilbert traced the allusions to, and revisions of, Rilke's life and work in Sarton's poetry; see *A Celebration for May Sarton,* ed. Constance Hunting (Puckerbrush Press, 1994).

Supervielle: Jules Supervielle (1884–1960), Uruguayan-born French poet, playwright, novelist, and short story writer whose poetry is marked by an innocence combined with a metaphysical quality of myth and allegory.

it is dedicated to you and Julian: Inner Landscape in its Cresset (English) edition, 1939, is dedicated to the Huxleys; the Houghton Mifflin (U.S.) edition, also 1939, is dedicated to Edith Forbes Kennedy. On 7 May 1939 Juliette wrote: "Did I ever tell you how proud and endlessly delighted I am with your including me in the Dedicase? It was quite the nicest thing which happened to me for a long long time & on your part a most loving thought."

Devance tous les adieux . . . : from #13 in *Sonnets to Orpheus,* the Maurice Betz French translation from the German of Rilke's *Poésie* (1922). Trans: Be in advance of all parting, as though/it were behind you like the winter that is just going./For among winters one is so endlessly winter/that, overwintering, your heart once for all will hold out. ¶ Be ever dead in Eurydice, mount more singingly,/mount more praisingly back into the pure relation./Here, among the waning, be, in the realm of decline,/be a ringing glass that shatters as it rings.

Chanson: French translation by Rilke, from *Dernières Poésies:* Trans: You, to whom I don't confide/my long nights without rest,/You, who make me so tenderly tired,/rocking me like a cradle;/You, who hide your insomnias from me,/tell me if, without surrender,/we will endure/this thirst that magnifies us?/For remind yourself of lovers,/how the lie surprises them/when the time comes to confess./Only you are part of my pure solitude./You transform yourself into all: you are this whisper/or this heavenly perfume./Between my arms: such an abyss priming itself with losses./They did not hold you back, and it's thanks to that,/surely, that I hold you forever. (Trans. by A. Poulin, Jr.)

Ma Vie N'est Pas . . . : from *The Book of Hours* (1899–1906). Trans: No, my life is not this precipitous hour/through which you see me passing at a run./I stand before my background like a tree./Of all my many mouths I am but one,/and that which soonest chooses to be dumb./I am the rest between two notes/which, struck together, sound discordantly,/because death's note would claim a higher key./But in that dark pause, trembling, the notes meet,/harmonious./And the song continues sweet. (Trans. by Babette Deutsch, 1941.)

[5 CHANNING PLACE]   Sunday Oct. 2d, '38

Juliette darling—what a month of human travail and horror—I have thought of you with my heart at my lips every day and almost every hour—and then came the news of your accident. O miserable donkey. It was so horrible—please don't let J. <u>ever</u> drive 60 miles p.h. again—the two accidents I was in (one so much like yours) could have been avoided at 40—the thought that you might simply have vanished into air in that moment! But thank heavens it doesn't seem to have been too bad—though the <u>implications</u> of it afterward will have shaken you, being a woman, down to your roots I know. Men in such matters are so much more facile emotionally, lucky devils. (This would make J. mad so don't tell him, the dear bear.) Kot wrote very sweetly to reassure me.

> "With so much hated still so close behind
> The sterile shores before us must be faced;
> Again, against the body and the mind,
> The hate that bruises, though the heart is braced."

That, apropos of Mr. Chamberlain's peace—is all I can find to say. Though "not war" seems better than war—almost—whatever the price—and even if it is only put off a year. Praying for peace seems such a futile pitiful thing—when it is only human intolerance and beastliness, the greed of man, his cruelty, and lying face that bring about war. But I do firmly believe that the hope of the world is in the infinitely slow personal progression—and there you must feel deeply involved in the future—with two sons who will perhaps grow to be better, saner, cleaner than we are. It is a childish argument, perhaps a romantic one, but it seems to me that one thing there is still to believe in—the private victory in each man.

I begin to teach next week—five pupils at a school in "Prose Writing" and one (so far) elderly school mistress (!) in Poetry, private lessons. But I hope it will end by being a small group. The year looks full of action and meat for thought which keeps the heart busy. I am learning to drive, am hoping to pay off debts—

There is no news. Grace is coming over in a month and I look forward to it of course—I feel really happy and quiet and pray it may last.

Please send me a letter someday—there is nothing in the world to replace your letters,

Very dear love and blessings—
M—

Am reading a good long absorbing Swiss novel called "La Pêche Miraculeuse" by Guy de Pourtales—Do you know it? It is solid like mahogany, first-rate, but a little dark and dense.

———

what a month of human travail and horror: The month of September 1938 brought the German-Czech crisis over the Sudetenland to a head, the most serious international

crisis since 1918 culminating on 29 September with Chamberlain's flying to Munich
to appease Hitler, promising "Peace in Our Time." The Second World War broke
out amid complete disarray.

news of your accident: Returning from vacation on the slopes above Lake Maggiore, the
Huxleys had a severe accident outside Abbeville, swerving sharply to avoid a straying donkey cart laden with children. They hit a tree sideways, escaping what could
have been a fatal crash. Francis was unhurt, Julian had a concussion, Juliette's forehead took a small gash, and the children on the cart were untouched.

"With so much hated . . .": unidentified.

five pupils at a school: the Stuart School in Boston, now defunct.

elderly school mistress (?) in Poetry: Elizabeth Rodman Swift, who had written Sarton about
The Single Hound; "Subtle, learned, out to catch me like a fish in her hands," Sarton
wrote of her to Virginia Woolf on 15 January 1939.

[5 Channing Place]   March 12th [1939]

Dearest Juliette—We are having a great silent Petrouchka snow—last night
it was too beautiful and mysterious for words and I wished we were walking under the trees

> You shall go shod in silk
> And I in wool—
> We shall walk in velvet shoes.
> Wherever we go
> Silence will fall like dews
> On white silence below
> We shall walk in the snow.

If my silence had been snow, it would be well. Your letter I have kept by
me and looked at like a dear treasure—and always thought I was going to
get to over a mountain of work. Dearest Juliette, forgive me—forgive me
for having taken so long to share in your unexpected and heart-rending
adventure. What is wrong with our complicated world today that "business" gets in the way of everything important? I would like to go with a
silver trumpet and pierce people's ears "Soon you will be dead and what
are you <u>doing</u>? What part of your day is living?" And I have been saying it
to myself so loudly that I feel quite depressed. All brought on I suppose by
the fact that I sent out over 50 copies of my book and so few people have
taken the time to answer—it is not that they are unmoved or don't care. It

is that they haven't <u>time</u>. Isn't that awful? You feel that if you knocked at the door and said "Look, I have found the truth" they would answer "No time this week. Call me up a week from Thurs" or if you came and said "See, here is my heart" they would answer "O, thank you so much. Just put it in a glass of water in the icebox. I am so busy today—tomorrow—" and so on. But it is more true of America I think. The struggle for existence seems to be more acute here.

Am glad you liked the Rilke—how distressing it is that people can never <u>be</u> their works, that if they could of course they would live and not write—but one hates to think of Rilke hating his own body—of Yeats, a small self-flattered man—of Duse an impossible intriguer—Perhaps the legend is the truth after all.

I must read Barrie's "David" and answer that part of your letter later. The great struggle here seems to be between those who interpret Christ's Gospel to the point of loving their enemies <u>more</u> than their friends i.e. in the interests of freedom of speech allowing a meeting in N.Y. of the Bund and even sending out 6000 police to <u>protect</u> the fascists from the angry crowd outside—and those, like me, who believe I am a Christian but think it is a faith that must be fought for—I am at war over this with many of my friends here. And of course the issues become sharper every day. The divisions are <u>awful</u>—I am filled with the <u>ache</u> of apprehension in all meet-ings—I seem at a word of being <u>severed</u> in spirit—and the dumbness that descends on me at a word so that I cannot persuade or convince but burst into tears and flee.

Kot's letters have sounded far away—I <u>felt</u> he was down or ill but do not want to hurt his pride and so haven't said anything. O Juliette, it has been so evident to me that my hearth home is in England these last weeks—What a pull to take up roots and embark—to see Kot and you and Julian and V. Woolf and Elisabeth—and now Ben Nicholson (V. Sackville-West's son) do you know him? A nice boy who is writing a book on Seurat and passed through Cambridge this winter. The thing one misses here is an emotional landscape—there is no <u>background</u>—people are painted on flat surfaces and they have no secrets. I cannot imagine an American boy of Anthony's age writing as he did about love (from what you told me once)—Is it do you think that in fear of dangerous emotions boys here have no "éducation sentimentale"—sophistication has no meaning unless it is a necessary tightrope over an <u>abyss</u>—here the Harvard boys acquire a sophistication before they even guess at the abyss—a tightrope two feet over a comfortable mattress.

Oh dear, I can't write letters anymore—and am catching the disease of "busyness"—two lectures to write this week—one on the young English poets and one on "Poetry as a Dynamic Force"—I think of Rilke's letters during the war—when he is so appalled to think it took <u>war</u> to produce the courage, the one-ness that poets had been trying to bring about "while we, the arts, the theatre called nothing forth in these very same people, brought nothing to rise and flower, were unable to change anyone. What is our métier else than purely and largely and freely to set forth opportunities for change—did we do this so badly, so half-way, so little convinced and convincing? That has been the question for almost a year."

And that now is the question for poets.

I feel quite inadequate and small before the necessity for greatness — My darling, how I <u>miss</u> you.

Love and love [   ]

In the months preceding the date of this letter, following an ultimatum from Julian to Sarton about physical intimacy, there was a lacuna in their correspondence. On 5 December 1938, Juliette wrote Sarton: "I hope . . . that you can care for him enough to be able to go on writing him as you do—if that is called 'caring' though not being <u>his</u> way of it." On 4 January, Julian wrote Sarton this poem, and soon after, began an affair with Theodora Benson:

> "Outer and Inner"
> I did not think our love could finish so:
> It seemed a single and undying thing,
> Which, though complete, could yet aspire to grow—
> Live as a tree, unbroken as a ring.
>
> The ring is cracked and the ends meet no more,
> The living leaves are falling from the tree,
> The singleness is with itself at war,
> And love infected with mortality.
>
> Yet my interior, my essential part
> Will not obey the mere external fact:
> Safe in its depth the living strands still twine
> The circling ring of love, and still intact
> The vital tree stands rooted in my heart
> With flowers that still eternally are thine.
>
> J.S.H. 4.i.39

On 7 May 1939 Juliette was to write Sarton, about to arrive imminently: "I don't know how you will find Julian—time has made—naturally enough—a sort of chemical change in his feelings. Don't worry about it—it is only part of the evolution towards a better friendship. Give it time to ripen."

Petrouchka snow: Igor Stravinsky's ballet *Petrouchka* choreographed by Michael Fokine opens in a St. Petersburg square in the midst of a wintry carnival fair.

You shall go shod in silk . . . : from "Velvet Shoes" by Elinor (Morton Hoyt) Wylie, American lyric poet, an important early influence on Sarton; see footnote to letter of 15 December 1939.

heart-rending adventure: Juliette suffered a miscarriage in late January.

50 copies of my book: Inner Landscape was published on 21 February. Sarton was additionally discouraged as at this time only forty-two copies of the Cresset edition had sold.

Rilke hating his own body: possibly reference to Rilke's long illness, which had incapacitated him from work long before it was diagnosed as acute leukemia and which diagnosis Rilke did not want to hear; despite intense agony, Rilke refused any drugs which might deaden awareness and was preoccupied with the conflict between the suffering body and the soul."We were such wonderfully good friends," he wrote, "my body and I, I don't know at all how it happened that we separated and became foreign to each other."

Yeats: William Butler Yeats (1865–1939), Irish lyric poet and dramatist, considered one of the greatest poets of the twentieth century. He remained a preeminent influence throughout Sarton's life and a model for what can be done with the lyric poem itself; she identified with him particularly at the end when she, as he, changed her style radically in old age; the product of that change, her volume of poems *Coming into Eighty* which won the Levinson Prize, was published in 1994, one year before her death.

Duse: Eleonora Duse (1859–1924), Italian actress, one of the greatest tragediennes of the international stage; an enigmatic personality who in seeking to avoid publicity made herself even more conspicuous. Sarton was fascinated by Duse during her own theater years and collected books on her which were still in her library at the time of her death.

Barrie's "David": Sir James Matthew Barrie (1860–1937), Scottish dramatist and novelist, is perhaps best known for *Peter Pan*; his last play, *The Boy David,* written for Elisabeth Bergner and played by her in 1936, treats the theme of universal childhood at the core of all humanity. Juliette had asked if Sarton ever considered writing of young David from the point at which Barrie left off, and whether David succeeded in living what he knew of charity.

the Bund: The German-American Bund, a Nazi organization active in the United States, was directed from Germany; although total membership amounted to only 8,300 in 1939, the Bund possessed more than eighty active cells, including twenty-two youth camps located near important military centers. Sarton may also be alluding here to the American Civil Liberties Union, on whose board she sat and which, in defending the rights of all people, often went too far, in Sarton's opinion, in defending the indefensible.

Ben Nicholson: Benedict Nicolson (1914–1978), eldest son of Vita Sackville-West and Harold Nicolson, art historian, editor of the *Burlington Magazine* and author of major books on the painters Terbrugghen, Wright of Derby, and Georges de La Tour; of him Sarton wrote to Koteliansky in 1939, "I am lonely here. There is no one.

Except that Ben Nicholson turned up and left. He is nice and might turn into a prop
for my old age."

"éducation sentimentale": By "sentimental education" the French mean an education in the
physical handling of the opposite sex quite apart from the spiritual, although it is the
spiritual which is Sarton's concern here.

"while we, the arts, the theatre . . .": Munich, 28 June 1915, to Thankmar Baron von
Münchhausen. *Wartime Letters of Rainer Maria Rilke,* trans. M.D. Herter (W. W.
Norton, 1940) p. 30.

———

35 ROSSLYN HILL N.W. 3   Tues. Aug. 1st, 1939

Dearest petite flamme, what was wrong with me last night? I felt so out of
key and couldn't get back to the right one—talking about poetry upsets
me now in the most stupid way and I did not mean to be cross about sitting so badly (it is quite true) but I suddenly felt in despair with myself and
then clung to the idea, the only spar, which is work—but what an arrogant
way of doing it. Please forgive me.

This year I have thought a great deal about Yeats and written and spoken of him, lived with him and Rilke in a way, and someday I must try to
explain better than I did last night. In Belgium I'll find some poems but
they are packed—I am sitting in a mess as a matter of fact at the moment
and can't find anything including myself. Partings are hideous. At the last
moment there was no emotion left and I couldn't even look at you. All this
year I have felt so strongly outside some inner circle which was before
open, a door shut irrevocably against me. You have been wonderfully the
same over the difference. But the difference is there isn't it? Something is
lost. I suppose that is what life does to one—it _is_ change. To wish it not to
be _is_ to refuse it and that is fatal. It is only the transitions that are painful
I have been sad that you never wanted to see me quietly by myself—and
it is not arrogance really Juliette that makes me want to read you my
poems, but the sense so strong that they are all I have to offer, that they are
the best of me—and also that I trust you and your judgement when you
show the great love and courtesy to make it (for I know how hard it is and
what an honor to be told the truth which you so rarely tell out of mod-
esty or something I don't know what). There are very few people in the
world whose sensibility one trusts when applied to work—yours is true I
believe. It is a treasure—to have been deprived of it has given me a queer

inner despair, flat and tolerable and deathly. When the day we were sitting looking out at the sunset and someone said something about saying a poem I wanted to say this one, but didn't dare—now I think I shall send it.

> Now goes under and I watch it go under, the sun
> That will not rise again.
> Today has been the setting in your eyes cold and senseless as the sea,
> Of friendship better than bread, and of bright charity
> That lifts a man a little above the beasts that run.
>
> I would have sworn, indeed I swore it;
> The hills may shift, the waters may decline,
> Winter may twist the stem from the twig that bore it,
> But never your love from me, your hand from mine.
>
> Now goes under, and I watch it go under.
> Farewell, sweet light, great wonder!
> You too farewell—but fare not well enough to dream
> You have done wisely to invite the night before the darkness came.
>
> Millay

I have said this in buses and subways to myself, not for the very goodness of it as a poem (for it is not so good) but because it is good to have things stated—the evil and the good goes out of them once they are spoken.

Before, I know that I talked too much, broke noisily into temples and behaved like a vandal of the spirit. I think I have learned something now. If I ever see you again, if I ever come back, though there was something final about last night—believe it Juliette. If there must be a transition let it be to a gentle end. I do love you and in my heart often praise you.

> *Your devoted*
> *May*

Give my love to the boys—the last week-end was so lovely—it was almost <u>real</u>, almost <u>right</u>, as it used to be.

––––––––

Tues. Aug 1st, 1939: Sarton had crossed on the *Normandie*, arriving in London 19 June.
that they are the best of me: Sarton suffered when her poetry was not received by those for whom it was written. In Ch. 10 of *A World of Light* she writes: "It took me years to

understand that the poem one writes out of love and brings to its subject as a present, is not always as delightful to receive as it is to give. For poems of this kind are always pleas and must, often, be warded off out of kindness."

Now goes under . . . : from "To a Friend Estranged from Me," in *The Buck in the Snow and Other Poems* (1928) by Edna St. Vincent Millay (1892–1950), American poet, famous during the 1920s for her poems celebrating love, unfaithfulness, and the right of women to as much freedom in matters of morals as men; her work of this period influenced Sarton's early poetry. On at least one other occasion did Sarton send this poem to a seminal friend; she did not herself close doors, and fought their being closed by others.

---

16 AVE. LEQUIME   August 12th, 1939
RHÔDES ST. GENÈSE
BELGIUM

Dearest Juliette, Here I was sitting in the garden under an apple tree with the little goat and the dog, in the sun, and such a sense of loss, such a hole somewhere inside, such a feeling of final parting as if never never again could I take a boat and cross the channel and see in the distance the block of the Zoo building standing out like a ship among the trees—and then your letter came. I can't tell you what it means, how dear of you to have broken through against your will, out of kindness and love, and tried to explain. I did want to talk to you but was shy always of asking as you seemed so busy and I had made one or two efforts which seemed inapropos. The night I left Kot said something to the effect that it was a pity I had come, that it was the wrong time, as if it had showed a lack of delicacy. And perhaps I seemed to have come like an American on a holiday, but it was not so. There I feel isolated because I am European—well, that is the strangeness of life, isn't it? As one grows older one's essential solitariness increases as perhaps one's humanity deepens, at least one hopes so. If personal isolation doesn't compensate for itself by some sort of communion, religious or simply human—if one cannot feel something like companionship somewhere, somehow, there would be nothing but an end to make of it. I do understand—and I think I somehow missed the way of being inside as well as outside, that was the trouble. If I seemed wholly outside of course it was quite wrong to have come—but there was also Julian. Perhaps in that too I was near-sighted—it is so difficult to know. I <u>felt</u> that it was necessary that I had some responsibility to fulfill, that with all the tenderness possible there must be no misunderstanding, and I have never honored him more than I do now. It is quite impossible to think of life without sharing some part of it with him, but he has been wonderfully patient and now I think it is my turn to be patient too, to be silent perhaps. I did after so many words and the sound and fury of last year feel prevented from speaking to you at all, as if discretion were now the only present I could make.

Don't answer any of this. I don't mean you to. I am just saying it quietly and thanking you as best I can.

This morning not knowing your letter was on the way I copied some Yeats for you and then despaired of sending it. It is evening now, I think I shall take the dog and go out and look at the fields—this is a strangely secret and closed garden—then suddenly one wants space and to see the whole sky. It has been a good day and I have worked like a beaver. Dearest Juliette, there are things that will remain whatever happens. One lives by essentials if at all. I hope Anthony will write some poetry, that you will someday take a piece of ivory in your hand again and carve it, that there will be evenings like this so intimately peaceful that in a moment one might begin to live a new life. I do love you and wish I had some great beauty to lay in your hands,

your devoted
<u>*May*</u>

Never think it was <u>dull</u> for me in England. It was like coming home. One does not want home to be exciting—even Kot seemed to think I expected some extraordinary event. I find friendship event enough, you know!

---

the little goat and the dog: Sarton called the Limbosches' "a Noah's ark of animals."

tried to explain: On 10 August 1939 Juliette had responded to Sarton with a plea for "normal values," without such "terrible stress on moments, on partings," said that one must now pray for the world and the future in peril, and that she felt empty of personal emotions and desires. But "you are right, absolutely," she wrote. "The only spar <u>is</u> work (It was not arrogance in the least, it was true what you said the other night). Yours has in it a rare quality—Don't <u>ever</u> despair about it."

[5 CHANNING PLACE]   December 15th 1939

Dearest Juliette—This is just to tell you that all is well. Your letter I have
carried in my pocket like a talisman ever since it came, and shall keep there
tomorrow to read again on the train (we are going to Florida for three
weeks to try to get Daddy feeling less tired) and shall finally answer when
I am rooted somewhere again. The last week has been terrific—with packing, getting Xmas all done ahead—and Julian. That of course is the great
news and why I'm trying to get this off on the Clipper although it can't
be a real letter and I don't like answering yours so hastily. Set this apart as
a news bulletin only. J. looks remarkably incredibly well considering the life
he is leading and a real miracle happened while he was here. I mean that
at last some peace has come to us and I really felt he was happy as I was
and that somehow all this hell we have been through hasn't been just
destructive, and I loved him so dearly and freshly all over again for being
all that he is—the blessed release from strain, the feeling of coming home
to the friend of one's heart (which is quite a different and ah, a better thing
than a lover, isn't it?). I feel a well of gratitude and deep joy to you and to
him, and as if a great peril in which one's soul was in the balance has somehow been passed. (But perhaps I am too sanguine.) I hope this makes you
happy. I have had the last lines of your letter on my lips a thousand times
before J. came and perhaps they had something to do with the miracle. You
at any rate are at its heart.

One night we gathered ten or twelve people here to discuss what
PEP is trying to do. I think it was valuable in a negative if not a positive
way as one must know the worst, all the marshes and pits on which the
foundations will have to be built. The woe of our age is I think that all trust
has gone. I want to believe but I cannot believe that in the end the Lords
and Masters (industrial, political) will not use all this to their own ends.
And then I think it is like this Blake drawing and we must bind the dragon, mustn't we? Somehow. But it cannot be done without the self sacrifice of Nations and I do not believe that is possible yet. There was a very
good man here called Ulich—prof. of Education, ex-German—who said
that he thought one of the problems was how to keep disenchantment out
of disillusion—and also that we must find the other side of the coin of
detachment—an attachment. How one misses it everywhere. There is no
faith in us to bind the dragon with. But there is Julian and he does believe

though it broke my heart that I was not quite convinced. The un-faith here in the Chamberlain government having a real change of heart and not just one brought about by emergency as an expedient thing—is slight. The French are savage. "Have we brought heart, have we brought mind up to this place only to turn them against both mind and heart?" rings through my mind.

Well, this was not to be a letter and I must think it all out quietly before I try to speak—anyway it is only instinct we women have to go on and that is sometimes a poor thing.

The Pitter poems have been the revelation of the last weeks for me. I haven't written her yet. But they are <u>absolute</u>, aren't they? They are not the trying to get through to something essential that one feels in most moderns. They are there, like the Muses upon a mountain, grave and changeless as if they had always been. One does not think of them as ever having been written but as having always existed—how blessed to find them. I like best "The Old Woman and the Moon," the first one, and "The Difference" and "O Come Out of the Lily" (because of the ermine's eye— doesn't it remind you of the DaVinci portrait—though that isn't an ermine but it has the eye of God).

I am going to work on my book. I see now that when I thought it was finished it was just beginning. Now the rocks have to be broken to get at the sources—

Dearest little blessed love, be happy about Julian.

> Faison de notre vie, illustré par ses pleurs,
> Une ville bâti au bord d'un fleuve immense . . .

You are right about Elinor Wylie—it is like a metal image instead of a plant as poetry. How beautiful the three poems you sent me—but I'll leave that for the letter you shall soon have.

Your devoted
May

---

like a talisman: Juliette wished her well with her novel, "but don't hasten it before its ripeness. You have such a sure touch for words and you send them spinning in your letters—other people's words are tarnished—<u>I</u> never have the right charge, but yours are magnetic."

Florida for three weeks: The Sartons left by train the following day for the Boca Ciega Inn at St. Petersburg; George Sarton was deeply depressed over having to give up *Isis*, the journal of the history of science which he had founded in 1912; despite the crisis at the time of this letter, he did manage to pull the journal through. For the forty years of his owner-editorship of *Isis* he met all deficits with his own resources; it was only in 1951 that he resigned his dual office. After *Isis* became the full responsibility of the History of Science Society in 1952, the officers and councillors of the society realized the burdens Sarton had shouldered, and the great service he had rendered to the society.

and Julian: During December 1939 Julian Huxley was in the United States, visiting the Sartons in the East and his brother, Aldous, in California.

last lines of your letter: Juliette's long letter of 22 November 1939 closes with "Tonight I wish to be forgiven and to forgive with more than understanding."

PEP: Political and Economic Planning, founded in London in 1931 as a nongovernmental planning organization; a war aims group under its auspices was organized in 1938.

Blake drawing . . . bind the dragon: possibly Plate 75 for the vast poem *Jerusalem* (1793) by William Blake (1757–1827), English poet, engraver, painter, and mystic. See "Binding the Dragon" in *In Time Like Air*.

Ulich: Robert Ulich, member of the Harvard faculty from 1933 on, author of *The Human Career: A Philosophy of Self Transcendence* (1955); married to Elsa Brandstrom Ulich, known as "the White Angel" during World War II.

an attachment: A recurrent tension in Sarton's work; see "In Time Like Air" in *In Time Like Air*.

Chamberlain government: In 1938 France and Britain, led by Chamberlain, gave in to Hitler's demands and signed the Munich Pact; in 1939 Chamberlain appointed Sir Winston Churchill First Lord of the Admiralty. Shortly after this letter and following Germany's invasion of Denmark, Norway, Holland, Belgium, and Luxembourg, British expeditionary forces of 250,000 evacuated the beaches of Dunkirk and Churchill became British prime minister (after Chamberlain resigned), giving his famous "blood, toil, tears and sweat" speech to rally the British.

"Have we brought heart . . . ": unidentified.

Pitter poems: The poems referred to in this letter are from *The Spirit Watches* (Macmillan, 1940). What Sarton calls "The Old Woman and the Moon" is actually titled "An Old Woman Speaks of the Moon" by Ruth Pitter (1897–1992), English lyric poet and friend of Sarton, whose work she greatly admired. See footnote to letter of 23 November 1941. Of these Pitter poems Juliette writes: "What line & quality of simplicity, of sombre beauty—of depth—of unhasting conquest."

work on my book: "Fire in a Mirror," unpublished; Sarton had originally believed she finished it on 27 November 1939.

Faison de notre vie . . . : from "Déchirement" in *Les Éblouissements* (Paris, n.d.) by Comtesse Anna Elizabeth Mathieu de Noailles (1876–1933), French poet and novelist. See epigraph to Sarton's "My Sisters, O My Sisters" in *The Lion and the Rose*. Trans: Let us make of our life, illuminated by our tears, a city built on the edge of an immense river.

Elinor Wylie: Elinor (Hoyt) Wylie (1885–1928), American lyric poet known for her vivid imagery and subtle love poems. In the early 1930s while she was working in the theater, Sarton immersed herself in Wylie's *Collected Poems*; in 1938 she was delighted when Samuel Eliot Morison (1887–1976), the American historian, told her that she had "already beat Elinor Wylie by a mile."

Dearest Juliette, I waited until we were here to answer your letter, until I should be back inside myself and able to contain experience again instead of feeling scattered in small bits over the world. We have just been sitting in front of our little house watching the light fall on the bay—smooth warm amber-coloured granite rocks covered with grey lichen going down to a sapphire bay with gulls dipping and screaming and then settling one by one on the water, a quiet gold sunset that tipped their wings and gilded their bellies and then gave them to the dark. Now there is just the sighing of slow small waves breaking. It is high tide. If anything happens to you I shall always consider the boys my little brothers and do all that an elderly maiden sister can for them. One has to face all possibilities. But I do not believe an angel will stop watching over you. One must prepare for and yet not believe in the worst. Thank you for making me one of the family.

I suppose that before this reaches you if it ever does we shall know the worst, the immediate worst. I do not know about America. But one has to admit that every country moves slowly and it takes a great deal to convince people that they _must_ fight. Nations do not do anything for reasons of chivalry. Munich, Spain were the chances for that. And here we are a mixture of idealism and cynicism, of fear and uncertainty and we are just opening our eyes after a sound, ignorant sleep. I do not see enough of ordinary people to know really where we stand except for immediate strong preparation for defence (we have a smaller army than the Swiss, less tanks, etc.). Every time I see an old friend I come home wounded and utterly lonely. Probably they feel the same. We have not yet reached the place where desperation makes for a certain clarity. The immediate necessity hasn't yet touched every individual and welded him to others. I expect that will come.

At present I feel close in spirit to my family and to everyone I know in Europe. The others are strangers with whom one must keep one's temper for the sake of international relations. The refugees are dead people. They live in no world and I see more of them than anyone. Why am I writing all this? What can one write? After my last letter to Julian about the

American position I trembled with the fear of <u>when</u> it might arrive, and perhaps I shouldn't have said anything. But we must somehow or other not allow the truth to be dulled. It must be our sword.

I have no beautiful transcendent poem to send you. And yes I cannot read anything but poetry and think I must at last write again. It is wonderful to be alone here, to have no friends, no telephone but only the healing sea. We spent the whole morning digging the little garden up and then going to choose plants for it—white petunias (which look so beautiful at night) yellow snapdragons, white cosmos, some extraordinary single annual chrysanthemums (like large daisies of the most subtle colours, strange dull pinks and yellows and browns), and lobelias, one set of Fra Angelico blue and six much deeper. Daddy dug with terrific violence, I with less and Mother with quiet persistence outlasted us both. But she is a real gardener not just a violent erratic digger. Now I wish you were here to sit, all four, quietly and watch the light go—for a little while to have the weight of anguish and terror and the tension loosened. I wish you were here—and yet one cannot wish people, even those one loves, to be outside the destiny. There are no people exceptional to common destiny—that is where Auden, MacNeice, Isherwood etc. are so wrong, to set themselves outside. One must somehow contain it, <u>be</u> it, take part. That is why I hate being here.

Thank you for sending me the scent of your childhood. It is true that the <u>instant</u> now is infinite. We are really always living very close to death—at such times one remembers it. The present is <u>charged</u>. But ah, if one had these experiences only for oneself it would be easy. It is the imagination for all the others who do not need such experiences, never asked for them. It is one's children and all the other children. I know. And yet you're right that one must take it as an intenser life as well as a more terrible nearness to death.

Have you read Julian Green's "Journals" you would like them. Somewhere he says apropos of Tchekov "L'humain, tout l'humain est en nous, au fond de notre coeur que nous connaissons si mal. Chaque homme est à lui seul l'humanité tout entière."

I'll send this—every letter one writes seems poor beside the events. I think of you often every day and send you my love. We have had no word from Belgium since the invasion. I'll write to Anthony.

Your [   ]

Thank you for making me one of the family: From childhood years when Sarton was separated from her parents for long and lonely periods, to adulthood as a woman alone, being made part of other families was precious to her. She is responding here to Juliette's having written in the midst of war torn London: "It is funny to think this might be my last letter to you. By the way, I wanted to say: if we die, will you think of our sons, and if you have a chance, keep an eye on them? They will need all the friends they know."

the immediate worst: On 10 June, Italy declared war on France and Britain; German forces occupied Paris; on 22 June, France and Germany concluded an armistice, and on 5 July, Marshal Pétain severed relations with Great Britain; on 1 July, the date of this letter, Germany warned the United States that the Monroe Doctrine could be legally valid only if the American nations did not interfere in the affairs of the European continent.

Munich, Spain: Munich: see footnote to letter of 2 October 1938. Spain: reference to the Spanish Civil War (1936–1939), in which volunteer brigades from around the world joined the Loyalists to fight Franco's forces; the nonintervention pact signed by twenty-seven nations failed and Franco prevailed.

my last letter to Julian: This letter does not seem to be extant.

Auden, MacNeice, Isherwood etc. are so wrong: Irish-born English poet Louis MacNeice (1907–1963) was closely associated with W. H. Auden (see footnote to letter of 3 March 1937) and English novelist, playwright, and short story writer Christopher Isherwood (1904–1986) as well as with other left-wing poets, but was not as closely committed to Marxist doctrines as were Auden and Isherwood.

the scent of your childhood: With the war machine grinding around her and aware she must live twice as much, Juliette had spent the day returning to her childood, the lake at Neuchâtel.

Julian Green's "Journals": The volumes referred to are *Journal 1928–1934* and *Journal 1935–1939* by Julian Green (1900–1998), French-born of American parents, novelist and journal writer whose work, of a mystical nature, searches for God and peace.

"L'humain . . . . : Humanity, all of humanity is within us; it is in the depths of our heart that we understand so badly. Each man is himself all of humanity.

seems poor beside the events: The events included Germany's invasion of France and entrance into Paris, the Vichy government's breaking off relations with Britain, and Italy's declaring war on Britain and France.

since the invasion: Denmark and Norway had been invaded by the Nazis in April; just two days before this letter, German armies without warning invaded the Netherlands, Luxembourg, and Belgium, where the Sartons had so many friends; France was to fall in a matter of weeks, and Churchill to appeal to the United States for military supplies.

[5 CHANNING PLACE]   Aug. 27, 1940

Dearest Juliette, we have no right to be silent who are here safe, sitting in the sun on the edge of the Atlantic listening fearfully and with anguish to the rumour of guns in England. But it is very hard to write. You are more sane than we are and what we say must ring high-pitched and false. We have not yet had to reach an inner heroism and share it with thousands. We are still isolated in private dreams and fears and petty disagreements. Yesterday I had a savage argument with a man here who is going to vote for Wilkie and thought I was a nazi because I said that Hitler had given his people food, work and faith and until we have done that here we will be in danger of fascism: from below where hungry people do not care who governs as long as their children have enough to eat and they have work to pay for it and will follow anyone who offers them these; from above where the irritable smug rich will admit anything as long as they do not have to make sacrifices—and anyway always believe that <u>they</u> will rule even in a fascist government. Why is it that peoples like people cannot learn from each other's mistakes but must each painfully begin again from the beginning, be cast down to the bottom before they can climb—and never on each other's shoulders. Mothers cannot pass on their wisdom to their children, must stand and watch them gain it for themselves. But it is hard to have to stand and watch.

Well, on my table I have the most elegant magical little bunch of all blues and purples from our tiny garden with a point of vermilion to set it off. Scabiosa and larkspur and my new love salpiglossis (isn't it lovely?), bachelor's-button and a flower that looks like an intense instead of pale blue forget-me-not. I have Vuillard's little portrait of Lugné-Poë in front of me which he had sent to me after his death (L.P. I mean)—a photo of it— and outside we have one of those silken blue September seas that sigh against the shore. Beauty does not diminish in the sight of pain. That is a queer thing, or does it? But people felt the beauty of dark London so intensely in war-time only now that bombs are falling it is all different I suppose.

I am horribly upset as I guess you all are at the treatment of Germans in concentration camps. I am trying to get a poor one out of the Isle of Man, a little furrier from Vienna who was gardening for our friends in Belgium last summer. He is separated from his wife and child and doesn't even know what camp they are in. It seems unnecessary. But again it is not for us to speak—only one can't bear anything English to be less than noble these days. We look to you with homage in our hearts. Nowhere must the deepest, the most essential of civilization be betrayed. That as I see it is the only answer to the nazis—even in war. <u>Even in war</u>, that is the difference between our civilization and theirs. Prisoners must be fed and especially those who have been exiled once by brutality and now must suffer it again. The suicides of Germans interned in England cannot be looked upon.

Why am I writing you this, to add another burden? I expect Julian like H.G. is agitating about it but I hope it is getting into more powerful and less partisan places than the New Statesman. A minor point but a possible important one politically is the effect such tidings would have <u>here</u> if they leaked out. So far they haven't. People at last are admitting the greatness of England. But there is still a stupid faction that talks about wars of Empires and could use that kind of dope very conveniently.

Yesterday I went on a long drive through the White Mountains of New Hampshire to where they look across the Connecticut River to the Green Mountains of Vermont. It reminded me of the Salzkammergut, gentle noble country, small towns of great dignity and self respect dominated by their white steeples, and so many small abandoned farms that I longed to settle in with a bee-hive and a cow. I was driving a young Dr. and his wife—she is a composer—to hear a ballet of hers played over the radio in a Vermont town. The orchestra is composed of young boys, 15 or 16, gathered from all over the country under the leadership of a young Russian-American, living together with hardly enough to eat and playing all summer. He hopes to build it slowly by summer into a real orchestra and meanwhile they play Bach and Beethoven and young American composers too in the villages. It was a very strange thing to walk off the main street of that little town with its usual drug stores, movie house, church, and Main Street, up a dingy staircase into the little studio and hear those boys playing a suite of Pergolesi's—a sudden jump into the 18th century—and my mind was full of images and the lakes and mountains and pastures full of Queen Anne's lace.

I am mostly planning and writing letters about the lecture trip across the country next year. It seems rather queer but it is one thing I can do for America. I mean whatever happens young people have got to have some citadel which can't be destroyed. Actually I haven't awfully many bookings and Daddy laughs because they are 1000 miles apart, and they are in queer out of the way colleges but I am glad of that.

I'll enclose two little poems from Supervielle from <u>Le Forçat</u>

Innocent—which you probably have—I got it out of the library—and one light important rhyme of mine.

Supervielle:

> Ne tourne pas la tête, un miracle est derrière
> Qui guette et te voudrait de lui-même altéré:
> Cette douceur pourrait outrepasser la terre
> Mais préfère être là, comme un rêve en arrêt.
> Reste immobile, et sache attendre que ton coeur
> Se détache de toi comme une lourde pierre.
>
> Je chosis un peuplier
> Avec un fleuve non loin,
> Je choisis le fleuve aussi
> Et je vous mets près du fleuve.
>
> Mais vous, vous, qui me dira
> À qui s'adresse ce vous?
>
> Je ne le sais qu'à demi
> Car l'autre moitié varie.

True Rhyme in False Rhyme

> Now you are air
> Who were here,
> And I bounded by
> Surrounded by
> An atmosphere
> As wind in hair
> As air on hand
> But alas wind
> Will never serve
> To take, to carve
> Resistant stone
> To grave you on
> Or keep your face
> A static place
> Whom absense hath
> Made into myth,
> Invented proof
> Of abstract love

> While baffled mind
> Hunts on the wind
> Impatient eye
> Scans the whole sky
> For who was here
> And now is air
> Who is nowhere
> And everywhere.

I sent Julian a poem for Lugné-Poë which I think is a <u>good</u> poem. Did he show it to you? Darling Juliette, I think of you with all my heart. Shall we ever meet again?

<u>Yes!</u>

[   ]

---

rumour of guns in England: Bombs were falling in London, Hampstead, and Whipsnade. "I wonder how long we'll be able to stand this," Juliette writes.

Wilkie: Wendell L[ewis] Willkie (1892–1944), American industrialist and political leader; at the time of this letter Republican candidate for the presidency; lost heavily in November 1940; the following year he did much to unify the United States behind Roosevelt's policies.

on each other's shoulders: An allusion to a concept of her father's. On 22 August 1934 he wrote: "I prefer to insist on . . . greatness in the Carlylean manner—for mankind can never rise except by climbing on the shoulders of giants who came before. It is no use climbing on the shoulders of dwarfs—or of people who are lying down in the gutter—one must climb upon the shoulders of giants, and if possible become a giant oneself. At any rate it is worth trying & the eventual failure is not dishonorable." Perhaps reference to Carlyle's central tenet, the worship of strength, and "All greatness is unconscious or it is little and naught."

Vuillard's little portrait of Lugné-Poë: Edouard Vuillard (1868–1940), French painter known for his intimate interiors. Aurélien-François Lugné-Poë (1869–1940), French actor, director, theater manager, and seminal friend in Sarton's life during the 1930s had just died; in 1893 he had taken over the Théâtre d'Art from Paul Fort, renaming it the Théâtre l'Oeuvre; he was the first to introduce Paris to Ibsen, Shaw, Strindberg, and other foreign authors. He appeared in many of his own early productions, and in 1908 was seen in Jules Renard's *Poil de Carotte.* Sarton kept this photograph of Vuillard's portrait of him until her death; it was sold at the estate auction in 1996.

like H.G.: H[erbert] G[eorge] Wells (1866–1946), English novelist and journalist, known for his science fiction and satire; vigorous socialist and long-standing friend of the Huxleys.

New Statesman: British paper known for its left-wing orientation.

Salzkammergut: the region around Salzburg and Upper Austria containing great salt deposits used from prehistoric times, and known for its early cultural remains; at this time a tourist resort rich in lakes, mountains, and towns.

Dr. and his wife: The Cunninghams, friends of Rozwell Hawley, a friend of Sarton's from Gloucester and sister of Margaret Foote Hawley, a painter who came into Sarton's life in July 1940, at just the time of Lugné-Poë's death: "These are the miracles, that when Lugné-Poë died life presented me at once with a great new friend, a woman painter . . . and I have started writing again."

a young Russian-American: Peter Page, adopted by a Miss Page of Hartford, Connecticut.

suite of Pergolesi's: Giovanni Battista Pergolesi (1710–1736), whose *Stabat Mater* remained an important piece for Sarton; he had known an almost unbroken succession of failures and was not recognized until after his death from tuberculosis at twenty-six.

lecture trip across the country next year: Sarton wrote letters to dozens of colleges throughout the United States offering to come and read her poetry for $25. The result was her first lecture trip west to colleges in the states of Connecticut, New York, New Jersey, Pennsylvania, Maryland, D.C., Delaware, Virginia, West Virginia, North Carolina, South Carolina, Georgia, Tennessee, Alabama, Louisiana, Texas, Colorado, New Mexico.

Supervielle: See footnote to letter of 19 July 1938.

Le Forçat Innocent: The Innocent Convict.

Ne tourne pas la tête . . . : Don't turn your head away, a miracle is behind/Which watches and would like to alter you./This sweetness could outrun the earth/But prefers to be there like an arrested dream./Stay still, and learn how to wait until your heart detaches itself from you like a heavy stone.

Je chosis un peuplier . . . : I choose a poplar tree/With a stream not far away,/I choose the stream too/And I put you near the stream./¶ But you, you, who will tell me/to whom this you addresses itself./¶ I only half know it/because the other half changes.

True Rhyme in False Rhyme: written in 1940, probably for Margaret Foote Hawley; unpublished.

a good poem: "What the Old Man Said"; see *The Lion and the Rose.*

Santa Fe [AS]   January 14th, 1941

Dearest petite flamme bleue, c'est que tu vois j'ai toujours l'impression qu'il faut attendre un moment de lucidité, de paix interieure, d'être un peu en lumière pour t'écrire. Je suis ahurie de voir que ta lettre est date du 19 novembre. J'ai l'impression que le temps est suspendu affreusement comme les montres glissantes de Dali. Où sommes-nous dans le temps? Tout est d'une vitesse (la destruction d'une église en une seconde) inconcevable, et d'une lenteur qu'on n'imagine pas. (Depuis quand dure la guerre? On ne se souviens plus.) Mais cette lettre me donne un plaisir profond. Comme j'aurais voulu entendre la conférence de Tony. Ma chérie j'ai parlé de Monteverdi depuis des années. C'était une passion et je le jouais tous les jours il y a deux ans. Il n'y a qu'une chose qui me choque un peu c'est le piano. I suppose that Boulanger did it to emphasize how this music speaks to us directly as if it had just been written, had always existed, but even so I wish it were an organ or a harpsichord. In some it doesn't matter. Anyway they are wells of delight and poignance and as you say the very soul of man.

I haven't heard from Julian in almost a month and am rather worried. It would be so natural if he stopped writing but I would only like to know that he is all right. Also no word from Kot for years and years. I am not good at letters and Christmas this year presented a mountain from which I haven't yet emerged. It seemed necessary to tell friends that one loved them more than usual—but what work! The pile on my desk never seems to be any smaller though I write and write.

When I asked Witter Bynner the poet how he happened to come here [Santa Fe] he said "O, I came here to give a lecture—18 years ago!" and it is really quite terrifying. It is like being in love what this landscape does for one. Everything so intense and <u>demanding</u>—my eyes ache with the color. I am exhausted after half an hour and sometimes cannot sleep for the moonlight on the mountains is something one cannot describe and I am continually thwarted in my longing to <u>say</u> it, but the longer one stays the less one can say it and one begins to feel like the Japanese painter who just sat and looked for seven years at the mountains! The thing I think that is moving is that it is so un-imprinted with man, so very aloof and solitary and standing apart from the Indians, the Spaniards, the Anglos, the Mexicans with a final indifference. The town itself is the color of adobe and disappears under the sky. Though inside all is bare and gay, white-washed walls, huge open fires that smell deliciously of piñon, lots of ver-milion and red Navaho rugs, soft white wooly goatskins. Outside one feels like an animal close to the land, nourished by it but never possessing it as English land is marked with man's pilgrimage. It is deeply refreshing.

I am working hard though it is not good to be forcing myself now to write so much poetry. After awhile one begins to feel like a bag of wind. But if I don't work I am miserable and have no anchor so I go on. I think perhaps these American poems are larger, saner, more open and human than anything I have done. They have no secret thorns to puzzle the read-er. They have no secrets at all, that is the trouble. And in getting the large-ness I have lost hard-earned technical proficiency and the steely line I worked so hard over. I am really and seem to have always been (that is what frightens me) in a period of transition. I comfort myself that this enlargement had to be for the sake of some work which I have not yet imagined, and that it is only a step. But perhaps it is leading nowhere. O darling Juliette I begin to sound almost as involved as Proust!

One sweet thing is that there are several people here who really want to listen to my poems and by listening give them life and make me believe for a moment that they are good. This has not happened since I used to read to you in London and always could tell by your silence and your listening what was false, what was right. The Atlantic has taken several but not yet told me which nor paid me which is sad. Perhaps in spite of everything I am growing a little patience.

I wonder if the Indian drawing I sent ever arrived? Perhaps it is at the bottom of the sea.

Did you hear Roosevelt's speech? To us here it was a great relief, at least an honest forthright speech to the people which should have been made long ago. But the rich are taking their revenge already on R. At a school here owned by a rich woman she terrified the teachers by announcing a cut in salaries, a "crisis" etc., all a fabrication of her mind and I'm sure she still has her two chauffeurs. When there is fear the people are punished. There is I believe still the very real danger here that there was in France of a fundamental lack of cooperation and throat-cutting for near-sighted political reasons. The whole of education must be changed to teach the idea of <u>service</u> and that will take years. But perhaps I am too pessimistic. At least there is no doubt now in anyone's mind that we are at war. A very distinguished sad Picasso-esque Spanish boy who works for a friend of mine said, "All my friends have gone. They are in the army. It is sad," and then later, "What happens in Europe reaches us slowly like a wave but it comes." He is sixteen.

I have a new friend who looks like Katherine Mansfield a French teacher from near Carcassonne who reminded me so of you (she has the same voice and does exactly the same things to English words, illuminating them, as you do) that the first time I met her I hardly listened to what she was saying I was so absorbed in the <u>ressemblance</u>. She reads me Valéry and Giono and I spend weekends in her house up on a hill in Santa Fe, rather like weekends at Whipsnade, the <u>rest</u> of providing meals, and making beds and doing homely chores with someone one loves, the immense relaxation and nourishment to the soul that that is. Her name is Marie Armengaud. She came here for t.b. and has that April-quality of the t.b.'s extreme variable sensibility that makes for intense joy and suffering.

I have no picture of your life now that is why I am talking so about myself and I am hungry for news. It is wonderful that Anthony is <u>quand même</u> having a fruitful growing time at Cambridge. I think of my little Francis (who must be enormous) often. Perhaps if the Indian drawing comes they will write and I shall answer them. I want to write but get buried. I'll copy you some poems. Chatto and Windus has put out a book by Richard Eberhart called <u>Song and Idea</u>, some of them very deep and dense and beautiful. I'll copy a few for you from his earliest book, <u>Reading the Spirit</u>. He is a queer divided personality who looks and behaves like a football player. The Yeats letters to Dorothy Wellesley have been my only meat for a long time.

My darling bless you in the New Year and always. Is there a certain ray of hope in English hearts? Here we feel it coming over as if from you. My love always.

[   ]

Have you seen it? It is very splendid of them to have done it in war-time.

———

petite flamme bleue . . . : Dearest little blue flame, you see it's that I always feel I must wait
for a moment of clarity and inner peace, to be a little <u>inspired</u> in order to write to
you. I'm appalled to see that your letter is dated 19 November. I have the feeling
that time is horribly suspended like those slippery clocks of Dali's. Where are we in
time? Everything is of an unimaginable speed (the total destruction of a church in
one second)—and of an unimaginable slowness. (How long has the war been going
on? One doesn't remember anymore.) But this letter gives me profound pleasure.
How I would have loved to hear Tony's talk. Darling, I've been speaking of
Monteverdi for years. He was a passion of mine and for a while two years ago I
played him every day. There's only one thing that shocks me a little and that's to
hear him on the piano.

les montres glissantes de Dali: probably reference to the bent and flowing waxlike clocks in
Persistence of Memory (1931) by Salvador Dalí (1904–1988), controversial Spanish
(Catalan) painter, book illustrator, jewelry and set designer.

la conférence de Tony: Anthony Huxley gave his first lecture at Cambridge to a small group
on Stravinsky.

Monteverdi: Claudio Monteverdi (1567–1643) Italian composer, dominant figure in early
Baroque music whose madrigals remained among the most evocative of music for
Sarton.

Boulanger: Nadia Boulanger (1887–1979), French composer and conductor, principally
known as an outstandingly influential teacher of composition. Sarton met her in
Cambridge and there was instant friendship. Boulanger was among the first in the

twentieth century to rediscover Monteverdi's madrigals and made her famous 78-rpm piano recordings of them.

Witter Bynner: (1881–1968), poet, critic, playwright, editor, pianist; having lived for many years in Santa Fe, he was greatly influenced by both Native American and Chinese poetry; the first American to translate in full a volume of Chinese verse.

almost as involved as Proust: Marcel Proust (1871–1922), French novelist, author of the monumental seven-volumn *Remembrance of Things Past.* In it he deals with the spiritual evolution of a narrator very like himself, neurotic, hypersensitive, asthmatic. See also footnote to letter of 31 March 1940.

several people here who really want to listen to my poems: Among Sarton's friends in Sante Fe at this time were the poet Haniel Long and his wife, Alice; the painter Agnes Sims; Dorothy Stuart; and Sarton's intimate Marie Armengaud.

The Atlantic has taken several: Ted Weeks cabled on 24 December that the *Atlantic Monthly* would use some of *The American Journal.* In the April 1941 issue the *Atlantic* published "Charleston Plantation," "In Texas," and "The Lady and the Unicorn"; and in the December 1942 issue "Poem in Autumn" and "Santos, New Mexico."

Roosevelt's speech?: On 7 December, when Churchill heard the news of the Japanese attack on Pearl Harbor, he knew England would live; a few weeks later he came to Washington to consult with President Roosevelt, and when Roosevelt delivered his Christmas Eve speech, 24 December 1941, Churchill stood beside him, as he did throughout the war. In that speech Roosevelt spoke of "arming" our hearts for the suffering and ultimate victory that lay ahead, that our strongest weapon was the conviction of the dignity and brotherhood of man, and that England had pointed the way in courage and sacrifice.

friend who looks like Katherine Mansfield: Marie Armengaud, who had tuberculosis and with whom Sarton fell in love, did, with her camellia-white face, high pure forehead, tender mouth, intellect, and spirit, remind Sarton of Juliette herself, and of Katherine Mansfield (1888–1923), British short story writer and critic, plagued by physical and spiritual conflicts, and longtime friend of S. S. Koteliansky.

Valéry: (Ambroise) Paul (-Toussaint-Jules) Valéry (1871–1945), French poet and critic with whom Sarton felt affinities; of his poetry she wrote to Juliette in 1938: "Isn't it delicious? Why is it so perfectly pleasing to the soul, to the mind, like a caress?" In his *On Poets and Poetry* Valéry defines with great precision the subtle, sensitive interplay between poet and poem, yielding rich insights for Sarton's own assertions and convictions about poetry. In the 1950s Sarton collaborated with Louise Bogan on translations of Valéry.

Giono: Jean Giono (1895–1970), French novelist whose works are set in his own domain of Provence; for sympathizing with the Vichy government he was blacklisted during the 1940s and wrote nothing during those years.

quand même: nevertheless.

Richard Eberhart: Richard Eberhart (1904–), American poet and teacher; later became part of the group made up of John Ciardi, John Holmes, Richard Wilbur, and May Sarton, who read and critiqued one another's poetry together in Cambridge.

The Yeats letters to Dorothy Wellesley: Dorothy Violet Ashton Wellesley (1891–1956), 4th Duchess of Wellington, poet, lived at Penns-in-the-Rocks, Sussex, where Yeats often visited her, as Sarton did later. *Letters on Poetry from W. B. Yeats to Dorothy Wellesley* (Oxford, 1940).

Have you seen it? . . . war-time: Richard Eberhhart's *Song and Idea,* (Chatto & Windus).

Enclosed with this letter are "For a Lamb" and the last two verses of "Necessity," both from *Reading the Spirit* by Richard Eberhart (Oxford, 1937).

[5 CHANNING PLACE]   Nov. 23rd, 1941

Dearest Juliette, it is such a long time since I've written and I think of you almost constantly, which is to say that you are never absent from some fibre of the heart—the other night I had a nightmare that you couldn't get enough liver and things and I was trying to get some packed in ice and off on the Clipper—one of those dreams with corridors, and constant frustrations! I was so happy with Anthony's new poems—they seemed to me to have a true <u>ring</u> about them, the real metal this time— and how lovely that he is living at home after all these years of growing up away.

I've become a bad correspondent—it seems an unholy effort to write a letter and I dread Sundays which used to be a vacation, a splurge of con- versations in writing—and now are the chore of <u>answering</u> the week's accumulation. Even Julian in his super-human busyness writes notes instead of letters so perhaps it is a universal disease. I am always looking "for the wide margin" to life, that Thoreau talks about. But it can only be achieved by a ruthless cutting away of non-essentials and who has the courage? The telephone rings and all my resolutions vanish—I see too many people who do not matter, too few, almost none who do. Almost none where friendship is a growing thing, an exploration, a renewal—that was always true with you.

Today it is raining, such a quiet pensive air it has—

> "Ces jours qui te semblent vides
> Et perdus pour l'univers
> Ont des racine avides
> Qui travaillent les déserts.
> La substance chevelue
> Par les ténèbres élue
> Ne peut s'arrêter jamais,
> Jusqu'aux entrailles du monde,
> De poursuivre l'eau profond
> Que demandent les sommets"—from "La Palme"—Valéry

It is the only poem that I have been saying over for a long time. But I've come to feel more and more the function of poetry in terms like these, <u>not</u> to try to take part in the immediate chaos or action, but to create a world <u>outside</u> the real one, to create and to keep expressed the <u>inner</u> reality—So it is that Ruth Pitter seems more necessary than anyone else writing in english except perhaps Eliot. More and more in a disturbed chaotic time one asks for <u>order</u> in art. Mozart and Bach—This it seems to me was a fundamental theme in V. Woolf's last book, on the whole so impoverished by the critics: "Dispersed are we; who have come together. But the gramophone asserted, let us retain whatever made that harmony." They were it seems to me curiously put off the track by her kaleidoscopic method. And on first reading I was disappointed by the book—one came to it too <u>emotionnée</u> by the fact that it was the last—I was such a mass of aches of delight and pain and couldn't catch the whole. On second reading it comes clear, seems more <u>organic</u> than any of her other books except The Lighthouse.—Did you see Elisabeth's beautiful review in The New Statesman? She said "To this reconciliation (between plot and vision)—a reconciliation so new in V. W.'s writing that one is aware of it here from the first page—certain elements in the writing might be said to be sacrificed; there is less anguish, less desire, and less surprise. The thickets of mystery between person and person have been thinned, though in no place levelled down. There is less speculation—but in its place, a perceiving certainty. One might say that the characters behold each other and the scene round them more calmly, and are beheld by Virginia Woolf more calmly, than in the other books. Actually, in this very calmness anguish, desire, surprise have reached rim-level: the miracle is that they are contained." E's review was the only really illuminating one I saw here or in England. The critics seemed a little <u>breathless</u> in general to do their homage or to withhold it. But it must be looked on as a work <u>in itself</u>, not as final work, which she herself never intended it to be. How <u>awful</u> it is, Juliette, that she had to die. It is unbearable. I cannot bear it. It's a hole nothing can ever fill. It took me months to get past the purely selfish inward cry—"Now there is no one whose opinion matters—I shall never be able to please her with her work" [sic]—But it is the world's loss, not anyone's—certainly not mine who hardly knew her.

Dearest, how are you really? Are you working at the canteen? I think it a bad necessity if you are, for surely there is someone else who can do that? It's like V.W. working at a canteen—a ludicrous misapplication of talents—How is Dora? I thought of her so often and couldn't remember the name of Captain Middleton's ship? Is he all right so far? What an agony for women, this waiting, outside action. Of course that is what is good I expect about women having jobs this time—the <u>difference</u> in inner life will not be so great between men and women—the awful gaps in understanding— Has Dora been able to do any work? I expect not.

I hear fairly regularly from Ruth Pitter and from H.D. but they are not writing (of course R's poems are all essences anyway so I expect she never writes in big creative streams)—I am fairly silent myself in spite of all the vitamins we get in the U.S.A.! I feel suspended in the air and am glad to be kept busy teaching and reading of American poems at schools (where it is exciting to watch them take action in the kids' minds and hearts)—have started a novel in the theatre but it is a slow brew and am not (for once) hurrying—I've become patient. You'll never believe it but it's true. I've become solitary and patient—I suppose one of those changes in rhythm that happens 3 or 4 times in a life. After all this is not a letter— but some desperate effort at communication, to reaffirm my love, to be sure you [words are cut off the page] the New Year begins.

.   [   ]

Met C.A. Siepman, Julian's friend, and liked him <u>tremendously</u>—it will be so sweet and strange to see J. again—I hope he can come up here and stay with us.

---

the week's accumulation: Sarton inherited from her father the lifelong habit of spending Sunday mornings at her desk for what she called "my Sunday religious service devoted to friendship."

Thoreau: Henry David Thoreau (1817–1862), American essayist, naturalist, poet, and Transcendentalist who remained a central writer for Sarton; in 1951 while teaching him she wrote to Jean Dominique, "Il était pûr et doux comme la neige" ("He was as pure and peaceful as the snow"), and to Katherine Davis, "Of all the American classics he is my nearest and dearest." At this time Sarton was reading *Walden.*

"Ces jours qui te semblent vides . . .": translation by May Sarton, 1954. See *A House of Gathering,* ed. Kallet (University of Tennessee Press, 1993), for Sarton's complete translation of Valéry's "Palme."

> These seeming empty hours
> When the whole world is gone
> Send avid roots and powers

Down through the desert, down
Like myriad fine hairs
The fruitful darkness bears;
Working their way through sand
To the entrails of the earth
Where sources come to birth
That the high peaks demand.

Ruth Pitter: See footnote to letter of 15 December 1939. Pitter produced a remarkably consistent body of work spanning sixty-five years and shared many affinities with Sarton. Not fashionable but powerful, her writing was grounded in the natural world, in common things and people, portrayed with love and painterly clarity. Like Sarton, as well, she affirms the miracle of rebirth; where Sarton chose the Phoenix as her symbol, Pitter chose Persephone.

except perhaps Eliot: T[homas] S[tearns] Eliot (1888–1965), American-born English poet, critic, and dramatist, one of the major poets of the twentieth century, whose poetry revolutionized literary conventions and gave expression to the spirit of the world after World War I.

V. Woolf's last book: Virginia Woolf (1882–1941), acclaimed as a pioneer novelist of extraordinary gifts, completed the writing of *Between the Acts,* but had not completed revising it at the time of her death on 28 March 1941. At 11:30 that morning, leaving one letter for Leonard Woolf and one for Vanessa Bell, Virginia Woolf, tormented by mental illness, crossed the meadows to the river and with a large stone in the pocket of her coat went to her death. See "Letter from Chicago" in *The Land of Silence. Between the Acts* was ultimately prepared for publication by Leonard Woolf.

"Dispersed are we . . . ": unidentified; possibly from *Between the Acts.*

emotionnée: moved.

The Lighthouse: To the Lighthouse (1927), novel by Virginia Woolf.

Elisabeth's review in The New Statesman: In 1932 Elizabeth Bowen had begun to review for *The New Statesman,* then under the literary editorship of Raymond Mortimer.

the world's loss . . . not mine who hardly knew her: Of Virginia Woolf's death Juliette wrote, "Yes, Virginia Woolf's death is very tragic. She was going mad again, and this time without the great Dr. Head who cured her before, without so many of her dear friends she felt she would not recover."

Captain Middleton's ship: the HMS *Ramillies,* on which Francis served as assistant navigating officer.

novel in the theatre: probably "Three Stages," a.k.a. "Fire in a Mirror," unpublished. "<u>Three Stages</u> it is to be called and that is an allegorical title—it is perhaps an allegory of the soul, what makes and what destroys it—seen through a single man and his creation of a theatre and final destruction by it, and escape to an imaginary world. It's based really on Copeau's life." Jacques Copeau (1879–1949), French actor and director; to Koteliansky, 12 March 1939.

and stay with us: Julian Huxley had been invited by the Rockefeller Foundation to lecture in the United States; he arrived in November 1941 and was to stay until spring 1942. On 16 December 1941, Sarton wrote to him: "My dear, I did write you a letter I hated to write to catch you before you left so that there should be no possible misunderstanding about <u>us</u>—but I guess it missed you. I am sad. . . . The reason I felt so free and warm and <u>with</u> you was because I thought you had had the letter and <u>knew</u>. Still, we can have some peace and comfort in each other, can't we? I do so hope so. . . . I feel toward you exactly like the photograph of the two birds with white crests whose beaks are meeting—and O dear, I know a woman is more comforting than a bird to a man but you will have to be content with a bird."

———————

[5 CHANNING PLACE]   December 29th, 1941

Dearest Juliette, well, I was quite right and Julian has now leapt to the stars from the bottom of the sea, seems much better and above all full of hope and confidence in what he can do here. Since war is declared at last, Washington plys him with questions and he can help enormously in the great fight to keep in certain government projects (educational and social) which the fire-eater will want to cancel as not necessary to defence. The minute one feels one is needed it makes all the difference.

It was quite a wild Christmas at least for our strong solitary Sarton life. Julian came up and also a dear German exile boy, Gerhart Speyer, sick with grippe, who had to be put to bed. Also I had planned a party Christmas Eve before I knew J. was coming, to invite all the waifs, refugees and old friends who might not have anywhere to go—50 people! From 8:00 to 11:30 I ran from place to place like the spitting image of Martha at her worst so I don't know what sort of party it was. Julian got into a corner with Bob Kennedy, a young architect in housing, and I knew this was an important conversation so left them at it for an hour, while the other guests got more and more irritated at not meeting J. But never mind. Daddy and Mother disappeared upstairs with half the party to listen to music. Cloudy sat on the front porch in haughty misery miawing her disapproval of so many strangers in her house. I was chiefly glad when it was over.

The next day I drove Julian up to Vermont to see Sipeman and to get a breath of air, some walks and a change of scene. We stayed in a tiny Vermont village, all still in the snow, in an inn which is also the county jail! I wish you could see these villages as they are a part of America which doesn't advertize itself (thank heaven!). They are built around a "common," in this case a quite magnificent courthouse (everything built of wood of course and painted white with green shutters) in American-Greek style with great white pillars, fan-shaped doors and windows. It sounds quite hideous but really has almost perfect proportion, grace and dignity. Then on either side low white buildings of inns and houses and a silly semi-

Gothic wooden church with a little pointed spire—beautiful trees and the great white space of the common in the center—mountains all around. It is the quiet. It is the dignity. There is nothing mingy or poor or mean in these villages. (Later on we did go up into the hills and saw incredible poverty and minginess, but that is not typical). There are hundreds of beautiful villages scattered over New England. There are lots of covered wooden bridges as in Switzerland, and lovely clear brooks, and rivers that pile up sinister blocks of ice to look like an inferno. One misses big trees, though there are great pine forests, and of course lovely elms in the town, and lots of birches outside, so delicate and white against the snow. Old apple orchards bounded by stone walls, beeches, butternuts, a few oaks. But no magnificent great forests as they were all cut down. Isn't that awful? The waste. I suppose the pioneer life was so hard they just couldn't bring themselves to plant again, and didn't realize that the apparent inexhaustible wilderness would someday vanish.

I really had a lovely time with Julian. He has so much gusto and is so <u>dear</u> and appreciative of whatever there is to see or do. We heard Churchill's speech which I thought magnificent.

Also it is an enduring wonder to me that we can be friends quietly and peacefully and with not too much strain on him. I think he really did get a little rested and didn't seem to mind my un-satisfactory-ness too much. Dearest Juliette I just wrote this quickly to reassure you after my last. I must get to work. With my love always

[   ]

---

war is declared at last: Three weeks before the date of this letter, on 7 December 1941, the Japanese bombed Pearl Harbor; on 8 December the United States Congress declared a state of war with Japan, and on 11 December Germany and Italy declared war on the United States.

Gerhart Speyer: German refugee whose brother, mother, and father were trapped in Europe and whom the Sartons took in and helped get papers for. Sarton herself raised money for him; as he was A-1, no one would hire him.

the spitting image of Martha at her worst: an allusion to the biblical Martha and Mary, sisters of Lazarus. Martha, the practical worker, was "cumbered about much serving" (Luke 10:40) and swept Jesus' house and cooked for him, while Mary, presumably more passionate and contemplative, sat beside him listening and anointing his feet. When Martha complained to Jesus that Mary was not helping, he said: "But one thing is needful; and Mary hath chosen that good part which shall not be taken from her" (Luke 10:42).

a young architect in housing: Robert Kennedy, brilliant son of Edith Forbes Kennedy, Sarton's age, married Gropius's draftsman.

great forests: Sarton was inspired by and often alludes to the great forests of Europe, such as the Forêt de Soignes and Bois de la Cambre, in poems and letters. To HD she writes: "I am like an affamée [one who is famished] getting back to Europe—just the trees in England make me new. I do miss great trees in America." See "The Sacred Wood" in *The Land of Silence;* "Old Trees" in *Halfway to Silence*; p. 16 in *Among the Usual Days;* and "The Two Forests" in this volume, letter of 8 July 1947.

heard Churchill's speech: Churchill gave a brief Christmas Eve speech from the White House Tree ceremony, broadcast to the world on 24 December 1941; his address to the Senate and House of Representatives in the Senate Chamber at Washington, arousing courage and hope, was broadcast to the world 26 December 1941. He concluded: "I avow my hope and faith, sure and inviolate, that in the days to come the British and American peoples will for their own safety and for the good of all walk side by side in majesty, in justice, and in peace."

[5 CHANNING PLACE]   Feb. 1st, 1942

Dearest Juliette, your letters are always events and to have two has made this month distinguished and dear. Since my first letter (I hope I wrote you, I think I did) everything has changed here because of the war and Julian instead of feeling out of touch is spending every weekend in Washington and sounds as merry as a cricket, extremely useful and not too tired. So I am a little ashamed of my worried first letter. It is the hell of distance that things change so fast. But you will—do—have understood, and some of the things are fundamental. I have a queer feeling all the time that Julian is unconsciously preparing himself by all these activities and curiosities, by having his finger in so many pies, for some super-job which the gods are leading him toward. And his sense of frustration is part of the preparation. Anyway I should say off-hand that the trip is turning out to be the fillip he needed and that is the main thing. He comes here tomorrow for three days, but I shan't see him much as he is lecturing up and down, at Amherst College, at Harvard (which alas I shall miss because I have a First Aid class that night). I'll write again briefly afterwards but decided this was the chance, the golden chance to answer yours at length.

War is much harder on the waiters and preservers, on the imaginative encompassers that women are, than it is on the <u>actors</u> I think (except of course when it comes to actual fighting). We <u>know</u> but we cannot <u>do</u>. We suffer and see and fill up our time with small useful jobs. I hate to see the women here rushing into uniform (it is quite different in England where a uniform is a necessity for a job—here it is all a fabrication still, the outlet for zeal and a superficial way to stop the gnawing sense of inferiority women have in war-time). I didn't expect to feel overwhelmingly inferior but I do. Edith Kennedy's youngest son, a charming red-head lazy brilliant creature, whom I have always rather despised for his easy charm and ability to get on in life without work, is now an air cadet. He gets up at 5:25, is dressed at 5:30, breakfasts and then goes up in a bomber with an officer sitting behind him shouting orders at him for two hours. Then he comes down and is allowed to lie down for half an hour (he says everyone is completely exhausted) and then hard intellectual work on navigation and so on all day with no break except for food until 9:30 P.M. when they fall into their bunks without a word, dead tired. They are dropping the boys at the rate of four a day. Thirty out of 150 will graduate as officers. The rest will be given lesser jobs. All the time I can't help comparing my devious, scattered, meditative, here-and-there existence to this concentrated tension and inferring subconsciously "You're a better man than I am, Gungha Din." This is not necessarily true but that is the way one feels.

I am so glad that Anthony has a real job. It should in the end improve his poetry and give him a sense of reality, and confidence in himself. And Francis to be called up. I can't believe it. Being a mother these days, as I see it, is just one continual ache. But I expect the moments flower now and then and one lives from moment to moment. I think their shutting themselves out may be part of the struggle they must have against how much they adore you—that awful process of breaking off from one's parents that has to be done some time in order to be able to breathe one's own breath. And once it is done, a perfect communion is again possible. I did it by running away into the theatre but the strain was awful just before that. And now I feel more truly intimate with Mother than with anyone else in the world. For English boys who see their mothers so little, it must be even worse. And you are such a perfect goddess of a mother. At this stage I suppose they are panic-stricken by your discernment and imagination about their lives. They wish you were an old Irish cook whom they could pat on the head and bring home candies to but who would know nothing about their secret lives. Instead of that you are more beautiful, younger, wiser, more charming, more deep than any girl they will ever see and I suppose

they mind that! Which is probably a lot of nonsense, but I have been thinking about your letter and thinking what a queer pain one's relation to one's
parents is. I really think I shall <u>die</u> every time I leave home and yet at the
same time I am relieved. When I am here as now there is something her-
metically sealed about my life. I am in a way untouchable. I am quite
absorbed in my parents and that is of course the charm of our life. We have
wonderful conversations at table and I fight with my father and we gleam
at each other across the table and each have our work. But still there is a
constant awareness of the umbilical cord. I couldn't for instance <u>possibly</u>
have an affair while living at home. It would be spiritually impossible. That
is why I think partly I was so wild in England those springs. It was all the
pent-up emotional energy finding its way out, a desperate hunger for Life
with a capital L and also a sense of escape and the intoxication of it—irre-
sponsibility, and the pursuit of sensation in consequence. What strange
creatures we are!

I wish I had seen Francis do Hamlet. How very moving to hear him
say those great words and feel them intensely and deeply. And what an
experience for him! "They all want to play Hamlet . . . /This is something
that calls and calls to their blood," as Sandburg says in a poem. And I am
sure Hamlet should be played by a <u>young</u> man. It is the depth and intensity and pain of adolescence, genius perhaps but adolescence just the same.
I wish I could have seen him. It would have been a draught of Life with a
capital L!

I haven't said a word about the war. The immediate reaction to Pearl
Harbor was hot anger and people flooded the Army and Navy, standing in
queues all night and all day without food or sleep, old men and young,
Germans, Italians, Greeks, Irish, Americans—to volunteer. There is no
doubt that it united the country as Dunkerque did England in a <u>fierce</u>
resolve. At the same time I am glad to say that people are grim rather than
hysterical (and here was the psychological value of beginning with a
defeat) and there is very little cheap hatred except among a certain type of
civilian. None at all in the Army. Our problem is of course that we shall
probably not be hit at our nerve-centers as you were and so I expect there
will be more civilian growling, less exalted struggle, less constant presence
of fear, and so less tension to produce what has to be produced and give
up what has to be given up. Sugar and tires are both seriously rationed
already. The problem of transportation in this huge country will be terrif-

ic. So many people live ten miles from their base for food and so on. But I guess there will be buses to replace private cars. I have had several letters from ex-students (girls) in college who are bewildered as to what to do— and the danger here is that we will drop all activity not directly concerned with war and so find at the end that we have lost the civilization we are fighting to preserve, and also have failed to train the young who must <u>build</u> afterwards. To these girls I write long letters telling them their job is to educate themselves as thoroughly and deeply as possible to be ready for leadership ten years from now, and if possible do one job like farm work in the summer for defence. I am hoping to go out next year, if I have to bicycle! to talk about the necessity for keeping the sources of the spirit open and the usefulness of poetry at this time. England has shown us the way there all right. But the pressures on the individual are really terrific. I found myself volunteering for motor transport and first aid although I believe there are plenty of people who can do this and few who can do exactly what I can do in poetry and speaking. But I felt ashamed not to be doing something practical. At the same time I am determined not to take a defence job that would use poetry—like writing for radio as they want me to do. I want to keep it free. I will do any practical useful thing and go on writing as I please and when I can.

I too feel I have been waiting to be seized by some demon for work. I have been very passive and still all winter, writing little and exerting no pressure on myself to the point where I begin to wonder if it is just laziness and no deeper instinct! But now I have an idea and perhaps it is THE THING—for a book of Modern Martyrs, legends in poetry of the people of our time who have been conscious of a mission in dying. Of such Matteotti of course leaps to mind. It means a lot of thinking and reading before any writing and if it is the thing I am certainly not going to hurry it. The poems should I think be essences rather than stories, something like the Duino Elegies with possibly a short prose biography at the beginning of each to make the reference clear. I am not suited to narrative poetry.

Are you going on with the pastels? I hope so. But what I am always hoping more and more is that you will keep a diary. It is so hard to do but on the other hand, you combine so many awarenesses and talents and discriminations and you have such <u>touch</u> on life and on words that it infuriates me that you do not use them to a concentrated purpose.

Have you read Davidson's Biog. of Edward Lear? I lay in bed with grippe and was melted with pleasure. What a dear <u>sad</u> man he was! And I remembered the little landscape over the yellow sofa.

I had a note from Leonard Woolf in answer to one of mine saying that it was June 30th 1937 when he and Virginia came to dinner at Whipsnade. How very long ago, through the looking glass, that was. Now the little giraffe is dead too.

This is a poem for Edith Kennedy when Eddie left for the Air Corps:

Airman's Mother

She hates the element of air,
The treacherous deeps, the burning radiance
Over the mist, the sudden currents there,
The sky's serene ambivalence,
When planes like planets secretly go over
She stubbornly turns down her eyes
Toward the earth, toward the frozen river,
For she will not be taken by surprise
Her curse what she must master, formless terror
Through which those perishable wings may move
Like stars within an orbit without error
As if ringed all about with quick-armed love—
Water and earth her steadfastness contain.
But air is now the fluid element of pain.

She sees too clearly what his errands are
She knows destruction is his curious mission,
And the heroic passage in the flying star
Becomes the image of a horrible decision.
That young men's richly-nourished blood,
That young men's fiery spirit must be spilled
To cure past ills with a most dubious good,
To right the errors that their fathers willed:
Hers the imagination, his the necessary act.
She will endure. She will not praise the fact.

Dearest one. I think of you with all of my heart.

                                                    [   ]

my un-satisfactory-ness too much: See footnote to letter of 19 July 1938 for what Sarton wrote to Julian on 8 June 1939.

super-job which the gods are leading him toward: Sir Julian became a world figure in 1946 with his appointment as the first director general of the United Nations Educational, Scientific and Cultural Organization, a post he held for two years.

a charming red-head lazy brilliant creature: Edmond (Eddie) Kennedy, whom Sarton first met when he was twelve in Paris and for whom she wrote "Navigator" (1942); see *The Lion and the Rose;* also "These Have No Dirge" (1943), unpublished; see Appendix.

Gungha Din: from stanza 5 of "Gunga Din," in *Ballads and Barrack Room Ballads* (1892) by Rudyard Kipling (1865–1936), India-born English poet, novelist, and short story writer whose glorification of empire alienated many but whose worldwide popularity was phenomenal.

And Francis to be called up: During the war Anthony worked in the plotting room at air force headquarters writing reports; Francis spent four years in the navy and was on HMS *Ramillies* during the Normandy invasion.

seen Francis do Hamlet: On 24 November 1941, while his father was en route to the United States, Francis played Hamlet at Gordonstoun, his school, which, with an exiled German as headmaster, had been evacuated from Elgin near the Scottish coast to Wales, which the War Office deemed safer. Of his performance Juliette wrote: "I was profoundly moved by the sincerity and purity of his acting. It moved from the heart & the whole play was held together by this youth living his destiny."

as Sandburg says in a poem: from "They All Want to Play Hamlet" by Carl Sandburg (1878–1967), American poet known for his free-verse poems celebrating agricultural and industrial America.

as Dunkerque did England: reference to the evacuation from Dunkirk, the rescue of British, French, and other Allied troops from this northern French port during the fighting which led to the fall of France in June 1940. An estimated 950 ships and small craft were employed in evacuating some 338,000 men between 26 May and 3 June. Sarton is referring to the privately owned craft and civilian crews which volunteered once the invasion was made public. One firm sent its lighters, the London County Council dispatched its hopper barges, the Port of London nine of its tugs. One ex-officer, on his day off, lifted more than 200 troops off the beaches in his motor launch, delivered them to offshore ships, and returned to work the next day, symbolizing the "Dunkirk spirit," which boosted civilian morale and helped involve the population in the crusade against Hitler.

do any practical, useful thing . . . when I can: As the war progressed, Sarton found herself drawn into lending her talent to the Office of War Information. See letter of 29 January 1943.

a book of Modern Martyrs: The poems for this book, celebrating certain individuals, remain unpublished; the book's concept, which was a central concern of Sarton's at the time, is reflected in "The Martyrs"; see Appendix.

Matteotti: Giacomo Matteotti (1885–1924), Italian Socialist politician, author of *The Fascisti Exposed,* containing detailed case histories of hundreds of acts of violence illegally carried out by the Fascists. On 10 June 1924 he was murdered by Fascists, some of whom were prominent in the party; when tried in 1926, they were either acquitted or given light sentences.

the Duino Elegies: Rilke's last great work, made up of "ten elegies which he wrote in a few days after waiting ten years" (May Sarton to George Sarton, 1954), the ultimate expression of his spiritual experience, in which he wished "from outward forms to win/The passion and the life, whose fountains are within" (from Rilke's "Turning," 1914). Of Rilke and her affinities to him, Sarton wrote to Koteliansky in 1938: "It seems to me that he exists at the places where other people cease to exist, or cannot admit existence, because that is such a solitary place they cannot stand it. (I am one of those)."

use them to a concentrated purpose: Juliette was doing no pastels at this time; the light had been bad and she simply had no courage. She had been keeping a diary since the Blitz, though not, as Sarton suggests, merely a factual chronicle; "I have burnt too many of the other kind." She did eventually write her memoirs, and in 1987 John Murray in London published them as *Leaves of the Tulip Tree.* Regarding the omission of Sarton therefrom, see footnote to letter of February 1986.

Lear . . . landscape: Edward Lear (1812–1888), English landscape painter and nonsense poet whom Sarton often quoted, and one of whose landscapes the Huxleys owned; Angus Davidson (1898–1980) published his biography of Lear in 1938 and worked for a time at the Hogarth Press.

he and Virginia came to dinner at Whipsnade: For a description of this dinner see pp. 220–21 of the chapter "Two English Springs" in *I Knew a Phoenix.*

now the little giraffe is dead too: During the Battle of Britain Sarton heard that "the baby giraffe had died of fright in a bombing, that gay gambol turned into a hideous terrified gallop and failure of the heart"; see *I Knew a Phoenix,* p. 221.

Airman's Mother: unpublished.

[5 Channing Place]   March 4th 1942

Dearest Juliette, in the first place I am haunted and enchanted by Francis' really magical lyric "'Why Does the Drum come Hither?' Hamlet"—it seems to me to show that he is a true poet, with a sense of the overtones of words, a remarkable ear (that lovely line "And straying of the leaves" with its slightly different stress). Well, he just seems to know all about it. Now I can only pray that he avoid cleverness and get to understand his own talent, not imitate what other people are doing, not be afraid to be simple and luminous and himself. I am going to write to him but you can tell him the essence of this if you like. The poem was an event. I have sent it to several people—it is magic. It is poetry just as a pig is a pig. This is what I have not yet felt in Anthony who is trying of course to say more complicated things (but don't of course tell him that). With A. I have felt an intelligence and a sensitivity working together to <u>make</u> a poem, and the awful thing is that a true poem is born not made. One can never admit this to oneself because one has to struggle all the time but it is really true. One can only prepare oneself for the coming of a poem. And while it is being born do the right things, and work like an expert obstetrician (it is hard work I hear!). But it was conceived in the act of imagination long before. I am so happy about Francis. It is a radiant happiness. I have always loved him like a darling little brother. If only now it can really take root in him, poetry I mean, so that he brings all he has to bear upon it. Talent is the beginning. There is so much discouragement and struggle ahead. Dear me, I sound like an old crone. I feel like one as I have a hurricane of a cold.

No word from Julian. I imagine him in the air on his way home. Do let me know. I live in terror that he will get bored with me as a friend. And why indeed shouldn't he? But it would break my heart all the same. I look on you both and each very separately and differently as two marvels in my life. Not in the least deserved and so perhaps doubly and fearfully precious. It is too tantalizing not to have seen the boys for so long, now that we have much to talk of and I could perhaps share a little in their inward lives. Blast this bloody war. It is hard to live near the core of that "perpetual ecstasy." It is hard to live at all. I have been in a funk for days. Put it down to my elephantine cold and pay no attention.

But I am ashamed that I do not earn my living and I chafe terribly at living at home. I feel like a pear wrapped in cotton wool going sour before it ripened. I adore my family but certain elements of life are shut out living at home. I become a domesticated deer and would like to believe that I am naturally a wild one. It is not, needless to say, a love affair that I am after! But what am I after? I suppose really and fundamentally one good poem to save my soul with. Nothing else really matters. But good poems are only written from the extreme reality of something so there is the rub.

Dear Juliette, what a lugubrious letter. And yours was all radiant. I hope you finished the poem—that the letter didn't interrupt it. Women are always being interrupted. It is one of the things V. Woolf was able to say, the miracle of feminine continuity in the multiple interruptions. I cannot get over her dying. It is simply unbearable. I dream of her often at night. Then I wake up and she is not.

Am reading Rebecca West's great fantasy and rhapsody on Jugoslavia—two immense rich tomes of anecdote, poetry, comment, history. A strange book and in some ways a great one. Rich and fruity like rich cake. It is not my genre, but I enjoy it. I mean I like form and essences.

Later

At lunch we were discussing and it seems that our income tax will be

$3000 next year—that means that I must get out and earn my living. We shall besides have to leave this house which we love dearly (the garden Mother has worked over for eight years) and look for something else. For me it is good. I shall simply <u>have</u> to find a job. Poetry is unfortunately not a profession. I was hoping that lectures would help make it one but last year I made 50 pounds on my poems and about 100 pounds on lectures and that is too little to live on. Actually it was a lucky year and I couldn't count on that much again. I have a spot of panic at the idea of being nearly 30 and such a pariah (is that the word?) but I expect something will turn up. The school I expect to fold up any day now as it is a luxury place and anyway that is only a help not a living in itself. It was a perfect part-time job for a writer to have. But now I shall have to become a professional at something besides writing. I have two ideas—one is something to do with education, any job to do with education which is offered, and two would be some sort of war work. The trouble with a full-time education job is that it takes all one's <u>vital</u> energy, but there are vacations. I do not even know if I could get one un-educated as I am and here there is a perfect fetish about college degrees. This is a very dull summing up but will give you an idea of the map of my mind.

Before deciding on anything else I shall have a stab at lectures for next year. But I would have to get 30 which is an awful lot. At present I have 3! But of course I have scarcely begun trying yet.

Here is a poem by Hodgson (he has brought out a little book I shall send to Kot)

> I've looked as far as I can see—
> Though that's not far—down into me;
> If you have seen as much of you
> And tell me it's a pretty sight,
> Look again, and take a light.
>
> On second thought don't trouble to,
> You may be right—
> And where's my introspection now?
> I missed that pansy in the slough.

Thank God for poetry! and for you—

Yours

[   ]

"Why Does the Drum Come Hither?"
Hamlet

Will the sennet come no more
No more trumpet blow?
Come with the winter and the wind
And with the falling snow.

Shall the raindrops wet the face no more
Or the wind wander over the hills?
Come with the autumn and the rain
And with the daffodils.

Shall night set the dew no more
Or birds sing in the trees?
Come with the autumn and the rain,
And straying of the leaves.

The sennet shall sound no more
Nor shall the trumpet blow
Come with the winter and the wind
And with the falling snow.

—Francis Huxley

Francis' lyric: enclosed; appears at the end of this letter.

to know all about it: The variation of the "slightly different stress" she refers to was for Sarton "the very essence of poetry." See *Among the Usual Days,* p. 75.

I am naturally a wild one: again the image of Sarton as a deer which appears in the first sonnet in *Encounter in April:* "We came together softly as two deer . . ."

I cannot get over her dying: See footnote to letter of 23 November 1941.

fantasy and rhapsody on Jugoslavia: Black Lamb and Grey Falcon (1940), the record of a pilgrimage the author and her husband took through the country of the Serbs, Croats, and Slovenes, bringing to life the whole recorded history of Yugoslavia; Dame Rebecca West (Cicily Isabel Fairfield Andrews), 1892–1983, English novelist, critic, and political journalist whom Sarton met and befriended in 1948 on board the *Queen Mary.*

look for something else: After uncertainty and some despair, the Sartons were finally able to buy Channing Place on 15 June 1944.

the school: Sarton had been teaching at the Stuart School, 102 Fenway, Boston, now defunct.

a perfect fetish about college degrees: Sarton never went to college; after graduating from Cambridge High and Latin, instead of going to Vassar where she had won a scholarship, she went into Eva Le Gallienne's Civic Repertory Theatre. Despite that fact, she went on to teach at both Harvard and Wellesley, and six weeks before her death was awarded her eighteenth honorary degree.

Hodgson . . . a little book: "The Pansy" by Ralph Hodgson (1871–1962), English "Georgian" poet whose main inspiration was always the enchantment of nature and man's abuse of it. The book is a small chapbook called *Silver Wedding and Other Poems,* published by Boerner Printing Company, Minerva, Ohio, in 1941.

––––––––

[5 Channing Place]   June 10th, 1942

Dearest Juliette, it was a relief to hear from you as I have had only newspaper comment to tell me how the Zoo war was going and a note from someone saying "the battle of the century at the Zoo"—Bryher, but she doesn't know you so it was quite un-satisfactory. I see it is more complicated than I had imagined even and you have had such a long siege alone first—I understand well all you say too about a different kind of problem when J. came back all ready to spur all the horses without looking back or ahead at the terrain! How anxiously I shall wait to hear ~~what~~ whether the reformed Council, that angelic possibility, comes through! But how long and difficult and straining of the <u>inner</u> muscles, it has been. I wish I were there to bring you masses of flowers, to make a perfect bower at the end of the balcony and then to sit on the yellow sofa and talk. It is awful how I miss you sometimes. It must have been excruciating having to summon the deepest kind of honesty and clarity to help Julian with—so much easier to <u>write</u> than to <u>speak</u>, for one thing. Because people's immediate reactions to criticism or suggestion are always anger and frustration and a feeling of <u>not</u> being backed up whereas it is <u>the</u> most difficult and noble backing up that wives have to do. And being a wife makes it ten times more difficult. But way down deep I'm sure it has added another stone to the foundation and J. is so generous <u>under</u> the fireworks of temperament. He will have seen later. I am stumbling along cursing letters for their black-and-whiteness but I expect you can read between the lines. Your letter made me feel so honored and so humbly grateful for you and for all that you and Julian mean to me, and especially perhaps for your confidence. I can't tell you possibly how precious it is and how I hope to be worthy of it.

I can hear Kot saying "perfect" when you ask how he is! I am sorry he has been ill again. It must be horribly bad for him, to have to contain and <u>repress</u> so much rage due to the war! But perhaps Traherne whom he writes about is a help. The purest cleansing fire, the purest cleansing water. I didn't know him at all before and am steeping myself in him now, and can't resist copying for you though you know them no doubt. I am always late in my discoveries! And this is thanks to Kot. Here, on thoughts:

> Ye brisk, divine and living things,
> Ye great exemplars, and ye heavenly springs,
>> Which I within me see;
>> Ye machines great,
> Which in my spirit God did seat,
> Ye engines of felicity;
> Ye wondrous fabrics of His hands,
> Who all possesseth that He understands;
>> That ye are pent within my breast,
>> Ye rove at large from East to West,
> And are invisible, yet infinite,
> Is my transcendant and my best delight.

It is a crystal stream.

We are staying one more year in the house. It is a <u>huge</u> relief. The garden brings in one glory after another—after the small fragile white and vermilion poppies, the lilies of the valley, the tulips, we have summer riches now—great single white peonies, still heraldic orange lilies, white Siberian iris, roses—there are only one or two bushes of each of these but that makes one look at them hard. The garden is an estate to me because I have been ill for almost two months now—longer really only I thought it was my old enemy fatigue. It turns out to be Colitis, that simple and irritating and fashionable ailment. I finally did collapse and went to bed with infinite relief for two weeks. Then they took x-rays found out what was the matter and now next week I go into the hospital for a few days under a specialist (I expect they will do horrid irrigations and plan a diet, but nothing serious). The main thing seems to be rest and no emotion or strain. I have never before given up all effort and I am terrified of its becoming permanent like a drug-fiend it is so pleasant. I am just living, just living in the air and the trees, lying out watching the shadows and light on the lawn with never-ending delight and wonder. I am reading novels avidly like a school-girl or very old lady, catching up on infant pleasures like scrap-books and sticking in snap-shots, seeing no more than one person a day outside family for not more than an hour. It is heaven. I think you had better get colitis so you can rest too! I am thinking over also quietly and without ambition or stress what I have done in the past ten years and what I hope to do now when I am better. I guess it will take the summer before I am leading a normal harried energetic life and "bankrupting the balance of energy" again! It is so true what you say about that. But what is the solution? I'm damned if I know. Everything in modern life makes for dispersal and not for concentration. Being ill I realized suddenly how full my life was of people whom I had no real need to see, of constant "appointments" which mostly meant small talk because there was never time to prepare oneself inwardly for a real conversation which pre-supposes time before and silence and time while it is going on. "Time's winged chariot" has become a dive-bomber making us start and run. Men avoid it by being guarded by their jobs and work. My father (though even he has a desperate feeling of never catching up with work) is enclosed in time as in a cocoon—because of his implacable routine. A woman's life is made up of interruptions, dispersals. I cannot understand how Elisabeth [Elizabeth Bowen] manages to be so mondaine and to accomplish so much work and to have such a rich emotional life all at once. I suppose the gods gave her a surplus of energy or imperviousness to certain things. It is constant awareness that is most exhausting, the kind you and I have perhaps, which makes small things as irritating, painful, or memorable as great ones. If I have been rather brusque on the phone (I hate the phone) I worry about it for hours afterward—such a ridiculous dispersal—but there you are. Sensitivity is weakness fundamentally, but of course it opens the world too, and we are here I expect to look!

Your story of Mr. Goode is enchanting. I have never seen him. I cannot believe it, it is so unexpected and wonderful!

There have been no events in my life except a flurry of excitement over what seemed like a perfect job (teaching 19th century lit in a college 30 miles from N.Y. in beautiful country) but it fell through due to my lack of any of the outward signs of competence (college degrees, blast them!). It irritates me because I really can teach and if there were a way of proving it, could prove it. And I love to teach. But I fear this is a bad augury (this job falling through) for they wanted me really—and wrote glowing letters—but were prevented by some higher board who said thumbs down. I am growing a passionate hatred of all Boards of Trustees, Councils, and

Governing Boards of Conservative old men who impede progress and the human spirit. Short of getting myself elected a Trustee or wangling an honorary degree I see no hope of a teaching job. It is sad. On the other hand, being sick makes one very passive. I refuse to worry. If worst comes to worst I shall get some lectures, live at home and put pride in my pocket and forget about the <u>elan</u> of longing for new places and new faces that made me feel I must get away from Cambridge and family. The trouble is that I am so perfectly happy at home and love my parents so passionately and take some comfort and joy in them that I make no effort about life outside. I don't suppose that at my age that is altogether healthy you know (shades of Freud!) in the long run. But another year shouldn't make me incurable!

June 13th

We are in the middle of a heat wave so this has lain unfinished. It is a poor letter in answer to your dear one. I am not in connection with my writing self, that is the trouble. I feel silent. Instead of writing more I'll copy you the only modern poem that has moved me in ages—by Rolfe Humphries. I wonder how you will like it?

Proteus or The Shapes of Conscience

This is Proteus, a god. He comes from the ocean
Sometimes, at hot noon, and crosses the beach
Looking for inland shade. If he comes within reach,
As he may, dive at his knees; do not be afraid
To bring him down to the sand with a flying tackle
And bind him, overthrown, with the rude compulsion
Of manacle, shackle, chain. And even so,
Ride him hard with your weight. Do not let go.

This god is worse than sly. In your hands he will turn
To utter fire, and roar in your face and eyes;
Or burn, burn like a beast, lion or tiger, bright
And hot and rank; or a lewd and ugly boar;
Or some unshapely horror, moist and brown,
Repulsive pulp to touch and foul to smell;
Or he may be a lovely river of silver
And blue and green, with delicate wave and ripple

Over the mottled pebbles. Hold him down.
Until the miracle do not let him go.

The final change you will never understand.
You will not know how he ever managed to rise,
Nor how you rose yourself to find him there,
An upright natural presence, facing you,
As tall as you, in the soft ambrosial air,
Smiling and looking you straight in the eyes like a man,
And telling you what it was you wanted to know.

I've been reading a lot, just now the ten volumes of Les Thibault—a queer
mixture of rather brilliant psychological analysis and melodrama—du Gard
evidently believes that "character is action or rather action is character" and
puts his characters through their paces rather violently. It has the coldness,
to me, of Romains—a queer detachment as if it were all worked out in the
mind and the characters never had a chance to exist <u>apart</u> from their cre-
ator. Have you read it? I guess I shouldn't judge till I am all the way
through.

Dearest Juliette, all my love, attentive and longing for the final news
of the Zoo—

Love to the boys and of course Julian—

Your [   ]

———

battle of the century at the Zoo: While Julian Huxley was in the United States from November
1941 until the spring of 1942, the Zoo Council, with Lord Onslow as president,
decided after months of tension with Julian Huxley to take advantage of his absence
abroad to suppress his job as secretary "in order to save expenses" and to declare the
post merely an honorary one. Despite attempts by prominent friends in official posi-
tions to fight the decision, and although he was still nominally secretary, it was evident the old council would make things increasingly difficult for him, hence he had
no choice but to resign.

Bryher: Winifred Bryher, Annie Winifred Ellerman McPherson, English novelist, lifelong
friend of H.D. from 1918 to her death in 1961; both were friends of Sarton; see
Selected Letters 1916–1954. Bryher and H.D. are together portrayed as Hilda in
Lawrence's *Lady Chatterly's Lover.*

Traherne: Thomas Traherne (1636–1674), English metaphysical poet and clergyman,
known for his emphasis on the pure, untutored perception of truth in children.

Colitis . . . fashionable ailment: Sarton had a long history of colitis, the earliest medical record
of it in the hand of her Belgian physician, dated 13 November 1914, when she was
eighteen months old. The problem persisted in various and extreme forms to the end
of her life. During the years of World War II many were diagnosed with "colitis,"
doubtless resulting from the intense tensions of the time.

reading novels avidly: Among the books she was reading at this time were *Hard Times,* Charles Dickens; *Middlemarch,* Eliot; *Only One Storm,* Granville Hicks; *The Colossus of Maroussi,* Henry Miller; *South Riding,* Winfred Holtby; and *The Medieval Mind,* Henry Osborn Taylor.

Time's winged chariot: from "To His Coy Mistress" by English poet Andrew Marvell (1621–1678), the last lines of which Sarton plays with at the end of "Now I Become Myself" in *The Land of Silence.*

Mr. Goode: Mr. Goode, whose real name was Moysheh Oyved, owned Cameo Corner, a jewelry shop in Museum Road off the British Museum, full of treasures from Rome, ancient Greece, the Middle East, and Europe. He wrote a book, *Jewels and Visions,* and worked gold into barbarously splendid rings; sometimes he appeared for tea at the Huxleys' carrying rings, brooches, necklaces, and precious stones in the pockets of his plum-colored velvet waistcoat. "Would you wear these pearls for a month or so?" he once asked Juliette; they had quite lost their bloom and needed the dew on a woman's skin, he said, to come back to life. The next time it might be an antique brooch which badly needed an airing. This story was of Mr. Goode's going every day to St. James Park and burying a small jewel; it was his way of giving back to the earth a small return for all her jewels; knowing it wasn't serious, he did it nonetheless, considering it a rite for his soul.

college 30 miles from N.Y.: Briarcliff Junior College.

elan: élan; transport.

Rolfe Humphries: (1894–1969), a leading American lyric poet, famous also as a translator of Latin, Spanish, and French works; editor of *New Poems by American Poets #2* (1957), which includes Sarton. His "Proteus" seized her imagination. Her own "Proteus" was published in the Spring 1951 issue of *The Prompter;* see *A Grain of Mustard Seed.*

Les Thibault: (1922–1940), in translation: *The World of the Thibaults* (1939–1940), in two volumes, eight-part novel series by French novelist and dramatist Roger Martin du Gard (1881–1958) in which two brothers, Jacques and Antoine Thibault, one simple and dutiful, the other rebellious and adventurous, react to their bourgeois environment; their personal stories are set against a sweeping background of world violence and chaos; both die in World War I.

Romains: Jules Romains, pen name of Louis Farigoule (1885–1972), French novelist, dramatist, essayist, and poet associated with Unanimism, a theory that the group is of prime importance and the individual, especially the poet, can attain significance only by merging with the social aggregate. His novel *Verdun* (1938 in French, 1939 in English), part of his *Men of Good Will* series, was recognized as one of the great war novels.

NEW YORK CITY   January 29, 1943
[HOTEL ALBERT]

Dearest Juliette, O dear it was not I who sent the marvelous parcel. I wish I had. I was out lecturing in November and December and did nothing at all about Christmas except to write a poem which only got printed in the middle of December and so will probably reach you on Valentine's Day! But it is good to have a word from you yourself. I have thought of you so much in that beastly time of illness. O, if only now you are really feeling better and it can look like a nightmare that is past and a new life beginning in the new house. But there are so many strains just now—there is no peace of mind. Of course Francis is constantly at the back of your imagination being battered about in the Atlantic. What are his letters like when they do come? I guess it is a pretty grim business. But has he made any friends? A great deal must depend on the group of men one is with. And Alan?

Julian wrote me of what a long disappointing business you have been through and the awful effect of the blood transfusion. I wish I had been there to bring messages daily and flowers and silly things. One resents being far away when people are ill. I resent the distance now terribly. It is too long since I have seen you. But O, the new house sounds lovely—and all that green so near.

And to think that by the time you get this in a month, it will be spring in England. Here we have had a great snow, it snowed and snowed and New York suddenly became a village with everyone plunging through drifts and laughing and it felt like sugar under one's feet. I am here, have been for a month, determined to get a job and earn my living. It was bad luck at first because I got grippe and spent the first week in bed and then staggered around for two more weeks, going to appointments and then back to bed, feeling desperately tired all the time. But that is past now. I had to make the plunge, get away somehow and it felt like tearing up roots to leave home—and perhaps being ill was just part of that uprooting and the panic of a new life to begin somehow. It was time I left.

For the last two weeks I have been haunting the OWI (Office of War Information) radio-script division and have now reached the point where I write them sample stuff and it is now being read by the top man so my fate should be decided in a few days. The suspense is rather awful. It is so much the job I want that I can't bear to look for another—a very good salary, a wonderful group of people—all the writers seem to be congregated there, and I would be working with men which I think I need. The alternative is teaching. I have turned down three badly-paid exhausting jobs teaching six and seven hours a day and have almost decided not to go to any more schools. A college would be possible but they will never have me without a degree. It is hard to talk about this at such a distance as everything will suddenly become a pattern again as soon as I have a job and meanwhile life is kaleidoscopic. Inwardly too, a sort of chaos, and I feel so nearly and strongly that all decisions I make in the next months will influence the next ten years and I tremble. People themselves become symbols and I feel rather like a character in a Kafka novel. O Juliette I wish you were here and we could talk. Not being here and being so far away perhaps I can talk to you as a radiant presence, as I could not talk if you were here. There is something dangerous in me, that longing to touch people, to reach them, to know them, to love them. It was bound to happen that I could do this and then involve someone much deeper than I intended. It has happened. It is part of this whole strange time in my life. The responsibilities are gathering and it is time they did. There are now two people—one is the head of the English department in one of the colleges I lectured at in the fall, a great large <u>sun</u> of a woman, one of the great givers (there are many in the small colleges) who had really given up all idea of a personal life or of looking for sources outside her work. As a symbol she is all the pure and inward life, the holiest and best, the giving life and to her one would want to give much, all there is, love should be poured over her. But she is far away. I can see her I suppose for three or four weeks a year at most. And O Juliette what a hunger there is in me for continuity and permanence, for peace and returning at night, for what marriage should mean.

The other person is the poet Muriel Rukeyser, a great dynamic girl who seems to hold in herself all of the currents of the time, the real creative person, the person who lives always at the peak of conflict which must constantly be resolved in poems, in action. She is now one of the top people in the poster division of OWI—making the images with which we shall try to make people understand the war, the enemy, our own potentiality as a nation, our dreams. It has been a long long time since anyone has entered my life with such seeds in their hands. Everything grows here and as someone said of her, "Muriel is a great moral challenge,"—and when I came to New York I was caught up in her life. And she is I suppose the symbol for the creative world, ruthless and powerful (not in herself, she is very dear and tender—but in what she <u>means</u>).

I do not see any solution to these two lives nor to mine just now. And it is terrible to be lying as I have had to do. I can't tell Florence (the teacher) until I can see her. And I see I think now rather clearly that this was coming and that I would have to face sometime this kind of division and make a decision. In love what is so frightful is that one perhaps cannot altogether make the decisions. They are lived into. There is a point where conflict is forever settled. Only one tries and tries to maintain a balance, to find the equilibrium.

And Muriel will go on. Things come to her and her life is very open and in the process of growing and many people will touch her life before she is through, before anything is solved for her. But I would be cutting Florence at the root.

I cannot go on with this. There is no point in talking anymore.

I wonder how Kot is?

What are you reading? If you want a gust of faith, a hyperdermic, a great wind get hold of Muriel's life of Willard Gibbs. Can't Julian get it somehow? I have no money. Another thing is that I am living on borrowed money here until I get a job. I wish I could send it. It would be better than raw liver!

There are branches of flowering quince against gray walls. This is a huge gray room where I work—Muriel's room—when she isn't here. I live in a filthy little hotel. New York is full of music and paintings. There is so much life here. One wants to be fully alive. When I know about everything, the job and everything else, I'll write better. I have not meant to present you with a problem. No one can solve this but me. I just wanted you to know what is happening, why perhaps I have been silent. It is hard just now to write letters.

As far as the war is concerned I am depressed by the confusion we are creating in North Africa and right here at home by not facing the deep issue, by this ancient evil compromise with the very things we are giving up so much, so many lives to fight. Will it all be a waste again? One mustn't ask that question. One must believe and yet you can't imagine how far from total belief or total inward action people are here. Nothing is clear. For that reason if no other I would dearly wish to have some part in the clarification. Julian is doing that. Writing radio scripts (for foreign consumption) is a small way. I would rather be talking to America. But I might be able to wangle something after—if I get in.

Dearest, dearest Juliette, at the worst times I think of you and what you have made of clarity and beauty and peace (Air-raid sirens suddenly!)

out of so much unclear, confused, wracking and troubled. It is a great lesson. I try to learn it.

With a kiss—

[   ]

The airman I wrote about is in <u>North Africa</u>—so he won't come.

―――――――

lecturing in November and December: Beginning in Buffalo, New York, Sarton read and spoke at colleges in Ohio, including Baldwin-Wallace, Denison, Otterbein, Muskingum, and Marietta, and at Bethany in West Virginia.

except to write a poem: "New Year Wishes" ("May these delights be yours in the new year . . ."); see *The Lion and the Rose.*

the new house: As a result of Julian's forced resignation from the London Zoo, the Huxleys moved to 31 Pond Street in Hampstead near the Heath, once a hunting lodge for Queen Anne's brother; parts of it were 250 years old. Lady Huxley remained there until her death in September 1994.

the blood transfusion: Juliette had been in the hospital for a blood problem.

the top man: John Houseman, born Jacques Haussmann (1902–1988), actor, director, producer; came to the United States in 1924 and worked in the theater in the late 1920s and the 1930s, particularly with Virgil Thomson and Orson Welles; during the war was head of Overseas Radio Programming for the OWI. Artistic director of American Shakespeare Festival; head of drama division of Juilliard; starred in popular television series *The Paper Chase.* Sarton's immediate superior was Phillip Dunne.

badly-paid exhausting jobs: Of these one was a school in Plainfield, New Jersey, another a Swiss school in Vermont.

will influence the next ten years and I tremble: To this Juliette responded, "Of course you tremble, yet whatever you do, why worry about the next ten years? They'll only spin on day by day & quite inescapably, fulfill your destiny which is yourself—as you were born to be."

character in a Kafka novel: The characters in the obscure, symbolic works of Czech novelist Franz Kafka (1883–1924) are tormented by unrelieved anxiety and have an almost allegorically symbolic quality.

head of the English department: Florence Hoagland, at Bethany College in West Virginia.

continuity and permanence: a perennial longing in Sarton; see "Because What I Want Most is Permanence" in *The Land of Silence.*

Muriel Rukeyser: Muriel Rukeyser (1913–1980), American poet, biographer, teacher, fiction writer, and political activist, with whom Sarton shared an apartment in New York during the 1940s and for whom she wrote "O Who Can Tell" in *The Lion and the Rose* and "Letter from the Country," unpublished.

life of Willard Gibbs: Willard Gibbs: American Genius (Doubleday, 1942), Muriel Rukeyser's biography of the brilliant physicist and scientist who formulated much of the scientific thought of nineteenth-century America.

confusion . . . in North Africa: An Anglo-American amphibious invasion involving 850 ships under the command of Gen. Dwight D. Eisenhower landed in French Morocco and

Algeria on 8 November 1942; Gen. Jean-François Darlan, party to the Vichy government, aided the Anglo-American forces in assuming control of French North
Africa and West Africa, before being assassinated on 24 December.
airman I wrote about is in North Africa: probably Edmund Kennedy, son of Edith Forbes
Kennedy for whom Sarton had written "Navigator," in *The Lion and the Rose*. At the
time of this letter he was reported missing in Tunisia; upon that news Sarton wrote
"These Have No Dirge" (January 1943), unpublished.

---

22 EAST 10TH STREET   October 1st, 1943
N. Y. 3

Dearest Juliette, autumn is here suddenly and it is one of those cold bleak
afternoons with great splotches of rain and a darkness everywhere. I am in
my new place, a room of my own after all these months of living here and
there—it is blessed. The room itself, a big gray studio with great studio
windows on one side and two ordinary windows on the other and they
look out on trees of the inner part of a block, divided up into small gardens, babies sleeping on the terraces (people build tiny platforms on anything, any piece of roof in N.Y. to get the air) and I myself have such a one
which I shall make into a garden with window-boxes in the spring. You
would, I think, like this place. It is cool and airy and light, with a great yellow armchair for guests to sit in, an emerald-covered studio couch with
yellow pillows for me to lie on, a big work table, a lovely little black
Chinese cabinet and that is all except a rather nice modern striped Belgian
rug with lovely greens and soft beiges in it. And lots of books up one wall,
Virginia Woolf and French poets and all the things I like best from
Cambridge. I feel I shall write poems here, and O I hope so!

It seems very strange to think of Anthony married, this shooting off
of life and growing up. It makes me feel rather lonely and old. Bless him,
I hope he will be happy. It may be you know that a more brilliant companion would not have given him the peace and comfort he needs. Perhaps
she will be his rock and his well. But it is horribly painful and <u>final</u> isn't it?
As you say, another kind of child-bearing which is all parting and no gift
(or seems so at the time). One thing makes me glad and that is that he has
married young. I am sure that is good if it can happen. As one grows older
it is harder to make the decision. One is more circumspect, more absorbed
in work, less touchable perhaps. I am all for marriage early. There is the

chance then to build slowly and well and to build together. You don't say much about what Anthony is like now. Does he write at all? Music or poems? I expect he doesn't have much time with a full time job and of course not during all the stress and first happiness of settling in with a wife. Does she have a job too? O I wish I could see them. I have a little pang that I didn't get to know him better before. I feel like Edward Lear

> But never more, O never we
> Will meet for eggs and toast and tea.

I will write Francis. It has been hard to write letters as I haven't felt settled anywhere for some time. In late August I got a miraculous two weeks off and went up to a little old lobster-fishing and boat-building New England town with Muriel. We went on long rows exploring islands in the river, and we lay on our stomachs in the sun and read E. M. Forster. Really how pure, how <u>good</u> they are with a depth of sweetness and humanity that seems to have gone out of literature with the 1914–1918 war. You have read them of course. I did not know "The Longest Journey" and like it. I wish you could see a town like Newcastle—it must be so different from your ideas of this rude country! It has a simple gravity and dignity that makes one believe in human beings again. And all is so light, the lovely wooden houses painted white and receiving the flowering shadows of great fountain elms, the open emerald lawns with no fences going down to the water or to the road, and the people themselves, extreme individualists and anarchists. We lived over a lobster-house and cooked our meals on the coal stove of an old lobster-man called Mr. Amazeen. He calls Wartime (daylight saving) "foolish time" (he reminded me quite a good deal of Kot as a matter of fact). He went up to the village constable and said, "You skunk, you wouldn't have come to this if you'd led an honest life." Mr. Amazeen is almost entirely self-supporting, has a cow, a vegetable garden, and sells his lobsters for cash. His amusement is going to law against his neighbors. He is a fine enemy and a terrifying friend. It was good to get out of New York. I would have liked to stay there all winter and write.

The job is still good and I work here in my room so it is rather peaceful, but my deepest mind is concentrated on poems now and I must get to them in the next few months. It is necessary.

I was glad to have news of Kot, of Dora (I am sorry she still has such a hellish time with health)—but nothing is a substitute for a sight of you, for the smell of English wet grass, for a picnic on the ground. I am putting some of my salary into war-bonds to pay my passage over when the war is over. But O I fear it will not be soon in spite of the optimism here. The political situation will be depressing until after our elections. At present I am sick with it all, and the fear that after the war we shall be the great con-servative power. But why talk about it? These things are building them-selves and we can only keep on and hope and do what we can. Hope is beyond reason or evidence—and hope sometimes triumphs.

Inwardly it seems to me the year until now has been sort of prepara-tion, not a thing in itself. I have established myself in the job, and got set-tled in mind over that, and established a good, a loving relationship with Muriel across the street which keeps channels of life and poetry open—and now I must get to work, the real work.

October 4th

I have held on to this letter because I have such a strange feeling about writing to you now after all the time and silences. I feel as if a letter should have some eternal quality as the form and color of the days simply can't be expressed—but after all it can't, and the main thing is to let you know, dearest Juliette, how much I love you and how that grows in the silence so you can expect quite a tree and perhaps even a little shade and some birds nesting by the time we meet again.

I must write to Francis. I wish I could see him

You have I suppose seen the Aragon poems—after all the fanfare I confess I was a little disappointed. The true voice of France, the voice one waits for must it seems to me be so pure and so stern. These are nostalgic and personal.

Enough—tell me how you are—a short note soon will be better than a long letter later!

Give Julian my love and much much to you O—O as the typewriter tried to say—

M—

a room of my own: After staying variously at the Breevort Hotel, the Murray Hill Hotel, the
    Village apartment of Ella Winter (see footnote to letter of 12 August 1947), an attic

apartment at 10 East 120th Street, and Muriel Rukeyser's, 5 East 10th Street, Sarton found a new apartment of her own on 3 September and moved into it on 16 September.

Anthony married: On 2 September 1943, Anthony Huxley married Anne Taylor, a young WAAF (Women's Auxiliary Air Force) officer.

But never more . . . . : From Edward Lear's letters to Evelyn Baring, ed. Lord Cromer.

I will write Francis: At this time Francis was midshipman on the destroyer HMS *Fernie*, and writing poetry. Juliette had urged Sarton to write him, as he "pined for letters."

New England town: Newcastle, New Hampshire.

E. M. Forster . . . "The Longest Journey": E[dward] M[organ] Foster (1879–1970), English novelist, short story writer, and essayist, about whose novels Sarton wrote to Bill Brown eight weeks before this letter: "They are the most human documents since the last war to my mind—warm and deeply human, English sensibility, tolerance and sense of justice at its very best—*civilized* novels." *The Longest Journey*, first published in 1907, deals with the protagonist's inability to distinguish between what is real and what is not.

Mr. Amazeen: See 'Song,' from "Mr. Amazeen on the River" in *The Green Wave* by Muriel Rukeyser (Doubleday, 1948).

news of Kot, of Dora: Juliette had written that Kot was well on the whole and "stamping most fiercely for the moment on Rilke and [Cyril] Connolly." Dora Clarke was still "greatly unwell" suffering from intense migraine; surgery was being considered.

get to work, the real work: At this time Sarton, inspired by Dame Myra Hess's wartime free concerts in the National Gallery in London, had persuaded the New York Public Library to sponsor a series of readings at which twelve poets, including W. H. Auden, Langston Hughes, and Marianne Moore, read from their work; the series, called "The Poets Speak," ran in October and November 1943, and a booklet by that name, including poems by each of the twelve with an introduction by Sarton, was published in 1943 and reprinted in 1976 by Granger Books, Miami, Florida. In addition, Sarton was working on one film for the OWI on the New England town meeting and another on the TVA and had just given a poetry reading at Harvard.

all the time and silences: Juliette's last letter was dated 22 August 1943.

the Aragon poems: Le Crève-Coeur by Louis Aragon (1897–1982), French novelist and poet who went from being a leader in the surrealist movement before World War I to becoming a leading writer in the socialist realism movement as well as a Communist, managing the Communist paper in Paris. *Le Crève-Coeur,* written between the mobilization and 1942, was the first collection of his poetry in which he had departed from surrealism and returned to rhyme and alliteration.

O as the typewriter tried to say: Playing on her typo, Sarton sends Juliette a hug with her customary O.

---

22 EAST 10TH STREET N.Y.C. 3   New Year's Day, 1944
N.Y.C. 3

Dearest Juliette, your letter was a Christmas angel, coming just the day before. I was able to get home, and sit by the fire with the family and so it was a good Christmas.

I was startled out of my skin that Anthony will be a father. When? It seems unbelievable. I feel just the same as ever but here is Anthony who was a child when I last saw him, grown up to be a father!

It was late November when you wrote and you were in bed, in a strange house, however comfortable, having an abscess. Surely by now you are well again—though I fear it may have been connected with your old trouble? I hope by now you are home and starting a new year. I am in several minds about this year. There is the possibility everywhere of a sort of purification down to essentials—a feeling that certain values are <u>essential</u> and one will fight for them in one's private life just as they are being fought for by soldiers everywhere on a grand scale. I was so deeply touched by a letter from Dorothea Singer in which she spoke of the "pools of happiness and culture" which bridge the dark ages and may make them shot through with radiance, when the final sum is added up. So in the darkness of France between the wars did Péguy seem to shine. And while we slowly create the forms, social and economic, for fruitful life for the many, there have to be people here and there who evoke by their very presence and nature, the reality of such a life, the <u>inward</u> reality. I have said this badly, but you will penetrate it, dearest Juliette, for it is just of such radiant centers as you that I am thinking. And even absence <u>distills</u> this essence and makes it the more visible.

I am, comparatively, at peace with myself for I have decided to take a long leave of absence, 4 months, away from the job and get back to poems—also perhaps to a new novel about a family in Belgium between the two wars and might have something in it of what I tried to say earlier. The Single Hound dealt with special people and this would be something in the same key but more universal and human. It is just at the back of my mind still and may not materialize but it is something to think about.

The main thing this OWI job has taught me is that even an ideal job (in the sense of variety of levels, interest plus short hours and good pay) seems so far from what I really know my life to be that it will never be a permanent solution. This year it was necessary to prove to myself and to the family that I could swing a full time job and earn my living completely. I am sure I <u>can</u> do so and now I am not going to worry too much about security again. I am going to use every means to be able to do my own work. And then whenever necessary economically take a job for awhile.

But I am simply <u>determined</u> not to get caught up into a standard of living that has to be "kept up" at the expense of the spirit. It is the one advantage of being alone that one can be so irresponsible! When I was at home I picked up d'Alembert on my father's table and opened to a page on which he said (and it seemed an augury) that the device of a writer should be "liberté, vérité et pauvreté" and that without the third the first two were all but impossible. I fear this country is going through an orgy of materialism and just because of that I will have no part of it. The other side of life will have to be ready to act and move people when this confused war state of mind passes. We do not suffer enough here, as I have written before!

As to outward life, I have now a most beautiful gray studio with a big table and my books. Muriel is across the street so there is always rich companionship and love nearby. I am, as far as one can be, in the midst of so much agony in the world, happy. I think of you very very often—how long will it be? Dearest Juliette, may the New Year blossom for you. It is nice that it will have a baby in it. Tell Julian I'll write soon—was so happy and honored to have his <u>Evolutionary Ethics</u>.

Love and a kiss
[   ]

Anthony will be a father. When?: Susan Huxley was born while Julian was exploring in West Africa, a trip he embarked upon on 15 January 1944 as a member of the Commission on Higher Education in the British Colonies.

abscess . . . at home: Juliette had an abscess on the leg from running about too much with Francis during his week's leave; she was recuperating at the home of a friend.

fight for them in one's private life: See "Innumerable Friend" in *The Land of Silence,* which deals with this theme.

Dorothea Singer: See footnote to letter of 27 October 1936.

did Péguy seem to shine: Charles-Pierre Péguy (1873–1914), who returned to Catholicism and poetry in his last years, celebrating the glory and greatness of France and, despite his involvement in the events of his day, decrying modern politics and the absence of old-fashioned virtues.

4 months away from the job: At the time of this letter Sarton was visiting schools throughout the city for the film *A Better Tomorrow: Progressive Education in New York,* for which she wrote the script with Irving Jacoby; she left the OWI on 10 March 1944.

new novel . . . Belgium: The Bridge of Years, a delicate, perceptive chronicle of a moral European family enduring and resisting the Nazi surge, published by Doubleday in 1946.

picked up d'Alembert: Jean Le Rond d'Alembert (1717–1783), French mathematician and philosopher, best known for his collaboration with Denis Diderot on the famous *La Grande Encyclopédie.*

liberté, vérité et pauvreté: freedom, truth, and poverty.

Evolutionary Ethics: the Romanes Lecture, delivered at Oxford in 1944, published by
   Oxford University Press in 1943.

———

22 E. 10TH ST.   September 25th, 1944
N.Y.C. 3

Dearest Juliette—I have been thinking of you more constantly than usual
ever since a letter from Freya Stark saying Julian had had a breakdown. It
is hard to know so little—how serious? I have felt him on the edge of
something of the sort for years, wished almost that it would come and
force him to pause for a few months. But I was thinking of a minor breakdown and a grim doctor who might take advantage of it to make him take
timeout from the fearful nervous pace he has made his own for so long.
Now I'm afraid it may be really bad—please let me know.

   I can imagine what this means for you, dearest petite flamme, and how
much sustaining, comforting, good humour and patience is asked of you. I
wish so terribly that I were there and could help a little. It is awful to be so
far away. You mustn't take time or energy to write a letter but if you could
just jot down the bare facts on a postcard, I would be so grateful.

   I wrote Julian at once. It seems to me so terribly necessary if he is to
be as useful as he must be after the war, that he stop and be quiet and think
and not force himself to produce before he has given himself time to reach
the deepest levels of understanding. Why am I saying this to you who
know it all so much better than I possibly can? Only perhaps if it is any
help and you are trying to get him to take enough time out, to know that
friends also feel strongly that he must.

   In his last letter, some time ago, I felt the awful fatigue. O, it has been
so long for all of you, beset by large terrors and constant small worries and
discomforts. You must all feel stripped down to the naked last little core of
strength by now. But, my dear, soon it must be over. How are you yourself? I have felt for months very far away as if it had suddenly been too long
since we have seen each other—and I dream of getting back to England,
but I wish I could find some way to be useful.

   It was very exciting to catch a glimpse of Freya Stark—and we cor-
respond now which means, I hope, that it is the beginning and not the end
of knowing her. She did not like America, but I fear she saw the worst of

it—crude ugly cities and empty people. It does sometimes feel like a wilderness for the spirit, but I believe that is always the failure in me, spoiled by inheriting an already created European civilization, unwilling to be a pilgrim moving painfully along the path toward a new life.

I am in a state of <u>total</u> ignorance about my new life—it is wonderful not to have a job, and to be working away at a novel again. But I have also a terrible feeling of isolation here—the kind of thing I most want to say is not what people here are anxious to hear. And I have terrors that I shall not be masterful enough as an artist to <u>force</u> the ears to open, to dazzle the eyes into seeing. Mostly I am aware of my own failure. Only now and then, in poems, I have moments of conviction that I am not altogether crazy to believe I am a writer. But they have no continuity.

In two weeks I shall go home to Cambridge to be with the family for four or five months, and finish the book I have begun about Belgium. In some ways it will be heavenly. I am so happy at home. It is so peaceful. But it is not <u>my own</u> life so it always seems a sort of cheating. I wish that I could marry now. It is time and for the first time in my life I think I am ready <u>inside</u>. But that is easier said than done!

Meanwhile there is work to do. I am hoping to work at the Negro Settlement in Cambridge—perhaps start a writing class there. The racial tensions are very serious now and I would like to do what I can, in a small way, to help solve that problem. It is profoundly a Christian one.

Dearest Juliette, I fear this is a gloomy letter, but I hope you see and feel the deep love shining through the gloom.

Your devoted and anxious

[   ]

Freya Stark: Dame Freya Madeline Stark (1893–1993), elegant, poetic travel writer, first Westerner to journey through many regions of the Middle East; she wrote in her *Traveler's Prologue:* "If we could make contours in hearts as we do in maps, to see their loves, we should learn what strange unexpected regions attain the deepest depths. Often we might discover that a place rather than a person holds the secret." Longtime friend of Sarton and the Huxleys. Visited Cambridge in May, 1944.

Julian had had a breakdown: Returning later in 1944 from his trip to West Africa, Julian Huxley was diagnosed with jaundice and severe depression; he was treated with electric shock.

wrote to Julian at once: "You have been burning the candle at more ends than a candle has!" she wrote. "All that you mean and stand for is going to be so terribly needed <u>after the war</u>, when as Kingsley Martin said the real war begins after this long <u>peace</u>—that now

your first duty is to get really rested and well, even if it takes a year. Your greatest work
will come out of silence and rest now I have never believed anything more deeply."

terrible feeling of isolation here: As a European, Sarton often felt herself an outsider in the
States.

Cambridge to be with the family: In March, Muriel Rukeyser had left indefinitely for
California; Sarton felt herself "grinding out" the new novel; all that, in addition to
financial pressures, made her decide to sublet her apartment at 22 East 10th Street
and return to Cambridge.

----

940 ACEQUIA MADRE   April 15th, 1945
SANTA FE, N.M.

Dearest Juliette, I have spent a half hour trying to find your letter in the
chaos of this room—so now I think I will answer it and it will probably
sail in on a breeze while I am typing. As a matter of fact, there is no breeze,
only a soft silent snow which has covered the little mud houses and lies
thickly on the trees and blots out the mountains. It is full of peace—after
so much sunlight that I was exhausted, too dazzled to live another day. In
Emily Dickinson's new book there is a poem that begins "A day! Help!
Help! Another day!"

This is the most extraordinary time of my life. A burst of poems, a great
creative tide that bears me along on its stream till I almost want to cry
"Enough." A real liberation after three frozen years when it seemed as if the
inner eye could only look at suffering and horror, silently—look and look.
But this is a holy place, the only one I know of in the States. It takes the
soul out of one's body. I will put in some poems and not talk about it here.
I have written twenty poems and two acts of a play in a month and I am so
happy all the time that I live in terror of sin. Gertrude Stein says that enemies and possessions make one forget Eternity and the Fear of Death. Here
both eternity and death are very present. The people are nourishing. The
old Spanish woman, Carolina, who works for us, is one. I talk to her and
sometimes make myself understood. I showed her the portrait of my mother and she looked at it a long time and then said, "I have no mother and no
father and no brothers and no sisters," (this with grave self-pity), "but I have
nine grandchildren," she said with a lonely smile. She is very old and she
works in a cloud of smoke as the one thing she loves is a cigarette.

Good things happen every day—like the two horses who wander in
and lie down on our front lawn every morning, no one knows who they

are. And the day Roosevelt died I was walking and thinking and a cart drawn by two great fat horses jingled past containing three merry old men and their ploughs in the back.

It has been a very lonely three days all over the world. I think of Roosevelt saying in 1933, "We have nothing to fear but fear," and of how he is perhaps the only leader of our time who seemed truly and generously to care about all the people everywhere and to believe in them. In France, in China, in India, in Russia he will be mourned as a friend—and in England surely. Now we all feel our responsibilities more deeply than before. I believe Truman will be all right. People seem to think so. In some ways perhaps more practical as a follower of the line laid down than a more visionary (and dearer) man like Wallace. Roosevelt was never loveable as Wallace is. His faults were more obvious, his greatness more devious. But as one looks back over the twelve terrible years that he was with us, he becomes very great. Because he always <u>believed</u>. And he was patient and a gay fighter.

What pierced me in your letter was that one sentence "I wish I had never been born," thinking of the horror and misery and infinite destruction, moral and material, that we have brought about in our time. The only answer to that is that I think an invisible society of caring and sharing people is being forged out of it all—a true international society of men of good will of which Julian is surely an important one and one who must be used to the full when he is really well again. After the necessary unity of the struggle against the oppressors, there will inevitably be a breaking apart and many wars within (as in France now) but I do not think this is anything but the labor pains. It would be an unhealthy poor world otherwise. Only the Germans think there is something rotten as soon as there is disagreement. The democracies grow through it. The people grow through it—provided the long term aids are <u>defined</u>. It is very often isn't it a difference of tempo—in France, the De Gaulle opposition complains that the great reforms are not being put through <u>at once</u>. De Gaulle I suppose is aware that until there can be elections all radical reforms could be overturned and considered illegal. In England too it looks from here as if the Tories and the opposition had an amazingly similar long-term view of what must be done, but differ in the <u>tempo.</u>

Have you heard anything from Freya Stark? I wonder where she is. When I last heard she was on the moors somewhere finishing her book which I fear was a tremendous effort and she was very tired. She hated

America—she saw, as all lecturers do, the very worst of it. She never got to know the people at all. She never saw or talked with a farmer, a garage mechanic, a small-town newspaper editor, a public school teacher. These are the country. The rest don't matter.

O the snow is beautiful—it falls and falls. I wish you were here. I wish you and Julian were here in a little adobe house and I could cook for you and read you poems and read Thurber aloud with you, and then we would laugh until we cried and we would embrace each other, and we would be happy and together.

Thank God he is getting better again. I cannot bear to think what this year has been for you both, and how you have had to lift your heart out of your boots somehow again and again and again and go on to the next day. I wish I could see darling Francis—is he writing any poems?

I am cook today (I live here with two other women in quite a large house and we take turns cooking) so I must stop. But I will put in some poems. You might pass them on to Kot. Perhaps after all these years they may be something I have done that could please him. I feel he has shut me out. I do not want to be shut out!

The play is about the resistance in France, about women, about Resistance as an idea for the future, the continuing revolt of the spirit that must go on, that must ask the most of itself, cling to the highest standards and never stop fighting from now until we have at least laid the foundations of the world in which we can bear to bring children.

I love you always, dearest Juliette. I think of you, and thinking of you is always good.

> *Your devoted*
> *May*

Four years ago I met your death here
Heard it where I had never been before
In a city of departures, streets of wind
Blowing down people, rigid stone,
Soft plumes of smoke dissolving—
City of departures beside an aloof lake.
Here where you never were, they said:
"Virginia Woolf is dead"—
The city died. I died in the city,
Witness of unreal tears, my own,
For experience involves time

And time was gone,
The world arrested on the instant of death.
I wept wildly like a child
Who cannot give his present after all:
I met your death and did not recognize you.

Now you are dead four years
And there are no more private tears.
The city of departure is the city of arrival,
City of triumphant wind lifting people—
City of spring: yesterday I found you.
Wherever I looked was love,
Wherever I went I had presents in my hands.
Wherever I went I recognized you.
You are not, never to be again,
Never, never to be dead,
Never to be dead again in this city.
Never to be mourned again,
But to return always, to come back yearly,
Hourly, with the spring, with the wind,
Fresh as agony or resurrection,
Fresh as every new love,
A plume of smoke dissolving,
Re-making itself, never still,
Never static, never lost:
The place where time flows again.

I speak to you and meet my own life:
Is it to be poised as the lake beside the city,
Aloof, but given still to air and wind,
Detached from time but given to the moment—
Is it to be a celebration always?

I send you love forward into the past.

Meditation in Sunlight

Who wear an envelope
Of crystal air and learn
That space is also hope
Where sky and snow both burn

Where spring is love not weather
    And I happy alone

The place the time together
The sun upon the stone.

Santa Fe, N.M.

———————

940 Acequia Madre: the home of Edith Ricketson, where Sarton was a paying guest and where on 6 March 1945 Sarton first met Judith Matlack (1898–1982), professor of English at Simmons College, with whom Sarton was to make a home for fifteen years, and with whom she maintained close ties until Matlack's death; see *Honey in the Hive.* Matlack's nephew, Timothy Matlack Warren, would become executor of Sarton's estate.

A day! . . . : the 4th stanza of "The Far Theatricals of Day" in *Bolts of Melody* (Harper, 1945) by Emily Dickinson (1830–1886), American poet whose terse poems rooted in nature Sarton frequently cited.

A burst of poems . . . two acts of a play: On the day of this letter she wrote "Meditation in Sunlight"; see *The Lion and the Rose.* In the days prior to this letter, she wrote twenty poems which became part of *The Lion and the Rose,* which *The Saturday Review* called "an achievement of the first quality," and also *The Underground River* (Play Club, 1947), dealing with the French Resistance; see footnotes to letter of 15 June 1947. The play was first produced in the fall of 1995, shortly after Sarton's death, at Watts Hall in Thomaston, by the Chamber Theatre of Maine; Erika Pfander, its director, had two years earlier produced, directed, and acted in the world premier of Sarton's first play, *The Music Box Bird.* Both plays had been written for Eva Le Gallienne.

Gertrude Stein: (1876–1946), American poet, novelist, and critic, expatriate in Paris for many years; one of the century's most publicized authors, she influenced three generations of writers, including Hemingway and Thornton Wilder.

the day Roosevelt died: Three days earlier, on 12 April 1945, Franklin Delano Roosevelt died suddenly of a cerebral hemorrhage at Warm Springs, Georgia.

Truman will be all right: Harry S. Truman (1884–1972), Roosevelt's vice president; succeeded to the presidency upon Roosevelt's death, making many momentous decisions, particularly to use the atomic bomb against Japan. Supporting the United Nations and formulating the Truman Doctrine, he generally followed his predecessor's policies in domestic matters.

man like Wallace: Henry A. Wallace (1888–1965) served as secretary of agriculture 1933–1940 and vice president under FDR (1941–1945). As secretary of commerce (1945–1946) he was asked to resign in September 1946 following his criticism of the government's policy toward the Soviet Union. He was presidential candidate in 1948 for the Progressive Party.

Freya Stark . . . finishing her book: See footnote to letter of 25 September 1944; *Arab Island, the Middle East, 1939–1943* (in England, *East Is West*) was published in 1945.

Thurber: See footnote to letter of 1 August 1937.

two other women: Judith Matlack and Sarton, paying guests in the home of Edith Ricketson, all enjoyed cooking for one another.

will put in some poems: In addition to the two above, Sarton enclosed "The Lion and the Rose" and "The Window," both in *The Lion and the Rose,* and "Evening Meal—for

Alice and Haniel," in *The Leaves of the Tree.*

resistance in France: The play is posited upon the belief that if one individual with courage is able to move from introspection to social action, then the collective conscience of righteous subversion becomes an underground river; see earlier footnote to this letter.

Four years ago I met your death here . . . : a substantially changed version of "Letter from Chicago, for Virginia Woolf" in *The Land of Silence.*

Meditation in Sunlight: See *The Lion and the Rose* for the final version; this version ends with two additional unpublished verses.

---

940 ACEQUIA MADRE   June 3rd, 1945
SANTA FE, N.M.

Dearest Juliette, your little letter with its breath of spring, of renewal—as if for the first time in years you were able to breathe without terror and anguish—came last week. I was glad. It is wonderful that Julian is pulling out. And I am so very anxious to know now where he will decide to plant his energies, where he will root his life. The trouble is that the possibilities are infinite! He has so much to give in so many directions.

You speak of Roosevelt's death. It seemed unbelievable here. And his greatness shone out of those days and on many people's faces. In some ways his dying was his most potent act. It laid responsibility squarely on all our shoulders where it belongs. I liked what a Merchant Marine boy wrote, "All the men write me the same thing—'We've lost our leader, but there is more of him in each of us. We have to finish his work.'" It is hard to tell about Truman yet. His whole policy seems to be conciliation. He has made some bad appointments—the important Secretaryship of Agriculture to a mere politician for the sake I suppose of Western votes (he comes from New Mexico). On the other hand this policy of conciliation is I think valuable just now when a balking Congress might as it did after Wilson's death, destroy the hopes of the world. The first big test, the debate on tariffs in which the low tariff internationalists won over the die-hard high tariff protect-our-own-interests guys lost. It is very frightening to think what difficult times lie ahead—frightening and inspiring too. I am encouraged by letters I get from American soldiers.

But what was so moving about Roosevelt it that he was really <u>loved</u> as I don't suppose any man had been by people all over the world. He reached out so far. Now if only the country can be worthy of him. But the people who hated and feared him are still very much alive and biding their time.

I think you must now consider yourself convalescent from this long and fearful strain, personal and public so to speak. Don't expect anything of yourself for awhile. I am so happy when I think of you gardening—what you say of the roots. O Juliette darling, try to <u>bask</u> a little (but that is easier said than done). I wonder what you hear of Francis. I expect he will be sent to the Pacific. My heart aches when I think of the boys who have fought through all the campaigns in Africa, France, Germany and who now cannot come home but are shipped off to another war in a totally different climate with a different enemy, not less terrible. How tired they must be. Does Francis still write poems? I treasure the one he wrote after playing Hamlet

> Come with the winter and the wind
> And with the falling snow.

I have often read it aloud when speaking at schools to prove what pure poetry can be written by people their age. It is a true poem. Then the girls want to know all about Francis and I know so little. Only I remember clearly our one day of drawing animals together at Whipsnade—so long ago. What fun we had.

I cannot imagine Susan. Have you a snapshot? I'll send it back. How strange human destinies are. I could not have imagined that Anthony would turn so soon into a family man! It must still astonish you. I wonder what he is like now inside. Is he using at all his special sensibilities—for music? for poems?

I wish you were here, basking with Julian. The air is so light here and always full of the smell of cedar, a fresh sweet scent that rises from the hearths. I find it very comforting and dear to be in a part of the world where religion is a natural and important part of life—a continual reality. I myself do not quite believe but I am comforted that others have this comfort. The churches are so gay and at the same time full of a simple acceptance of agony and human suffering. The stiff primitive Christs hanging on wooden crosses and then the so human saints. There is one favorite here called Santiago, always dressed in Spanish clothes (which the women make) and on horseback. He has to have many pairs of new shoes as he wears them out going out at night on errands of mercy. Today, Corpus Christi, there is a great procession in which the Archbishop carries the Host through the streets and everyone kneels.

And then going along beside this new religion, hand in hand with it, for there are missions and chapels in all the Pueblos and Franciscan priests, streams the ancient Indian religion, out in the open air, drenched in sunlight with its beautiful sense of the relation between man and the elements, man and the earth and sun. It is extraordinary after one of the Indian dances to see the Indians go to kneel in full costume before their patron saint, and bear him back into the church. (They bring him out to watch the dances.) Even more strange when the Indian chant suddenly changes to a liturgical one.

I was in an ecstasy when I got here. Now after writing a host of poems and a play about the Resistance in France, I am beginning to feel written out. But I think it is a matter now of going down deeper than the landscape, the shock of joy, and that new poems will come. It has been one of the marvelous times of my life. And I hate to think of going back to crowded little New England in August. Except that it will be good to see the family.

Such lovely things happen here partly because the tempo is less fierce than in the East. Three women friends and I drove out one spring day to a little town in the mountains where a family has carried on the tradition of carving saints for three generations. I found there a little white wooden tree with fat formal leaves on each of which sits a bird or a squirrel or beaver, a tree alive with animals and I got it for Daddy. Then we came back through the ancient land, watching young boys plough (the men were all at war) and old women sow, and the fruit trees all in flower and the marvelous running brooks, miraculous always in this arid landscape. After that day we all wrote poems and now there is a little book to celebrate the day for which I have painted a cover with a phoenix on it. These are the precious things. It is like a taste of what life should always be. Wherever I go, I take poems to read and it seems perfectly natural. In the East it would be un-heard of!

Have you read Osbert Sitwell's memoirs? It gave me hours of delighted astonishment and wonder. And I hear Ruth Pitter's new book is very fine. Over here Auden is a great pet, but I am very sick of his sophisticated stuff. It is just too clever and I cannot believe his religion at all. When one has read many of his poems one feels that human life is a pretty shod-dy affair. I do not believe that it is!

I will stop to copy poems. Do write. How long has it been, six years, since I have seen you in a vermilion cap, or eaten a cucumber sandwich under a tree with you and Julian and the boys. Dear dear times. Often and often they come back like a song.

With dearest love

[   ]

What of Kot? Alan?

Landscape With Figure

At last we came to the small valley where
Green flowed the wind upon the ravished air,
Sweet flowed the sun upon the young fruit-trees
That flowered suddenly before our startled eyes.
Clear flowed the water in the snow-rich stream
Where all was bright and classic as in dream.

And there we saw a solitary and triumphant boy
Ploughing a long field to the shape of joy;
His young hands turning the old memories under
Made of the crooked furrows a straight splendor.
The air around him burned. The boy was spring.
And he was very old and he was very young.

The Gifts

There was nowhere without
A mountain. The horizon
Opened like a shout,
A peal of silence, a huge organ
Building wave upon wave
Of music far and near:
The high peaks rang
So sharp and clear
Sound shivered like a glass

Struck in the air,
And the rocks sang.
The light was music, and the music, light.
It mounted from green foot-hills
To blue ranges out of sight.
We heard the sound the mountains make.
We heard the rocks sing.
This was the first gift, for joy's sake.

We opened wine and drank the sun
Until the open vein was gold and warm
And wine and sun and we were woven into one.

But then the vision grew—
As if the iris that reflected all the sky
Opened to the black pupil of an inward eye:
The whole tortured world was what we knew.
And all we listened to was children weeping,
And all we cared was: they are in our keeping.
And all we knew was our responsibility
To build on earth the children's holy city.

The mountains shouted and were stilled
By the great cry that the heart spilled.
So we were given back ourselves again:
The second and the greater gift was pain.

All the Children Have Hello to Say

All the children have hello to say
On the curving road
When you walk to town,
They always say "Hello," whoever goes that way.

The little girl in red is always there
Waiting for you to come,
And though you have no name
She is waiting for you alone, whoever you are.

And the two dirty cherubs by the gate
Stop playing school
To give a quick hail
(And maybe you are Love and maybe you are Hate.)

For all the people in the world go walking by
Sooner or later, now and then,
The whole world of men
Passes the calling children, passes them by.

The children in the garden smile and stare
When Death himself goes by,
"Hello" to him they cry,
And whoever he may be, he answers "Hello there."

Whoever goes down to town by the mother stream
Thinking the ways things are,
Too lonely and poor and hard
All over the world, dreaming a saving dream,

Always, whatever he knows, the children are there
Playing the ancient game,
For whatever may be his name,
They are wanting love, they are asking him to care.

They are waiting for an act, for a word, for some
Stranger who will know
The answer to "Hello"
The stranger who will say "Your Kingdom come."

[12 April 1945]

---

breathe without terror and anguish: After three weeks of air raids in London, months of domestic misery, and news of the concentration camps, Julian was very much better and Juliette was sowing a garden.

a mere politician: Clinton P. Anderson, secretary of agriculture from June 1945 to May 1948.

what you say of the roots: "I like to think of them," Juliette wrote, "with that blind instinct which the films bring to our eyes. Power of life."

what you hear of Francis: Francis Huxley had been transferred from HMS *Ramillies* to HMS *Vengeance,* an aircraft carrier on a mission to the East. See footnote to letter of 1 February 1942.

with a different enemy, not less terrible: On 1 April 1945, U.S. marines and army troops invaded Okinawa. Between May and August of that year in the greatest air offensive in history the U.S. forces destroyed or immobilized the remnants of the Japanese navy, shattered Japanese industry, and shelled populated cities. On 6 August an atomic bomb, secretly prepared by American and British scientists, was dropped on Hiroshima. On 9 August a second atomic bomb was dropped on Nagasaki. The Japanese signed a formal surrender on 2 September.

Come with the winter . . . : from "Why Does the Drum Come Hither?" See letter of 4 March 1942.

his special sensibilities: Anthony Huxley became a botanist and horticulturist, writing over thirty books on these subjects, including *Green Inheritance*; Francis became a biologist and anthropologist, writing *Affable Savages* and *The Way of the Sacred* among other books.

cedar: actually it is piñon or nutpine, burned in New Mexico, that is so redolent; see "Of the Seasons" in *The Lion and the Rose.*

called Santiago: Santiago, the apostle St. James, brother of St. John the Evangelist; patron saint of Spain and many Spanish-speaking countries; his bones are said to rest at Santiago de Compostela, Spain, one of the most famous places of pilgrimage in the Christian world.

Today, Corpus Christi: Corpus Christi, Body of Christ, a feast commemorating the Eucharist, observed on the Thursday after Trinity Thursday.

a little book . . . with a phoenix on it: "Garland for a Day," a booklet still in Sarton's possession at the time of her death, contains poems by Judith Matlack, Dorothy S. McKibbin, Edith B. Ricketson, and May Sarton, including "In a Dry Land," later published in *The Land of Silence.*

Osbert Sitwell's memoirs: Left Hand, Right Hand! (1944; a year later in the United States), the first of a five-volume family memoir by Sir Francis Osbert Sitwell (1892–1969), English poet and writer of unusual grace and richness, brother of Edith (see footnote to letter dated 7 December 1936) and Sacheverell, all iconoclastic, eccentric aristocrats, who gave public readings together.

Ruth Pitter's new book: The Bridge Poems (1939–1944) Cresset Press, 1945.

cannot believe his religion at all: From the Marxism of his youth, Auden had moved to Anglo-Catholicism.

Landscape With Figure: unpublished; also known as "Spring Day," the first in a series of poems entitled "New Mexican Spring."

The Gifts: unpublished; also known as "In the Mountains," the second part of the "New Mexican Spring" sequence.

All the Children Have Hello to Say: unpublished; appeared for the first time in *Selected Letters 1916–1954*; also known as "Always the Children Have Hello to Say . . . Acequia Madre, Sante Fe."

---

139 OXFORD ST.   Nov. 26th, 1945
CAMBRIDGE, MASS.

Dearest Juliette, O petite flamme bleue, your letter came very fast and I read it in great excitement. It has seemed a long time except that I think of you very often and do not feel in spite of all the silence and the time that the connection is lost. A kind of wireless goes on—but your letter made me sad, sad for you, sad for Julian. I had hoped somehow that his long period of fatigue and illness and all that time for quietly thinking would have brought him out to a new sense of life and not back to the old one where he depended so much on whipping himself up emotionally. I have just called Shapley who seems to think J. may be on the Queen Mary so perhaps I shall see him. I would love to. But it all makes me sad, also deep down revolted and angry—though who am I to be angry? My darling, I am counting on getting over this summer somehow to see you and to go to Belgium.

Are you gasping on the shore now instead of drowning? Are you getting real rest and sleep? The hardest the really intolerable things are those that have no solution where one faces and faces again the pain and knows that there is no healing. But I am very glad indeed that you have talked with Julian and I hope made him realize some things. I wonder if we in our time have not made some fatal mistake in believing that happiness was the most important end in individual life. Psychoanalysis with its emphasis on integration, on releasing the inner drives, badly understood no doubt by most of us, seems to me to have had a poor influence. And in seeking happiness above all, <u>of course</u> we never find it. It is a by-product and not the end of life surely. And all personal relations depend so much on patience, on living through the deep places, the bored places, the dark places <u>together</u>. Women know this better than men I think. They are more rooted or perhaps the roots mean more to us, I don't know. It is very hard to write about it all. I only wish I were there and we could go for a long walk quietly through a wood—and talk if we felt like it—or not talk. The awful thing about a letter is that one <u>must</u> talk. But it is really—and you know this I'm sure—in the silence and in thinking about you with all my heart that I feel close to you now and always.

How extraordinary to think Alan, the gipsy, is wandering about. I wish he would find a way to the Southwest—he would like it there. Perhaps by now you will have heard where he is.

Yes, I am back in New England. And for the first time living in Cambridge but not with my family. I am living in a dear shabby old house with a friend whom I dearly love—a woman a good deal older than I who teaches in a college here. We met in Sante Fe and had a good five months of testing how we got on. I feel like a man who finds haven after years and years of tossing about on foreign shores. It is really very good I think. Things apart from "love" though that is very real and deep too make it good. Now at last I can live in the frugal way which is the only way possible for a poet to live. That means that without working all the time I can earn months of solitude to write in. Judy is away all day. It is peaceful here and then we cook our supper and read aloud. Every now and then I go off

on lecture trips and get a look at this country and try to do a little something in the colleges for poetry. It seems as if I had at last reached the main-
stream of my life. It was a tremendous relief to have the novel accepted (it
will be out in the late spring) and so to have a little confidence again. Now
I can wait several years even if things are rejected and still be of good cheer.
I still cannot get a publisher for the poems but they can keep. And eventually I am sure it will be possible. The novel is also now with my English
agent. I wonder if it will fall into Kot's hands for Cresset. I sent him a small
Christmas package of tea and jam and have a great longing to communicate with him again, but the silence has been so long it is like a wall.

My only trouble is again a bout of great fatigue which ever since the
time some years ago when I had to really take three months off, scares me
a little. So now I am trying to make very quiet days and not push myself
into beginning a new book which is simmering. I have so much I want to
do that it is depressing to be pulled back by a mere weak stomach! But I
did live very high and produce a great deal from March of this year till
August and I guess it is time as the Coca Cola ads say for "the pause that
refreshes." To arrive at this place of peace and communion, of camaraderie
douce, Judy and I went through some pretty grim times. She had, I think
and quite naturally, grave doubts about it as a way of life. But now I believe
she is really happy and without any doubt. So it is good. I just pray that
being given so much I will at last be able to prove that I am a builder and
a person fit for an enduring relationship. That is, I think, up to me.

About Elisabeth—what you said was exactly right I think about "static reflections in poisoned waters." It is a very strange thing that Elisabeth
seems focussed inwardly at her best almost always on extremely perceptive
children's awareness of the grown-up world. I have just read a long story
in Horizon called "Ivy Gripped the Steps" but have not seen the collected book. Somewhere or other she seems to me trapped inside herself so
there is no clear flow out to life or of life into her—it is immensely clever,
immensely self-conscious, full of perception. But the heart is not beauty or
love or anything positive or glowing but somehow, as you suggest, death.
Surely she is one of the most interesting of living writers. But I wonder
what in the end the total work will add up to. I never hear from her and
hope perhaps to see her if I get over. We are all it seems pieces of people;
it would be a great thing to come across a whole person, a whole person
who would write of love and God from wholeness. Did you by any chance

see a very fine and critical review of Aldous's anthology in The New Republic by Alfred Kazin? It ends (but you must read it all) and it is written in the form of an address to God, "Lord, you who condemned Aldous Huxley to dislike life or to write novels; to seek you in libraries and amid the fumes of Hollywood; to love the Indian scriptures but not the Indian masses; to know everything about a man as a specimen and to believe so little in him, on sight, as an ultimately irreproachable being—Lord, will you not show him that all these texts are a defence against a real faith and not the road to one; that he really fails you most by failing us? Will you not show him that the idea is not the pinnacle of thought as it rises into faith but the enemy of thought when it evades the life which grounds it? We have had enough, Lord, of 'dying to self'; the self is still only honored or dishonored, it is not lived; and because it is not, there is not self-love either, but only a trembling to be what we are not and to deny what we are. And where we are denied, the love of you is gone forever."

Well, I must stop though I have so much to say. I'm glad you liked the poems, the letter about Santa Fe. I am fearfully depressed by the world we are in—the atomic bomb—the fear of Russia—fear and suspicion everywhere—a sort of deadness instead of a quickening. But it is worse here in this great healthy giant of a country without imagination and without faith. I think of you often and dearly. Take care of yourself, of the blue flame. With love always and bless you for writing as you did. M—

---

139 *Oxford St:* As explained in this letter, the house in which Sarton and Judith Matlack made their home in November 1945.

do not feel . . . the connection is lost: Juliette had been suffering from what the doctor called "combat exhaustion" as well as from "a long perilous journey of agony with Julian."

just called Shapley: Harlow Shapley (1885–1972), American author, astronomer, director of the Harvard Observatory.

perhaps I shall see him: Julian Huxley came to New York City for a rally against nuclear weapons held at Madison Square Garden and was an observer of the Preparatory Commission of UNECO, soon to become UNESCO (United Nations Educational, Scientific and Cultural Organization) after he and Joseph Needham, a Cambridge biochemist, had led a delegation pleading for science to be part of the project.

Alan . . wandering about: Alan Best, Canadian naturalist, sculptor, later became zoo director, Juliette's lover. At this time he had reached New York, jumped his ship, and disappeared into the United States.

whom I dearly love: Judith Matlack was fourteen years older than Sarton. See footnote to letter of 15 April 1945.

to have the novel accepted: Doubleday took *The Bridge of Years*.

publisher for the poems: The Lion and the Rose was not published by Rinehart until 1948.

had to really take three months off: After Sarton's theater failed, she had a breakdown and recuperated at Anne Thorp's in Sudbury, Massachusetts.

a weak stomach: See footnote for letter of 10 June 1942.

camaraderie douce: gentle companionship.

as a way of life: See footnote to letter dated 26 November 1945.

an enduring relationship: Although of Sarton's passionate attachments she could write "Now frost has broken summer like a glass" (see "Der Abschied"), friendships were a different matter. She did not drop friends, and at the end of her life retained many she had known for more than sixty years; it was a matter of principle to *work* at healing rifts. Although the nature of her relationship with Judith Matlack changed over the years, Sarton was attentive to her even after Alzheimer's rendered communication impossible.

the collected book: The story "Ivy Gripped the Steps" by Elizabeth Bowen appeared in *The Demon Lover* (1945; in U.S. under the title *Ivy Gripped the Steps and Other Stories*, 1946.)

Aldous's anthology: The Perennial Philosophy by Aldous Huxley (Harper's, 1945); see footnote to letter of 20 January 1948.

Alfred Kazin: (1915–1998), American literary critic and autobiographer.

bless you for writing as you did: Juliette had not written since June, she explained, as she had been recovering from "combat exhaustion . . . yet it isn't the war & the world which sent me on a long perilous journey of agony, but a minute wheel revolving within my heart, lacerating with its sharp edges till only pain remains . . . yet this time, the first time, I have spoken of it to Julian—& let him take his share."

---

5 Channing Place   July 13, 1946
Cambridge (until Sept. 1st)

Juliette darling, I was panting for a word from you—after that abrupt, teasing meeting which was no meeting! But I am very cross that you can even for an instant have allowed your little blue flame, so pure, deep and distinguished that shines wherever you go and on whomever you see to be dampened by an idea of competing with those empty sterile New York shop window models. In the first place do you really want to look like them? I don't! Stark Young is a fool. It is the foolishness of the fairy and he has to be forgiven because he is such a good critic, but don't for heaven's sake think what he thinks matters to a <u>woman</u>. Fairies always want women to look perfectly unreal and disgusting. They do not want them to look like women, they would be scared to death. They want them to look like dolls (which are no menace) or tropical birds or anything at all except a WOMAN. You are a woman, thank God, and not a doll or a bird. But I think at first N.Y. makes

everyone feel fearfully insecure and there is a kind of false security in looking like all the others. One can hide behind a dress and a coiffure. I used to
feel it terribly and I was cured by living for a time with Muriel Rukeyser
the poet who looks like a large Kwan Yin and wears no corset and seems
always so relaxed, and whose clothes are fearfully odd and often dirty and yet
no one minds (I do mind the dirt a little!) in the end it is what one is—
clothes are an armour, that is all. And I know how you felt, but I think what
you forget is how utterly and unbelievably charming you are—better and
deeper than that, how your wisdom shines out and everyone feels it. I was
very sad about Julian. I do not feel that he has very much to give. You really
have to give the appearance at least of having time to get anything at all out
of people. He breaks every chance of a sequence anywhere with his ner-
vousness and speed. He is worse than America to me or at least perhaps he
allows America to jazz him up like that. But it is not good. I do love him so
much and was happy to see him—but sad too. I had hoped that that long
period of quiet would have created some deep calm inside from which he
could move out into the world. He rushes around like a humming bird tasting this and tasting that, but does any of it get digested? Is it real? Perhaps I
am too severe. After all, it is all very rushed—but I think that impatience is
dangerous. He will break things that he needs—will miss so much.

I'm glad you liked the family. I hope Daddy didn't exhaust you that
rhinoceros and glass-flower morning. I come back to them and bask and
find them more interesting and charming than almost anyone I ever see.
They are both so young because they are both so pure in heart. Is that it,
I wonder? Anyway they loved you and I'm glad you loved them. Some
people have thought that Daddy was Paul in the book but he is not at all!
I shall be anxious to know your final impression. I think the first part is the
slowest and later also the dimension enlarges, at least I hope so.

I wish too that you could have met a few more of the real people.
There are many, but also, you are right, there is such a welter of things,
money, speed, bigness. I often despair. I hate the whole advertising business
and that of course runs the country—runs publishing and everything else
as well. The miracle is that there are still places like the small New England
towns (though they are smug) and Sante Fe and also that right in New
York there is so much going on that you can't imagine at first sight. I think
of a sculptress friend of mine who is a holy person, always having to work

for a living and doing her own work at night, never embittered, full of real joie de vivre—people like her—and there are many. But the hugeness bewilders and makes people passive and selfish—a kind of inertia—you feel "it is all so big, I don't count so it doesn't matter whether I write my congressman about the loan to Britain or not." The really violent antipathy to England is something I find it hard to understand. I suppose it is a sense of inferiority but it is unfortunate and especially just now when you have so much to teach us.

Have you read Kierkegaard? I am plunged into it up to my ears. Wonderful stuff that you have to mine for—for his tortuous style and fearful self-consciousness puts off a natural animal like me, but under it all, it goes so deep. It is so absolute in this world of evasions and compromise, of appeasement on every side. He asks everything of the person and that is a tonic. One emerges glad to be human and to meet such a challenge, even though one fails. This for instance: "And now the Instant. It is short, indeed, and temporal, as every instant is, fleeting, as every instant is, gone like all instants, the following instant, and yet it is decisive, and yet it is full of eternity. Such an instant must have a special name, let us call it the fullness of time." Your special genius it seems to me, darling, is to make every instant seem like the fullness of time. It is a very rare genius.

But of course Kierkegaard goes on to say—and here alas, I cannot follow him: "'The instant does not need to be long, for it is a leap.' 'If only the instant posited, the Paradox is granted.' An instant, if it is only an instant in time, is 'filled with emptiness.' What fills it with eternity is the apprehension of the paradox that God became man. It is then the decisive Instant of faith."

An instant, incidentally, which I don't believe Eliot has ever experienced. One reason his poetry is so moving to me is that it seems to be the place where we all are, the longing for faith—without ever having faith. I found it fascinating to see how my ignorant, immature students fell on Eliot (after disliking Yeats) and really managed to understand him. It was exciting and I have written Eliot to tell him so. So many people brush him aside as a "difficult poet," the critics' delight, but they have never bothered to read him with wide open ears and eyes. Do you see him at all?

Now I hope you are in Switzerland and perhaps this will be forwarded—I hope not opened on the way to you!

With dearest love. Take a breath of the mountains and the pure air—
and write to me sometimes—

Your devoted

May

---

abrupt teasing meeting: The Huxleys had been in New York where Julian, now a world figure with his appointment as first director general of UNESCO, had explained
UNESCO's aims to the United Nations General Assembly.

sterile New York shop window models: Confronted with New York's fashion scene, Juliette
had "succumbed to the withering blight of feeling dowdy."

Stark Young is a fool: Stark Young (1881–1963), American drama critic for the *New York
Times* and *The New Republic*, whose work was considered among the best theater
criticism ever written; he abuptly stopped writing on theater in 1948 and turned his
attentions to painting, autobiographical writings, and translations. He had expressed
chagrin at Juliette's clothes, adding, ". . . but you can *wear* your clothes well."

Kwan Yin: Kuan-yin, the Chinese goddess of mercy, often pictured as a large white-robed
woman sitting in meditation.

Daddy was Paul in the book: Paul Duchesne, who is based on Raymond Limbosch, not
George Sarton, lives a contemplative life in *The Bridge of Years*; a philosopher and
writer, he works at home, receives no notice upon publication of his work, and has
an inner sense of failure; he shares Sarton's own conflict between life and art.

sculptress friend of mine: probably Theodora Pleadwell.

Kierkegaard: Søren Kierkegaard (1813–1855), Danish philosopher and theologian, for
whom man's relationship with God was the lonely, agonizing experience of a man's
inner solitude.

And now the Instant. . . . Instant of faith: from *Kierkegaard* by Walter Lowrie (Oxford, 1938),
p. 312.

Eliot: T. S. Eliot; see footnote to letter of 23 November 1941.

in Switzerland: Juliette often returned to Neuchâtel, Switzerland, where she had grown up
and where her mother, Mélanie Antonia (Ortlieb) Baillot, still lived.

---

*There are no extant letters between 13 July 1946 and 14 June 1947. On 9 April
1947, for the first time since the war, Sarton sailed for Europe, crossing on the HMS
Queen Elizabeth. The ship was stuck in mud in Southhampton, then further
delayed due to fog; Third Class finally disembarked on 17 April. After seeing friends
in London, Suffolk, Sussex, Rye, Kingham, and Manchester, Sarton left for two
weeks with the Limbosches in Belgium and time with Jean Dominique. Early on
the morning of Saturday, 24 May 1947, Sarton left Belgium for Paris, where she
spent the first night at the Huxleys, sharing a room with their friend Violet
Hammersley. Most of that first day they spent together in the forest of
Fontainebleau, having tea under the chestnuts and a picnic supper. Although she
moved to the apartment of M. and Mme. André Mayer, Sarton spent much of the*

following days with Juliette; it was of this brief time they shared together that she
would write months later:

> This gift of passion we both give and take,
> That translates friend to dearest enemy
> And love itself into a dazzling stranger,
> So all between us that was safe and deep
> Is made uncertain, sharpened upon danger. . . .

───────

first night at the Huxley's: The Huxleys had rented out the Pond Street house and moved
to 2 Avenue Alphand in Paris in January 1947.
Violet Hammersley: Violet Mary Hammersley (1878–1964), an old friend of the Huxleys
whose stepchildren Julian had tutored during his undergraduate days. Hostess and
patron of the arts.
M. and Mme. André Mayer: André Mayer was director general of the Food and Agricultural
Organization of the United Nations; he and his family were old friends of the
Sartons.
This gift of passion . . . . : originally unpublished, from sonnet sequence "These Images
Remain" (June 1948); first published in *Among the Usual Days* (1993).

───────

SATURDAY AFTERNOON   [14 June 1947]
18 AVE. LÉQUIME
RHÔDES ST. GENÈSE

These are the bad days, darling, because all communication has
stopped. I am having a bad <u>crise de nerfs</u>—I tried yesterday all day to reach
you by phone. (I went off with the keys. What shall I do with them?) I
started at eight A.M. and finally got through to <u>la bonne</u> at 11:15 when of
course you were out. I started again at eight at night and at 12:30 A.M.
went to bed in tears of exasperation. Telephoning from here is really a
Kafka nightmare and I shan't do it again. But I am pushed by time and by
silence that will descend on me next Saturday on the boat, and I have been
a little mad with the frustrations so that I imagine now that my letter will
get lost. One to the family took 18 days sent air mail from here! The tyranny of postmen, telephone operators, things, furniture makes a great opaci-
ty and I do not find you through it. Tell me that you are well, safe, happy,
that you think of me. I need to know something. Il y a des abîmes autour
de moi. I shall have to spend half the week getting visas for Holland and
perhaps (?) Switzerland or France. But the time runs out so fast, like sand

in a glass—it frightens me. However, don't take any of this seriously. It is, as I said, a <u>crise de nerfs</u>. My heart is at peace really—or will be when I have heard from you and know how to plan, whether we shall meet again, what sort of equilibrium to create, how to live.

But I remember everything: how the light flowed on the pavement outside Socrates, how the Arc de Triomphe looked, the little chairs under the chestnut on the Ave. Foch, the David leaves, your piercing loveliness as we drove toward the Orangerie and I looked at you, the palms of your hand, Mr. Prière. You see, I am full of incredible riches, and when this first darkness of absence of parting is healed, I shall be full of light. Just now I feel tired.

But I laughed very much with Jean-Do yesterday. We agreed that if the boat were ours we would simply tie it in a canal near a post-office and write poems and drink wine like Chinese philosophers. I see her revive when I come and it is so good to be able to do this. And she understands everything <u>without a word</u>. Such a blessing. So you see, there is peace here too—and you must not worry about anything. Now I must dress. An old friend of my father's is coming to take me out to lunch—in a car, there is a trolley strike here!

Let me know something by Wednesday if you can about plans. That would still give me two days to make arrangements. If you can't don't worry. The only killing thing in my life is suspense. Everything else can be transformed in one way or another. I am so full of poems, of marvelous <u>inépuisable</u> joy!

Dear one, be at peace.

M

Shall I mail the keys to the concierge at 2 Ave. Alphand or what? How stupid of me.

The tyranny of things has just proved that it is true: the door of my room (a sliding door) suddenly fell down! Tu vois!

I wrote yesterday three possibilities
1) to fly to Neuchâtel Wed. July 2d. for 2 or 3 days without my heavy luggage and come back <u>here</u> afterwards.
2) to meet you in Paris, 3d or 4th (Julian I suppose will get in before the

6th?) If it is this I <u>must</u> know by Wed. to make arrangements before we leave

3) to meet in England after July 10th and before the 25th when I sail

Perspective

The glittering leaves are still
That shook down light and shadow
Until the static pavement flowed
Under our feet like broken water.

Now all the trees are still
Opaque and green: the golden bough
Has vanished and the constant stirring
As of wings in the air is no more.

The heart looks down the avenue of silence,
A long perspective where the formal trees
Lead only to a strange and empty space:
Where is the arch of triumph now?

Absence throws green upon all glory
And dulls the eyes that saw with lucid joy
The stone itself flower in the late light.
Now all the glittering leaves are still

And the triumphant arch dissolves in tears.

June 14th

————————

crise de nerfs: fit of hysteria.

la bonne: the maid.

the boat: The Limbosches had arranged for a week's boat trip to Holland for all of them on a small, primitive sailboat with no comforts. Sarton dreaded it.

Il y a des âbimes autour de moi: There are great caverns of emptiness around me.

Switzerland or France: On 20 June Sarton decided not, after all, to go to Switzerland to see Juliette.

Socrates: Juliette Huxley's milliner.

David leaves: Reference to *Landscape* by Gerard David, of which Sarton writes in "The Two Forests": "The painting is a forest so complete/It is the secret testament of leaves." See letter of 8 July 1947.

Mr. Prière: unidentified.

friend of my father's: Irénée Van der Ghinst, scientist.

inépuisable: inexhaustible.

Tu vois!: You see!

Perspective: See *The Lion and the Rose.* Sarton's original manuscript for this book ended with the
letter of 1 November 1948; at that time, it was her wish that this poem close the volume.

––––––––––

SUNDAY MORNING   [15 June 1947]
[CHEZ LIMBOSCH]

It makes me very cross that I seem unable to condense everything as you
do with your real mastery of words, into one short evocative statement—
so my letters are far too long. But perhaps I shall learn this from you. I realize now all that I didn't say last night. One reason I want very much to see
you—after you are settled and back in the groove—is to once go over the
poems with you. Your instinct and taste are simply unerring. You are quite
right about Perspective. I have been working on it, but it isn't right yet. I
wanted a sort of dissonance, to make the sound of absence, but there are
too many words, far too many. Anyway the last is better now: "And the triumphant arch dissolves, dissolves." I am trying to cut one stanza entirely. I
think line two of Definition will have to stand, but I might cut both eight
and ten, what do you think? I wonder what you will say of the last ones—
the leaf one still is rough. I might leave out the two lines about laying hands
on the trunks as it is perhaps another poem and too much here. In Spring
Song I am trying to find the word for when the fruit is made. In French it
is "la fruit se <u>noue</u>" and "My love, my love, the fruit is already knotted"
would be much stronger than "growing." I think we must have a word and
when I get back to Cambridge I can look in a dictionary. It would make
the poem to have one strong and unexpected word I think.

    As for the play I'm amused about Jean—I hadn't thought of it. The main
trouble is Act II I think. I should have been able to contain the play in
Madeleine's room. Fontanes is Lugné-Poë as you probably guessed. It is at last
going to be published by a small publishing house for amateur production so
I may eventually have a chance to see how it plays. That would be fun. But it
is too romantic and hopeful—only perhaps someday I can write a good play.
You are darling to have read it. To have sent it back so fast, so registered!

    I love to see your window and it is before me now. How mysterious a
window is—framing and somehow making a person in it eternal. Do you
know Rilke's French poems? There are several very fine ones about windows.

    I go back to your letter, full of questions. What, I wonder, do you have to forget? What do you have to know? What hurts me is never anything to do with me—please believe that. You can't hurt me. Everything you do and are blesses, nourishes, makes magic for me. Your words are magic. Your silence is magic. What you say and do not say. What you feel or do not feel. It is all <u>good</u>. No, what hurts is not your relation to me, but your relation to yourself. It's when you talk of "naked starving souls" for instance. Or "penchée sur ma sècheresse." Those words hurt very much. I am haunted by them. All of this happened partly at least because of such words. And I suppose, yes, what is awful, is that I can do nothing. I think any love, even the lightest, the most imaginative, is a weight. And in another letter you speak of the "links in the chain of possession—lips, eyes, beauty and the joys of love." I suppose that yes, if we were ever together a great deal that might be true. As it is, there is blessedly no danger. Whatever takes place between us takes place within a very rigid <u>form</u>, the established form of your life and the form I am trying to establish for mine. Form is always a safety. I do not even dream of possession. I think perhaps your equivalent in my heart is poetry. How could I <u>possess</u> poetry? It is always a divine demanding <u>question</u>. We are both really <u>given</u> to someone else. Then how can the gift be made again in any physical sense? How can one even speak of love without the whole person being involved? That is the mystery which I don't pretend to understand. But I have felt no guilt which astonishes me. What I would hope—but O darling, forgive me if this is pure arrogance or cruel misunderstanding—is that somehow or other I could be salt or leaven or something or other, some enlivening ingredient in your life, without doing <u>harm</u>. What I know for myself is that it does not touch my relationship with Judy at all, but of course I don't know what will happen when I see her. Only I feel that she represents continuity, peace, the chance to build a long-lasting relationship where all the small daily things of life are of great importance—and that perhaps is marriage.

And on your part I understand how deep your marriage goes. It is a very beautiful and difficult creation, a true creative act on your part. But also I have no guilt about Julian because for a long time now it seems he has not been able to nourish you, but only to take from you. If I could give anything whatever to you, I would be giving it <u>also</u> to him. I think I shall try to come to Paris. Would you dread it very much? I shall be so far away so soon. If I came it might be Thursday, the 17th or Monday, the 21st [of July]—but probably the 17th—<u>not</u> a weekend as I want to see you alone once for an hour. You can say <u>no</u>, you know. You can say anything that you <u>feel</u>. You do know that? I would only be hurt by <u>not</u> loving you, not by anything you might do, except to be <u>less</u> than yourself.

[   ]

---

your mastery of words . . . short evocative statement: There are no extant letters from Juliette during this period.

the leaf one is still rough: Probably "The Leaves" at end of letter of 22 June 1947.

Spring Song: See *The Lion and the Rose.*

the play: The Underground River, see footnotes to letters of 15 April 1945 and 15 June 1947.

Madeleine's: Madeleine Closset, a poet and teacher, enraged by her own impotence in the face of France's surrender to Germany and resolved to help her country, is all but destroyed at the hands of the Gestapo but her powerful spirit remains intact.

Fontanes: close friend of Madeleine, an elderly, ailing gentleman who has spent his life in the theater and who, though as angry as she, is incorrigible about extricating joys from even war-torn moments. Fontanes is based on Lugné-Poë; see footnote to letter dated 27 August 1940.

write a good play: Of its production forty-five years later in 1995 by the Chamber Theatre of Maine, the *Free Press* reported: "*The Underground River* not only says something singularly important about the period in history it describes, it strongly evokes the possibility of history repeating itself. . . . Sarton's characters are both passionate and compassionate." Sarton had greatly looked forward to its production that October; she died twelve weeks before it opened.

a person in it eternal: See Sarton's "The Window" in *The Lion and the Rose.*

Rilke's French poems . . . about windows: Sarton was reading the Éditions Emile-Paul Frères edition (1946) of Rainer Maria Rilke's *Poésies Françaises,* in which there is a section of fifteen short poems titled "Les Fenêtres."

penchée sur ma sècheresse: leaning over my withering.

Form is always a safety: Whether in poetry, music, gardening, or love, whether within the structure of her day or her year, form and routine were essential to Sarton's inner and outer worlds. See pp. 7–13 in *Among the Usual Days.*

my relationship with Judy: Judith Matlack, a Quaker, was uncomfortable from the start with the idea of physical intimacy, and that aspect of her relationship with Sarton did not last beyond the first six months; it was the continuity of home and communion which remained at the heart of their union for the fifteen years they lived together. Matlack was stoically accepting of Sarton's love for Juliette.

---

18 Ave. Léquime   Sunday morning [22 June 1947]
Rhôdes St. Genèse

My little marvel, your letter came after all, <u>the</u> letter and with it the gust of tears I have held back so long, and now it is a new beginning. It was at breakfast and when I came down no one said anything, bless them. They are true friends. It is rather terrible that instead of quietly experiencing what happened I have forced you and myself to think ahead to what might happen. But I believe that it will be wise to think that we shall not meet again this time. Heaven knows, your life is complicated enough and then I always am afraid of planning such things. Like the night when we came back from the theatre. It is all flame and air and we cannot hope to hold it. Also I am really afraid of so much emotion. I am no longer capable of much suffering of this kind. Strange—but perhaps that is growing up. When I think how far ahead of me you are in every way, it seems a true miracle that for an instant we were together outside time and you could say "I am with you." Those words are my greatest treasure. Never, never shall I come to the end of it or cease to rejoice and praise God.

The little poem is very beautiful. Whose?

If only now I could be alone and work instead of the fearful gaiety, comradeship, physical life ahead in these next six days. But life is always unexpected in its gifts—and I do not know, perhaps a long time on the moving water will be a good limbo.

For you I dread the ten days with your mother, all the business, and the suffering of not loving. That is bad because it can't go out and create but only go in and blacken. The only comfort is, as usual in your extraordinary life, in the certainty that you will give her much. So many children cannot do that for their parents.

As I write all this, it feels like a farewell (beautiful word!). Everything is good, darling, you know that. It has taken ten years or nearly for this to flower, then ten years from now perhaps there will await us some wonderful strange fruit. More than anything, because I am so frightfully quick, I love and adore slow things. Let us be very slow then, slow and tender and wise. I have so much to learn. Amongst all its other gifts, love humbles. One has to go down so deep, not to die.

I think of you by your lake which I shall see some day and look for your reflection.

It is Julian's birthday. Last night, thinking of you both and our walk on the Ave. Foch that hot night, I wrote a poem. On the reverse you will find it.

If in the end you should come to London before the 25th, it would be of course marvelous. But I have truly renounced all violent hopes. There is only a glimmer which every letter of yours will keep alive. And that is all that matters.

It will be a long time before you get this. Write to here until July 10th. After all Célia [Bertin] is not coming and it will be peaceful here. I leave for England the 9th or 10th and will send my address. Of course if J. came back later and you said come I would come. But meanwhile, all is <u>well.</u>

With all the silences these words interrupt

M-

The Leaves

We walked under heraldic trees
Under the hot bland street-lamp's flare,
Three shadows in the heavy air
That flowed like water though our knees,
On every side the strong dark breathed,
And overhead the serried leaves,
Leaves stiff as feathers, very black
Shifted like tiny screens,
Mounted the stairs of wind:
Leaves became massive towers,
And all was formal balance, poise,
Arches and domes and bowers
And a little rustling noise.
We smelled night in the green
More potent and more fertile
Than all things heard or seen.
We had to press our hands
On the rough trunks to be sure.
I asked "Where is peace, where?"
"In leaves" was all you said.
From then on it was clear
We would be three, not two,
However separate each shadow
One grieves, one lives, one gives,
But I do not care or know
Which is he or I or you.

June 22nd

[ ]

---

your letter came after all, the letter: On 1 December 1947, at Juliette's request, Sarton burned all of Juliette's letters from this period, this one among them.

never shall I come to the end of it: Sarton never did come to the end of her love for Juliette; it was as magical for her at eighty-two as it had been at thirty-two. And yet, as with Judith Matlack, what physical intimacy there had been was an ephemeral and not easy part of the early weeks only; Sarton remembers it in a later letter as having been just one week. She always believed she was a better friend than lover, and in old age recalled a visit when she and Juliette had gone to the zoo, and both suddenly "very physically aware" had rushed home, but the moment had passed—a vignette which stands as a metaphor for the sensual side of their love. But as poet, letter writer, and friend, Sarton kept the passion alive, and no other woman in her life ever again focused the world or called forth the Muse for her as consistently as did Juliette Huxley. One of the final poems May wrote was "Lunch in the Garden" in *Coming into Eighty*, the title, as well, of a novella she began but was not well enough to complete; the characters at the lunch were Juliette, Juliette's lover Alan Best, and May, drawn from one of Sarton's last visits to Lady Huxley's garden on Pond Street. See p. 228 of *Encore*.

next six days: See footnote to letter of 14 June 1947.

of not loving: Juliette had always had a difficult relationship with her mother, which she describes in her autobiography, *Leaves of the Tulip Tree* (John Murray, 1986).

The Leaves: unpublished; first appeared in *Selected Letters 1916–1954*.

HANSWEERT, ZEELAND   Wed. June 25th [1947]

Escape! I have got off by myself for a couple of hours, <u>first</u> to find a bath because I couldn't stand being so dirty and we were here in the port overnight—a tiny village at a lock. A café owner who had been in America finally understood after I had asked the butcher for a "warm bath" and he showed me the end of a sausage hopefully. Anyway the owner of the sad café heated water in a pail and I had a <u>wonderful</u> splash—Heaven! Now I have on clean clothes and am drinking a gin (in another café because that man though so kind wanted to talk and I wanted to write!). The poem I wrote Sunday afternoon in the middle of packing—and in the somewhat overwhelming <u>physical</u> state of realizing that I probably shan't see you again. In my <u>woe</u> in the boat (for it is <u>damned</u> uncomfortable, brutish and nasty—and I <u>hate</u> the captain who boasts constantly in a shouting Flemish—hideous language. He is like a wallowing seal, very fat, very coarse, and utterly lacking in tact.) in this woe, I have invented a game of imagining that perhaps I shall see you but I <u>believe</u> it won't be—so don't let it add a featherweight to all the little and big weights you juggle, <u>dar-ling</u>, my dear wonder.

Holland is such an utter contrast to your lake and mountains. It is such a <u>human</u> country, no grandeur, no cristal or snow or lake—only a rather <u>flat</u> place, and little snug houses and little snug lives. But it is very charming to see so many people in white coifs and the delicious tight bodice and full skirt—and I love the lines of trees, the immense skies.

Only <u>I</u> now know <u>nothing</u> ever seems good to me unless I can have solitude, a few pieces of paper, a room to myself. We get up at 5:00 or 6:00 and begin what I consider a <u>hellish</u> day when we can never stay in one place for more than a few minutes because the sail must be furled or there is a meal to get. Thank goodness the girls feel as I do and we get the giggles when Mamie (inexhaustible cornucopia of maternal energies) keeps saying "Au moins, vous vous reposez, mes enfants!" I sleep curled up in a ball in the airless bow of the boat which <u>thumps</u> the dock every few seconds—and then I think of you because this is so delicious, consoling, infinitely exciting and wonderful a thought that it makes even the boat seem bearable. I am <u>not</u> a water bird.

How are you? I wonder when you get to Neuchâtel. We go to Middleburg and Veere tomorrow—by <u>bus</u>—thanks be to God.

With all my love,

[   ]

Wed. June 25th [1947]: At the top of this letter is typed "Magnet"; see *The Lion and the Rose.*

Hansweert, Zeeland: a stop along their boat trip.

the immense skies: These skies, part of "the country of my birth," haunted Sarton; see "Homage to Flanders" in *The Lion and the Rose.*

the girls: The Limbosch children, Jacqueline, Claire, and Nicole.

Mamie: another of Sarton's names for Céline Limbosch, who, until her death, was a second mother to Sarton.

Au moins, vous vous reposez, mes enfants: At least, my children, you are resting.

LONDON C/O JANE STOCKWOOD   July 5th, 1947
12 ORMONDE MANSIONS
106 SOUTHAMPTON ROW W.C.1 <u>CHANCERY 7036</u>

Darling, these are bad days. I have walked up and down with the wind outside making the whole air and earth restless, trying to reach you with my heart, trying to stop the waves of now real anguish, since your two letters about Kot, about yourself, the little poem which I cannot reread without a sort of rage. It's the rage of absence and I am so tired of trying to explain in words and have written pages which now seem utterly sterile and useless. Ah, if you were here and we could walk in the forest (which is my equivalent of your lake) and not say anything for a long time. A letter precipitates one into words before one is quite ready. Only the poems have a silence round them but I can't write anymore. I must see you first. And where are you? Perhaps packing, getting ready to leave your mother, to be suspended again between your lives, with so many things to be done—and Kot's pain close around your heart like an iron band. It is all stifling.

You say such fearful things: "I could not receive another person's gifts." It is a sin to say that when it is you who have given so much, in spite of the state you are in. It is you who have performed miracles in these last weeks. And if inside yourself you are something quite different, then all the more wonderful that you have been able to create a person within yourself who is not yourself, but who has all these riches of tenderness, understanding, depth, delicacy, this pure soul. Darling, how can you lie to yourself any longer? You surround Julian with a cloud of attentions, a sort of radiance. If you have taken his guilt upon yourself to do it, is not that a triumph? Why resist your triumph now? Why not rejoice in it? Because I think—it is the only possible answer—you resent your gift and so you have not really made it. It is not the transference of guilt which is killing you, but that fact that you have not got through to love, you have not really accepted. And how can a person made for love, not resent not having love? Of course you resent it and it's the living part of you that fights and fights in a vacuum. That's what I sensed. That's what drove me to all of this. Do you think I love you out of some illusion I have invented? Or because you are beautiful (though you are)? No, I love you for no reason perhaps at all. Why have reasons? Why imply that I have created this love out of what I think you are? Why not accept that I love you just because of all that you hate in yourself? That would be much nearer the truth. If you now deny this love, this riches which has come out of poverty, then you will make us both poor. O darling, don't do it. Accept me with all I am, if you can, for I am no saint, God knows. I am all torn up with egotisms and desires and selfishness and wanting you for myself. How often do you think I arrive at the serenity of that poem and after what struggles? It seems to me that you are the one who does not see me. We are both poor struggling human beings who by some miracle have much to give each other. That is why I say it is good. And it is good. Even these last two days, even being very much torn as I am now, I know that it is good. And even it seems very big, very deep now—a sort of greatness is implied. There has never been anything quite like it for me. I feel all the time on the brink—

Of course I who see you with love see the real you, and you who see yourself without love, don't see the real you. What in the world can be seen without love? Darling, you are quite mad if you won't admit this. And I am mad to try to persuade you out of it. No, there is nothing to say. Only let me come on the 17th. Do not say no. I know it is asking a great deal, but I do ask it, because I must.

I have said nothing of Kot. I feel dépourvue. I hope to see him in England. But you must not blame yourself for not having gone. You could not have helped. This depression has been growing in him for a long time. No one can do anything, I'm convinced, and that is what is so awful. So heartbreaking. I can't even say I feel empty—and in all this I love you terribly, more than ever—

[   ]

I had a sweet letter from Francis. Is Julian all right? The paper said he was hurt in an auto accident.

———

Kot: After some months of severe depression, on 7 June, Kot tried to commit suicide by cutting his throat; his wounds healed but he was confined to Holloway Sanitorium, Virginia Water, for treatment. His faithful friend Marjorie Wells, daughter-in-law of H. G. Wells, who watched over him during his final years, wrote Sarton telling her that he had asked to have her letters read over to him several times.

can't write anymore: Three days after this letter, on 8 July, Sarton wrote "O Saisons! O Châteaux," one of the most important poems she ever wrote for Juliette; see The Lion and the Rose.

this riches which has come out of poverty: Although not written at precisely this time, "Where Dream Begins" in In Time Like Air, written several years later, pins down, particularly in its lines "Go rich in poverty/Go rich in poetry./This nothingness/Is plenitude," the richness of the poetry Juliette inspired, and the enduring friendship which nevertheless prevailed between them.

dépourvue: bereft.

an auto accident: While in South America on a trip for UNESCO, Julian was taken to see the sights at Petrópolis outside of Rio; the car crashed into a truck; Julian fractured his collarbone and bruised a rib.

TUESDAY, AND AFTER TOMORROW   [8 July 1947]
C/O JANE STOCKWOOD, 12 ORMONDE MANSIONS
106 SOUTHAMPTON ROW, W.C. 1

O darling, what a relief that there was a letter this morning (yours of July
5th with the news of Julian which I had already seen in the paper). You had
the same wind and the same strange anxiety I have been having for three
days. Yesterday I mailed a letter to Paris not marked personal but with Mrs.
very clearly marked. Chase it down if you never got it. It was a poor
attempt to answer your very wonderful letter about yourself. I shall not
really live again until I see you and thank God you say to come. I was afraid
so afraid you would say not (and I would have understood and I would
have managed somehow but it is good that I can come). Of course I will.
I shall have time to see Kot as well as I only sail the 25th. I shall go at once
to get my visa when I arrive in London, and to make a reservation for the
17th, and stay at least through Saturday morning. What comfort to be able
to do this, to see you again. It is wonderful beyond words.

     Yes, I know that we have entered a new season. But I do not see you
differently only it goes deeper and I have been suffering from the poverty of receiving more than I can give. Something is huge and dark now,
and imminent. I don't know—Kot, all this, and your letter which broke
down all my defences, way beyond tears. But if in this new reality I see
you differently, no that is not true. I do not see you differently. Only I
love you more, if that is possible. It has taken on a new dimension and I
am a little frightened because I am so afraid I shall fail you, become suddenly too selfish, or suddenly demand your love. It is very hard not to.
Sometimes a pain goes down from my heart right to the womb. Yesterday,
in the trolley. What is trying to be born? I do not feel quite great enough
for whatever it may be. And so I am a little frightened and I need the
reality of <u>you</u>, with all your lightness and ability to break the tensions and
not to <u>appuyer dessus</u>. My sin I know is always to want to break through
and it is not good. But you know, when we meet all this will make an
equilibrium. We shall find each other. That is all that is needed—an end
to the strain of so many words around a great deep Silence. Love.

The poem to France has to be entirely redone. I really sent it just to send you what I was doing. I wanted a great souffle, a long line like wind in a sail, but it hasn't arrived yet. Perhaps I will be able to work on it later.

Yesterday I saw Jean-Do for the last time. But you know in spite of all the anguish, she is always healing. We have arrived at communion and that means that even time, even distance, even perhaps death, no longer is cruel. I felt it very much when I left her yesterday. First I cried like a lost child in the street and then suddenly I was at peace. Only I have felt in these last days so fearfully anxious and strange that I feared that I did not have much to give her. But she made all all right as she always does. What has been awful with you is that we have not had time to arrive wherever we are bound. So distance has been cruel, time has been cruel. Death I do not dare even to think of where you are concerned. We have so far to go— and where? And how?

It was strange to have the news of Marie and I shall be so anxious to hear all Julian has to say about her and Mariette. She never writes but loved Julian that summer and I think helped me to love him better.

I think about Kot of course a great deal. What frightens me is that I do not see the future. I feel this depression has been growing for a long time as he cut one branch of life off after another, as his friends died around him. In a terrible way he has cut himself off—without work, without responsibilities, without the things that make one go on somehow, quand même. Kot, pure and naked, is really a soul prepared for death. This is his marvelous quality and also perhaps his weakness. There is something piti-less and ruthless behind all this. I feel it and can't say it. And I dread seeing him.

Francis wrote a very happy cheerful letter to me because I had asked him to tell me where he got the pin so I can when I'm rich get you some earrings. Such a gay happy letter and looking forward to the isolation of the mountains and the island and the birds. You will have heard too of course.

I shall be anxious to hear how Julian really is. I hope he won't mind my coming but perhaps he will enjoy telling me about Marie and all. I wonder if he saw Eugenia in Chile? And I shall look forward immensely to seeing him. All this is so strange, darling. But I think I can be happy with you both—as long as you and I have some time together and that we shall have during the day. I dread the nights without you. But I must learn all there is to learn before I go. I must try to contain it all, you and myself and Julian and Judy.

God be praised—

Ah love—

[   ]

I'll be in London at 5:00 tomorrow evening. I wonder if you will be in Paris by then? I am <u>hoping</u> the apartment will work.

The Two Forests

Forêt de Soignes and Landscape by Gerard David

This forest is a pattern so complete
It echoes on and on, musical phrase
The slender perpendiculars repeat.
Against the broken brilliance of the light,
Leaf upon leaf, precise and eloquent
Sings like stained glass in towering shade.
Chord upon chord, this marvelous forest
Makes a final statement upon form and space,
On light and shadow—and it does exist.
Here as a child I came and still do come
When all reality has become a dream.
Here I brought my love as lovers bring
Their hopes to the cathedrals in the spring.

The painting is a forest so complete
It is the secret testament of leaves;
Each has become a presence, each a soul,
We stood there once together and they spoke.
We heard the timeless leaves that feel no wind
And in a great throng, we were all alone,
Seized by a dream so real it could unbind,
Set free and change all memories we have,
Outside the real lives that we still must live,
Outside of time, it holds for us both
As do the painted leaves, its passionate truth.
Here I have thought, love that can have no rest
Still might find peace in an imagined forest.

[   ]

not to appuyer dessus: not to emphasize them.

souffle: sustained gust.

news of Marie: Marie Stiasni ran the Schwarzwald pension at Grundlsee (see footnote to letter of 1 August 1937) and was director of Dr. Schwartzwald's school in Vienna;
 "Mountain Interval" in *Encounter in April* is dedicated to her.

Mariette: Mariette Lydis, friend of Stiasni, an Austrian artist who later emigrated to
 Argentina, as did Marie.

quand même: nevertheless.

Eugenia in Chile: Eugenia Huneeus, Jungian analyst who studied with Jung and worked at
 the Jung Foundation; originally from Argentina, she often returned there. In May
 1947 Julian made a flying trip to South America for a UNESCO conference; Sarton
 gave him her name, thinking they would like one another. In later years she settled
 in England.

apartment will work: The Huxleys had found an apartment on the Avenue Foch.

The Two Forests: unpublished.

MON. 11:30 P.M.   [probably 21 July 1947]
106 SOUTHAMPTON ROW

Dear love, my deep peace, I write that and am silent. I feel as if you were
still very near and that perhaps I do not have to find words yet—still
enguirlandée as I am by your hands, by your words, by the things you give
knowing and all the thousand others you give without knowing, my secret
treasures like the sunlight on your hair. I feel these three days crowding up
like the land as the plane tilts for a landing and all I want is time to think
of you, time to write the poems. Instead I must get up early, wash all my
clothes, start telephoning about Kot (Marjorie was out tonight) and so on.
Shall I have time to make the little book before I go so you have clean
copies of the poems? I hope so. If not I'll do it on the boat.

 I do not think at all about the future. It seems interminable without
you. But I think about every instant of these last days. I learned the day I
cried what it would be to lose you. I know it now so well that it must
never happen. We will not let it. Now all is radiance and peace and my
heart is full. Please be happy, rejoice in it all and even in our separate lives,
so different, and each so rich and giving. Perhaps it sounds arrogant to say
that, but I believe it. When we meet is Heaven and I suppose one can't ask
for that very often in this life—or continuously. Meanwhile the soles of my
feet miss you very much. There is a lonely place where once you laid your
head on my shoulder on the red sofa. I do not think we need to worry

about anything. I think somehow that it is all <u>with</u> life, not against it. And now what we have must be given, what we are must be used. You have made me so rich, I have much more to give than ever before. This is what I know tonight. I wear you in the living of my heart and on my breast. You are with me. You go where I go. You can't help it, darling. It's done! Glory be to God!

Tues. morn.

Marjorie has not yet been allowed to see Kot but is going this afternoon—and will call me tomorrow morning to see if I can see him on Thurs. (it looks doubtful). O dear, it is sad. He had narcotics for two weeks and then a week <u>out</u> but they say he is still "too bewildered." Marjorie was interested to know what nursing home J. was in and also <u>what</u> narcotic treatment was used. I said I would ask you. Kot does get his mail. I do hope M. can see him today.

Darling, darling, darling, darling—wasn't it good of it to be a <u>new</u> moon the other night? Shall we have a full one someday?

Your
[   ]

----

still very near: Sarton is just back from four days at the Huxleys' Paris apartment at 17 bis Ave. Foch.

enguirlandée: garlanded.

Enclosed: "Perspective" (see letter of 14 June 1947 and The Lion and the Rose); "Song" (see Appendix).

[LONDON (JS)]   July 23rd, 1947, Wednesday

How are you, my treasure? My heart is very full. I have been to Acacia Road and sat at the table upstairs to have a long quiet talk with Marjorie. I think I shall not see Kot. He is still so very weak. Yesterday M. saw him for the first time and I will try to remember everything. When he saw her he began to cry and then he said, "I thought you had come to take me home!" Then he asked, "What happened? Why am I here?" and at first she put him off and then I'm sure rightly told him that he had tried to commit suicide. And he cried and said, "Why did I do it?" They brought him tea with an egg while she was there but he didn't eat anything and she will take him the cheese (which I forgot but am mailing) and some of his black bread and butter today when she goes. He asked if the house was still there and was very much relieved to hear that it was—and that this is not a permanent removal. It is so awful to think of these nightmares of uncertainty and darkness. Thank God M. has finally got through the Doctors. They sound rather awful, jocular (!) but she feels it is a good place and while she was there various attendants and nurses came and went and Kot said several times, "That's a good girl," or "That man is all right," so at least he doesn't hate them. They have been giving him shock treatments (first they did then they stopped—the first narcotic treatment at home was not deep enough, now they have given him a very deep one <u>and</u> shock). It is wonderful that M. managed to get him in as a voluntary patient: Rau wanted to have him certified. Rau has been rather brutal I think. There is still the danger that they will certify him if he doesn't get well. You are technically considered mad if you attempt suicide.

While she was there Kot said he had had a lot of letters but couldn't read them, so M. brought them out and laid yours and mine and Beatrice Glenavy's each in a pile and read them to him and he cried a great deal. I believe it is good that he cry. He didn't at all in the first week after he tried to commit suicide. He just begged to be allowed to die and begged M. to give him something. Now he hasn't mentioned dying (that is a good sign) and wants to come home. I fear it will be some weeks—and then what? I am with M. in her conviction that he must be allowed to try to live his own life at Acacia Road. Anything else risks further depression. They could have him at the Wells. Violet Schiff has been wonderful apparently. There is plenty of money—some anonymous person gave £200. There is enough for a year.

The Dr. asked M., "Who is Marjorie?" and then "Who is Juliette?" and when she told him who you were, he was <u>very</u> impressed, so perhaps he will begin to understand that Kot <u>is</u> someone. I <u>hate</u> doctors!

I am writing everything as I remember it so it is rather jerky. All I can think of is from the Bible. "Goodness and mercy shall follow me all the days of my life." If only one could lay some balm on his heart, his pure heart of a child. Marjorie kept saying, "He is so simple really and perhaps because he is he can be helped." Kindness moves him so. How we all need love!

I liked Marjorie <u>very</u> much, but what a terrible strain all this is for her, the responsibility, the decisions, the continual attention, time, love, patience. It is very wonderful that there is such a person. She said it was awful that I couldn't stay and I had such a pang, darling, but it would mean staying six months if at all, and I don't see how. I haven't the <u>right</u>, or my love for Kot isn't the very center of my life, enough to make it possible to break that center to do it. I hope I am not failing—and I will try to come back in the spring. But of course the crucial time will be when he first comes home. It is awful.

I hate these days—no time. Yesterday when I came home from Ruth Pitter's at eleven I had a bath and set to work to finish a poem that had been growing in my head, and I counted on this whole empty morning which has now gone. I worked till two A.M. then left it and now at eight before rushing off to Acacia Road I finished it off (ruined I fear) and put it in the book which also went Air Mail at 9:30 so I hope it will reach you before I sail.

None of this seems real yet. I do not know that I have parted from you. It is just as well I guess, but I fear the knowledge when it comes. Only now you are with me every moment—the leaves, the pavements, all my friends say your name whatever else they think they are saying. Ruth read a beautiful poem and I had a good time there. Now I go to lunch at Elisabeth's, to have my small pox inoculation, to a Noel Coward new play with Jane tonight. Yesterday I bought lovely books—Sidney Keyes poems—so beautiful. I can't bear it that he was killed <u>at twenty</u>. It makes one feel terribly responsible to have escaped. Darling, you have spoiled me terribly with such a mountainous check. I got Sachy Sitwell's book on English architecture, a novel by Hartley (I loved <u>The Shrimp and the Anemone</u>—did you read it?)

I hope the party is all settled. I hope Julian is steadily better, but I fear these days with their nettles of impatience to be suffered, inevitably, and all the little strains. Still you shine—dear love, dear love—

[   ]

Acacia Road: home of Kotelianksy.
Rau: Dr. Leo Rau, the Huxleys' physician as well as Kot's.
Beatrice Glenavy's: Lady Beatrice (Elvery) Glenavy, wife of Gordon Campbell, Lord

Glenavy, governor of the Bank of Ireland; mother of the humorous writer Patrick Campbell and of the novelist Michael Campbell. Irish friend of Koteliansky; she befriended but later turned upon Sarton.

Violet Schiff: Violet Schiff [pen-name Stephen Hudson] wife of English novelist Sidney Schiff (1869–1944), and sister of English novelist Ada Leverson. The Schiffs were friends of Mansfield, Wilde, and Proust, whose work Sidney Schiff translated.

"Goodness and mercy . . .": from Psalm 23:6.

home from Ruth Pitter's: Pitter lived in Chelsea.

before I sail: Sarton sailed on the *Queen Elizabeth,* leaving Friday, 25 July.

a Noel Coward new play: Both *Present Laughter* and *This Happy Breed* by Noël Coward were produced in 1947.

Sidney Keyes poems: the Routledge 1946 edition of *The Collected Poems* by Sidney Keyes (1922–1943), English poet killed in Tunisia in World War II.

Sachy Sitwell's book: Sacheverell Sitwell (1895–1987?), English poet and writer on art and travel, brother of Edith and Osbert. The book may be *British Architects and Craftsmen* (1945), which went through six editions.

novel by Hartley: L[eslie] P[oles] Hartley (1895–1972), English novelist whose *Sixth Heaven,* the second novel in his Eustace and Hilda trilogy, was published in 1946; the first in the series, *The Shrimp and the Anemone,* was published in 1944.

THURSDAY AFTERNOON   [probably 24 July 1947]

I had gone out with a great cavern of emptiness inside me to have my hair done, and then came back to find your letter. How it reverberates and seizes me, each word of yours, so that almost when I have read it once too fast, too violently, I can't read it again. But I have read it again now after sleeping for an hour. I can't sleep at night. They are so long and like deserts, these nights. I shall be better after the sea-change. The sea numbs, helas, above all <u>separates</u> one thing from another.

Now I feel I must tell you everything quickly before I go, and at the same time I feel silent, silent as a rock. I'm glad you say you felt sick. It is the one comforting line in the beautiful cold blaze of your letter—wonderful letter, darling, but all for me and not for you. Everything was meant for you. O tell me there is somewhere in you the seed of simple happiness?

But do not be sad that you did not love me. I think there was a deep wisdom in it and perhaps an instinct which was defending you. If you had loved me, really, everything would be so much worse than it is. And things that grow slowly into whatever shape they must have are best. There was no physical magic this time, even for me—you know that. Partly because of my curse. Partly I know because something did crack in the flood of my feeling

for you after the first night and morning. I had come so very open and frightened and loving—then it seemed all cut off, so absolutely cut off, and then
my heart cracked and I couldn't get back any more quite to where I was.
There is no regret in this and you must have none. It is one of the facts we
have to deal with, that's all. And perhaps it saved us and gave us something
else, more durable and better. When I kissed you I was full of tears always. It
was very strange. It is all very strange. We shall understand better later.

But it would have been awful if I could not have touched you at all
or come close to you and the physical expression is fearfully important to
me. I don't mean that it isn't. Only that the angel didn't come down. There
was nothing greater than we to lift us and lift the weight of hearts. But all
the time love was there, so beautiful. There is so much love in you towards
me. You mustn't say there isn't. I feel it all the time. And that is all that matters in this world.

I find it so hard to write. And for so long there will be nothing but
words to tell you—I simply can't go on. I may be able to write from the
boat again. After that you won't hear for 10 days or so. I think nothing so
wonderful has ever happened to one as this. God bless you, darling, for it all

[   ]

and for your letter—<u>marvelous</u> words like flowers—they all sing in me—
I do not deserve such words.

Yes, the dress—but how <u>beautiful</u> you looked—forever and ever—

———

nothing greater than we to lift us and lift the weight of hearts: This paragraph touches upon the
essence of Sarton's sense of intimacy and passion and upon what she means by physical expression being "fearfully important" to her. What ultimately propelled Sarton
into and throughout the greater parts of her more extreme and tumultuous relationships was, with all its intensities and furies, the search for poetry, and not wild,
promiscuous sexuality. She said it to Louise Bogan in 1954 when she wrote: "When
I say I love you, I am saying that I love poetry."

———

MIDNIGHT THURSDAY   [later, the same day of 24 July 1947]

My darling, I've just called—your voice was so lovely, so cool like a
snowflake. If only I could be one and not this lump of tears. (I don't

expect you can read a word of this, I am crying so much I can't see what I'm doing and am afraid I'll wake Annie and Jane if I type.) I'm so <u>glad</u> Julian is better and the conference begins well. Sometimes I forget what a large and complicated world you make the living <u>feeling</u> centre of—and it is very exciting to think of it. I <u>love</u> your life, never forget that. It means a great deal to me and many other people, just as it is—you and Julian. At this moment it seems very wonderful to me—and so it must be, for at such a moment it is hard to think so and to rejoice. But your voice was the voice of someone who knows what she is doing, and is doing it superlatively well. I leave with great faith in your powers, a great rejoicing in them—and not least perhaps in your relation to me. For—without love, as you say—you have accomplished a miracle of love. All is <u>fruitful</u>, all <u>flows</u>, all <u>enriches</u> that comes from you to me. I hope you are a little proud of yourself. I know it has not always been easy. It is very difficult to be loved, much more difficult than to love well. And it seems to me you have done it with infinite imagination, tenderness and what I can only call <u>savoir faire</u>. That is a cold and worldly word, but I mean something of the <u>spirit</u>, the knowledge of the soul, very delicate, subtle and powerful which goes into every relationship you build. Be happy in this. It is, I think, a real triumph.

I hope you will not be upset by my letter of this morning. I feel the only thing one <u>must</u> do is to tell the truth whatever it is. Other people may have time to let the truth tell itself. We have had so little time and I at least have had to live so fearfully fast and deep within it, that it will take a long time to really understand just what has happened. Little by little you will know it through letters and poems. But as time goes on <u>of course</u> our letters will be less personal. It's only <u>now</u> that I feel I must try to explain everything, to be sure you understand. And I want to know <u>all</u> you are thinking. But that is life outside time and I want to know all about the days.

I had a wonderful time with Elisabeth [Elizabeth Bowen] on Wed. She is so warm and real. I wonder why people imagine she is <u>cold</u>? I always feel the warmth, the real wisdom, the real love of people, an infinite tenderness for people, not without <u>wit</u>, but it is always tempered by tenderness. There were wonderful flowers in the room and we drank red wine and talked about Virginia Woolf. E. may be coming over in Feb. and if so will come to Cambridge and stay with Judy and me. How exciting!

Today I was so tired I did nothing but pack, write letters (I owe so many), have my hair washed and take Annie and Jane out to a nice drunken dinner at Le Gourmet. They have been <u>so</u> good to me! Then call you, O my darling.

Now to sleep. It would be wonderful to sleep. I haven't been able to and such <u>fruitless</u> nights, these last two. I think of you very much. I do not feel sad at all, only terribly keyed and <u>wrung</u>. It will all fall into place eventually. Time is a great thing—and I think of it in the branches of the pine trees at Chantilly.

I hope these months are rich and gay and full of <u>you</u> (that is the best thing I can imagine!) Be happy, my darling—I am.

[   ]

Thurs. morning

Your <u>first</u> letter only arrived today and I've just called Alice—had a good talk with her, and will call Ann in a moment. Then must rush to finish packing.

How <u>peculiar</u> to find a part of your letter copied out! but I had to think about it so much, that part, and copied it out to have it beside me when I was working on a poem I think.

<u>Does</u> Julian guess or mind? I wonder. <u>Poor</u> Ann has chicken pox—is at her mother's.

Annie and Jane: Annie Duveen Caldwell and Jane Stockwood, with whom Sarton was staying in London. Jane Stockwood worked on the staff of *Harper's Bazaar* and wrote reviews for *Queen's* magazine.

conference begins well: UNESCO was having its Council Meeting at the Hotel Majestic in Paris.

All is <u>fruitful</u>, all <u>flows</u>, all <u>enriches</u>: an intentional counterpoint to the French proverb both Juliette and Sarton often quoted: *Tout casse, tout passe, tout lasse, hélas,* "Everything crumbles, everything passes, everything fades, alas."

savoir faire: tact.

stay with Judy and me: Bowen did stay at Wright Street for a week in 1953 and again in 1955 when she lectured in the United States.

pine trees at Chantilly: area northeast of Paris, home of famous racecourse, with a beautiful forest south of it which Sarton loved.

Alice: the Huxley's faithful Scottish maid, Alice Pirie.
Ann: probably Anne Huxley, Anthony's wife.
<u>*Does*</u> *Julian guess or mind:* Julian Huxley did not ever learn about Juliette and Sarton.

[139 OXFORD STREET]   Sunday morning, Aug. 3rd [1947]

Sunday morning—Judy is at Quaker Meeting and the house is still, full of flowers and silence and your marvelous long letter which came yesterday. This is a great boon, but I am a wreck. Apparently the smallpox inoculation can make one quite sick and I am a mass of fevers and chills and pains, all panache gone, a broken reed. Everything seems a mess I shall never clear up, I mean all the papers and stuff, unanswered letters, unfinished stories, old mss. lying around and even <u>your</u> poems not typed out properly as they will stand. Today is Mother's birthday and I am too sick to go over. I did stagger out for tea yesterday to take presents, but apparently it was not a good idea. All this will be well past by the time you get this. It is nothing, only I had counted on plunging with no time to think into this life, and I resent being weakened and so exposed to my own doubts and fears. Yesterday I did nothing but cry. Judy is an angel beyond words. Last night I told her about you and she said that she knew and that she knew also that it was necessary for me and that I needed you, and this morning all was the same. I had so feared that she would have a depression. She used to have awful ones, closed in a box which no one could open, but she has not had one since we have lived together. Of course I have now got rid of my burden and laid it upon her and only time can tell what this will do, but I have a deep inside feeling that all is well and will be. This is entirely because she is, where people she loves are concerned, of an almost infinite generosity and imagination. I do not deserve so much. Now if I can feel well again and get to work, I shall be all right.

I wish I dreamed of you—I haven't yet. It would be lovely—and I am furious because I can't find the photo of you and Kot. I wanted to have it framed last year and must have mislaid it somewhere. Also, darling, your letter sounds as if there had been a letter to the boat as well as the telegram. It never came and I can't bear it. Will it turn up somewhere? I hope you put your address on the back?

Perhaps you will be in Vouvray soon. I do hope you have a day or so in that peaceful elegant house. It's a well of peace and so is Grace. It is marvelous that you are getting off. Altogether your letter sounded happy, rich in life. How I feasted on the description of the Lully pavilion, of the party. I would love to have Le Diable au Corps when you get back. I have never read it. It is very wonderful to have the two lives I have now, yours and mine. And if it can also make everything have a double meaning for you, that is very good. Only I have this awful fear now that you won't get letters as you are away. I hate not to know where you are sleeping, what you see when you wake up. It disturbs the image, makes me feel as if I had no roots. But this is nonsense.

What does "caniculous" mean? I looked for it in my dictionary but couldn't find it! You used it about the heat. The heat was a real death when I arrived, but now it is blessedly cool. Cambridge is a leafy bower, Mother's garden and little wood so dear. I hate not seeing her on her birthday. The real reason is that some awful loud French people are expected some time today and I simply couldn't face them.

I found the exact meaning of "plangent" and it is just what I wanted: "(of sound) thrilling, vibrating, moaning, insistent."

Yes, wasn't it fine to have found the unicorn? Daddy sent it to me in an issue of Life, the dear man. I rejoice in my parents, but the awful thing is that even when one loves one's parents, the tensions are very great. I worry so much about Mother. And dreamed of cooking for her and now this beastly bug has got me (it is grippe added to the inoculation so the doctor says). Please forgive a dull letter, darling. I wonder if it will reach you and I'll copy some of Sidney Keyes' poem "The wilderness" for you. Then I will get drinks ready and peel the potatoes for Judy's return.

All is well, really, except my bones!

I'll copy the poem in my next. Too tired.

[   ]

Judy: Judith Matlack; see footnotes to letters of 15 April 1945 and 15 June 1947.

letter . . . as well as the telegram: among what Sarton burned on 1 December 1947.

that peaceful elegant house: Le Petit Bois, home of Grace Eliot Dudley in the Vallée Coquette, deep in the Touraine, three miles from Vouvray, France.

would love to have Le Diable au Corps: considered one of the most delicate love stories ever written, the first novel by Raymond Radiguet (1903–1923), worked on between his sixteenth and eighteenth years; his death at the age of twenty from typhoid fever is described in Djuna Barnes's story "The Little Girl Continues," also known as "The Grande Malade," in which Radiguet appears as "Monsieur X." Radiguet was a pro-tégé of Jean Cocteau (1891–1963), French poet, playwright, and novelist; both were associated with the surrealist movement. This volume inscribed by Juliette was in Sarton's library at the time of her death.

"caniculous": probably "canicular," meaning of or related to the dog days, a very hot and sultry midsummer period. The theory was that the Dog Star, rising with the sun, added to its heat, and the dog days (about 3 July to 11 August) bore the combined heat of both.

plangent . . . just what I wanted: See "Magnet" in *The Lion and the Rose.*

[139 OXFORD STREET]   Aug. 6th, 1947

Dear heart, I've written you two rather dreary letters but it is because I have turned into the Bong with a Luminous Nose and have been really very miserable with a huge boil on my nose, awful fevers and chills and swollen glands and general debility. Today I begin to rise up. I have made my bed and swept the floor and my room begins to look human again, and I rush to the typewriter to tell you that all these days (only five, but it feels like a year) I have been lying with such vivid images of you under my eye-lids, secret magical treasures: you in the car in your blue suit (cad or not, it is very becoming!) when we were on our way to the Flemish exhibition, for some reason one of those moments which becomes photographed for-ever on the retina—and then lying looking up at the pine branches and their pattern against the sky at Chantilly—and your voice saying "Oh my dear," when I called from London. The echo of your voice which I only really heard long after, for at the time I suppose I wanted more than a voice could give, and later your voice seemed to have given more than I could take. I go on hearing it. It makes me think of the strange immense gulf between love and passion, the gulf and at the same time the fact that it is only a <u>nuance</u>, a shade, a shutter that opens or closes in an instant no one knows why. Love really does open the world, I think; increase all one's sen-sibilities, generosities, flows out in all sorts of ways to all sorts of people beyond its special object. Passion is so exclusive and violent. It closes out the world. So all things considered I have come to believe that for us the absence of passion is a saving grace—perhaps <u>the</u> saving grace. Especially as in a state of such delicate equilibrium it may happen at any time. That makes the excitement, the extra-mundane light, the X which may at any second solve the equation or prove it insoluble. Without the possibility of passion, love would lose its mystery in part. Or wouldn't it? Anyway I feel all the joy come back now that I am a little better and not the prisoner of my body. How wonderful it all is, darling, wonderful beyond words.

I had a dear letter from Julian which I have just answered. I do hope you get to Grace Dudley's. My only fear is that she will fail to answer your letter in time as she is very absent-minded. I know she wanted you to come very much. I transport myself into that cool spacious house. You will feel I know what a work of art, and of <u>heart</u>, it is. It will be lovely for her to have you share it

I have ideas for six stories if now I can only summon the will and imagination to write them. The one I began on the boat may not work, but I shall have another try at it, maybe tomorrow. The theme has haunted me for a long time, but I fear it should be a short novel, not a short story.

I have hundreds of other things to tell you, but I have to lie down now. The main thing is to send you this return of <u>la joie</u>—the cool and blessed light of my days, you.

Have you had a rest on these days?

[ ]

Your letters are full of riches. I explore them slowly. More soon.

––––––––

Bong with a Luminous Nose: She means "The Dong with a Luminous Nose" from Edward Lear's *Nonsense Songs* (1871).
Flemish exhibition: On 11 June 1947, May and Juliette had gone together to an exhibition of Flemish paintings including Pateners, Davids, and Memlings.
absence of passion is a saving grace: an underlining tenet in both her life and work; see pp. 87–90 in *Among the Usual Days.*
la joie: joy.

––––––––

139 OXFORD ST.   Aug. 12th, 1947

It is so hot that even the crickets are silent and Judy has gone out in the dark to lie in the garden and try to see the meteors (she will call me if they start falling—what an exciting thought, but she says they are supposed to fall and I do not believe her). I lay down and tried to sleep but then I began

to think of all the things I would forget to tell you tomorrow. This morning came your letter with its ambiguous repetition of the word "candid"
and other things which made me stop and think. But O how glad I was to
hear at last and that you are having a rest and that Julian is so quiet and
dear. Only I am worried about the pains, and if it happens again you must
go and have X-rays at once. But it was worth it perhaps if it made visible
all the tenderness and love which is there of course in him for you. I am
very happy about this, darling. It is awful that daily life and bad little habits
of no real importance like J's impatience can at times obscure the great
reality of your long life together. What a pompous sentence, but now and
again I feel a little stiff and under the stiffness you will read the truth with
your "candor." Darling, I do understand about the uncandidness and am
not meaning to tease. We always said we would understand more as time
went on. One of the things I am understanding is how difficult it is to
write when one is never alone (I expect you are not very much these days
and I am not unless I am working until Judy goes to college in Sept.) and
now what seems to me the real miracle is that you were able to be all that
you were those last nights—not what was lacking, not failure—heavens,
no, but the great extraordinary success of it under the circumstances. For
never with Julian in the house would you feel free, if you ever would again
with him away. Why did I not see this at the time is quite beyond me. Such
blind spots one has when in the midst of things. Only at least now I do
understand and am grateful. That is all.

It is lovely to think that you two are perhaps at Grace's now, sleeping in that cool quiet room where I have slept so often alone and where
I wrote many poems long long ago. I love to think of you three in that
beloved house. I hope you will feel Grace's special charm. It is not a charm
I would find it easy to define, not dependent now on beauty (she was very
lovely) or even on great intelligence, but something far less tangible and
more subtle. In this world where everyone "is" something or "does" something I suppose it is rather peaceful and wonderful to discover a woman
who simply lives in depth. But really what a poison the Whitaker is, a little mad I expect. The truth is of course that she after William married kept
writing suicidal letters and said she had gone into the lake up to her ears
and would drown herself next time etc. and he with his sickly New
England conscience couldn't stand it and asked her to come back and live

in the house with G. and him—and then Grace left. After that for years he punished Whitaker, treated her like a servant, gave her no money (Grace used to give her money and then it was so awful) and never came over to Le Petit Bois until I was there that summer and talked to him like a Dutch uncle. But by then it was too late. Strange violent tender man, he looked like the head on a Roman coin, was rather like a faun or a wild mythical man. Together he and Grace were the eagle and the dove, too much so. I think he was a friend of Jo Davidson and I expect you had the story from him. I have always heard about Jo from Ella Winter, Lincoln Steffen's wife, whom Jo D. calls Pete. He must be marvelous, but I think you are right about him as an artist. Perhaps Flaubert is right that one can't have too much life and still have the essence left for art, so Brancusi thought, didn't he?

I have before me a Greek Aphrodite I found in the British Museum. It is a most tragic face, too human, Greek at the point of decadence, just on the brink, too lovely perhaps and not stern enough. Are there two Aphrodites? What about them? I do not, like Aldous, travel with the encyclopedia so you will have to tell me. Unless I remember when I am at Channing Place, full of such lore. But it was your hair on the Chantilly picnic that made me think of Aphrodite and of the myrtle, the golden branch on the black pot in the British Musem. Forgive the image—you are not a black pot! This made me laugh. Do please go and see it when you are in London.

Today I also had two letters from Marjorie [Wells]. By now you will know the news, that Kot really seems to be getting over the depression and might go home next week. Isn't it wonderful? I was quite light-headed all day with your letter and that news. I worked very hard all morning on a story about Mr. Socrates and an English girl called Joyce Fraser who is very frightened of herself and discovers something or other by means of a hat. I am afraid to tell you because I haven't finished the story myself!

Then I went to lunch with Ed Spiegel at the Civil Liberties to talk about plans and what to do now that the saint who was the secretary is dead. I have to write a poem, that is one thing. Spiegel foresees a great fight here—and in the flood of the reaction Civil Liberties will have a lot to do. I am glad to be in it. One can at least be sure one believes in that, though we shall be doing nothing but defending communists for the next few years as the Red Hunt goes on. Betty Sanger died from overwork fighting a bill on un-American activities which we and other organizations succeeded in getting squashed before it came up. There are a few good people in this country, darling, please remember. She was one. She was always ill, practically blind (everything had to be read to her) and never stopped fighting and never stopped being gentle and kind and awfully endearing all the time she was fighting. I think of her with great tenderness. She did not fail. When people like that die one feels one's responsibilities enlarge. When Roosevelt died the feeling of individual new responsibility was tremendous. I got it in letters from practically every young man I know.

After that I had a drink with Bill, my sort of brother, who drove down from the country to show me a painting. He is growing very fast. Oh what a treasure, so sensitive he knows what you are feeling almost before you do yourself. I hope you will meet him sometime. He is sure to land in Paris sooner or later. And I think he will be a good painter.

Then I came home and read Henry Adams' letters and laughed because he defined himself as "a seeker of the Lord, praying for light; a worm crawling towards the asphalt in a spring rain; a pilgrim, very seasick, looking for the harbor of Paris."

It is so hot darling, and you must be getting very tired of this letter— I hope you are not. I hope it seems rather exciting to be back in the doux et grand apartment. I am happy because I shall know where to think of you and my heart drops a yard when I remember that after September I shan't know.

I can't help feeling rather nervous that J. will see the poems, but I am glad too. I hate not being honest with him. It seems like a poor kind of love. But I trusted, do trust to your wisdom and it is for you to know and to decide. What I said about the star was right you know. Happiness and aliveness and a greater capacity for love of everyone one touches—this if it could have, all would be well. And if it is a star, that is how it will be. That is what it is for me except at moments when suffering comes in and the awful ache of absence and the knowledge that so it must be. And anything else would be destructive, and then guilt would come in. How delicate and difficult and how absorbing. It is just a day over two months since I left you in Paris, found you in Paris—it seems a lifetime.

Next morn.

We did see <u>one</u> meteor, beautiful, like a tear of light. How is your health really? Should you have a complete going-over by the doctor?

[   ]

I got <u>Friends and Relations</u> out of the Athenaeum and am rereading it.

---

where I wrote many poems long long ago: Sarton first met Grace Eliot Dudley in 1938 cross-
ing to Europe on the *Normandie;* during that year she lived at Grace Dudley's home,
Le Petit Bois, for six weeks from late April to June and returned again for most of
July; a very fertile period for work.

what a poison the Whitaker is: Whitaker, an old flame of Grace's husband, William.

Jo Davidson: (1883–1952), American sculptor whose work is in the Luxembourg, Paris, and
the rotunda of the Capitol in Washington, D.C. He did a bronze bust of Julian
which was acquired by UNESCO.

Ella Winter: English writer married in 1924 to Lincoln Steffens (1866–1936), American political
writer. They divorced and in 1936 she married actor and author Donald Ogden Stewart.
Sarton wrote a poem (1945) for her son Pete's twenty-first birthday, unpublished.

Flaubert: Gustave Flaubert (1821–1880), French novelist, whose letters Sarton read throughout the summer of 1941 and whose struggle deeply moved her. To Koteliansky she
wrote: "He is a saint really, but he had to shut out life altogether and one sees him
cutting off his arms and legs, cutting out his heart little by little concentrating everything and then working for two days on a single sentence, pursued by a sense of failure, always ill with rage and impotence. So humble and so uncompromising."

Brancusi: Constantin Brancusi (1876–1957), Romanian sculptor, settled in France, known
for his radically simplified, almost archetypal forms. On 8 June 1947, Juliette took
Sarton to Brancusi's studio, where he talked for hours about his life and work; Sarton
was impressed by his simplicity and purity, the light and space of his studio, the sanc-
tity of art when it is great. See third and fourth stanzas of "A Recognition, for Perley
Cole" in *A Private Mythology.*

on the black pot in the British Museum: See "Invocation" in *The Silence Now.* "Your hair gold
as the delicate branch of myrtle/Laid on the Grecian grave-jar . . ."

Mr. Socrates: Sarton used Juliette Huxley's milliner, Mr. Socrates, in her story "The Paris Hat."

Ed Spiegel at the Civil Liberties: Ed Spiegel was a lawyer for the Civil Liberties Union. The
ACLU's charter alleges the uncompromising defense of the so-called Bill of Rights,
the first ten amendments to the United States Constitution. Sarton was an active
member, believing in the ACLU's principles, but despairing when those principles
meant defending a Communist or never firing a fascist.

saint who was the secretary: Betty Sanger, for whom Sarton wrote an unpublished poem.

letters from practically every young man I know: Sarton had been particularly touched by a letter from the twelve-year-old son of her Santa Fe friend Edith Ricketson; having
never known any president other than Roosevelt, he was worried about the peace
and wrote: "If we should fail, I think I had better start a savings account," about
which Sarton writes to her parents: "It made me feel more than anything the trust

Roosevelt held, that even the children felt <u>safe</u> and now do not. Of course it means that everyone's responsibility is greater than ever."

Bill, my sort of brother: William Theophilus Brown (1919–), artist, amateur musician, and lifelong friend of Sarton; she first met him by chance in 1939 at Harrison Smith's on the eve of their both sailing on the *Normandie;* they met again on the *Normandie's* last voyage back. "Unlucky Soldier" in *The Lion and the Rose* was written for him. Brown did eventually meet the Huxleys for lunch; he is today nationally known and shares artistic affinities with Richard Diebenkorn, David Park, Elmer Bischoff, and Paul Wonner. It was Brown's flowers, wired to her in hospital from California on 13 July 1995, which were the last flowers Sarton was to see.

read Henry Adams' letters: Henry Brooks Adams (1838–1918), American historian and man of letters, best known for his *History of the United Sates of America During the Administration of Jefferson and Madison, Mont St. Michel and Chartres,* and *The Education of Henry Adams.*

after September I shan't know: The Huxleys went to the UNESCO conference in Mexico that fall, stopping off in New York on the way.

for you to know and to decide: It was Juliette's wish that Julian not know about her intimacy with Sarton.

Friends and Relations: a novel by Elizabeth Bowen published in 1931.

Athenaeum: the Boston Athenaeum. Founded in 1805 by an exclusive association of Boston literary men, the Boston Athenaeum, an outgrowth of the Anthology Club, was patterned after the Liverpool Athenaeum in England.

––––––––

[5 CHANNING PLACE]   Sunday, Sept. 7th [1947]

O darling, spending the weekend here at Channing Pl. I went to the old file and found all your letters—<u>marvelous</u> letters which make me see all over again and freshly how deep all this goes, made up of much suffering and <u>bursts</u> of light. In April 1937 (more than 10 years ago) you wrote, "I have seen the tree with its twin flowers of love and friendship—and it's like Jean Giono's great pile of golden grains, offered in the frozen earth under the frozen sky; it is a magnet to all the wings of the air. My thoughts have gathered there—and yours—and Julian's. We are all a little afraid—I am. These two flowers are not ordinary flowers. Who knows—and who can tell what fruit they will become?"

That was ten years ago but no one knows still what the fruit will be. O dear, how strange, how marvelous life is. Je n'en reviens pas. Then you often wrote to me in French and called me Minette (do you remember?) and Alan was jealous, perhaps that's why you wrote in French. I think of all the things we must do together before we die: one is, to hear Maggie Teyte sing the Debussy and Fauré songs; one is to have a week somewhere—<u>one</u> week in a lifetime. Shall we ever have it? Would you be bored? Not really, if the place were beautiful enough. There are so many things we should see with our four eyes. Without you I feel cut off from so much, that intensity which made everything leaf edged with fire, every change of light in the sky <u>immensely</u> important.

And then in the next breath I wonder whether any of this can seem <u>real</u> to you. I don't see how it can. It seems much too "impossible" to be real to me. I think I must have invented that single night. It never <u>hap-pened</u>, did it? It was a dream. You are, you always did frighten me by being so beautiful and now I am more frightened than ever. I suppose I shall almost die of it as meeting draws near and everything must crystallize— only it doesn't <u>have</u> to, darling. I think that whatever you do, whatever you are will be good to me. As long as I can see you now and then and we can look at paintings—and music. Just imagine, we have <u>never</u> been to a con- cert together!

Writing to you I am putting off what I must do, which is to read over the Santa Fe novel and think what to do with it—perhaps begin all over again?

Good night, dear dear one—

[   ]

Tues.

I think the book must be <u>completely</u> rewritten, alas—but perhaps some- day it will be good. I have hopes. I <u>long</u> for a letter. Lately I have been miss- ing you very much.

———

Jean Giono: The works of French novelist and short story writer Jean Giono (1895–1970), set largely in his native Manosque, are rich in poetry and images of nature.
Je n'en reviens pas: I can't get over it.
Alan was jealous: Alan Best, Juliette's lover.
Maggie Teyte . . . Debussy, Fauré: Dame Maggie Teyte (1888–1976), English operatic and concert soprano, studied with Debussy and is best known for her superb interpreta- tions of his songs and those of Fauré.
I must have invented that single night: Reference to Paris, May 1947; this and the days just prior to 4 May 1948 were the entirety of their sensual communion.
the Santa Fe novel: "The Astounding Air," unpublished.

———

O my love, such a dark gloomy day with long streaks of heavy snow–rain falling past the window, on top of the ancient dirty drifts of past snows. Yesterday I had a black day of rage because Cooks suddenly told me they couldn't get me passage over in April (I applied last August, you know, and they never warned me that it would be very difficult though they knew way back then and I could have planned to come in March, but now have lectures I can't put off). I lay awake a long time thinking of you and wondering what it would be like if I couldn't see you—and it all seemed like a windy darkness. But now in the morning I think I can get there in one way or another, perhaps fly, perhaps move up a class in the ship, though it is stupidly more (20 pounds more for Cabin Class right away and God knows how much more for First). It means writing a short story and I can't bear to interrupt the novel just now. Oh my dear.

> My beloved has gone away,
> Alas, why has she so?
> And I am so sore bound
> I may not come her to.
> She hath my heart in hold,
> Where ever she ride or go
> With true love a thousand-fold.

And you say that thinking with your heart is to no avail or pleasure. But surely it is the only way to think at all. Pascal would say so. I suppose the wind and the darkness come in when you do. I feel very far away from the real inside you. There are screens of journeys and extraordinary tropical flowers and bare mountains and all you have seen looking outward, between me and you heart. But I like to know how it is getting on. That is what really interests me most in this sorry world. I think partly the sea got you down. It is so sad, the sea, so lonely. "Lonesome," the American word is better. And now you are with your mother. I'll send this there hoping it will reach you, though letters in winter even with wings take an awful long time. She will be so happy to have you in her nest for a little while.

My own darling mother is in a wild state of nerve and agitation due to various things. We have had an awful time getting the drug we are sending over to our cousin who has t.b., the one who was tortured by the Gestapo. The dr. friend who was to have done it has proved entirely unreliable—and so the stuff didn't get off for two months and now we get awful desperate accusing letters from Jean Sarton saying we are letting him die etc. etc. Mother doesn't sleep at night and trembles like an aspen and I rage at the cruelty of it all. That procrastinating doctor has stolen a year of her life. Well, now at last the stuff has gone and must be there. But this has cost too much. Daddy is no help, doesn't even know what we are doing, money being the one awful abyss in their lives together which there is no crossing. He is a queer man, round and cheerful, and never seeing Mother's tiredness. Perhaps that is a good thing. When he does see it he becomes terribly upset and writes letters all over the world explaining what it is to have the <u>burden</u> of a sick wife (!). Men are terrible creatures. Their selfishness is beyond telling. But I suppose they have to be forgiven because they do so much work! And because we love them <u>quand même</u>.

(Mother has just called me and called Cooks and as usual performed miracles and extracted a promise that I shall get passage in April. Hurrah!) I am sometimes terrified of the sweetness of seeing you again because it must always be so brief, broken and poignant—in the nature of our lives. And I expect you may sometimes worry too. But you will see and I shall see how presence smooths all the fears of absence away. As long as I can see you now and then for an hour alone I am perfectly happy whatever happens. Do remember that when you get nervous, if you do.

What nonsense I am talking!

Kot described my letter coming through the window while you were there. I gather he did not want to tell you about the selling of the letters, as he said, "Alas, Juliette recognized your writing," and I pondered over that, alas, a long time! But that was it, I'm sure. I was awfully jealous of you both and wished it had been me instead of a letter handed through the window. Actually he is asking such a lot for the letters I fear he will not be able to sell them—at least not with Lawrence eclipsed. But that will change as people grow wiser and L. is reassessed. The same has happened to V. Woolf.

It is now the end of the morning and between page one and two I have worked, more or less, at least taken five typewritten pages out of the typewriter. This is the illusion of work at any rate and I am through for the day. Balzac worked twelve hours a day—how I wonder? And sometimes I think I do not push myself to the limit. It's really only beyond the limit that anything good occurs. But we shall see. I wait for the book of poems now like a pregnant mother! It should arrive any day and I have no idea what the jacket will look like. I hope not too awful!

There is no news to tell you except work. And the endless snow. And my extreme longing to see you, to look into your eyes.

There have been two charming rather longer reports on the Mexico UNESCO meeting, one by Ritchie in the <u>New Statesman</u> and one by a woman in the <u>New Yorker</u>. If you don't see them let me know and I'll send them along.

With all my love, darling, <u>tous les jours</u>.

[   ]

My beloved has gone away . . . : from a Middle English lyric, author unknown: My lief is faren in londe,/Allas, why is she so?/I am so sore bonde/I may nat come her to./She hath myn herte in holde/Where ever she ryde or go/With trewe love a thousand-folde.

Pascal would say so: Blaise Pascal (1623–1662), French mathematician and mystic. Sarton is probably referring to Pascal's belief that "it is the heart that feels God, and not reason," that the heart is understood as an order higher than reason rather than as its complement or substitute.

cousin . . . tortured by the Gestapo: Jean Sarton, of whom she writes to Kot in January 1946: "A cousin of ours, the most mingy little man, proved himself a hero and was terribly tortured but did not tell anything. He will never be well again, poor man. He was a clerk in a bank. It is so moving to think of these poor human beings who seemed to be so little and then found in themselves the heroic qualities they did not imagine they possessed. Jean Sarton was one of those." His experience was the seed for Sarton's "The Tortured" in *The Lion and the Rose*.

procrastinating doctor has stolen a year of her life: Eleanor Mabel Sarton was to die of cancer in less than three years, on 18 November 1950.

money being the one awful abyss in their lives: Remorse over her mother's struggle with money plagued Sarton to the end of her life. To Judith Matlack she wrote typically from Montreux in 1948: "I was horrified to find that [Mother] had just 25 francs left as pocket money and Daddy won't give her any, just expects her to ask for every stamp etc. This is the only blot and it is a small one as Mother has rightly made up her mind not to let it spoil anything."

selling of the letters: Koteliansky was in the process of trying to sell his letters from D. H. Lawrence (1885–1930), English novelist, short story writer, poet, and essayist who served as editor for a number of Koteliansky's translations of great nineteenth-century Russian works. For some of Lawrence's letters to Kot see *The Quest for Rananim: Letters to Koteliansky, 1914–1930*, ed. George J. Zytaruk (McGill–Queens University

Press, 1970). More than three hundred letters of this correspondence were bequeathed to the British Museum.

not with Lawrence eclipsed: Lawrence's reputation was tarnished when *The Rainbow* (1915) was condemned as obscene and *Lady Chatterley's Lover* (1928) was prohibited both in England and the United States; after a prolonged court case in 1960, the ban on *Lady Chatterley's Lover* was lifted, and Lawrence came to be seen as somewhat of a classic.

Balzac worked twelve hours a day: Honoré de Balzac (1799–1850), French novelist of whose château at Sache Sarton wrote to Judith Matlack in 1957: "It was very moving to go up to the small almost monastic room—narrow bed, big table, coffee pot. He drank innumerable cups of coffee and worked all night. One felt in that quiet place the shadow still of the terrible battles of creation."

wait for the book of poems now like a pregnant mother: The Lion and the Rose.

Mexico . . . Ritchie: The Huxleys had gone to a UNESCO conference in the fall of 1947. Ritchie Calder, Scotch scientist, prolific author, professor of international relations at Edinburgh University, friend of the Huxleys.

tous les jours: every day.

---

139 OXFORD ST.   Jan. 14th, 1948

Darling, balm of my heart, I must have written two days ago to Neuchâtel but can't resist a moment more, to reach you there again before you leave for Paris and all the efforts again. I am sad at your sadness and the little letter from London brings it to me vividly so that I wish only we were sitting somewhere under a tree, in some sort of <u>silent</u> communication. After all these words—But you must put down part of it to the ocean and part of it to the immense fatigue you must have. Some reaction was inevitable, I think. I had hoped so much you would have those ocean days <u>alone</u>, without having to respond to anyone, even Julian or perhaps especially Julian—that you would sleep and be still and become friends with your soul again as one can't when there are so many people and so little time. You get wrenched out of your orbit by all these journeys and efforts, of course—anyone would. And then Julian doesn't help, just when a word would be balm and saving—I know. You live with the impossible all the time and still draw a small daily victory from it, your angelic patience, understanding, loveliness, radiance—these somehow or other survive the blows. How? But sometimes I think the very tension and the despair is part of it all, that without your agonies, you would fail to be supported—for in a strange way your whole difficult, painful, joyful, always surprising journey by Julian's side is your support, your life, the great reality of it. I have to remind myself of this when I rage sometimes at J. Take J. out of your life and the very building would fall—for it is a construction of yours made with, it seems to me, almost infinite love and foresight and care and something like passion, the passion to endure and to understand, quand même. I am not saying what I mean, I never do at this time of day when I have finished work and am too excited. Oh, if only you were here, my blessed one! I would make you some soup and we would sit by the fire—

By now surely you will have found my letters in Paris and know that the silver glory is wedded to my neck and only leaves it in sleep—and then perhaps does not, metaphorically speaking.

How lovely that Francis could meet you! How strange to be in London and not at Pond Street. Strange people come to see Channing Pl. now, prospective tenants, turn up their noses at the old fashioned bathrooms and leave. Poor mother! It is awful to think that here the absolute and only standard is the bathroom! But I think we shall find someone who will see what a dear and liveable house it is and will appreciate the value of tea in a garden, even if the bathroom is not designed by Crane and the towels are not an inch thick!

Today a great thing happened. William Rose Benet, the poet and chief critic for the Saturday Review wrote me out of a blue sky to say he had seen proofs of the book of poems and then wrote a paean of praise. Amongst other things "I think My Sisters O My Sisters is one of the most extraordinary poems by a woman that I have ever read." and ends "Not often can poets cope both with the actuality and the dream. Your intensity is the sinew of the real poet." What a relief! I have been really in an awful state of nerves about what the critics would say. I am so unfashionable and plain really—but maybe this is an augury and anyway, in itself, very precious. I respect W.R.B. He wants the same things of poetry that I do, that it be a real inward experience and not just a clever play with words, for one thing. I'm so happy James liked the New Year Poem too— it all comforts me in my travail on the novel. For whatever happens to it, I shall be with poetry again in April,—and be with you at latest in May. How shot through with glory and even the dull days are—when I think of you, darling.

And now I must go to the P.O. and mail this and other things.

With dear, dear love. Let us believe that miracles will happen in the spring—to the world—to us—

how lovely the single tree in London!

[   ]

Today we heard too that the medicine for Jean Sarton has arrived safely— at last mother can <u>sleep</u>.

———————

silent communication: Silence had been at the center of both life and art for Sarton from "Request" in *Encounter in April* (1937) "Silence/is infinitely more precious to me/than any word"—to "The Silence Now" in the volume *The Silence Now* (1988)—"immense . . . deep down, not to be escaped." See also pp. 68–76 in *Among the Usual Days.*

the silver glory: a silver choker which Sarton wore until the end of her life and which was sold at the estate auction.

prospective tenants: The Sartons were looking for tenants to rent Channing Place while they were to be in Europe, sailing on the *Queen Mary* on 19 February.

Today a great thing happened. . . . What a relief!: See *Selected Letters 1916–1954* for her reply of 14 January 1948 to William Rose Benét (1886–1950), poet, editor, husband of Elinor Wylie, older brother of Stephen Vincent Benét, one of the founders of *The Saturday Review of Literature* and writer of the column "The Phoenix Nest." At the time of this letter about *The Lion and the Rose* he was assistant editor of *The Saturday Review,* in which Martha Bacon reviewed the book favorably.

James liked the New Year Poem: James Stephens (1882–1950), Irish poet and novelist, best known for *A Crock of Gold;* close friend of S. S. Koteliansky about whom Juliette Huxley wrote in her memoirs: "He was Kot's opposite, yet his twin brother, so tangible was their unspoken solicitous tenderness." See Sarton's "A Letter to James Stephens" in *Inner Landscape* and footnote to letter dated 20 January 1946. Sarton's 1948 New Year's poem was "The Invisible Bridges," published as "Innumerable Friend" in *The Land of Silence.*

with poetry again in April: In April 1948 Sarton would stay variously with Jane Stockwood, Basil de Sélincourt, and Rebecca West. The reference is to England, where she worked so well, and to where she always "came home to poetry,"

———————

139 Oxford St.   Jan. 20th, Tuesday [1948]

Darling, just a quick word before lunch to welcome you back to Paris. I shall be anxious to hear how you found your mother? Was so happy to have your letter of Jan. 13th on the chaise longue at the Bristol—to know that at last you had got my letters. But you labor under a delusion if you imagine that I write good letters to <u>anyone</u> but you. You are my joy and writing to you is just necessary for my own inner _équilibre_, setting everything in its place. And sometimes I imagine that I hardly experience my life until I have sent pieces of it off to you in a letter—but I have become a rather tired correspondent. I never get to the end of the pile of letters I owe and it is really rather a burden. (Edward Lear used to write 15 letters before breakfast, but 15 a week is about my speed, and even that seems too much!) I only write real letters to you and Jean-Do and occasionally, Kot. Kot by the way has written twice to say how young and beautiful you look and that the only justification for UNESCO is how it becomes _you_—which makes me quite furious that I can't see you with my own eyes this minute.

I am now a little ashamed of the effusion I sent to Switz. about your life. Who am I to say anything? But the one word "irascible" about J. set it off. Do forgive. Now I gather from this Paris letter that he has mended his ways and let you see some of the immense ocean of love he has for you and allows to be buried under the petty irritations of the day. So my letter is quite irrelevant. That is the way with letters. The magic is how rarely yours ever are. I do not say enough about yours, but just take it for granted that you know they are my heart's food and drink and without them I would pine away, develop a meagre unimaginative heart and finally perhaps atrophy altogether. How you managed to write such beautiful ones in the midst of Mexico I don't know. But someday you will read them again and see how wonderful they are.

I don't wonder that you feel unreal about UNESCO a great deal of the time. Your job is so crucial and at the same time, always on the _periphery_, not at the center as J's is. At least he knows and is part of the actual work. You are everybody's relief and treasure, the balm, the oil on the waters, _the charm_—and still not at the center. I think this is a very difficult thing to sustain and that you do is a miracle. Of course you underestimate so frightfully the inner fountain you have that rises to meet each person as if they were a treasure—that is your one fault. But it is a very BAD ONE—this continual underestimation of yourself and your powers. If only you could come to accept yourself as a natural wonder. It will happen in Heaven, but I would like to see it happen before I die, before we both vanish into the air.

I hope you go to a dr. now and then for a thorough checkup. I have become quite terrified for all I love. So many of our friends are dying horribly of cancer. Three people on Channing Pl. this year. Now I just heard that Elsa Ulich (that living angel of strength, Elsa Brandstrom she was, and known as the White Angel in the last war) is dying in horrible tortures and nothing to be done. And so many useless people live. How hard it is to accept, to understand. <u>Why</u>? Why she of all people, why have to suffer so much when her whole life has been a gift, a warm, large happy spending of herself for others? I cannot resign myself to it and tremble for my mother, for you, for Judy. Who next? It is terrifying. Please be sure you are all right if you have the slightest shadow of a pain <u>anywhere</u>.

I am almost at the final wave of the novel—impossible to tell whether it is a horrid bowl of mush (as I fear) or a luminous definition of the inner line of a spirit through six months of crisis (as I hope!). Probably somewhere between the two, actually, very far from what it might be. But I shan't I think write a good novel for another five years. It is much more difficult than poetry for me. And one must know and see and feel so much all around everything, not just darting to the center as a poet does, like a dragonfly.

Tomorrow I read poems for a college—around four words: delight, discipline, growth, freedom, in that order. It will be fun. And then I have to race over to the State House to speak for the Civil Liberties at a hearing on four very dangerous bills that are coming up, ostensibly to keep commies out of gov. jobs, from voting or running for office but actually so worded that they would affect all liberals. Anyway you cannot fight ideas by repressing them and that is what I am going to say, by flattering the ignorant Irish Congressmen to the best of my ability. I put great faith in a great-great-grandfather whose name was Tims. What could be more persuasive than Tims?

The poems won't be out till about Feb. 10th. I had hoped sooner, but did I tell you that I got a wonderful letter about them from Benet? Such a relief.

I must go now and steam some clams for lunch. Judy is home as this is exam time. I wrote a lot this morning and feel rather weak in the back as a result. Bless you always. How I shall be hoping that you find a flat with a square room! I hope I shall be there when Aldous is, but maybe it would be better not, that you have one distraction at a time! It is lovely that you feel as you do now about Maria too. It is good when people grow up.

I wish I could send you an elf-packer to pack for you—the endless packing and unpacking of your errant life.

A kiss X
M—

Elsa Ulich: Elsa Brandstrom Ulich lectured throughout the United States from 1921 on, on
the subjects of human suffering and the hardships and dislocations of war; author of
Among War Prisoners in Siberia (1921); wife of Harvard professor Robert Ulich.

shan't I think write a good novel for another five years: Shadow of a Man, originally entitled *A
Man's Shadow,* was published in 1950. In the *Chicago Tribune* of 7 May 1950 Fanny
Butcher wrote: "Even if the reader . . . did not know that its author is a poet of distinction, it would be obvious that, sung or unsung, poetic genius vibrated thru every
line of the book." Sarton can be seen in the character of Bostonian Francis Adams
Chabrier, and Juliette in Parisienne Solange Bernard, who opens Francis's eyes to the
complex realities of life and love.

whose name was Tims: (John) Timms Hervey Elwes (1771–1824), of Stokes College, Essex,
England, took the name Timms in 1793.

the poems: The Lion and the Rose.

from Benet: William Rose Benét; see footnote to letter of 14 January 1948.

Aldous . . . Maria: Aldous Huxley (1894–1963), novelist, essayist, and satirist, brother of
Julian and half brother of Andrew (born 1917 and 1963 Nobel Prize winner in phys-
iology). Aldous's wife was Maria Nys, a Belgian who had come in 1915 to live at
Lady Ottoline Morrell's Garsington, near Oxford. Juliette Baillot Huxley, a Swiss,
had come the same year to be governess-companion to Lady O's daughter Julian.
See foreword to this volume by Francis Huxley. The Aldous Huxleys came to Paris
in July 1948 before going to Italy, where Aldous was to write the screenplay for one
of his short stories, "The Rest Cure"; they were in Paris again in September.

----

139 OXFORD ST.   Jan. 25th, 1948

My treasure, what a wonderfully quick letter from Switzerland (it arrived
on Friday, three days ago just as I was on my way over to Channing Pl. for
a weekend of cleaning with Mother). I had to laugh at your <u>fantaisie</u> on
how poets are treated in this country. Alas, the book will hardly be reviewed
and then months after it comes out, no pictures, no fanfare—but still I must
admit I am excited. They say now that they won't have bound copies till
Feb. 5th and that means I shan't see it for several days after that and I am
suddenly very impatient. I have <u>no</u> idea what the jacket looks like or anything, but I'll send one over first class as soon as I have one. I am already a
<u>little</u> sad that I think I had better sign this copy for you <u>and</u> Julian—but it
is better, I think, to make me a little sad than to make him a little sad. And
it seems exaggerated to send you each a copy—just one more thing to pack!
I think I shall be hugely relieved to have it out, and be finished with all

those poems forever. I threw away bundles of mss. over the weekend and realized how many times I had remade the book and how much I finally left out (all to the good!) but once a book is out it is finished. I think one has lost all emotion about it by then and even people's response seems about someone else, for by then one has grown a little and changed a little and feels one can do better. But until it is out of the way, it is a millstone, so the relief is huge and the anxiety about critics and all that seems so foolish once it is launched and does not even make a ripple (which has always been my experience so I am old and cynical by now about failure). You know, I gave 70 copies of Inner Landscape away and lots of people didn't even bother to write me about it. Now I expect nothing—except of course a long and very critical letter from you which I shall read and think about and make into new and better poems when we meet.

The slight tinge of melancholy in this letter is, I must explain, that I have again a most monstrous cold which makes me feel big, slow and unwieldy like an enormous puffing pillow. I am cross because this is the last week of the novel (I hope) and now I fear I'll have to wait till I feel a little thinner and brighter.

We have had our 8th or 9th immense snow (over a foot on top of all the rest) and it is bitter cold. A little boy about ten years old is plunging about now in our back-yard up to his waist, laughing with the joy of it, climbing up on the fence and plunging in as if he were diving into deep water. I spent the weekend cleaning out my study at Channing Pl. throwing away whole parts of my life: scripts from theatre days, packages of love letters from people long dead (it leaves a fearfully ashy taste, all that accumulation of things and people) and I realize how many of my friends have died and it is sad—sad because so often people leave such a small record behind them, and because their letters tell so little of what they were—a most beautiful girl I knew in Paris who died at eighteen in 1933 and whom I hurt. How cruel and exclusive love is when one is young. Narrow and piercing like the thorn of a rose. But one does learn I think—that is comforting. One learns a lot. All my life I have been learning slowly how to deal with passion and how to love people better, to build and not destroy. But one has so far to go. And it is never ended, is it? And a good thing too!

I think very much about you and J. You are generous about my letter. As I wrote I felt it was bad, but I think of you both and wonder sometimes what went wrong in the very beginning. Only it doesn't matter, because you have somehow made it a triumph all its own, unlike anything else on land or sea. How lovely that you had that peaceful time together in Switzerland.

Darling, how I shook at the State House when I had to speak on Wed. I had to lean against the table facing the semicircle of inattentive senators, not to fall! But the audience applauded very much, so much that the head of the committee banged down his gavel and said after this, no applause from the audience. Most people read their speeches and I said mine which made it a good deal weaker in form (I left out a lot) but a good deal stronger in spirit. I was relieved not to be heckled and afterwards an old Negro woman beamed at me and shook my hand and said, "There should be more people like you," and there was no seat left and another woman squeezed over for me and said, "You deserve a seat," all of which was very human and cosy and I just sat there, sweating quietly with relief and wished I had done better. A legal mind and a ready wit are really what make good speakers at these things, neither of which I possess. Conviction borders on passion and I had enough of passion and—wind!—after listening to the proponents of the bill rant and tear their hair and damn the communists. However it is very moving to see democracy in action: the patience of the committee, the willingness to listen to anyone and everyone who wishes to speak for or against, and the infinite variety of people who do speak, many of them with thick accents, like me immigrants, and proud to be Americans now and to be able to take part in the government and not to be afraid—and above all to feel that their opinions _matter_. Apparently the bills will be squashed. So our work is done for the present. Though there are sure to be others, better worded and so less open to attack, than these.

On Thurs. nite with my cold a misery, Judy and I went to hear Maggie Teyte. The tickets were in the toe of my Christmas stocking and we had looked forward so long that we had to go. Maggie Teyte is getting old so that her first group of songs made me despair, but she warms up and by the end of the evening is very fine, especially the French songs, Fauré, Debussy for which I have a passion. It was a wonderful evening.

I wonder whether Percy Lubbock knew when he began the Wharton book how much he disliked her? Or whether he found it out as he accumulated evidence, always wishing to show her shining and brilliant and always somehow or other ending by a negative appraisal. I think it is a fascinating construction, don't you? I wonder too what Berry was really like. There was certainly a real affinity between them. I fear in the end she had many of the vices of the aristocrat and few of the virtues—least of all that divine ease. It was all a little too well planned, wasn't it? Her life, I mean.

My lecture at Tufts was called off as we had a snow storm that day (the same day as the State House thing). There has never been such a winter but I'm awfully glad we're getting it instead of Europe.

Of course I'll fit my plans into yours. I wonder if you will go and I expect you will, to Jugoslavia—but if not perhaps we could have a week in Paris? (I imagine you would go to your mother for most of the time?) All that will fit into place when the time comes.

How exciting to have sculpture in your solar plexus. When all this is over and you and J. retire years and years from now, it will come back again and inhabit your solar plexus. You are right of course about the limits in work, that it creates them. The true fact, I fear, is that this book is just not it. It fails. I'll read it over this week even if I can't work and maybe that will create the final push to finish. You are dear to write as you do. Your letters fill me with a desire to work. What more can I say? All my love, snowy and cloudy though it be.

[ ]

I hope you find a flat, but wouldn't a hotel be easier in some ways? And warmer?

---

little boy about ten years old: probably Binks Barrett, a neighbor.

letters from people long dead . . . how many of my friends have died and it is sad: In the years preceding this letter, Sarton experienced, among others, the deaths of Mary Chilton, whose letters this is probably reference to; Jacques Limbosch, Sarton's "little brother" and the only son of Raymond and Céline Limbosch, who died in a mountain-climbing accident; Elizabeth McClelland, Cambridge friend of Anne Thorp and the Sartons; Ernesta Greene, childhood friend, daughter of Henry Copley and Rosalind Greene, who committed suicide; James Stephen's son, who was killed in Spain; Jean Dominique's nephew, killed in a car accident; Hermann Schwarzwald, who ran the inn at Grundlsee; Sarton's grandmother, Eleanor Cole Elwes; Richard Wheeler, to whom she wrote the poem "To R. W." (unpublished); Virginia Woolf, who committed suicide; her dear friend Edith Forbes Kennedy; Elizabeth Swift, friend from Cambridge; Jean Tatlock, classmate from Shady Hill who also committed suicide; and Hendrik van Loon, father of Sarton's close friend Willem.

a most beautiful girl . . . whom I hurt: Mary Chilton. See "That Winter in Paris" in *I Knew a Phoenix*.

Maggie Teyte: See footnote to letter of 7 September 1947.

Percy Lubbock: (1879–1965), English biographer and critic, author of *Portrait of Edith Wharton* (1947), which while written with stylistic grace is most notable for its subtle malice toward its subject, Edith Newbold Jones Wharton (1862–1937), American novelist and short story writer.

what Berry was really like: Walter Van Rensselaer Berry (1859–1927), Paris-born American lawyer of international repute who at one point might have married Wharton.

the limits in work, that it creates them: See "Reflections by a Fire" in *Cloud, Stone, Sun, Vine:* "I wonder if the secret of dimension/Will come to me if I can pay attention,/And if I chose this house because I guessed—/And hoped that I would pass the crucial test—/That if the form was there I'd learn the rest. . . . So that both life and art may come to be/As strict and spacious as this house to me."

wouldn't a hotel be easier in some ways?: The Huxleys found a flat the following month on the Quai Louis Blériot, on the Seine.

---

139 Oxford St.   Feb. 16th, Monday [1948]

O my darling, how far away you are and how I love you! I think I am an iceberg presenting a tiny surface to the sun but most of me, a great mountain concealed under the surface, and that is all my love. In these last purgatorial days I have thought of you much. Judy brought me your letter on Sat., no Friday, as we struggled in the last desperate throes of cleaning out every cupboard in the house, washing all the shelves, putting away silver, making beds, and thank goodness I was there to be her hands and feet and to make her go to bed for her meals even if she had to stagger up between. She planned so well and it was really at times an impossible problem with so many details to plan. You see, tenants move in today and the house had to be ready. But she never allowed herself to become panic-stricken and we just quietly did one thing after another—but what Hell! In the midst of it came my book. We never had time to sit down quietly and look at it, but I did manage to get one off to you Air Mail so it should be there by tomorrow or the next day I think. I like it quite well—I mean, the format. Shall be so eager to hear. It was sad having it come when there was no time, after all these years; but when I came home, there was a dear letter on my desk from Judy to say that she thinks all the personal poems so beautiful, and doesn't mind who they were written to, but just rejoices. That was balm. And I felt I was coming home after a long exile, though actually I only slept at Channing Pl. the last three nights!

My darling, I shall be so sad if you have to live with furniture you don't like. How well I remember the awful apt. on Ave. Foch and I hope you will have the strength to hold the suspense a little longer, even against J.'s impatience, for surely you will discover (as you did last time) a roof under which you can feel yourself. But if you don't, it is amazing how soon one forgets furniture and finds one's own little places, a table where one can write, a chair which seems right etc. and with your books and flowers so much can be done. I shall be terribly anxious to hear. I wish I could somehow by long distance telepathy make the woman who rented you the beautiful Ave. Foch go away for a year! Can't she be persuaded that Paris is no place to be just now? Have you tried her? Can't she be bought off? Or appealed to as a citizen of the world? Dear Madam, the work of UNESCO depends on your getting out immediately. How could she refuse? I could not.

I loved the description of the Fath opening. Oh dear, what a strange world. I had a letter from Freya today from Barbados, speaking of the fear of war in Italy. She sounds happy and finished her book, lucky woman! I do not dare look at mine until I feel a little better. I am still in a perfect nightmare of sinus, can't sleep at night, etc. but some of it may have been worry about Mother, so I shall wait and see. And my Dr. whom I see tomorrow is wonderful.

Before I forget, here are the Mayers: Mr. André Mayer, 47 Rue de Vaugirard (littre 94–29). Do have them with not too many other people. She is not half the person he is. She is French in a Jewish way, exclusive and a little smug and anti-British(!), once made Mother cry. But she does really love and admire my work (and of course that makes me forgive her for much, I fear!) and it always surprises me and makes me so grateful when people do. She loved the Unicorn which I wrote in their house. And really reads and really cares. But André Mayer has all that and the largest most generous spirit, as well as much wisdom and knowledge   a great, great man. He looks like a French douanier with a white moustache and very blue eyes. You will love him. But they are no good at small talk. You must engineer a real conversation. Julian could learn a lot from Mayer if he only gives him a chance—and Mayer from him. She has no charm, but she is something underneath. I long for you to meet them both. If not now, then when I come, but don't wait if it is possible. Of course André is always off on FAO meetings at the ends of the earth and there is no point in seeing her alone.

Demian after all was disappointing. It goes off into fantasy and I was in the end, disappointed.

But what you say about having so many true selves may be true in some senses, but not I think in the deepest sense. Finally one makes a choice, one <u>becomes</u> one of the possibilities and the awful tragedy is that so many people discover this too late, when the choice has been made, when it is irrevocable. All one's life I think one struggles to live more and more so that <u>never</u> will one have to be less than one's true self, paring down, eliminating, choosing closer and closer to the marrow. It is much easier for men than for women, of course, because women's selves are usually involved with a man's and the problem is to <u>still</u> be oneself and to be someone else's. Darling, what a confusion of words! This is something to talk about. [D. H.] Lawrence of course based the true self so much on sex and maybe he was right, I don't know. I have sometimes imagined that the spirit only flowers when the senses flower in their own true way. There is a clear stream of physical passion in each person and if that is blocked it does sometimes block everything. And yet some people can be their true selves with no lived out passion at all in their lives—such as Jean Dominique, for instance. For myself at least as I grow older sex seems less and less important and love more and more important. More than any other beauty (though it is true of all beauty except in art) passion seems to me to have the seeds of its own destruction in it.

Of course one is different selves for different people, a matter of response, but deep down inside <u>to oneself</u>, one is always somewhere it seems to me the <u>same</u>. In some people the buried real self never comes into action or into life and I think that's what <u>Demian</u> is about maybe, and all life is about.

What a jumble! But we will talk. I do not dare to think too much about seeing you. It becomes frightening. Do you realize that we have had only about eight days together in all our lives in love? Those, and that brief meeting in New York. So even weeks can be a century—and so it will be. It will be the purest happiness. I have no doubt of that. Even tears are dew not rain when there is so much love, so I really have no fear and you must not. My fears never have anything to do with the essence of the matter, but only things like where I shall sleep and how far from you.

I go off a week from Friday, Feb. 27th, and you'd better write here. Everything will be forwarded as fast as possible. One can't count on air mail time. Sometimes it takes a week and I only stay two days in each place. Back March 21st.

There is a Hellish amount to do still before I get off, but I look forward to the lectures and being able to concentrate entirely on poetry and on "being my real self"—no laundry, telephone, dishwashing, housecleaning for three weeks. Hurrah!

I still haven't my passage, damn Cooks! Oh my love, be well, be happy, be mine!

[   ]

---

putting away silver, making beds . . . make her . . . meals: Because Eleanor Mabel Sarton had been ill in bed and the cleaning woman was ill and unable to help, Sarton prepared the house at Channing Place for the Taylors, tenants expected during the Sartons' absence in Europe.

came my book: After the Sartons' departure, Judith Matlack, their friend Ruth Harnden, and May celebrated the arrival of *The Lion and the Rose* together on Sunday, 15 February, with old-fashioneds and chicken.

the Fath opening: fashion designer Jacques Fath (1912–1954).

Freya: Freya Stark; see footnote to letter of 25 September 1944.

the Mayers: André Mayer was director general of the Food and Agricultural Organization of the United Nations; he and his family were old friends of the Sartons.

loved the Unicorn: "The Lady and The Unicorn—The Cluny Tapestries" in *The Lion and the Rose*, written for Juliette Huxley.

douanier: customs officer.

FAO: Food and Agricultural Organization of the United Nations.

go off a week from Friday, Feb. 27th: Sarton's lecture tour beginning on 1 March took her to Mary Washington College in Fredericksburg, Virginia; Pembroke State College in Pembroke, North Carolina; Emory and Henry College, in Emory, Virginia; Bridgewater College in Bridgewater, Virginia; and North Carolina College at Durham.

---

139 OXFORD ST.   Tues. Eve. Feb. 24th [1948]

Darling, your letter of the 19th here so wonderfully quickly with its vision of the flat on the Seine, its windows, its white walls. I hardly dare to pin it down in a hope it sounds too lovely and surely you must get it somehow. Is it fearfully expensive?

And all you say of the book. As long as you like it, that is all that matters. It is a huge relief to hear. Later you can tell me more. But it was awful last night. I had dinner with an old friend, headmistress of the Winsor School (the Boston equiv. of Eton—for girls!) and she asked me to read from the book, as we drank apricot brandy and I felt an utter and complete revulsion as if I could never look at one of the poems again. I did read, but badly, but I expect it is all tiredness and still being ungirded for life by this old davvil sinus. I can only see the poems through other eyes, now, not my own. They have gone from me and it is a good thing. The only ones I like are yours.

Today a big day. I took a huge lot of parcels to the P.O. 15 of my books, an immense bundle of clothes for Marie-Anne Kuntze in Germany, some notepaper for a friend in Eng. and the mss. of the novel which I have at last sent off to the publisher, so it is out of my hands at last. Then I had two old fashioneds for lunch to celebrate a friend's new flat, and slept for an hour and began almost to feel human about four when Judy came home for tea, for the first time in weeks. Perhaps I am getting better. So now the red coat feels less incongruous.

The cocktails sound so good, what a blessing for all the people now to feel included and as if they mattered. It is very important that you do them and I'm so glad the response is warm. I am all for a wives' club, old feminist that I am! and do tell me what happens.

But this is a very sad night and I can think of nothing but Czeckoslovakia and this second death. Elmer Davis for once was quite moved in his news broadcast, said he felt he was sitting for the second time at the deathbed of an old friend. How blind people are in their belief. Matthiessen who spent last winter at the Univ. in Prague assured me that this would not happen, that everyone was quite free, no pressure on the socialists etc. etc. And I felt like a rat not to believe him but the grain of salt I took it with almost choked me—and now already this has happened.

And Palestine. I got into a perfect rage yesterday when I read the Jews had killed British soldiers and accused the British of blowing up that block in Jerusalem. But then tonight one reads that the British provide King Abdullah with eight million a year for his army (he has the Arab Legion) and supply him with 48 top-ranking military aides. It looks awfully dirty and one wonders—oil, I suppose. But America is playing its own little horrid game of hands off and not taking any real stand, and above all not willing to send troops to back up partition. What a mess it is, with so much suffering wrapped up in it, so much wrong on all sides.

I have been thinking (because of the book) very much of Lugné-Poë, rereading his heartbreaking notes all through the years up to Munich and then the gradual dark. He died luckily before the fall of France but not before his heart was broken: "Se verra-t-on jamais avec ces heures qui me font si mal," and this which finding again meant so much to me today (1938): "Mais ta lettre a l'air (assez?) filtrant la lassitude. Ah non! Pas ça de ta part—si toi tu manquais d'enthousiasme où irions nous? Tu comprends ce n'est pas pour jeter la manche après la cognée qu'on bon destin m'a dit à moi: tu laisseras tes armes en dépot aux mains de cet enfant qui poursuivra ici où là," and "ce qui me rend furieux c'est qu'il ya des heures de lumière où ce qui se passe dans l'humanité me parait ignoble et que j'enrage d'avoir été inscrit sur la liste des passengers de ce monde!" and finally, "Les forces me manquent et le mal ma vite. J'en suis à m'interroger si je pourrai atteindre mai et aller jusqu'à Paris. Tu es arrivée à temps de ma vie pour que j'ai pu t'entrevoir mais la vie des hommes d'aujourd'hui à fait du mal à l'idiot sensible que je suis resté et les nouvelles de chaque jour me tuent."

Some of this you will find in the poem for Lugné, but now I feel I must write another. It takes a long time fully to understand, darling, what any relationship holds doesn't it? And now the riches of Lugné pour over me and I think it is a miracle that we met, he so old, I so young. I was nineteen, he was over sixty when we first knew each other and then he stopped writing suddenly and only much later told me that it was because he had been warned about his heart and couldn't bear to become attached to another human being he would have to leave. He was always such a violent angry man one did not always see the tenderness which made him angry. You would have loved him. He would have loved you.

I must go to bed, my treasure. I think of you. My heart is very full tonight. Life is so mysterious, so rich, so very beautiful and goes by so fast.

[   ]

---

headmistress of the Winsor School: Valeria Addams Knapp, who had been headmistress of Concord Academy from 1937 to 1940 and for whom Sarton wrote "A Letter for Valeria" (February 1940), unpublished.

the only ones I like are yours: Among the poems in *The Lion and the Rose* written for Juliette are "The Lady and the Unicorn, the Cluny Tapestries," "Question," "O Saisons! O Châteaux," "Perspective," and "Song."

Marie-Anne Kuntze: "la fille du Général," Frau Dr., one of six sisters; lost her position as professor under Hitler for her liberal views; friend of Céline Limbosch; visited Sarton in Nelson in 1967.

a friend's new flat: Ruth Peabody Harnden, friend of Judith Matlack and Sarton.

Czeckoslovakia . . . Elmer Davis: The Communists threatened a coup d'état, securing

President Benes's signature to a predominantly Communist government under Klement Gottwald, and in a drastic purge lasting several months, democratic Czechoslovakia was transformed into a Communist-run "people's democracy" and Soviet satellite. Elmer Davis (1890–1958), American essayist, novelist, scholar, and journalist, one of America's leading broadcasters during the war, was appointed by President Roosevelt as director of the new Office of War Information, which was to become one of the most powerful agencies of the United States government in the struggle for democracy. Sarton is probably referring to Davis's trenchantly witty analyses of the news, which won him three Peabody and myriad other awards.

Matthiessen: Francis Otto Matthiessen (1902–1950), American educator and scholar whose most significant contributions to literary criticism were his efforts at finding a unifying tradition to American literature. He taught history and literature at Harvard University and lived in Cambridge; Sarton did not know him intimately, but his great integrity, personal agony, and ultimate suicide affected her deeply and were the basis for her novel *Faithful Are the Wounds.*

And Palestine: The immigration of Jews into Palestine had risen sharply during the war. As the war ended, both Jews and Arabs maintained military organizations in the Holy Land in a state of uneasy truce. At the time of this letter, terrorist activities raged; the British government, unable to solve the problem, withdrew its forces. Three months later on 14 May the British mandate over Palestine ended, and on the same day the Jewish State of Israel was proclaimed under David Ben-Gurion, with Chaim Weizmann as president; within two days it was recognized by the United States and the Soviet Union, and immediately attacked by Arab armies from Lebanon, Syria, Jordan, and Egypt.

Lugné-Poë: Aurélien-François Lugné-Poë (1869–1940), French actor, director, and theater manager, an important person in Sarton's life during the 1930's; see footnote to letter of 27 August 1940. The character of Fontanes in *The Underground River* is based on him; see also "That Winter in Paris" in *I Knew a Phoenix,* and "What the Old Man Said" in *The Lion and the Rose.*

"Se verra-t-on jamais . . .": Will one ever see the end of these days that make me so ill?

"Mais ta lettre a l'air . . .": Trans: "But your letter seems full of weariness—if you lose your enthusiasm, where shall we be? You understand, it's not in throwing the ax after the handle that destiny said to me: you will leave your arms in care of the child who will follow here and there," and "what makes me furious is that there are days when what occurs among humanity is horrible and I rage at having been listed passenger of this world," and finally, "My strength is leaving me—and I'm overtaken by illness. I wonder if I will last until May and be able to go to Paris. You came into my life when I could still understand and perceive you—but today's world is hard on the sensitive fool that I still am, and each day the news destroys me."

poem for Lugné: "What the Old Man Said" in *The Lion and the Rose.*

---

139 Oxford St.   March 23, 1948
Cambridge, Mass.

My treasure, dear sprite, Radiguet arrived yesterday to make me feel alive again. Also it was a lovely warm day and you could smell the earth, and I am so happy to be home, and at last I definitely have my passage on the Queen Mary, April 7th. Now I am eager to hear what you can plan and whether perhaps I cannot see you for a week-end alone. Air Mail from your side takes six or seven days so if you cannot get it to me here, send plans to c/o Jane Stockwood, 12 Ormonde Mansions, 106 Southampton Row, London W.C.1. I'm sorry about a depressed and rather cross letter I sent—something in your letter froze me, I think, and now it is really time that we saw each other again. I find it suddenly very difficult to write. I think of you a great deal but it is not a word-making thinking, perhaps. And I think of Paris and the great serene spaces and the trees. I am so tired, darling, that is the trouble with me. I feel as if I had not settled anywhere, deeply settled for a long time, but all has been effort and hurry, climbing up and down the days, a great lack of savoir vivre as I really do not have so damned much to do, nothing compared to what you have to do. But there it is, the ends all frayed and the deep messages not getting through. Living on nerve, one loses one's soul.

But now people are beginning to buy the book. It is hardly out yet and no bookstore in Cambridge has it at present, but orders are in and people call up excitedly and the Times book sup has reprinted two of the poems, "In That Deep Wood" and "Santos, New Mexico" in two consecutive issues which is good free advertising. Kot said you had written Spender—how very kind. I feel that he doesn't like me, but I think no male poets ever like female poets really. It is the taking over a masculine, creative function which annoys them. Profoundly inside they want women to be passive, the receivers not the givers. Malraux was very interesting that day at lunch. He took the other side, that women were natural poets but men poets always monsters—Keats (t.b.), Byron, lame etc. etc. It is fruitless really, only one minds the perhaps not necessary sense of being on the defensive, of having invaded someone's territory, all unasked. I got terribly angry at a very condescending review of Woolf's Common Readers by Diana Trilling. She is an acute critic, but the fact is that there is great conflict always about the woman writer and this was very evident. D.T. blames Woolf for not ever saying the definitive thing about any writer, entirely missing the point as I see it of The Common Reader, and even of the title which was not, I believe, ironic, but meant exactly what it says. They are personal essays, springing out of the pleasure of rereading and meant to make other people wish to read. Heavens, we have PhD.'s to cover the whole ground and make the final statement. I think the limitations of any genius are one of the most interesting things, because almost always with-out them the genius would never have been exactly what it was. The limitations are a positive, not a negative. To expect Woolf to have the tough-ness of a truck driver or the masculine analytic mind, or to blame her for not making syntheses when her genius was something entirely different, seems to me just stupid. I wrote Trilling an angry letter but thought better of it. It is a pity because she is actually one of our few critics opposed to "reviewers." Perhaps it is partly that with any greatly praised writer, there has to be a period of debunking before the final reassessment and Woolf is out of fashion now.

O darling your letter of March 20th arrived this minute. How quick, how blessed! With the wonderful news that we might have a few days together in May—and that perhaps I might catch a glimpse of you in London, for I shall be there à partir du 12 ou 13 avril, and until about the 25th. However, if we miss each other there, how lovely May will be. This is a great relief to my mind to have some plan—and I loved the flowing river. It reminded me of Eliot's quartets:

> I do not know much about gods; but I think that the river
> Is a strong brown god—sullen, untamed and intractable—

only the Seine is beautifully tamed and tractable.

This was interrupted by a long sherry-drinking conversation with our dear painter friend from Santa Fe, Agnes Sims, who has been visiting us since I got back and has just left in a taxi. So now for the first time the house is silent and I am alone. It is noon but all I can think of is sleep and the dentist in a few minutes. I wait for you to appear to make time not a long treadmill but a flight, a marvelous parabola, an extension of love.

I devoured half of Radiguet, a very passionate book, marvelously written. How it seizes one!

I am sorry about the maid, except that if you didn't like her you may unearth a wonderful treasure instead.

Descartes, alas, I haven't here. It's at Channing Pl. with half my books or I would try it again. But I think it is true that one looks now for absolutes, for the absolutely pure. There is nothing else. I must write Julian about his book on ethics which I read with very great interest and admiration. It is a

very <u>usable truth</u>, and so it is comforting. But always now I feel in his work
with its astounding ability to synthesize, that some middle step is missing, the
place where once the synthesis is made it can settle down inside the personality like motes in a sunbeam or particles in water, and that <u>only then</u> would
be the time to do the writing. The ideas themselves are so magnificent, rich
and full of faith and somehow the writing fails. Am I wrong? Soon when I
feel a little more bright, I'll try to write him a letter about the book and what
it meant to me. These criticisms are not important.

Love and love, darling

[   ]

Here is the beginning of Maritain's intro. to a book of Leon Bloy in translation I bought in the South. It made me think of you because you always
believe you feel poor because you give so much: "We can give nothing we
have not received, being in the likeness of Him who had received everything from His Father. That is why the more one gives, the more one needs
to receive, the more one is a beggar."

Radiguet: See footnote to letter of 3 August 1947.

cross letter I sent: There is no extant letter between 7 March and this of 23 March.

savoir vivre: Sarton means "knowing how to live" rather than "good manners" or "good
breeding."

buy the book: The Lion and the Rose.

written Spender: Stephen Spender (1909–1995), English poet and critic, friend of Julian
Huxley's who is represented in *Forward into the Past,* the festschrift honoring Sarton's
eightieth birthday. His obituary appeared in the *New York Times* opposite Sarton's
on Tuesday, 18 July 1995.

Malraux . . . interesting that day at lunch: André Malraux (1901–1976), French novelist, art
critic, archaeologist, left-wing activist, flier with the Republicans in Spanish Civil
War, allied himself with de Gaulle and became minister of culture in the Fifth
Republic. In an unpublished journal entry for 28 May 1947, Sarton writes:
"UNESCO luncheon—I sat between Malraux and Hill [Henri Hill, critic, worked
at UNESCO, was editor of *Fontaine*]. . . . Theory that all male poets are sick: Byron,
Rimbaud, Baudelaire etc. whereas its not true of female poets." She was deeply
impressed by his greatness in both creative work and action, his purity, and his lack
of pretense.

review of Woolf's Common Readers by Diana Trilling: Diana Rubin Trilling (1905–1996), cultural, political, and social critic particularly known for her acuity, her sharp, unfor-
giving pen, and her marriage to Lionel Trilling (1905–1975), one of the century's
foremost literary critics and teachers. Virginia Woolf's *The Common Reader* (1925)
and *The Second Common Reader* (1932) are collections of critical essays.

wrote Trilling an angry letter: Sarton's letter to Trilling of 23 March 1948, never sent, appears in *May Sarton: Selected Letters 1916–1954.*

à partir de 12 ou 13 avril: as of the 12th or 13th of April.

I do not know . . . : the opening lines of T. S. Eliot's "The Dry Salvages," in *Four Quartets.*

painter friend . . . Agnes Sims: A Pennsylvanian transplanted to the Southwest, in whose home in Santa Fe Sarton had been a paying guest, Sims was an archaeologist, sculptor, and painter; her portrait of Sarton, which Sarton never liked and kept in a third-floor office at Wild Knoll, was featured as the frontispiece in F. O. Bailey's catalog of the Sarton estate auction in May 1996; it now hangs in a private guesthouse overlooking Sabbathday Harbor at Islesboro, Maine, and is reproduced in this volume.

Radiguet . . . a very passionate book: The Devil in the Flesh by Raymond Radiguet, who died at twenty (see footnote to letter of 3 August 1947), is one of the most delicate love stories in literature; written while the author was sixteen and seventeen, it deals with an adolescent's love affair with an older woman. In his introduction to the Black Sun Press edition, Aldous Huxley writes: "Radiguet set out in possession of those literary virtues with which most writers painfully end."

Descartes: René Descartes (1595–1650), French mathematician, philosopher, and autobiographer, who believed that the science of mathematics held the key to understanding the nature of all life.

Maritain's intro . . . book of Leon Bloy: Jacques Maritain (1882–1973), French Roman Catholic humanist and metaphysical philosopher, among the first twentieth-century philosophers to urge Christian involvement in secular affairs. He came to America after the fall of France in 1940 and taught at Columbia, Notre Dame, and Princeton. Léon Bloy (1846–1917), French writer whose work greatly influenced the twentieth-century revival of Catholic literature and to whom Maritain owed his conversion to Catholicism.

the more one is a beggar: Perhaps evidence of Sarton's having shared this reading with her father, six months later, on 3 September 1948, George Sarton wrote in his journal: "It is clear to me that the main purpose of a man's life is to give others what is in him. Such a matter is not a question of selfishness or unselfishness. Mozart was probably rather selfish in a childish way but he gave the world what was in him (he could not help it) and WHAT a gift! We only have what we are, and we only have what we give. That is, we only have what we are, but on condition that we give all that is in us."

[ON BOARD THE *Queen Mary*]   11 April [1948]

My treasure, your sweet note did find me just before I sailed but there was no time to answer. It has lived in my billfold among the pounds ever since and been reread several times. Of course this is in limbo. I have no feelings or ideas, only sensations: hunger, sleepiness. I read and sleep and find it almost impossible even to write letters. Today there is a deep under-swell and the boat creaks and heaves. I'm in a cabin with only one dear soul, mother of a G.I. bride coming back to England after a visit. The people are much more fun than on the <u>Elizabeth</u> and I think I like this boat better. Soon I shall go on deck to be wrapped up and finish reading a new biog. about Newman's Anglican years and conversion. I've devoured a wonderful <u>witty</u> novel called <u>Prevalence of Witches</u> and various other things. The great thrill has been Rebecca West to whom in a fit of boredom and daring I sent my poems. She came down from first twice for drinks and was so <u>eager</u> and warm. I liked her very much. She really seems to love the poems, which is nice.

I wonder so much if you will come to England as you once said you might—or are you by now in Switzerland? Perhaps I'll have news in London (where I'll be till May 1st).

How sad that Francis was in a distant mood, but it is difficult being a son. It must be. Children and parents, what an infinitely perilous relationship—and Julian tired and impatient will not have helped.

Now, my love, please do not torture yourself about anything concerned with me. I am happy and peaceful and think of you with rushes of excitement, but no <u>pang</u>. I am really rather tired and very gentle, you know, and getting old, so please "take it easy" as we say in America. All will be well—all will be <u>very</u> well!

I can't believe at the moment that there is such a thing as you on earth—but it is marvelous to know that both will be visible soon!

With dear dear love

[   ]

---

limbo: The metaphor of this particular sailing as limbo, and the central image for her "To Those in the Limbo of Illness" in *The Silence Now,* was repeated during Sarton's final hours when, "on that last mysterious voyage everybody takes toward death" (from "Coming into Eighty" in *Coming into Eighty*), she encapsulated her state of mind to this editor in the single word "limbo."

Newman's Anglican years and conversion: John Henry Cardinal Newman (1801–1890), English churchman and author, famous as leader of the Oxford Movement. Converted to Roman Catholicism and continued to engage in bitter controversies, particularly with the Protestant clergyman and novelist Charles Kingsley and the Catholic Cardinal Manning. His most famous work, *Apologia pro vita sua* (1864), a history of his intellectual development and conversion, was written to refute charges against him by Kingsley.

Prevalence of Witches: The Prevalence of Witches (Scribner, 1948), a first and highly successful novel about the difference between tribal and British civil law in a remote Indian province where a Limbodian chieftain is accused of murder under British law although according to his own law it is not a crime; by Aubrey (Clarence) Menen (1912–), English novelist and essayist of Indian and Irish parentage.

Rebecca West . . . sent my poems: Dame Rebecca West, pen name of Cicily Isabel Fairfield (1892–1983), English novelist, critic, and political journalist whose *Black Lamb and Grey Falcon,* a study of contending nationalisms in Yugoslavia, Sarton admired more than she did West's fiction; their meeting on the *Queen Mary* was the beginning of friendship, and Sarton was invited immediately thereafter to the farm at High Wycombe where West lived with her husband, Henry Andres.

She came down from first: Sarton was in Cabin Class; Rebecca West, in First Class, had come down at 8:15 P.M. to arrange for Sarton to join her there for lunch the following day. Permission denied, West and Sarton had drinks in the Cabin Class bar that evening and several subsequent evenings.

[London JS]   April 14th, 1948

Darling one, Kot gave me your letter when I went there this afternoon under the cloudy skies, looking at all the flowering trees and wondering whether I should see you in London—and now I am quite lost among the dates. I go to Belgium May 1st (to catch the family) and because I thought you had said that if I came to Paris the 15th J. would not be back for a few days, but I must have two weeks in Belgium. Now Kot says he will be back May 11th! I miss you here and could come there later etc. etc. O dear, well, it doesn't matter. Plans always tempt the furies, the light-haired and dark-haired ones and I do not really mind (I expect it would have been rushed in London for you) and perhaps it is just as well for Julian to be there when I arrive. Let the barrier be life itself and not your heart—if there must be a barrier (and I have felt gloomy ever since I arrived). Jane and Annie show the effects of this winter, of the long bleak struggle and I feel guiltily fat and tall, immense with American energy and wishing I would take them away to some warm climate and spoil them and feed them and take care of them. I can do little things like the standing in queues which I really enjoy, because it is all an adventure, and taking them out for meals and so on. What makes me sad too is everywhere the violent reaction against the Labor Gov., the sense of the price being paid, of one kind of life having to go—that another may be born. But what kind of child is being born? There is a curious sort of sterility, of waitingness as if people were not really <u>focussed</u>. Lack of incentive? Awful fatigue from all the years of worrying and making do?

My one hope has been and still is England. If England cannot find the middle way between communism and fascism then there is none, and this I would hate to have to admit.

Kot was so angry because his tobacconist called while I was there and there is a new tax and I felt the frustration and anger in him too—And some women I have never seen, came and brought him some Spam—and interrupted us. And mostly I am cross and worried because you do not tell me when you leave Switzerland or where you will be if letters take so long. I am making a carbon of this which I'll send to Paris in case you have left Switzerland before it arrives there.

After May 1st I'll be c/o Limbosch, 18 Ave. Lequime, Rhôdes St. Genèse, Brabant, Belgium.

You are very sweet about the novel. It really does not matter. It is strange but it doesn't. I think I will write a good novel but not for about five years and it will keep. Meanwhile, yes—stories—but I have no ideas at all. But tomorrow perhaps I shall. I must write one or two now or I shall suddenly have no money at all and my only way of not becoming abysmally depressed is to have money enough to be able to do things for people— you know.

My treasure, what is awful is that whenever you get a chance to rest when Julian is away, you have so many other responsibilities, like your little mother. Of course you are tired and emptied out and I hate to think of your having to use your last ounce of heart-energy to make her less nervous and more happy.

I got quite cross with Kot today, though I did not tell him, because he seemed quite surprised that A. V. Hill had been at my father's lecture. After all, G. S. is in his way a very great man and everyone who knows anything about his subject knows it. Why should it be surprising that some Englishman goes to the lecture? I sometimes think the abysses, the preconceptions are so immense between peoples that there is no hope ever of their being bridged. One or two people can cross, but no more. We all have our treasured implacable prejudices. We are all snobs at heart, even the vulgarians. Even the pure in heart like Kot. But he did cheer me up by saying that if we drop an atomic bomb on Moscow it will liberate Russia and everything will be all right! Of course I don't believe it, but it is the first time I have even imagined what the world might be like if this giant fear of oppression were removed.

Russell Square is all feathery green and astounding white cherry blossom, so heavy it looks like some heavenly fruit and not a flower at all. I walked across it this morning thinking of V. Woolf.

I read your letter again and feel all its tender dearness and love, so precious. Do not please worry. Trust your feeling, which is right for you and probably for me. I trust it—your feeling I mean—so much. Nerves can be destructive, but under them we have I think a solid foundation. Meeting will be awful I expect, but after that how lovely to walk, to look out at Paris. I feel joy in the air all around me, a beating of wings when I think of it.

Forgive this tired cross letter. The world is too much with us. I'm so glad Julian was pleased with my letter.

Love and love, dear heart,

M—

How wonderful to talk instead of writing!

Jane and Annie . . . effects of this winter: Jane Stockwood and Annie Duveen Caldwell; see footnote to letter of probably 24 July 1947. It had been the most severe winter in Britain since 1894.

making a carbon of this: Sarton rarely made or kept carbons of her letters except for purposes such as this, in cases of unusually important or final letters, or in cases of letters not sent. Concerning those in this volume: All letters from Juliette Huxley to Sarton not destroyed on 1 December 1948 and covering the years 1936 to 1951 were deposited by Sarton in her archive at the Berg Collection (see footnote to Editor's Preface) in the 1970s. Those from Juliette between 1975 and 1995 which had been in Sarton's files at York are now in the possession of Francis Huxley. In the 1970s, Juliette returned all the letters Sarton had written her between the years 1936 and 1948; those after 1948, after Paris, Juliette had destroyed; those between 1974 and 1995 were returned to Sarton in the spring of 1995 by Francis Huxley. Except for what he now holds, all other documents are at the Berg Collection.

write a good novel . . . not for about five years and it will keep: Shadow of a Man, dealing with her relationship with Juliette Huxley, was published in 1950: Francis is Sarton, Solange Juliette, and Fontanes Lugné-Poë.

to have money enough . . . to do things for people: Sarton's generosity was legendary, beginning in adolescence and inspired by her mother, who, despite a limited budget and George Sarton's objections, sent $30 every month to the Baranovitches, a white Russian family living in Florence. Sarton herself supported Jewish refugees, poets and writers, political activists, neighbors in Nelson, the children of whom she continued to help to the end of her life, and the lost and lonely who found their way to her door; her entire estate was bequeathed to establishing the Sarton Fellowships for poets and historians of science in perpetuity. As for Juliette, toward the end of her life her money was running out; Sarton sent $10,000, and a video machine, some-

thing which she herself had only recently acquired and from which she was deriv-
ing great pleasure.

A.V. Hill: Archibald Vivian Hill (1886–1977), English physiologist and biochemist who
investigated the liberation of energy in muscles; won the Nobel Prize in 1922 and
1923.

---

12 ORMONDE MANSIONS   Friday, April 16th [1948]
106 SOUTHAMPTON ROW, W.C.I

Dearest one, since I got your second letter yesterday when I went to Kot's
a great peace has descended on me and I feel at last that I have arrived am
not suspended somewhere between air and earth, Purgatory and Heaven.
This morn I went to Cook's and changed my ticket for one for Paris, leaving on the 9:20 train from Victoria (not the Arrow)—Ap. 28th. I'll send
you a <u>wire</u> to Quai Bleriot the day before to give time of arrival, as you
say you will be there on the 27th. I'll leave for Belgium Monday morn, my
birthday, May 3rd. We are both tired, you with reason Heaven knows, I
with none, but I am curiously empty and tired and have terrible nightmares—so we'll be very peaceful, and perhaps have a picnic and sit in a
wood on Sunday? I wish there were a good concert and perhaps there will
be. It is very good for me to come from here as I can use pounds and I
have more pounds than dollars at the moment. Please agree now that if and
when we go out for meals <u>I</u> pay for them. I shall be terribly cross and violent otherwise and make your life miserable. Also, if you are broke, you may
be glad to hear that I wasn't able to find the vague blue blouse. I went to
6 different places, finally found just the thing, only to discover that a button was missing and they had no other. The buttons were covered with the
material and that was part of the charm so it seemed Hopeless. But I did
get the stockings you asked for. So much for <u>les affaires</u>. Except to add that
I would very much like to come back late in May, first see you and then
perhaps Julian whom I do want to see too. I'm delighted to be able now
to stay three weeks in Belgium as I must do some work and that will be a
good time and place. Daddy will be lecturing in Paris at the end of May.
It is my fond hope that we can get you and the Mayers and them together one day for lunch or something.

    Kot is in wonderful fettle. People pour in and out, all bearing gifts and he is really like some god who receives little offerings (the bearers of which live in terror that he will not be placated). The poor woman who brought some Spam was not thanked! I brought beef and was better treated. Yesterday James was there, whom I confess I like less and less because he is always acting and playing the part of James Stephens and it is very tiresome. Especially in contrast to Kot. But there was a dear man called Fulton and one of the Wells boys, adorable. A boy that age melts one's heart to butter. Kot has solved the Negro problem in America and gave a long impassioned discourse on the solution: to ship them all to Liberia. His ideas about UNESCO make me laugh till I cry: Julian simply telling everyone they are blighters and know nothing and must wait 200 years till they are wiser and meanwhile take orders. A world run by Kot would be rather terrifying really—if one were not of the elect.

I am so happy because Mother has really found again her dearest friend, Aunty Lino (Melanie of my book) and it has been so long, I was a little afraid. Also they love Daddy which they have never done before, though how could they help it? But they thought Mother was much too good for him, and perhaps that is true. Women are always too good for men as far as I am concerned.

I hope that in spite of the tension, you are resting a little, just being in one place without too great social responsibilities must be something of a rest. Can you sleep in the afternoon, a real long two-hour rest? That, I think, is the way to manage, then the day is divided in two.

I've read nothing to do anyone's heart good except Cry, the Beloved Country which I'll bring with me for you to read en route to England. I am so happy that you will have a weekend with Francis in Oxford, in his climate. That is good. I am sorry not to see Anthony this time but the days fill up terribly and I will not see more than one person a day. It just means being half there. Kot is dearly demanding and that is my main reason for being here, with Jane and Annie of course. On Monday I go to Kingham to the de Selincourts for four days of peace in the country, though I rather dread the extreme coldness of their house (I never dare turn on the electric heater). I still have an almost perpetual stiff neck and pain in my shoulder from that beastly long infection this winter. Or else, perhaps, old age? I feel about a hundred years old and only hope I don't look it! Yesterday I cried in the hairdresser's (though nobody saw) because they gave me a terrible permanent in the U.S. and the man at Antoine's was quite rude and told me it would never look like anything. Be prepared for the worst!

Dorothy Wellesley, out of the nursing home, has begun to drink again so I shall not go there, at least without Ruth Pitter.

That is all the news.

Dearest love—how splendid to have a definite date when we shall meet at last!

Yours [   ]

---

got your second letter yesterday: among those destroyed on 1 December 1948.

to Quai Bleriot: The Huxleys had moved to 38 Quai Louis-Blériot.

les affaires: business matters.

the Mayers: See footnote to letter dated 13 July 1946 and text of letter dated 16 February 1948.

dear man called Fulton: Probably Dr. Fulton, a Scotch scholar, keeper in the Department of Oriental Printed Books and Manuscripts at the British Museum, for whom Kot had great affection, calling him "little Fulton." Interestingly in their Catalogue 27, Summer of 1992, Waiting for Godot Books of Hadley, Massachuetts, listed a copy of *Encounter in April* inscribed by May Sarton in year of publication "For Dr. and Mrs. Fulton from the author—May Sarton. Feb. 15th, 1937." The cost was $450.

one of the Wells boys: The oldest son of Marjorie Craig Wells, daughter-in-law of H. G. Wells, who had been married to Wells's older son George Philip (Gip); she was among Koteliansky's dearest friends and watched over him in his later years; Sarton admired her.

Aunty Lino . . . Melanie of my book: Céline Dangotte (Limbosch) loved Eleanor Mabel Elwes from the time they were in school together and never ceased loving her to the end of her life; Céline called May her eldest child; when young, May called Céline "Mamie," then "Aunty Lino," and "Lino," and, finally, as an adult, "Celine"; she appears as Mélanie Duchesne in *The Bridge of Years.*

Cry, the Beloved Country: by Alan Stewart Paton (1903–1988), South African novelist and humanitarian. Published in 1948 and one of the few novels to have come out of South Africa to stir the emotions of readers all over the world, it tells of a Zulu minister who, in coming to Johannesburg to find his sister, discovers that she has become a prostitute and his own son a murderer. Maxwell Anderson translated it into the opera *Lost in the Stars,* with music by Kurt Weill.

to the de Selincourts: Basil de Sélincourt (d. 1966), author and critic whose first wife, Anne Douglas Sedgwick, distinguished American writer, died in 1935; brother of Wordsworth scholar Ernest de Sélincourt. He lived with his second wife, Jay, in Kingham, Oxfordshire; one of the first to recognize Sarton as a fine poet in a long critique of *Inner Landscape,* "The Blessing of Augury" in the *Observer* (London) in April 1939: ". . . the intense experience which underlies and unifies [her poetry] has engendered an uncompromising determination to forge and refine the tool for its expression, a tool which is . . . deep searching to the point of ruthlessness, and very delicate." For his visit to Nelson see *Plant Dreaming Deep,* pp. 158–60.

Dorothy Wellesley: See footnote to letter of 14 January 1941.

———

18 Ave. Léquime   Tuesday morning
Rhôdes St. Genèse   [4 May 1948]

My dearest treasure, how strange, how lovely it is to be back again in this high room over the bower of trees—where I came last year, thinking of you and so dazzled and torn because you were off to Italy and couldn't be reached by letter and I tried to phone Paris and O dear, how difficult it all was with the poems spurting out and so much hope and so much fear to carry all alone. Now the storm of flowers is over and all is green and at peace and fulfilled and silent. It is a crystal clear day and I was woken by the sun and by the birds (instead of by cramps for the first time in days!). Everyone thinks the bread in Paris is the answer and I think it may be. Anyway I am eating charcoal madly and penicillin and getting well as fast as possible so that I can work.

When I first came up to the room yesterday afternoon before I unpacked I missed you so horribly, the world seemed desolate and I lay down on the fur rug on my bed (rabbit not ermine!) and then the dear cat came and licked my face and sat on my stomach and purred and I went to sleep. When I woke up I opened the little silver box and read what is inside and all was well.

Stories of my father and mother pour over me here and last night I was too tired. Lino is so upset because Daddy hasn't given Mother one cent of pocket money since they left and lets her pay for flowers for friends etc. and only by miracle, a gift of a friend just as she left, has she anything at all! It hurts her so much, this infernal business of money and now I must try to get Daddy off and somehow find out as if I didn't know that he isn't giving her an allowance and make him do it. Quelle delicatesse cela va demander! He is just like a porcupine, you know, and one can see his quills rise at the very mention of the word money. On Friday I go to Bruges to have lunch with them, which gives me three peaceful days here and I am so glad to have them.

I am afraid you will be horribly tired and I dread the very full days for you, but there will be Kot and Anthony and Francis, and I hope you will take a pill and have some long deep-sleeping nights. Don't try to write letters. Just send me a line one of these days. I do not have to have letters this time. Puisque tu es là, "toujours—Juliette."

I have been thinking of what you said about doing an objective job of writing. I think I know what you meant of the dangers of depending so much on feeling. But darling please remember that for nine or ten months of the year I am sober and thoughtful and give lectures and think about politics and writing technique and then when I come to Europe every-thing explodes, so it is not <u>always</u>. But even in these last days at times I am revolted by having a nature which exploits itself to such a point! I think I am aware of the dangers, more than I used to be. Now what seems impor-tant is continuity, is the deepening and deepening. Is it Gide who says somewhere: "Il faut beaucoup penser pour que un peu de droit à la joie s'achète," (horribly bungled but that is roughly his idea and that I believe), but actually I now remember that it is exactly the other way round and that is even better: "Il faut beaucoup de joie pour qu'un peu de droit à la pensée s'achète," and you see, I am talking nonsense.

I found when I got here a very good analysis of the novel from my publishers which I'll show you when we meet. Everything they say is true and I'm glad to be able to trust them. The failure of the novel is a failure of intensity, so that half the characters are not really <u>created</u>.

What else, my love? I wish to stop and write a poem. Last night I was a little sad because they all seemed to have forgotten it was my birthday and there was apparently no message even from Mother. Then at supper, Nicole brought in a tray covered with lilies of the valley around a magnif-icent cake with all sorts of little presents hidden under the flowers—so dear. Mother has given me a lovely little topaze ring which Grannie wore, Aunty Lino a Chinese plate. I am horribly spoiled! There was a cable from Judy.

But of course you know what my real birthday is—

> this is the birthday of my life
> Because my love has come to me.

I am ashamed of having said superficial things to tease you (the effect of pernod, an evil drink) the other night. And better than say things you won't believe, I shall be silent now. But O my darling, it is good to be loved by you, <u>how</u> good you can perhaps not know.

Theoda is beautiful. More about that when I have finished it. I read quite a lot on the train—very slowly and with great pleasure.

[   ]
May-Juliette

----

all is green and at peace and fulfilled and silent: May had arrived at Juliette's on 28 April and left for Belgium on 3 May; Julian had been away for UNESCO. Of this visit she writes to Bill Brown on 5 May: "The main thing is that what I hoped and staked much on has happened—I think Juliette is out of her darkness and her desert and that means that things are better with Julian than they have ever been. She has accepted once and for all all the bitterness and sterility that that relationship has in it—and this would not have been possible I am quite sure, without love, another love, my love. After twenty four hours of sheer Hell in which I became violently ill with cramps and indigestion and sinus out of nervous tension, we had three unbelievably passionate days and I understand now how much I needed passion and how rare it is——and how also perhaps it never should last because it is too intense. I remember in The Single Hound saying 'Love like this is like a liqueur, one can have too much of it.' It is better to be forever hungry, as I shall no doubt be, than to reach the point where the body lives more intensely than the soul. And this will never happen to us as we shall see each other so very rarely." There was never again to be such a time between them. It was these three days, together with those referred to in her letter of 16 February 1948, which set their seal on the passionate side of what Sarton forever termed their "love affair."

the bread in Paris . . . it may be: Sarton having had nervous indigestion and dysentery believed it might have been caused by the bread.

a gift of a friend just as she left: probably Anne Thorp, who often helped Mabel Sarton and to whom Sarton sent flowers with a note of thanks from Eleanor Mabel Sarton on 16 February, the day the Sartons left for New York to sail on the *Queen Mary* on the 19th.

Quelle delicatesse cela va demander!: What tact that is going to take!

Puisque . . . Juliette: Since you are there, "always—Juliette."

Il faut beaucoup penser . . . : It takes a lot of thinking before we can earn, even a little, the right to joy; *exactly the other way around . . . even better:* One needs a great deal of joy before one earns the right to truly think.

this is the birthday . . . : "Because the birthday of my life/Is come, my love is come to me." Lines from "A Birthday" by Christina Georgina Rossetti (1830–1894), English lyric poet and author of devotional prose.

Theoda: Théoda, a novel by Sabine Corinna Bille (1912–1979), published in Paris in 1946.

[BELGIUM]   [7 May 1948]
FRIDAY NIGHT

Petite flamme bleue, et je t'ai nommé il y a bien longtemps sans savoir! Just back from an adorable day with the family in Bruges—where I did not stay the night because I thought there must be a letter from you and, thank God, there was! I can't type because everyone is asleep and fear you will not be able to read a word. How awful that Anthony the archangel, will have another little burden tied to his feet, but perhaps it will be a marvelous boy to astonish the world and I think he would like to have a son. I love to think of you all day with the babes whom you <u>can</u> kiss and enjoy and adore with all the privilege of being a grandmother, though of course it is quite impossible for me to imagine it—a grandmother all fire and so terribly wonderfully young. But then the only people who are interesting in this sad world are the people who keep their innocence (so much <u>deeper</u> than any other sort of wisdom). On the train I read the <u>Maitre de Santiago</u>—rather <u>grand,</u> in a way, except that the end seems unconvincing. In the preface he said this (which I carried around with me all day, waiting to lay it in your hands):

> Il y a le réel et il y a l'irréel.
> Au delà du réel et au delà de l'irréel,
> il y a le profond.

Now words have so little meaning—and so much. I walk round and round them, searching for the <u>exact</u> truth. All the horizons are pushed very far out for me. Je souffre de tant d'espace, cette perspective infinie où tu es toujours au bout, tant désirée. <u>Darling</u>, I have to come to Paris <u>May 24th</u>, willy-nilly, to hear Daddy speak at the Collège de France on the 26th. Will it be all right? If Julian is there all will be well and I'll stay 2 weeks if you can bear it and see him when he comes back. If, for any reason, you would rather not, I can go to the Mayers. Let me know. But I hope, I hope—though I shall never <u>expect</u> anything, you know.

Bruges was such fun. We sat for a long time in the sun drinking coffee outside after lunch, tasting each other's smiles. Mother (who looks frightfully tired) said she felt like a butterfly opening and shutting its wings very softly on a flower. Then we saw the Memlings (how <u>vividly</u> it brought back to me the day when you and I saw them together in Paris!) and then took a slow put-putting boat and wandered lazily among the canals. We saw two swans gravely doing their courting dance, their long necks just not touching. How I thought of many things, source-qui-donne-soif.

Baltus, the painter-uncle of Maria Huxley was here yesterday when I got back very tired from a long afternoon with Jean Do and called today to say he must make a drawing of me. I dread the time but perhaps it will be good and I can give you a photograph of it. His second wife is a poet.

I wrote Kot, also very circumspectly, and told him the last 3 days were close to peace. I'm glad my cramps served a purpose! But of course, darling, he knows everything in essence, if not in fact. Only we know the facts, or should know them, so that is all right.

I think very much about the delicacy of your face, when it suddenly becomes transparent. Whenever I shut my eyes you are there, so now I'll shut them.

[   ]

But where to send this? You don't say when you leave for Paris! I have an awful cough, but am otherwise all right—cramps all gone.

Petite flamme bleue . . . . : My little blue flame, and I named you that a very long time ago, before I knew!

like to have a son: The Anthony Huxleys had three daughters.

Maître de Santiago . . . seems unconvincing: Le Maître de Santiago (1947), a play by Henri de Montherlant (1896–1972), French war correspondent, novelist, essayist, and dramatist who for a time during the occupation turned on his own people and made peace with the enemy. Set in 1519, the play concerns Don Alvaro Dabo's devotion to meditation, his soul, and his daughter.

Il y a le réel . . . : There is the real and the unreal./Beyond the real and beyond the unreal/is the profound.

Je souffre . . . . : I suffer from this vast space, this infinite perspective where you are always there at the end, and so greatly longed for.

we saw the Memlings: The works of Hans Memling (c. 1430–1494), German-born Flemish painter, which hang in the reliquary of St. Ursula in the hospital of St. John in Bruges, Belgium.

swans . . . not touching: This scene was the genesis of "The Swans," in *Leaves of the Tree* (see *Collected Poems 1930–1993*), of which she writes to Bogan in 1954: "I think I can honestly say that no poem in the book was written without a real experience back of it and the necessity to write it."

source-qui-donne-soif: spring which makes one thirst.

Baltus, the painter . . . wife is a poet: The painter Georges Baltus, professor of fine arts at the Universty of Glasgow, well over seventy-five in 1948, had recently remarried; his first wife had been Sylvia "Vivi" von Hildebrand, daughter of "the Rodin of Munich," Adolf von Hildebrand; his wife at this time was the poet Adrienne Revelard. His drawing of Sarton, which hung in her dressing room in York, is now at Westbrook College, Portland, Maine, and reproduced in this volume.

18 Ave. Lequime   May 10th, 1948
Rhôdes, St. Genèse, Belgium

My treasure, how I loved your letter about Susan and Lucinda tulip-high in Regent's Park and I'm glad the flowers arrived. I suggested various things but they sound as if they had been all right. I wonder what color the carnation was? I wonder when you arrive in Paris as you didn't tell me and I am a little shy of having a barrage of letters there but it cannot be helped. I am sending under separate cover a letter for Elisabeth [Bowen] who is supposed to be in Paris the 11th or 12th for a week, to explain that I shall miss her. I expect <u>Newsweek</u> and its address are in the telephone book. If it is not, just throw the letter away and I'll write later to London. I hope it is not too much of a bother. I put some stamps on the envelope but perhaps not enough.

All morning I've been working at a story about Alyosha, a Russian circus rider who has no horse. It is rather fun—made up out of something one of the girls said one day, a little image which took root. Yesterday I worked and worked to try to get the swans into a poem and I think, failed. But there is this small image of a horse we saw in Bruges:

The Belgian Horse

Great was the pride of the horse
As he danced the cobbles down
Golden and warm his pride
Rippling the glossy shoulder.
Others might prance. He walked
And his walk was a dance.
His walk was a slow pavane
And he was not defeated
Only made great and holy,
Dragging the dirty cart.
He breasted the air like a god
In the power of his joy
That rang like bronze on marble
Long after he had passed.

I made nearly 50 drafts to get even this and it is not much. The swans are much more difficult.

I have my ticket to Paris for May 24th arriving on the 1:20 train—but how far away it seems! Mon Dieu, comment t'attendre tous ces jours et toutes ces nuits? I have written the Mayers hoping that we can both go, you and I, to Daddy's lecture at the Collège de France on the 26th—if you would like to. I think he has surprised people everywhere and at times he can be very fine. Sometimes he is too nervous and over-passionate. Of course if Julian is there you may not be able to go. I wonder what his plans have turned out to be and how all the worries are doing at UNESCO. I fear these will be difficult days for Julian and he must be so tired.

I shall be very anxious to hear about the weekend with Francis and also to have a letter answering mine—as these two of yours were written before you had had any letter. I find it very hard to write. There is too much to say, and too little. Je vis dans un grand silence plein de lumière. Je t'attends aussi. Je t'écoutes. Je te regarde tout le temps. Il m'est horrible-ment difficile de détourner les yeux et je me plonge dans le travail comme dans le sommeil pour me reposer de tant de lumière et de cette nostalgie folle de tes yeux, de tes mains, de toi—la douce impossibilité qui me pour-suit et dans laquelle je n'arrive pas encore à croire. J'ai peur que tu changes. Et j'attends.

The garden here is like a heart. Everywhere one looks at some unex-pected beauty: brilliant crimson tulips, three, standing in the grass, a gorse bush which is just pure gold without a bit of green showing, clematis over the arbor, the loveliest pale purple and white with iris at its feet. And at tea-time the three geese waddle out to beg for crumbs, the cat sits in the grass lapping milk and the dear half-chow dog who is as soft as a teddy bear lies and watches jealously until someone notices him. Things are a little better here though R. is in one of his black moods, does not speak at table and thinks he has grippe.

I read part of St. Ex's Citadel last night. It is really a series of short concentrated myths told by the king of an imaginary country, too con-centrated to be read much of at a time.

On Thursday my darling little mother arrives here for two weeks while Daddy is in Paris. I am longing to spoil her and put her to bed and walk around in the garden with her in the evenings. But also a lit-tle afraid—as all I really want is to be left in peace to write poems and not have to be anyone's child or mother, puisque je suis en ce moment tellement

et

Toute à toi

[   ]

Susan and Lucinda: Anthony Huxley's daughters.

Alyosha . . . image which took root: "Alyosha and His Horse," short story about a Russian circus rider, Alyosha, and a rich, barren woman drawn from Theodora Pleadwell, sculptor, apprentice at the Civic Repertory Theatre and later member of the Associated Actors Theatre; published in *World Review* (English), 1950.

The Belgian Horse: unpublished.

Mon Dieu . . . : Dear God, how am I to wait through all these days and nights?

Je vis dans un grand silence . . . : I live in a great silence, full of light in which I wait for you, listen to you, look at you all the time. It's terribly difficult to turn my eyes away from you to plunge myself into work, as into sleep, to rest from so much light and this mad desire for your eyes, your hands, for you—this peaceful impossibility that haunts me and in which I still cannot believe. I am afraid you will change. And I wait!

the three geese: Of these Sarton immortalized two in "Franz, a Goose" in *A Private Mythology.*

R. is in one of his black moods: Raymond Limbosch, whose bursts of temper, withdrawals, and savage remarks often made Céline cry, came to life on weekends when the children returned home and rekindled his charm.

St. Ex's Citadel: Citadelle by Antoine de St. Exupéry (1900–1944), French novelist, essayist, and aviator who disappeared while on a reconnaissance flight over occupied southern France in July 1944; first published in France in 1948, it appeared in the United States as *Wisdom of the Sands*, a collection of notebooks, in the hypothetical voice of the monarch of a desert empire, written by the author over many years.

puisque . . . toute à toi: because at this time I completely and entirely belong to you.

[BELGIUM]   [early May 1948]

Darling, isn't it marvelous how different our lives are? Yours especially fills me with wonder, more than mine. You bring me children and grandchildren (that lovely image of Kot and Lucinda whom I must see when I go back to London) and a husband and all this intricate web of relationships—and your mother, all a woman's life, and so much more—dazzling riches and gifts. And I take it all and swallow it up and think about it and enter into it through you. And that is wonderful. Yes, you are quite right about the greenness of the poems. I am going to stop, though it [is] awfully hard to stop. The trouble is that it is awfully hard to write about happiness and as I look out of the window onto the garden I am simply steeped in happiness. My head is so full of images all the time and I try to put them down just to get rid of them, as I write to you exasperatedly to stop thinking about you! Two of the snapshots are very good indeed, the other awful. Nobody but you could look so delicious after a champagne lunch and all the rest of it!

It is so lovely having Mother here—and today I went in town about my June ticket to Lausanne and for once didn't have to wait at Cook's or the P.O. and so had a lovely sense of time and walked very leisurely up the Chaussée Charleroi, stopping for <u>filtré</u> and to read the paper, and to buy <u>pain d'épices</u> for tea and chocolate for Mother and a dishmop for Aunty Lino—and the sun was shining—lovely day and lovely to come back from town and come back to my room and the evening light. I have had a migraine for two days, the curse I expect, and so have done nothing useful except to type off "Alyosha and His Horse" and send it to N.Y. I wonder what you will think of it. I must read it to you when I come—between the rings of the telephone! I know you will be busy this time and I shall have to see the Mayers and Lucile Sumpt and various busynesses—and perhaps by then the poems will be riper. It's a good deal a matter of form, really. I must find the <u>form</u>.

Mother is very tired and has slept all day, also with a migraine but when she wakes we talk and talk and there is so much to hear—and to tell, and we keep remembering new things.

I also had a simply adorable letter from Beatrice, about Michael and Kot and my poems which she read so thoroughly, really paying attention. I am grateful. I wrote Kot but haven't had a word from him. I think he must be tired from all the joys and people.

I shall be very anxious to hear how Julian is—how beastly to get intestinal trouble just at the end.

I listen to all you say about the poems and bless you for it. It all helps and gets used and you must feel terribly useful darling, bless you.

When will Monday come? The days are much too short and much too long, but the 24th keeps bobbing up nearer and nearer—and I am there already, shining with happiness.

[   ]

---

filtré: filtered coffee.
pain d'épices: gingerbread.
Lucile Sumpt: Mlle. Lucile Sumpt, a social worker whom Sarton had known in Cambridge
    as a child and saw several times in Paris after World War II.
about Michael: Michael Campbell (1924–198?), son of Beatrice Lady Glenavy, schoolmas-
    ter at Hampstead, journalist on London staff of the *Irish Times*, and novelist; in her
    letter to Sarton of 8 May, Lady Glenavy thanks Sarton for being so kind to Michael
    and quotes him as writing: "May Sarton is the only human being in Paris."

---

18 Ave. Lequime   May 18th, 1948

My angel, what a lovely dear surprise your letter of Saturday arriving on
the holiday yesterday for breakfast. I was feeling horribly depressed after
four days of sinus headache and perhaps also the necessary reaction to such
a fury of work. It is incredible that you have managed to write so often,
and instead of feeling it is little, you should know how marvelous it is to
find time in all you are doing, and to write me so beautifully and justly
about the poems. My darling wonder! Please do not talk about poverty or
about ton coeur creux de ta pauvreté. It makes me so unhappy. I know
only too well what a self-indulgent lazy life I lead compared to yours. But
I can give you perhaps a little taste of this and you give me all your life—
and it is so <u>rich</u>. Of course it would be better if you could have more time
and more peace to live it all inside you, but one can't have everything! And
I think of the so much more difficult poems you create each day for all
those around you; how in the midst of so much detail, so many small material soucis and préoccupations, you still manage always to seem alive to all
the beauties and wonders of the world, and to your friends, and to me.
Can't you for once pin a large invisible medal on your chest and rejoice in
these extraordinary powers? For such they are and for them I love you.
When you get to the door of Heaven you know St. Peter is going to look
at you with great severity and say, "Yes, you were almost an angel on earth,
but now you have got to go to Purgatory for several hundred years until
you have learned to love <u>yourself</u> a little better, and to rejoice in yourself."

    However, I know, I know, darling how the day gets all split up into
particles of this and that and you have so little time to gather yourself and
them together into a whole—and it is a painful and continual dispersion

of your essence. But that is how it will be until UNESCO is over, so you might as well make up your mind to it and seize the precious free hours when they come, as you always do with such extreme <u>virtuosity</u>. (There is really no other word.) I am very cross that you make me say all this again— "I have said it once. I have said it twice. I have said it very loud." But as I have also said, as far as I can see my present work on earth is to try to persuade you of how wonderful and adorable you are and every time you say these awful things I feel that <u>I</u> have failed. Ah, if you were here I would kiss you now and we would not say another word.

Yesterday I spent the day sitting for Baltus in his lovely dirty studio looking out on an immense acacia and a wild ragged garden. I was so tired and sinusy I was glad to sit still (though I felt unbeautiful, my hair is awful, like Haile Selassie Mother says). Baltus did a pastel, a rather startled and very beautiful goddess who has no resemblance to me whatever. I hope he will try again. His wife came and read me poems half the afternoon, not very good, but I enjoyed listening to the words and to her rather overemphatic slow way of reading. It was a nice day, but I was dead when I got home, one hour of hot trolley. We are a niché de misères, as a matter of fact. Mother is so tired, poor lamb, Oncle R. has grippe and is in bed, Nicole has grippe, I am a miserable creature (but I'm better today and shall be well by Monday. How fast it comes! O darling!) I realize now that I misread your letter and that I may miss Julian at this end, but surely I'll be there when he comes back. Whatever happens is good.

I long to see the silvery blue dress. Wonder how the opera was and the great grand party, and the cocktail? Well you can tell me everything next week. You say the dress is <u>white</u>—I thought it was to be pale blue?

I'm glad you like the sonnets. I'm working on the second. I'll enclose a copy of the first swan poem I wrote. Perhaps after all it is better than the second. I felt it lacked spontaneity. You will tell which is best and which to work on. And that is all. I must prepare what I am to say to Jean-Do's class of elderly women profs. this afternoon.

Soon we shall make the hours into days and the days into years and gather everything up dans cet immense embrassement de douceur et de flamme.

[   ]

ton coeur creux de ta pauvrete: your heart hollow from poverty.

soucis and préoccupations: anxieties and concerns.

"I have said it once . . .": unidentified.

Haile Selassie: (1892–1975), emperor of Ethiopia from 1930 until a coup in 1974; modernized his country and brought it into both the League of Nations and the United Nations. Reference is to the wooliness of his hair.

Baltus did a pastel: See footnote to letter of 7 May 1948.

niché de misères: nichée de misères, nestful of miseries.

Nicole: The Limbosches had three daughters, Claire ("Clairette") the oldest, Nicole the next, and Jacqueline the youngest. A son, Jacques, had been killed in a mountain-climbing accident in 1935.

the first swan poem I wrote: See Appendix; this is an earlier version of "The Swans," in *The Leaves of the Tree,* see *Collected Poems 1930–1993.*

Jean-Do's class . . . this afternoon: Before this day, Jean-Do had never heard Sarton read for an audience; Sarton was grieving at this time over Jean Dominique's onsetting blindness and for her reading chose among others "After Teaching"; the last part of "To the Living"; "The Work of Happiness"; "The Lady and the Unicorn"; "What the Old Man Said"; and ended with "Return to Chartres."

dans cet immense embrassement . . . : in this immense embrace of tenderness and passion.

Thursday, May 20th [1948]

My darling love, this is my last letter before I see you and will not be one, as I am struggling through an ocean of correspondence so the decks will be clear when I come. I had such a heavenly dear time reading my poems to Jean Do's little class—et elles en étaient éblouies, parce qu'elles ne s'attendaient pas peut-être au vrai souffle, mais pensent que j'étais la petite amie de Marie et voilà tout. They had brought flowers and a huge box of chocolates and after all the greetings I sat in Jean-Do's chair on the platform in that familiar classroom where I sat as a child, and read first a French translation of each poem and then the poem in English. Jean-Do herself has never heard me read publicly and of course it is much stronger and better when one can use a louder voice—so she was very moved. I ended with Chartres and when I had finished she went over to the wall and unpinned a large photograph of the angel of Chartres and gave it to me. All of this was just formal enough to seem like music and I was awfully happy.

I have been thinking of you, apart from me, very much these days and the sonnets I'll stick in are an attempt to say some of what I've been thinking. You will protest, but don't—accept—ah, that is hard, I know, darling, but just accept and be happy and know that whatever happens to us is good and also that I <u>expect nothing</u>, as I already have more than my heart can hold.

Yours, à lundi—13:20—and don't come yourself if it would be more restful not.

J'éclas de joie!

[   ]

I have to go to the Mayers to dinner the <u>26th</u>.

Variations on a Theme for Juliette

This is the cruel poverty of one
So rich in gifts, so luminous and rare
That where she sits no shadow has the sun,
That where she walks no wind ruffles the air
And in her clear gaze lovers see their love
Grow as the magic coral under sea
Delicate branches that no tempests move,
A world within and a mysterious tree,
And yet she tells them that her heart is hollow,
And yet she walks in poverty alone,
Driven by this self-hatred still to follow
A desert path of sterile rock and bone,
Refusing to admit—lovely, immoral—
The rich sense in her heart that feeds the coral.

Dear innocence, dear wisdom, dearest treasure,
Ask in the dark when you are most alone,
And empty of the day and its full measure,
When heart can speak to heart and bone to bone,
Across this distance and this lonely air
Where you lie open-eyed drinking the night
And I beside you here as thirsty stare,
Ask yourself then if you still have the right
To speak of poverty, if you still dare—
For surely an excess of riches is the key
To this perpetual state of civil war,
And love, poor love, so lost in mystery

Juliette Baillot at
about nineteen.
Courtesy: Francis Huxley

Juliette Huxley,
early 1930s.
Credit: Dorothy Wilding
Courtesy: Francis Huxley

Julian Huxley before portrait of his grandfather T. H. Huxley by John Collier. On left side of mantel, bronze head of a Kikuyu girl by Dora Clarke.
Credit: John Collier
Courtesy: The Berg Collection

Juliette Huxley.
Credit: May Sarton
Courtesy: The Estate of May Sarton

May Sarton at Hampshire Downs, 1936.
Courtesy: The Berg Collection

Sarton at Grundlsee, 1937, with copy of Kennington portrait of Julian on her desk.
Courtesy: The Estate of May Sarton

May Sarton, 1939.
Credit: Crosby Studio
Courtesy: The Estate of May Sarton

Juliette, Julian, and May, picnic
at Savannah Wood, June 1937.
Credit: Alan Best
Courtesy: The Estate of May Sarton

Juliette Huxley.
Courtesy: The Estate of May Sarton

Holograph with hieroglyph,
5 December 1936,
New Haven.
Courtesy: The Berg Collection

Sarton and Julian Huxley at
the Huxleys' apartment at the
London Zoo, c. 1937.
Credit: Juliette Huxley
Courtesy: The Estate of May Sarton

Juliette and Julian Huxley.
Credit: May Sarton
Courtesy: The Estate of May Sarton

Juliette and Julian Huxley.
Courtesy: The Estate of May Sarton

Julian Huxley, birdwatching.
Credit: May Sarton
Courtesy: The Estate of May Sarton

Juliette Huxley in the library
at 31 Pond Street, 1950s.
Credit: Tom Blau
Courtesy: Francis Huxley

Juliette Huxley at Les Diablerets
in Switzerland, c. 1930.
Courtesy: Francis Huxley

Portrait of Julian Huxley by
Eric Henri Kennington
(1888–1960).
Courtesy: The Berg Collection

Drawing of May Sarton
by George Baltus, 1948.
*Courtesy: The Estate
of May Sarton*

Sketch of Sarton by
Elizabeth Bowen, at
2 Clarence Terrace,
4 June 1937.
*Courtesy: The
Berg Collection*

Pencil drawing of
May Sarton by Polly
(Ethel) Thayer, 1936.
*Courtesy: The Estate
of May Sarton*

Portrait of May Sarton,
1936, by Polly (Ethel)
Thayer.
*Courtesy: The Fogg Art
Museum, Harvard
University Art Museums.
Gift of Paul J. Sachs
through Polly Thayer
and May Sarton*

Portrait of Sarton by Agnes Sims,
Santa Fe, New Mexico, 1945.
Courtesy: The Estate of May Sarton

Julian's first party as Director General of Unesco in Paris, 15 July 1946, with Walter Laves, assistant Director General, and his wife from the United States.
Courtesy: Francis Huxley

Julian Huxley, about to be knighted, 1958, beside the Kennington portrait.
Courtesy: The Estate of May Sarton

Julian and Aldous Huxley, c. 1950.
Credit: W. Suschitzky
Courtesy: Francis Huxley

Juliette and Julian looking for gorillas in Uganda, 1960.
Courtesy: Francis Huxley

Sarton in the garden of Le Pignon Rouge, the Limbosch's home in Brussels, Belgium, where she wrote so many of the poems for Juliette. *Courtesy: The Estate of May Sarton*

Juliette Huxley.
Courtesy: The Estate of May Sarton

Juliette and Julian Huxley in the library at 31 Pond Street, 1960s. *Credit: W. Suschitzky Courtesy: Francis Huxley*

Sarton at Wild Knoll,
7 December 1986.
*Credit: Beatrice
Trum Hunter*

May Sarton, from
"Live Reading—1987,"
Ishtar Films.
Courtesy: Martha Wheelock

"And my dress . . . the
sleeves open like brilliant
wings . . . brilliant patterns
which remind me of my
mother's designs."

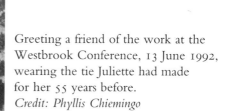

May Sarton at
Wild Knoll, 1992.
Credit: Don Cadoret

Greeting a friend of the work at the
Westbrook Conference, 13 June 1992,
wearing the tie Juliette had made
for her 55 years before.
Credit: Phyllis Chiemingo

May Sarton, 1992, a photograph she dubbed "the bliss of old age."
Courtesy: The Estate of May Sarton

Sarton, receiving her eighteenth honorary degree at the
University of New England, 13 May 1995,
eight weeks before her death.
Courtesy: The Estate of May Sarton

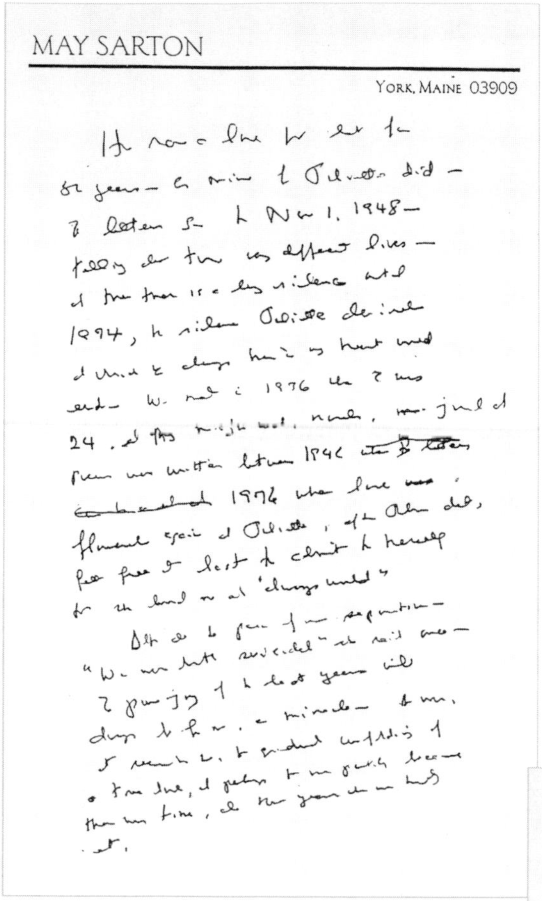
MAY SARTON

YORK, MAINE 03909

Holograph of "Fragment Three"
from Drafts of Introductions
by May Sarton, 1995.
Courtesy: The Estate of May Sarton

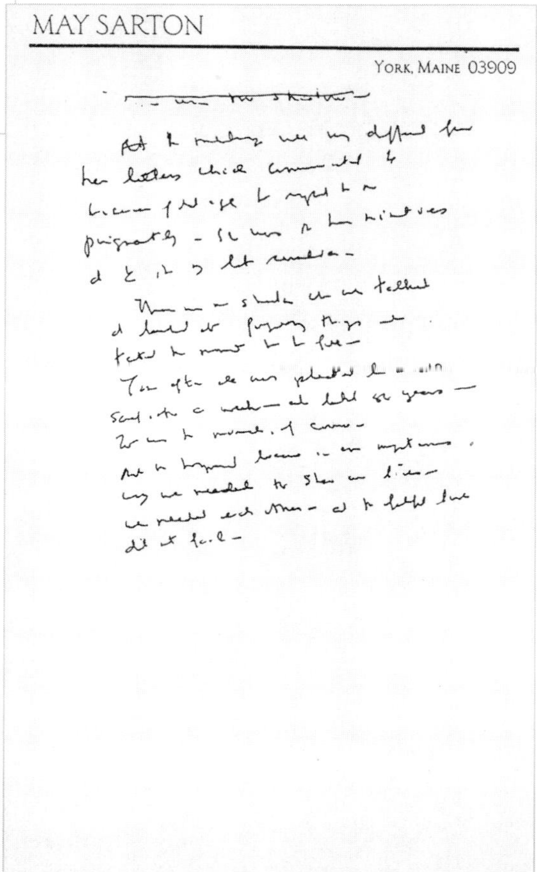
MAY SARTON

YORK, MAINE 03909

Holograph of "Fragment Five"
from Drafts of Introductions
by May Sarton, 1995.
Courtesy: The Estate of May Sarton

Sarton at Wild Knoll, 1992.
Credit: Susan Sherman

Resolves the question if you could but live
To measure what you have by what you give.

When I consider your lie and its scope,
So small in peace, so multiple in stress,
In time so long, and yet so brief in hope,
In essence deep, in action various,
So rich in its demands, so poor in space,
Where the world tends to scatter and disperse
The kernel of yourself, your human face,
I marvel that you do not rage and curse
But spend so lavishly your little treasure,
The single hour saved from the busy day
And all delights and graces without measure
Pour out in these rich letters where you say
You starve for lack of what you most possess,
A lavish heart, love, and inwardness.

I do not think the key stone of the arch
Where many tensions meet and are made one,
The single stone that holds the entire church,
Mastered by all and yielding still to none,
Could ever be called poor or even humble,
But rich beyond all telling, it sustains
The full weight of the arch and does not crumble,
And proud beyond all dreaming, it remains
Simply itself and never breaks apart.
Now in the image of this princely stone
I set your name within the poem's heart:
Call yourself poor and humble and alone,
Yet still admit you join and hold in balance
This arch of triumph founded upon silence.

[ ]
May 20, 1948

————

et elles en étaient . . . : and they were dazzled because they had probably not expected to
   hear a true voice, thinking I was merely Marie's young friend and that's all.
the angel of Chartres and gave it to me: This photograph remained pinned on the wall opposite Sarton's desk in York until her death.
the sonnets I'll stick in: "Variations on a Theme for Juliette," four unpublished sonnets, part
   of the larger series "These Images Remain"; see *The Land of Silence.*
á lundi—13:20: until Monday at 1:20.
J'éclas de joie: I am bursting with joy.

VOUVRAY, LE PETIT BOIS,   June 4th, Friday Eve. [1948]

Mon très doux trésor, tu es partout et nulle part—tu es déjà là avec Kot sur le sofa jaune devant mes yeux, et j'ai le petit paletot bleu sur moi (Dieu, qu'il fait froid dans cette maison inhabité depuis tout l'hiver!) et Le Sourire de Paris est là sur le mur et l'ange de Chartres. Mais malgré tout cela je ne suis vraiment ce soir qu'un cri éperdu qui te cherche. Et comme tu seras loin et étrange déjà dans des pays que je ne connais pas quand tu recevras cette lettre! I am not yet, darling, in that state of grace which the long working days ahead will bring and when I hope I shall have become used to not seeing you or only in those intense flashes of memory. It was a marvelous drive down here. At Versailles we had engine trouble and it was so cold and miserable but in an hour all was fixed and we set out and suddenly there was the sun and great clouds and the immense plateau of the Beauce with hundreds of poppies down through the wheat and bluets and then fields of purple clover mixed with poppies and bluets, the richest tapestry. And finally the twin towers of Chartres far off in the distance. I felt that I was in the center of France. We hardly talked and it was very peaceful. Grace drove the whole way and seems to have survived though we are both nearly dead now after unpacking the car and ourselves and tea and getting food in the village and facing all the domestic problems of bedmaking, getting things a bit straightened out. How lonely it would have been for her to come alone and I am glad I am here. By Monday I hope the daily rhythm can be established, the maid really found (she is several possibilities at present) and the weather warmer. They say the new moon comes Monday and the weather will change so perhaps you will have a lovely flight.

I think of you, I'm afraid, all the time. And I am still full of those stars you sowed so prodigally last night. Now I am going to close the gate for the night and to see if I can make us some supper. I had a small glass of whiskey and was fearfully grateful to you for it. I am glad of the last poem because it comforts me too. I hope it comforts you. I hope you miss me. I shall finish this in the morning.

9:00 A.M.

I've just gone down for breakfast. Grace is asleep. The sun is out and I forgot yesterday to speak of the air which is so gentle and soft it is like a caress.
It's not cold out, only inside the house but I have invented a system with
a hot water bottle on a pillow under my feet and wrapped like an Indian
in a huge blanket, I feel fine. And where are you, my bird?

　　　This is no letter. I have to be silent now and try to grow. I think a lot
of what you said of pleasure and joy. I think of the peace of that last night,
the immense final peace. How deep the heart is opened and how will it
ever close?

[　]

Now silence speaks for me, grows like a weed
Up through the day. There are no singing words,
Only the dull dark absence and the empty need,
The night is full of sad and silent birds.
Poems accuse me that I cannot learn.
They have one word and it is absence, absence,
And this word does not sing and does not burn,
Is dark and heavy, full of sleep and nonsense.
I am nothing. I have lost myself in dreams.
Climb the interminable stairs within the heart
And never find the window or the hidden streams,
Only this prison and the doors that part.
At night I am a voice crying your name—
Where is the pure song and the fervent flame?

[　]
Vouvray
June '48

June 4th: On 25 May 1948, Sarton writes to Bill Brown of the eleven days between 24
　　　May and the date of this letter, days which Sarton was to spend at the Huxleys' apart-
　　　ment on the Quai Louis-Blériot: "I was very happy to find your letter when I got
　　　here, rather battered last night—as Julian who was to have been away for a week in
　　　N.Y. is ill and can't go—it is, I must say, a rather terrific blow and I am staggering.
　　　. . . I am learning a lot about myself and life in general. I am more and more con-
　　　vinced, aren't you? that passion is by its very nature tragic and must always end trag-

ically—and the greater it is, the more inevitable the tragic end becomes—(as in the great love stories, Tristan etc.). It is something <u>outside</u> life and that is what makes it so tremendous and so impossible. I am more and more grateful that my relationship with Judy has never really been passionate (I understand better now that it never really was) as that is what will make it last. But how hard it is to learn these things and how much one must suffer to learn them." And to Judith Matlack on 26 May: "Julian finally went away for two days to London and so I have been able to recapture a little peace with Juliette and that is good as I was near to distraction. When they are here together the tensions as you know are terrific." And on 1 June to Matlack: "The house is full of roses opening, too open—they are almost falling and I feel a little like that. I wonder sometimes what makes one consciously and with eyes perfectly open walk into such self-made Hells. But I shall be out of this in two days with such a store of suffering that I expect to outdo Shakespeare in a sonnet sequence. But one keeps on learning and as you know, at the root of all this is my real love for <u>both</u> Huxleys and that is what makes it easier."

Mon très doux trésor . . . : My sweet treasure, you are everywhere and yet nowhere—you are there before my eyes on the yellow sofa with Kot, I am wearing the little blue coat (God it's cold in this house which has been empty all winter) and 'The Smile of Paris' and the angel at Chartres are here on my wall, but in spite of all that I am nothing but a lost soul searching for you and as you are already in a faraway and strange country, I don't know when you will receive this letter.

la sofa jaune: The yellow sofa. In a photograph appearing in this volume, Sarton and Julian are seated on this sofa. In 1942 Juliette had written that "in spite of every chance of its being blitzed next week" the yellow sofa Sarton had loved had to be recovered in a serviceable, unglamorous beige. "It doesn't shine like a bee's wing and make you think of sunny banks."

already in a faraway and strange country: On 6 June the Huxleys left for Czechoslovakia, Hungary, and Yugoslavia, a trip postponed from 1947.

immense plateau of the Beauce: The Beauce, the ancient district of north-central France, is now part of the departments of Loir-en-Cher and Eure-et-Loir; Chartres was its ancient capital.

twin towers of Chartres far off in the distance . . . center of France: "We came to Chartres, riding the green plain,/The spear of hope, the incorruptible towers,/The great tree rooted in the heart of France/Blazing eternally with sacred flowers." From "Return to Chartres" in *The Lion and the Rose.*

Now silence speaks for me . . . . : unpublished sonnet from the sequence "These Images Remain" in *The Land of Silence.*

VOUVRAY   June 6th, 1948

O my darling, what images of you I have, what a treasure—the blue dress, the pink hat and you all gold and shining at the station the first time; you kneeling before Janet and looking about fifteen; you sewing the lace on your slip having an awful time threading a needle with an obstinate look which I loved; and running away from the car on the Ave. Kléber in a black suit and your legs like a deer's so nervous and delicate and you asleep, a secret child; and you with a brilliant scarf at your throat in a black dress in the restaurant, and once looking down into the table as if you were for once really pleased with yourself. I who forget everything remember these things precisely. It is a great joy.

Life here still feels rather strange, though at moments I breathe the time and the space and know that all will be well. I did not expect to feel quite so cut in two, nor quite so desolate and for 24 hours I was frightened, not daring to lie down on my bed for fear I would begin to cry and if I once began would never stop. But a certain order and rhythm is beginning to be possible. We have a maid. But alas, this morning she was to have made our breakfast and when I went down to open the gate at half-past seven in the rain I discovered that the electricity was en panne (all the current cut off till six tonight!). Finally I went down and heated some water for our breakfast on a neighbor's gas range. We shall have to go to town for lunch which is bad for Grace. She is really ill, poor lamb, and so about a third of a person. But last night we did have a long talk about Scweitzer (we have a mutual acquaintance who has gone out to Lambaréné to be a nurse in the hospital) and there are many tales of the people around here which I glean little by little. These are noble people. Whenever I come here I realize again that this is France, not Paris. I have never seen such poverty maintained with such complete dignity and absence of self-pity. Yesterday we met Mlle. Penautot in the village—a woman who lives in one room, sleeps on a paillasse, hasn't even a candle at night to light her and lives by charring and raising rabbits. But she walks and talks like a princess speaking of a child as "having great distinction." We met at the butcher's Roberte, who worked for Grace last year. Roberte was deserted by her husband, a prisoner of war, before her baby was born and now is wholly responsible for a paralysed grandmother and the baby, gets up at five, cooks for them, makes the beds, gets the old lady settled in her chair and then works in a button factory, comes home to cook the noon meal, etc. She looks like a pretty delicate girl, no sign of bitterness or of the huge hopeless burdens she carries. My heart melts when I think of these people. It is humbling.

The day we arrived—did I tell you?—we stopped at the Javarry's farm. There they were with a great mountain of peas on the table, eating their noon meal at four as they had been to get a new hive of bees—and we talked of peas and bees and tasted the 1947 Vouvray which is a marvel. Madame Javarry is rich as people go here, but walks the three miles back and forth to town every day. Her son looks like a Spaniard and spent two years in bed with t.b. after the war.

But have you time to read all this? I am talking as if you were here as indeed you are. You live in my room and when I come upstairs I come back to you and to my real self. Darling, I haven't thanked you for all the things you piled in at the last minute—and all so useful! The rye biscuits have been keeping Grace alive. The gin has been keeping me alive! And the potato chips!

But as I think of it all, I think too of what it means to run a house as beautifully as you do and this is one of your talents which I have seemed perhaps not to notice, but I think I can imagine what it means in imagination and forethought, just one more of the multiple threads you hold so apparently easily in your hands. You make wherever you are, on a picnic, in a strange apartment a wonderful shelter.

There are other things for which I can't thank you yet. But I shall instead copy part of one of those prayers of Péguy for Chartres. You can take it as a secular poem, for the moment:

> Voici le lieu du monde où tout devient facile,
> Le regret, le départ, même l'événentent,
> Et l'adieu temporaire et le détournement,
> Le seul coin de la terre où tout devient docile.
>
> Et même ce vieux coeur qui faisait le rebelle;
> Et cette vieille tête et ces raisonnements;
> Et ces deux bras raidis dans les casernements;
> Et cette jeune enfant qui faisait trop la belle.
>
> Voici le lieu du monde où tout est revenu
> Après tant de départs, après tant d'arrivées.
> Voici le lieu du monde où tout est pauvre et nu
> Après tant de hasards après tant de corvées.
>
> Voici le lieu du monde et la seule retraite,
> Et l'unique retour et le recueillement,
> Et la feuille et le fruit et le défeuillement,
> Et les rameaux cueillis pour cette unique fête.

Voici le lieu du monde où tout rentre et se tait,
Et le silence et l'ombre et la charnelle absence,
Et le commencement d'éternelle présence,
Le seul réduit où l'âme est tout ce qu'elle était.

It was a great blessing to have your little word yesterday (how quickly it came on the wings of the morning!) and the two cards, the strange impassive smile of the god. I stole the car and rushed down to send a wire late that afternoon as I suddenly realized the P.O. would be closed today and I couldn't reach you for so long.

Darling, I hope the little book will be filled with images of places and lakes and churches and new and wonderful people who believe they are making a new world, and that perhaps you can believe them. I shall be so anxious to hear, but do not try to write more than a card now and then. Sleep when you can. Think of me—as I do of you with all my heart. And above all, <u>be happy</u>. Que notre joie demeure. At night I lie on your shoulder at peace.

[   ]

Marcus!

———

kneeling before Janet: Janet Flanner (1892–1978), American journalist and novelist; settled in Paris in 1922, and in 1925 began writing the Paris letter in *The New Yorker* under the pseudonym Genêt, given her by Harold Ross; these Paris letters provided a vast record of social, political, and cultural events covering half a century.

en panne: broken down.

long talk about Scweitzer: Albert Schweitzer (1875–1965), Alsatian philosopher and theologian whose ethical beliefs were based upon his "reverence for life"; noted musician, expert on Bach, and founder of a medical mission at Lambaréné, Gabon (then French Equatorial Africa). Nobel Prize in 1952.

paillasse: straw mattress.

Madame Javarry is rich as people go here: Mme. Javarry, a *vigneronne,* or winegrower, had a stone farm near Grace Eliot Dudley's Le Petit Bois in Vouvray.

Voici le lieu du monde . . . . : verses from "Prière de Résidence" in *Cinq Prières Dans la Cathédrale de Chartres* (Five Prayers in the Cathedral at Chartres) (Gallimard, 1947) by Charles Péguy (1873–1914), French poet and essayist whose work is marked by his patriotism and faith. Trans: Here is the corner of the world where all becomes light/Regret, departures, even emergencies/Farewells and diversions/¶ The only corner of the world where all becomes manageable./And even this old heart that played the rebel/And this old head and its reasonings/And these two stiffened arms in their barracks/And this young infant acting the beauty./¶ Here is the place where all return/After so many departures, after so many arrivals/Here is the one place in the world where all are stripped down, poor and naked/After so much unforeseen, after so many labors./¶ Here is the only corner, the only resting place/the unique communion and meditation/And the leaf and fruit and deflowering/And the branches gathered for this transcendant celebration./¶ Here is the place on earth where all enter and are silent/And the silence and shade and absence of desire/And the beginning of holy presence,/The only sanctuary where the soul is all that it ever was.

making a new world: Reference to the Communists who had gained full control of Czechoslovakia and Hungary.

Que notre joie demeure: May our joy abide.

Marcus: unidentified.

Vouvray   le 11 juin, 1948

You are everywhere and nowhere. Your hand is on me. You are kneeling in the forest. You, who are water which makes one thirst, where are you? And what are you doing, little blue flame, so faraway. Are you seeing the same crescent moon as I am, with the same very brilliant planet beside it, perhaps it is Venus? Above what city unknown to me, above what towers of what church—or over what great empty space full of absence? During two days of anguish I stopped smoking. Everything in my life seemed a mess, a mad expense, meaningless with no place of secret refuge, so that I just wanted to hide away and be silent. But then yesterday after a day of marketing in Tours with Grace staggering, suddenly poetry returned. I resumed smoking like an old Turk. Birds are singing in my branches—nothing very good, a little groan, but I feel alive again after such difficult days—if you were here we would laugh. Grace is truly ill, poor thing. She can't digest anything and she looks like a wraith. And all that with the most admirable courage. It must be horribly discouraging—this condition has lasted a year now. We've been to a doctor, but the drugs only make her feel worse—she must see him again. I said that if you were here we would laugh, and it's a little strange to follow that sentence with this about poor Grace's illness, but as she is ill, she becomes rather vague, rather like a cloud, forgetting to order meals, becoming maniacially absorbed by "things," afraid that I am going to pour coffee on my skirt or get a drop of wine on the tablecloth, to the point that I become so nervous I will doubtless break all the dishes out of sympathy with her fears. But then it's not my house and I have no authority so everything is very disorganized. Finally, I finished a short story—not bad. When I feel smothered in the garden and its walls close in, I go out into the country and look at the red poppies—and the great fields of wheat trembling in the wind. I love my room, my books, my little table, the flowers which make it an arbor—and I don't really understand why I am so sad, horribly sad, or where this sadness comes from which I don't want and which overwhelms me.

I am waiting for news of Marshal Tito and his "hat of roses." Ella Winter, Jo Davidson's friend, came back dazzled by Yugoslavia—among other things by the Marshal himself, whom she spoke of as a handsome god, powerful and bold. She said there weren't any "neurotics" in that country. I must say I don't see the charm of a country so deprived.

Interruption while I have a long talk with Ploujou, the gardener (lovely name) who helps out the 80-year-old Père Bonot who works here. Long talk about the bill, about les limaçons who are devouring the garden, and all this reported to Grace who is in bed, the ghost of herself, gazed at tenderly by the deer we painted on her wall years ago.

In Tours I discovered my train, which leaves Tours at 9:06 A.M. Sunday and arrives in Paris at 12:45. I wonder when your plane arrives. I expect UNESCO will be closed on Sunday? But I'll be there anyway and do send a wire to 38 Quai L.B. if you don't get off. Michael sent me his story re-written and much better after my suggestions. It is more than I have done with your suggestions, darling, and I feel ashamed. Here is something by Bergson about joy and pleasure which you might like:

> Philosophers who have speculated on the significance of life and the destiny of man have not sufficiently remarked that Nature has taken pains to give us notice every time this destiny is accomplished; she has set up a sign which apprises us every time our activity is in full expansion; this sign is joy; I do not say pleasure. Pleasure, in point of fact, is no more than an instrument contrived by Nature to obtain from the individual the preservation and the propagation of life; it gives us no information concerning the direction in which life is flung forward. True joy, on the contrary, is always an emphatic sign of the triumph of life. Now, if we follow this new line of facts, we find that wherever joy is, creation has been, and that the richer the creation, the deeper the joy.

(execrable translation but I haven't the French).

I have been meditating on this paragraph and hope to do something with it. The question is perhaps what does passion create when it doesn't create children? For me, of course, poems. For you, it could be joy, but I wonder? Does one lose oneself to find oneself? And if the self is not found then there is something wrong. But passion itself is also a creation, a creation which creates <u>peace</u>. Sometimes there seems no other way at all to peace.

Soon the mailman will be here—with a letter? I am terribly curious to hear all your impressions. Ella came back on a great wave of hope and enthusiasm. What will you think?

All my love, darling. I'm sorry the poem is sad. But that is finished now. I am back in myself. I am finding the riches hidden in your absence. I am happy.

[   ]

This letter, up to "Interruption while I have a long talk with Ploujou," is in French; see Appendix for original.

kneeling in the forest: Forêt à genoux; virtually untranslatable. Possibly a reference to Juliette's "kneeling before Janet"; see letter of 6 June 1948.

Marshal Tito and his "hat of roses": Leader of Yugoslavia Marshal (Josip Broz) Tito's hostility to the Soviet Union culminated on 28 June 1948 with the Cominform expelling Yugoslavia from membership; three weeks later in July the Yugoslavian Communist Party gave him a vote of confidence, and the party was purged of Cominform supporters.

Ella Winter, Jo Davidson's friend: Ella Winter, English writer, author of *And Not to Yield;* divorced from Lincoln Steffens, married Donald Ogden Stewart, one of the "Hollywood Ten," friend of Sarton and Muriel Rukeyser. Jo Davidson, sculptor, friend of the Huxleys who lived at Bécheron in Tours and sculpted most of the famous people of his time. His bronze bust of Julian was eventually acquired by UNESCO.

les limaçons: the snails.

Michael: Michael Campbell; see footnote to letter of early May 1948 from Belgium.

Bergson about joy and pleasure: Henri Bergson (1859–1941), French philosopher; this passage is quoted in *The Re-Creating of the Individual* by Beatrice M. Hinkle.

all your impressions: of Yugoslavia.

THURSDAY AFTERNOON   [17 June 1948]

Darling angel, how happy I was to have your long letter from the packard. How did you ever do it, so tired and with so much ahead and behind? And now this is not to answer but just to tell you, in case you get in on Sat. as my hurriedly taken notes suggest that you were to leave Vienna for Prague on Sat. and hence I imagine you might have flown to Paris Sat. and not Sun. as I thought? Anyway my train gets in at 12:45 P.M. on Sunday so if you are there wait for me and we can go round the corner for lunch. I should be there before 1:30 unless I can't get a taxi, in which case I'll phone.

We are off to Tours for the second time today in a rafale of pluie et vent to have Grace radiographiée. If by chance she has to be operated we would drive to Paris Sunday but if so I'll wire and anyway will be there by tea time.

I can't quite believe I'll see you and perhaps indeed this is being written to an imaginary person for whom imaginary red carpets are laid down in Zagreb and Belgrade and who charms imaginary Ministers. It will be interesting to see if you are real—ah, love!

[   ]

I have written one real poem at last, but it needs work and your critical eye.

---

letter from the packard: Apparently Juliette had written a letter while riding in a Packard; said letter is not extant.

in a rafale of pluie et vent: in a downpour of rain and wind.

radiographiée: X-rayed. On this day Grace Dudley had x-rays of her stomach and intestines taken.

one real poem at last: Probably sonnet #2 of "These Images Remain"; "Even such fervor must seek out an end . . ." in *The Land of Silence.*

The following day, 18 June 1948, it was determined from her x-rays that Grace Dudley had a definite obstruction. Doctors told Sarton privately that it was surely cancer; Grace Dudley believed it an ulcer. On 20 June, Sarton returned to Paris to see Juliette, who had returned alone from Central Europe, Julian traveling on without her. On that day Sarton drove Grace Dudley from Vouvray to the American Hospital in Neuilly, staying at the Huxleys', and because she had to remain in Paris until Grace was operated on, was unable to meet her parents as planned in Bex, Switzerland. Grace's operation was unexpectedly postponed when her doctor was called to Brussels. She was operated on at three in the afternoon on Wednesday, 30 June; the entire stomach was removed, and the doctors felt confident that the can-

cer had been contained and would not return. During the days May lived at the Huxleys' at 38 Quai Louis-Blériot, she and Juliette walked around Nôtre Dame, attended the ballet and art exhibits, sat for hours at the Deux Magots, had lunches at home and dinners out, and shared friends, among them Janet Flanner and Freya Stark. By 28 June they were preparing for Julian's return. The evening of 30 June, the day of Grace Dudley's operation, May wandered alone through Paris because the Aldous Huxleys had arrived and wanted to be en famille; *she had been made to feel redundant. Although Juliette had awakened her at two-thirty that morning to watch astounding fireworks over the Seine, the following day, 1 July, in a cryptic date book Sarton wrote simply, "The terrible night." The next morning the Huxleys left for three days in the country while Sarton stayed on in their apartment, entertaining Bill Brown, who was in Chartres for a month with the Experiment in International Living. On 5 July the Huxleys returned and Sarton writes of that last night in Paris before leaving the next morning to meet her parents in Montreux: "One of the peaks [with Juliette] . . . a long talk and afterwards I read her all of the poems very quietly—later by a miracle we were able to spend most of the night together—so I am leaving with all my wounds mended." Later Sarton would write to Juliette of this time, comingled in memory with the early days of May 1948.*

MONDAY, 8:30 A.M.   [July 1948]

O my treasure, your letter of Thurs. arrived this minute, held up by the douane because of the ticket I expect. Healing letter and I am ashamed now of the sadness of my last. I've just read the Gide (which I had marked <u>of course</u>!) and will take your letter in my pocket for we start out through large ominous clouds and probably rain in a little Renault which I shall drive to Sion and perhaps Sierre, hoping the valley may be less gray than here. Your letter brings me back my love. O darling, I had got into such a tangle a jungle of nerves and fears, trying to read your silence, imagining that you hated me and knowing too well all the reasons why you might— what is known as a tailspin! How foolish—forgive me. I think perhaps I've really caught a small germ and it is physical and not mental what is wrong with me—a slight fever and an almost continual migraine headache. If it doesn't go tomorrow I shall stay in bed.

How sad the party wasn't better—perhaps everyone too tired? And the maudite femme de chambre—but have you been able to get Nellie back? The attendant angel with her laughter? How can Louise be tired out so soon? O my dear, what a damnable business it is.

Last evening was a perfect serene evening with that mist at the foot of the mountains so they looked transparent above a deep green lake and the trees all shining in the light—and we sat out and drank an aperitif on the terrasse here for the first time. And now these heavy clouds.

I think of you all the time, but I had lost my joy these last days—agonies of self-reproach from which nothing good ever comes. But your letter makes all well—and I kiss your wrists and your eyes. And we must go.

[   ]

---

douane: customs.

sadness of my last: not included in this volume.

the Gide: On 23 June in Paris, Juliette presented Sarton with André Gide's Journal 1889–1939 to replace the copy Sarton had lent to her friend Gerhart Speyer, who had lost it; this volume, inscribed as a gift from the Huxleys, Paris 1948, was still in Sarton's possession at the time of her death.

Sion: Capital of the Swiss canton of Valais, where Rilke lived in the Château de Muzot from 1921 to 1922 and where he wrote the Orpheus sonnets and Duino Elegies. See "At Muzot" in In Time Like Air; see also footnote to letter of 19 July 1938.

the maudite femme de chambre: the damned chambermaid.

Nellie: possibly the old faithful who looked after Leonard Huxley and his second wife, Rosalind Bruce.

HOTEL BRISTOL   Tuesday, July 13th [1948]
[MONTREUX, SWITZERLAND]

We are again wrapped in silver and soft clouds, feathers of cloud lying in the crevasses of the mountains opposite and just above the lake a great bank out of which the dark peaks emerge, and further away mountains change into mist and become transparent, the lake very pale grey-green and slightly ruffled so it doesn't reflect. With my breakfast, the book and your long letter. O darling, how rich and wonderful your letters are. How I devour

them and eat them and rejoice in them and you. But before I answer this
I must tell you about yesterday, our fabulous day into the Valais, la Noble
Contrée, so gentle and valiant, in the funny gasping old Ford 6 which
almost blew off the road and panted up the hills like a small dragon. You
will never forgive me, I think, for being so glad to get into real country and
away from this lake which I admire but have no feeling for. The minute we
came to the amber fields in the valley, to the steep hillsides shelved in vines,
to the sturdy old farms, all that green set in relief against white peaks—I
began to feel well and happy and at ease with the earth. How lovely and
rich and dear and secret. I longed for you so much, having dreams of coming here with you before we die for a long month or even a week and
wandering and discovering and lying in the grass, of finding wild flowers
and being wild flowers ourselves. We aimed for Sion—do you know it?—
with its two steep hills, one crested by a mediaeval castle in ruins and one
with a 13th century church? It looks exactly like the magical scenes one
glimpses through the windows of 15th century portraits. The town itself
below rather grand and Catholic, sumptuous houses with tiers of iron bal-
conies and large courts, a bishop's town, you know, with I am sure a small
jealous aristocracy. We stopped for coffee while I went to ask the police
where Muzot, Rilke's little chateau could be found and they didn't know,
so on we went to Sierre where there might be hope. Here the valley opens
and smiles and there is room on the gentle slopes for innumerable villages
and church towers. This is La Noble Contrée:

> Chemins qui ne mènent nulle part
> entre deux prés,
> que l'on dirait avec art
> de leur but détournés,
>
> chemins qui souvent n'ont
> devant eux rien d'autre en face
> que le pur espace
> et la saison.

I ran into a hotel to ask again, and everyone was so apologetic explaining
they had only been there a year. The old Italian porter beamed and said he
himself wrote poems but had never heard of Rilke—and then a little maid
came and said, "But it is just up the hill, the next on the left." It seemed
like a miracle and off we went, winding round and round, panting and

coughing and the engine steaming like a train engine, higher and higher till we came to a most beautiful ancient village gathered round a church and what looked like Rilke's house—a steep rectangular forbidding stone building—and looking down into the valley, to the Rhône and the most luminous mountains. But it was not. It was Venthone instead and we had gone too far and missed a turning, so we crept down again and into gentler pastures and saw the little house in the distance. Here, after a terrible long silence, years, Rilke wrote "The Sonnets to Orpheus" and the great Elegies all in three weeks. It is an adorable place. We wandered all around it, through thick grass fairly springing with water, so you felt a fountain might jet up under each footstep, streams running down on every side, channeled very carefully and here and there bursting into tiny waterfalls over a rock. We looked through the fence into the very much loved and cared for garden, just careless enough, just secret enough—and then we lay down in the grass for awhile and ate our lunch and waited hoping the guardian would come back, the "demoiselle" a little boy told us lived there. But she never did and so we left the magic place and drove back to Sion where Daddy was determined to climb one of the mounts and see the Museums—Mother and I now hot and tired—but it was worth the climb to be once more in these airy places, les pentes remplies de vignes, les grands aperçus adoucis par tous les travaux de la terre, une ampleur, une douceur partout.

The museum was interminable because the <u>gardien</u> was very lame and took hours to descend each stair and also was so conscientious that he must tell everything about each object. Daddy, inexorable, and we obedient. I felt like a goat let out of a stable when finally we found the sun again and leapt down the rocks to find the car and tea and make for home. Altogether a golden day. Darling, we must go there together.

> Mais non seulement le regard
> de ceux qui travaillent les champs,
> celui des chèvres prend part
> à parfaire le lent
>
> aspect de la Noble Contrée.
> On la contemple toujours
> comme pour y rester ou pour
> l'eterniser

dans un si grand souvenir
qu'aucun ange n'osera,
pour augmenter son éclat,
intervenir.

Daddy spent the evening writing Rilkeian postcards to undeserving profs. He loves almost as much as I do to make literary pilgrimages!

Tomorrow Meta, Mother's old flame, comes. I am longing to see her. She has had a most gruelling life of one incredible tragedy after another and now she has married, alas not for love, but somehow she has kept her <u>fougue</u>, her joy, her amazing temperament through it all, a wonderful woman.

Yesterday I hurried to get a note off that I forgot to thank you for telephoning Grace and now in this letter for the further news. Of course it is sheer Hell, this convalescence. Thank goodness Ellen is there. And my sweet love, I never said a word about Mimi—and this awful shock. Of course as the daughter of a historian of science who gets purple with rage at the very idea of such nonsense, I have to smile at your going to the <u>guérisseur</u>. However as he is a Basque he must be all right. I feel about the Basques as Kot does about the English: they can do no wrong. I fear though that he can't do much about the roots of your anxiety, which are so deep in your life. I am all for drugs or, better, religion. No, that is not as lightly said as it sounds. Isn't it that one must somehow at such times <u>lose</u> oneself? Who am I to talk? I have been in a most non-state of grace ever since I arrived here and saved not by any inner triumph, but by your yesterday's letter. On such sweet love does my <u>équilibre</u> depend. Of course my own idea has always been to conquer your anxiety by squeezing you tight, and by marking your wrists with my nails so perhaps the man has some sense.

<u>Of course</u> you were knocked out by Anne all over again. It is a real nightmare. Black.

Before I forget, in case the threatened strike of Postes Télégraphes etc. does happen on Thurs. my train seems to get in at 6:25 but perhaps one is allowed to stay on till seven. Charles will know and seemed quite happy to meet me, early as it was. That is Wed. 21st at 6:25 or seven. I am very tempted to stay till Sunday because of the lack of beds, a paradox which you will understand. But we'll see. I have no ticket for Brussels and will just buy a second class one and take a train when it seems best. If by any chance J. is to be away Tues. night, my family leaves here Monday and I could come by day Tuesday. I only have awful fears always of trying to <u>arrange</u> anything. At the moment just to see you seems enough. How lovely it will be. This letter has gone on much too long as I am supposed to be working seriously and not dreaming of impossible lives with you in the high mountains!

Dear heart, I do worry about your not sleeping <u>still</u>. I wish these next three months were over. I feel the pace of anxiety accelerating. Perhaps there is nothing to do but live each day as it comes along and say to yourself, chambermaids come and go but I am still here (like Tennyson's brook!).

An adorable letter from Bill all about Chartres, "this most marvelous skeleton demanded by their religious fervor." He longs to see you and will I expect turn up sooner or later—not without warning.

I'm glad you liked the sonnets—and for all you said. The trouble is nothing satisfies me now and nothing is enough, exact enough, deep enough and perhaps in the end only silence is the answer. I would race through the years to meet you at the other end. And it seems like years already.

Two things have been haunting me and I can't get them out of my head so here they are. One, Valery:

> Mais les amours sont les plus précieuses
> Qu'un long labeur de l'âme et du désir
> Mene à leurs fins délicieuses.

and another of the Rilke French poems:

> Eau qui se presse, qui court—eau oublieuse
> que la distraite terre boit,
> hésite un petit instant dans ma main creuse,
>   souviens-toi!
>
> Clair et rapide amour, indifférence,
> presque absence qui court,
> entre ton trop d'arrivée et ton trop de partance,
>   tremble un peu de séjour.

They are really opposites. I wish I could write a real poem, but now I think I am almost ready. It is you who open all these doors and when I feel safe in your love, I grow and breathe and put forth leaves and it loses its <u>obsessive</u> quality. For then I hate myself and almost you. My treasure, so much love.

[   ]

---

la Noble Contrée: the Noble Country, as was called the remarkably beautiful part of the Valais where Rilke had found his Château de Muzot.

You will never forgive me . . . away from this lake: The resort of Montreux, a group of villages forming the communes of Le Châtelard and Les Planches in Vaud canton, is at the east end of Lake Geneva; Juliette was born in the small fishing village of Auvernier on Lake Neuchâtel, to Sarton a similarly impersonal landscape.

Sierre: a quaint town situated among the hilly remains of a prehistoric landslip, known as a health resort.

Chemins qui ne mènent . . . . : quatrain #31 of "Les Quatrains Valaisans" in *Poésies Françaises de Rainer Maria Rilke* (Paris, 1946). Trans. by A. Poulin, Jr.: Roads leading nowhere/between two meadows,/as if detoured from their/end by design,/roads that often have/nothing ahead to face/but the season/and pure space.

Venthone: Venthône, between Montana and Montana-Vermala, northwest of Sierre.

the great elegies: Duino Elegies, Rilke's last great work, named for the Castle of Duino, which stands on a rocky headland of the Adriatic above Trieste and where, during a lonely winter sojourn in 1912, some of the poems were conceived; but it was not until after ten tortuous years of silence, and in the castle Sarton describes in this letter, that Rilke's silence broke and these ultimate expressions of his spiritual experience burst out in an indescribable torrent.

"demoiselle": young girl.

les pentes remplies de vignes . . . . : the hillsides covered with vines, the great vistas made human by the work of farmers, an amplitude, a peacefulness everywhere.

gardien: the keeper.

Mais non seulement le regard . . . . : quatrain #34 from *Poésies Françaises de Rainer Maria Rilke.* Trans. by A. Poulin, Jr.: Not only the gaze of those/who work the fields,/but also that of goats takes/part in perfecting the slow/aspect of this noble country./We always contemplate it/as if to remain there, or maybe/to eternalize it/in so great a memory/that no angel, to brighten/its luster, would dare/intervene.

Meta, Mother's old flame: Meta Budry, whom Eleanor Mabel Sarton had known in school, dearly loved, and for whom she had been a great confidante; after Mabel Sarton's death May Sarton fell in love with Meta who, after a glamorous city life, married Marc Turian, a simple man who adored her; their home, La Roselle, with its vineyards among the Jura mountains in Satigny, Geneva, became one of Sarton's havens; after Meta's death she visited Marc alone there. See Ch. 7 "Marc, the Vigneron" in *A World of Light.*

fougue: fire, mettle.

Ellen: Ellen (Mrs. Richard) Paine, Grace Eliot Dudley's sister.

Mimi: unidentified.

guérisseur: faith healer.

your yesterday's letter: among those that were destroyed.

équilibre: composure.

paradox which you will understand: Sarton writes to Bill Brown on this date: "I had meant to leave Friday but now hear that Anthony [Huxley], his wife and baby were to arrive Friday and as there are so few beds J and I would have to sleep together in her bed, so you can see it is rather tempting to stay the extra two days."

still here (like Tennyson's brook!): "For men may come and men may go,/But I go on forever," from "The Brook" by Alfred Lord Tennyson (1809–1892), Victorian lyric poet.

from Bill all about Chartres: Bill Brown (see footnote to letter of 12 August 1947) at the time of this letter was in Chartres with the Experiment in International Living.

Mais les amours . . . . : But the loves which are most precious/are those which long labors of soul and desire/lead to delicious endings. From "Le Philosophe et la Jeaune Parque" by Paul Valéry.

Eau qui se presse . . . : #18 of "Vergers" ("Orchards") in *Poésies Françaises de Rainer Maria Rilke.* Trans. by A. Poulin, Jr.: Hurried, running water—forgetful water/drunk by a distracted land,/linger a while in my cupped hand,/remember!/Between all that coming, all that leaving,/clear and rapid love, indifference,/almost a running absence,/linger, trembling.

[MONTREUX]   Wed., 14 juillet [1948]
                                                  just after lunch

O my darling, I am so sorry about the maid and the whole damnable maze and to have frightened you with a possible arrival on Monday. Please forgive but the family is leaving Monday and it seemed too silly to wait here if you were to be alone. First, have you considered getting Nellie back in the morning and a <u>man</u> as butler and what not and to serve at table and look after Julian? This was one idea that seemed quite possible before.

Now as to me, please do not worry. I can go to Belgium <u>Thursday</u> (even Wed. if it seemed good for you) so it will not be a long nor a difficult visit. Also l am very good at making beds, as swift as lightning. Also at early morning tea and breakfast. I'll bring coffee, soap and soap flakes as many as I have francs (which is not many).

Gray day again, and the swallows flying low, but Meta arrives this afternoon to make us all sit up and be a little more than these exhausted selves.

So, I'll look for Charles at the Lyon at 10:25 <u>Tuesday</u> evening. I hope you get off somewhere to the country for this weekend and get some rest and that by then there will be a solution to these intolerable domestic problems. I can't bear it for you.

I could of course go to the Mayers but it would seem a little cruel as well as rather complicated because of repacking. Do not be afraid however to treat me as a friend—for that is what I really am—and that means packing me off at once if it seems best. With dear love, my darling

[   ]

I won't write again, just look forward to seeing you. Also don't <u>come</u> to the train. I'll be really cross if you do—just a waste of time and energy.

———

juillet: July.

———

[CHEZ LIMBOSCH]   [23 July 1948?]
                                           Friday Eve, 6:00
                                           and so still and bright

My darling love, how I wish I could get this off tonight, but we are deep in the country and if I walk in one direction I come to the great forest and if I walk in the other I come to the open fields and nowhere a mailbox, so it will have to wait till tomorrow morning when I shall make the long and rather tedious expedition to the village to get my ration books—and it will be nice to have an epistophilic reason as well. It was so lovely to arrive here alone—the garden full of its summer flowers, the two little mountain ashes on either side of the door covered with vermilion fruits and the purple clematis, dark purple over the arbor (instead of the pale lavender one which was open when I left). I just walked into all the green and the stillness and no one was there except the adorable teddy bear dog Sadji who gambolled with joy and then when I went upstairs, all in the silence, the cat asleep on the fur rug on my bed. Aunty Lino and Oncle R. out to the dentist's. The Flemish-speaking maid to help with the bags. Mail on the hall table and the most wonderful feeling of coming home. How I love this house and this garden and this room, high up over treetops, red tiled roofs in the distance, full of all the poems and thoughts of you, last year's and this year's, so I come back to you here and find myself in you and yourself in me, and all is well.

Now I have unpacked and put up Chartres and my beaver and the adorable Viennese ash tray and I have gone to sleep and woken up without that fearful weight on my heart which made waking so awful. O ma douceur, ma douce et profonde douceur et ma paix et mon plus cher amour, sois en paix toi-même. I shall think of you tomorrow morning among the boats and fountains and lionesses with Susan, your gold and her gold. And I shall be anxious to hear too about Royaumont and about the lunch, and above all that some of the peace you let fall into my heart like dew on a desert early this morning came to you too and that all is well.

On the train I read Mauriac's fine article on Eugénie de Guérin, and also a good review of a book of reflections and maxims by a woman called Myriam Le Bargy (Fayard ed.) called <u>Démaquillages</u> which might be worth looking into.

Before I forget it, Mary Trevelyan's address is Hotel Bellevue, Chardonne sur Vevey, Vaud.

Instead of being bored here I am terrified at how fast the two weeks will go—and on Monday I hope to start to work. Tomorrow, odd jobs like my huge laundry, getting ration books etc.—Sundays are conversational days here. The Baltuses come to lunch and sit around till tea and always four or five other people come to lunch—but one can come and go. I rest and then join them again for tea.

I'll add a word to this tomorrow.

Sat.

No time. Oncle R. will mail this in town. Love and love

[   ]

Did you go back to the witch? And how is the solar plexus?

Aunty Lino and Oncle R: Céline and Raymond Limbosch.
O ma douceur . . . : Oh my sweetness, my gentle and absolute sweetness and my peace and my dearest love, be at peace yourself.
with Susan: Susan Huxley, Anthony's daughter.
Royaumont: founded in 1228 by St. Louis in the Val d'Oise, outside of Paris, one of the most beautiful of thirteenth-century abbeys.

the peace you let fall . . . early this morning: After three difficult days and a terrible parting from Juliette, Sarton left Paris on 23 July.

Mauriac's fine article on Eugénie de Guérin: François Mauriac (1885–1970), French novelist, essayist, and dramatist; his style of French clarté, a style Sarton saw as deceptive clarity rather than deceptive obscurity, was one with which the French-speaking side of Sarton felt affinities. Eugénie Guérin (1805–1848), famous for her posthumously published *Journal.*

The Baltuses: The painter George Baltus and his wife, Adrienne Revelard.

how is the solar plexus: Regarding the tone of this letter, on 26 July in her date book she writes the single line "Still hate me if you must but not my love," and on 4 August to Bill Brown: "We write circumspect letters with no feeling in them and everyone hurts. But all this will pass . . . at the bottom of this there is a great deal of love on both sides. But we have hurt each other so frightfully, so it has all become too complex and too invaded by analyses and _words_."

[26 July 1948]
Monday evening

My treasure, O, if only we could go there together, what <u>balm</u>. I have just come back from seeing Jean-Dominique, from tea at the peacocks, from the long delicious trolley ride along la lisière de la forêt at the end of this hot day. And now I must in a minute see that Mother's tea things are by her bed, and biscuits, and go and pick some flowers when the sun is down. She arrives tomorrow morning. I am still all surrounded by the golden mist of this afternoon and want to write you quickly, quickly before it goes for from now on and for a long time you are to have nothing but happy letters, full of petals of roses and ribbons and leaves and small very digestible pieces of love like the finest Huntley and Palmer thin biscuits which have disappeared long ago from anything except a letter. We are making plans for Mother's birthday which will be feted like mine in a series of events, including tea at Jean-Do's and here and I imagine a shower of gloves and books and lavender and photographs.

I wish I could describe this afternoon because if you could see it you would know everything about Jean-Do, sitting in her tiny armchair, the great owl-eyes looking so clear and deep and straight at one through immense dark glasses as if she could see—and I really believe she must—the small dry delicate hands, warm and dry like leaves warmed in the sun, always a little fine collar and a bow at her throat and her voice which is the voice of poetry itself, <u>ashes</u> where there has been great fire. And what did we talk about? A good deal of the time about where and how she should be buried, but in <u>fits</u> of laughter, because she has discovered it is so expensive to have a permanent grave and is determined not to, and we talked about it really as if we were buying a house or renting a flat—and laughed and laughed. But I could not after all promise that there would be no plaque because of course people will want to know where she is. People will be reading her poems, you know, long after—and it mustn't be like Mozart. As I explained. But it was so good to be able to talk about all this—holding hands, and so alive and laughing. I feel so sure now that she will live through the winter and I was not sure before, and that I shall see her again. There are the packages of letters—so many things to be decided about. And we talked of Camus and <u>La Peste</u> which they are reading aloud with gratitude. Jean-Do feels it is as important to us of this time as perhaps the great Russians were at their time. And I am very relieved as I feared they would not like it. And we talked of you—whenever I can for a moment recreate you in this way, bring your presence into a room where I am with someone I wholly trust and love, how beautiful it is, what a blessing, darling. I came home with such a flood of gratefulness in my heart, all open, all free and released and knowing the essence again, and thanking God for you and all you have been and are. Only not telling you today because I do not want to enrage you with what you will cruelly call a compliment.

And I told Jean-Do how wise she is and she said, "Je suis sage parce que je suis fou," bending her head like a bird with that indescribable half-bitter, half-gentle laugh. How I wish you could see her once before she dies, she you!

And then we went down to tea with the other two, Blanche Rousseau and Marie Gasparre—Marie hurling slices of bread at me in one of her sudden gestures, always the laughter, the bouquet of their laughter, and tea with crushed red currants, whipped cream cheese, the cat's shadow appearing against the white curtains to get his saucer of milk. (He is a very ugly thin cat and spoiled rotten.) Blue and white checked cloth, blue and white cups, beautiful blue plates on the wall, and pewter. Of course the trouble is that when you spread everyone's bread with so much honey, you are inundated with people who need honey and they are quite exhausted with visits.

Also, a lovely thing has happened. A beautiful book has appeared in France called <u>La Guirlande des Muses Françaises</u> from Desbordes-Valmore through Marie Noel and Jean Dominique is there, the only Belgian. She laughs about this too, but I think she is pleased and I especially am very pleased, though the selection could be better.

And that is all. Now it is after supper, the light is going—a very pale gold sky, and every leaf still in the heat. We have been watering the plants in the little greenhouse and now the doors are locked. The dog is in. I must stop typing as everyone will be asleep in about five minutes.

Tuesday morning

My little tuffet is here looking remarkably well. And now your Sat. card is here for which my darling, bless you. I have decided to stay here till Monday Aug. 9th, a little longer than I thought so as to have a longer perspective of quiet days and to give a story time to form itself and get written. Deeply, deeply all is well. So whatever your anxieties in these days, let them not to be me. Rest in the thought that I am at peace and here and happy and always very gently by your side. Do not try to write until you feel like it.

You have given me the flower, the rare flower—<u>peace</u> in the heart—cannot I give it you—perhaps someday, even if not now—Let me know where you will be after Friday? On Sat. I am having my hair cut short and curled. I shall be a new person. Baltus makes a drawing Friday.

---

la lisière de la forêt: the outskirts of the forest.

mustn't be like Mozart: When Mozart died impoverished in 1791 of rheumatic fever, he was buried, in accordance with Viennese custom of the time, at St. Mark's Churchyard in a paupers' unmarked, mass grave.

Camus and La Peste: Albert Camus (1913–1960), Algerian-born Nobel Prize–winning French philosopher, novelist, dramatist, and journalist. Sarton wrote "One Man Goes Down, For Albert Camus," unpublished, in February 1960, one month after his death in a car accident. His novel *The Plague* (1948), considered one of the great novels of the twentieth century, is a parable depicting the life of a modern city during an epidemic of bubonic plague.

what you cruelly call a compliment: Regarding what Sarton withholds from this letter: in her date book for the day before this, 25 July 1948, Sarton only quoted from Raymond Limbosch: "Now rinse the troubled mind and bitter eye."

Je suis sage parce ce que je suis fou: I am wise because I am mad. Perhaps an allusion to *The Madwoman of Chaillot* by Jean Giraudoux (1882–1944), French dramatist, essayist, and diplomat, recently produced in Paris in 1945. In later years Sarton often quoted it; to Louise Bogan in 1965 she wrote: "Do you remember all the Madwoman's wisdom about how to *manage*? . . . How fine to be mad enough to be sane."

Blanche Rousseau and Marie Gasparre: Blanche Rousseau, Marie Gaspar, and Jean Dominique lived together; in life Sarton called them the peacocks; in *The Single Hound* she called them the owls. See *I Knew a Phoenix*, pp. 121–53, and Ch. 12 in *A World of Light*.

from Desbordes-Valmore through Marie Noel: Marceline Desbordes-Valmore (1786–1859), actor and author of gentle, unsophisticated genuine lyrics; French symbolist poet Paul Verlaine (1885–1896) included her in his gallery of *poètes maudits* [gifted poets ignored or misunderstood by society]. Marie Noel (Roget) (1883–?) author of *chansons*, often written with musical accompaniment, and lyrics of religious inspiration.

My little tuffet. one of Sarton's pet names for her mother.

[5 ACACIA ROAD]   [10 Aug. 1948]
9:30   Tues. night

Dear Juliette, it is very kind of you to send me the check and I should have gladly and gratefully accepted it if I had really needed it, but I don't so here it is back again. I heard from Heath's this morn that they had sold two stories over here, one "The Paris Hat" for Eng. rights (35 guineas) and one "The Desert" which I wrote last summer and which never sold in the States (25 guineas) so I shall even arrive home with enough to live on for a month, an almost unheard of state of affairs. It is, I must say, a great relief, if only to show that not everything I touch goes wrong these days. It had gotten so that I couldn't buy a ticket without some small calamity taking place. England is kinder. I got my flight for Ireland in five minutes (for the 28th) this morning.

Kot I think looks tired, but we are having a peaceful time. I was here for lunch and all afternoon, then went out to dinner with Katharine Taylor who was much impressed by the UNESCO Teacher Training conf. at Ashbridge which she visited—no speeches, real workshop stuff and much accomplished. Tomorrow I have dinner with Jane and Annie but shall be here all day. Marjorie comes to tea. I shall work in the morning.

In case you have any qualms or fears, I am not telling Kot anything about us. He is very cross that you haven't written, but I told him that you were feeling rotten and of course he really understands and I gave him your message.

This is the next morning. Kot seems to be very cross and I expect I have done something awful but I can't imagine what. Ruth Pitter will be able to put me up for the ten days I'm in London. Address 55A Old Church St., Chelsea.

Yours as ever

May

Heath's: A. M. Heath Ltd., Sarton's English agent.

sold two stories . . . unheard of state of affairs: Sarton wrote a short story using Juliette Huxley's milliner, Mr. Socrates, called "The Paris Hat," which was published in *Cosmopolitan* in 1948 and in *Woman* (English) in 1949; "The Desert" was published in *Everywoman* (English) in January 1949.

Katharine Taylor: Miss Katharine Taylor (1888–1979), headmistress of the Shady Hill School from 1921 to 1949 and a great champion of and inspiration for some of Sarton's earliest poetry. After retirement she devoted much of her time to service for children here and abroad; see also pp. 114–19 and p. 139 in *I Knew a Phoenix*.

Jane and Annie: Jane Stockwood and Annie Duveen Caldwell; see footnote to letter of probably 24 July 1947.

Marjorie: Marjorie Wells; see footnote to letter of 5 July 1947.

Kot seems to be very cross: It is unclear precisely what the intransigent Koteliansky with his "imaginative genius for understanding people's inner directions," this demanding, ultrasensitive friend, was angry about here. But it is clear that he raged over what he could not control, and clear, also, from his letters, that he had always had the greatest tenderness for and dependence on Sarton, as well as belief in her work. With what Lady Glenavy's letters suggest was hostile encouragement on her part, and despite Sarton's saying she had not told Kot about Juliette, he must have felt increasingly abandoned by what he heard of and saw as her passions for others.

KINGHAM   Friday, Aug. 13th [1948]

Darling, I agree with you about silence, if we can feel <u>together</u> in it, if it is not a piling up of barriers, all the <u>unsaid</u>, if above all it contains hope. I know that I have a great deal to learn from you now, but at the moment there are very great barriers because perhaps you do not feel with me but only against me and often I do not feel with you but only resent the suffering instead of being able to learn from it and to use it. It has taken all the days since your letter from Bécheron telling me the plans and stating the bare fact that I shall not see you again, to be able to write this letter. I must write it honestly now and really open my heart to you once more, and even if it is to be for the last time, because it seems to me there can be no love otherwise, even the kind that lives in silence and on silence. But that love presupposes real communion and above all the sense of being included and not excluded. Just because our natures and our needs are so very different, we must <u>include</u> each other or everything breaks apart. I know that in order to make this happen I must learn to love you less terribly and more simply and less intensely. But that will take time and with time it is very possible, I think. Only now you mustn't leave me quite outside. If you can make a small act of faith in my direction, then the greatest barrier will fall at once and I believe we can begin to build the foundations of our true relationship as it will grow in the years to come.

However hard these last weeks have been, I have never for one moment doubted in my deepest self that they were necessary and that they would not be wasted. But it has been a matter of remaking that faith every day, of weeding out hatred every day, and then often beginning again half the night. This I think is excessive, in that there must be some rock to which one might hold. I turn to you today and ask your help.

You see, darling, I have come to you so often full of that most vulnerable joy of meeting and love, only to be slapped down and shut out. I know there are valid reasons why it had to be so for you and you couldn't do otherwise, and this is not to blame; and in my letters since I left you, I felt I must go always toward you still and wait and be hopeful and patient, but then every letter held only negatives. You could be tender and anxious about all my small anxieties and never about the big one. And they came <u>after</u> what was a very real torture of the spirit. The fact that it was clear last time that you must be allowed to be extremely cruel but I was not to be allowed to suffer if and when you were. My suffering seemed to become the great sin. To the point that you could write to me over and over "be <u>happy</u>." I wonder if the explanation of this is not that you have so decided that I am "over-intense" and excessive that you confuse this real failing with the reality of my feeling. That even the tears were not <u>real</u>, and therefore the love not <u>real</u>. Oh, I know that another sort of person could do you good where I have done only harm, could have helped not hurt, could have meant peace and comfort. I have hated myself not to be that person, to the point of almost not being able to be the person I may be able to be. It has all become a jungle of negatives, of refusals, of <u>refoulements</u>. The only thing that can make it change, make some peace and clarity is if I can know there is something of me you can still love and believe in. If you can say one positive thing and mean it. It is, I know, a very great deal to ask and I only ask it in humility and because I have come to the end of what I can do alone in this. But if you can't then don't answer this letter. We shall have a real silence and perhaps that would be best.

O my darling, think of me, please try to remember some of the good.

[   ]

The worst thing has been your assumption apparently that everything was happy and peaceful, your saying "do something definite" etc. That is saying to someone with a raging toothache "Why don't you think of something else?" What I don't understand is that now when you know you will not have to see me, perhaps ever again, you cannot be kind and help me through this bad time. It is true that since I left you I have perhaps not done any serious work except a short story and a few poems, but it seems a great deal to expect. There again perhaps we are different. I mean I must live through this out to the other side, and then of course I must get back to work and to life in the U.S. At the moment I parcel out the day into times, into a routine so as not to think too much, but one has to lie down at times. There is no absolute defence against pain, against this frightful loneliness for you. I miss you and miss you and it never stops. How strange it is that to say this to someone one loves risks to seem unforgivable. But I feel now that I must risk it.

Bécheron: the manor house of Jo Davidson in Tours.
refoulements: forcings back into oneself.

SATURDAY, KINGHAM   Aug. 14th, 1948

Darling, after the rain and the wind it is a perfect clear day. I had your letter with breakfast in bed. It is so very good of you to take time to write and I am grateful. I look over a thatched roof, one ell of this house and out to a golden field of grain, half of it lying flat from the wind, and then a line of trees and sky. This is a blessed peaceful place because I know Basil believes in me and we go for silent walks to visit the horses in the far pasture, sit on a tree and talk about nothing in particular. But for a few hours at a time I emerge from the state of leperdom I am in. I feel like a leper because of suffering. It is such a useless thing and affects every relationship like a poison.

You ask about Kot. It was not really a very happy time. We had some good talks, but I felt more than usual his sometimes lack of humanity, simplification of everything to an absolute black and white (perhaps that is wisdom?). On the last morning the charwoman came and I felt that Kot hated to have me still there, so off I went into town to a newsreel, wandered round Soho (to get my umbrella which I had left in a restaurant), had lunch and saw him for just a few minutes before leaving. I am having tea there on Wed. to pick up my big bag and take it to Ruth's. Kot was most difficult about my leaving it there and four dresses hung up as it is so damp. It became a small nightmare as Jane couldn't have it and at Ruth's I am sleeping first on a couch and then in a room after a few days and I hated to ask them to crowd in clothes and a bag. There was Kot's whole empty house! Finally when I was near to tears he capitulated but the whole thing left us both slightly sore, as we say in American.

I'm delighted to have the Du Bos. Here I have been reading von Hügel. I think myself that it is a great insult to God to turn to him out of suffering. Because it is not a matter of being <u>found</u> by God (comforted in) but of being lost <u>in</u> Him. One should only praise God and only look to Him in joy and for the sake of purefying joy and feeling its true human proportions perhaps, but <u>not</u> out of despair. Von Hügel says "The great rule is, variety up to the verge of dissipation; recollection up to the verge of emptiness; each alternating with the other and making a rich fruitful tension." I've been reading also Dorothy Osborn's charming letters because I have David Cecil's <u>Two Quiet Lives</u> with me and wanted to have the letters first. And a book by the Abbé Bremond called <u>Prière et Poésie</u>, less rewarding than the title. I don't know exactly what is meant by the inner current, but I think the writing of a poem presupposes at least a <u>temporary</u> solution of conflict, so that it must be at the end of the struggle which precedes it not the finding of oneself but the touching of the humanity in oneself, the place where one is universal just because one has gone down deep enough into oneself—and I suppose that might be the current for a poet: his humanness. It is the opposite of negative brooding of which alas I do far too much.

The Breslau conf. sounds very exciting, almost too many people. How will anything real emerge? In three days? But I suppose the very gathering together is a sort of testimony, a witnessing. I shall be excited to hear how it goes.

I am so happy that you seem to feel back in your real self, reading and all. You seem safe, darling. That is so good. Your life looks very marvelous and whole from here.

Thank you for the news of Grace [Dudley]. It really does seem now as if she were pulling up.

The only troubling thing is "infiltrating." What does that mean? Was it the result of an infection? Yes you must get well for Breslau. Can you stay in bed and telephone from your bed all morning? Please be wise.

Bill [Brown] will be coming, I hope, before you leave. But it really doesn't matter. I shrink from it. O, I see now that he only arrives in Paris the 23rd from Haute-Savoie. So that is that.

I am more and more aware that suffering really is a sin. But it is like being in Hell. One can't even imagine the way out. One just creeps along from day to day. There is a common myth that time heals. I have never found it so, not in the real things. One buries it finally, but it is buried alive. What is awful is that I have lost all faith in myself. I don't see what I am going to do or be anymore. I feel like a leper. "This is a sufferer. Noli mi tangere."

Diarmuid is quite hopeless about selling anything. He says that it is affecting all his writers (all "literary blokes") as there is an imperceptible tightening of the market and so only sure-fire formula stories get sold. I can't do that, though it is not altogether contemptible to be able to.

When does Mary come? Give her my love when she does.

And again all you have to tell me is that you made a great mistake in loving me once because of differences of temperament etc. Is there really no one positive to be found? Is it just nothing for you but a hideous mistake? There was joy once and fun and tenderness. I think of how we laughed about the Clermont-Tonnerre, so many other times. Is it never never to be again?

[   ]

---

and I am grateful: To Judith Matlack, Sarton writes on this date: "Until this morning I had not cried once and thought perhaps I was over the bad place, but today another let-

ter from J. (she tries to be kind!) which left me in a flood of tears. Luckily I was having breakfast in bed."

Basil believes in me and we go for silent walks: By the time of this letter in 1948, Basil de
Sélincourt had given up writing entirely and had become a farmer. He believed in
Sarton from the beginning; in his review of *Inner Landscape,* "The Blessing of
Augury" in the London *Observer,* he writes: "If her verse deserves notice, it is
because the intense experience which underlies and unifies them has engendered an
uncompromising determination to forge and refine the tool for its expression, a tool
which is . . . deep-searching to the point of ruthlessness, and very delicate." Her
poems, he wrote, tell the story of "human passion, unique, holy and unforgettable."

to Ruth's: Ruth Pitter; see footnote to letters of 15 December 1939 and 23 November
1941.

delighted to have the Du Bos. Charles Du Bos (1882–1939), French critic. Sarton still had his
Journal, 2 vols. (Eds. Corrêa, Paris) inscribed "with dear love from Juliette, Paris, 12th
August '48" at the time of her death.

von Hügel: Baron Friedrich von Hügel (1852–1925), Roman Catholic theolgian born in
Italy, naturalized British subject 1914. The quotation is probably from his *Letters to
His Niece.*

Dorothy Osborne: (1627–1695), wife of Sir William Temple (1628–1699), English statesman. *The Letters of Dorothy Osborne to William Temple,* originally published in 1888,
were edited by G. C. Moore Smith and republished in 1928.

David Cecil's Two Quiet Lives: Two Quiet Lives: Dorothy Osborne, Thomas Gray (1948) by Lord
Edward Christian David Cecil (1902–1986), English literary critic and biographer.

Prière et Poésie: Abbé Henri Bremond (1855–1933), French literary critic and historian,
withdrew from the Jesuit Order in 1904 to devote himself to writing; his chief work
is an eleven-volume literary history of religious sentiment in France, of a contem-
plated fourteen-volume work. *Prière et Poésie* was published in 1925.

the current for a poet: his humanness: In the 1979 Ishtar Film production *World of Light: A
Portrait of May Sarton,* Sarton says: "I think the deeper you go into the personal, the
more universal you are, if you go deep enough, that's the thing. And if it's no longer
just a 'look at me, I'm in pain' poem, which I see such an awful lot being written
now, that seem to me never to get down to that universal. And, of course, the image
is what does it, the image is what does it—the mollusc image, the field, the metaphor
is what does it. When you have the metaphor, you've got it." And in answer to the
interviewer's final question "How would you like to be remembered?" Sarton
answers, "For being fully human, if I am."

Noli mi tangere: Touch me not (Latin). The words Christ used to Mary Magdalene after his
resurrection (John 20:17): "Jesus saith unto her, Touch me not; for I am not yet
ascended to my Father."

Mary: Mary Trevelyan Moorman, friend of the Huxleys' who worked at UNESCO; wrote
a two-volume biography of Wordsworth, published in 1965; revised the second
1969 edition of the *Letters of William and Dorothy Wordsworth,* edited by Ernest de
Sélincourt; sister of Humphry, daughter of George and Janet Trevelyan.

Clarmont-Tonnerre: Duchesse of Clermont-Tonnerre, Elizabeth de Gramont (186?–194?),
French grande dame whose birthright gave her entry into the highest circles of
European society; translator of Keats, author of the memoirs *Au Temps des Equipages*
(1928) and *Les Marrioniers en Fleurs,* and of biographies including *Robert de
Montesquieu et Marcel Proust.* About her, Sarton wrote to Judith Matlack from the

Huxleys' in Paris on 29 June 1948: "We were just sitting down with a drink when the doorbell rang. There is no chamber maid now and it was the new cook's first night so I rushed to open, only to be confronted by two fabulous women one about sixty looked like an exaggerated and ancient LeGallienne. She had on a skirt to the floor; a very 18th century red brown corduroy coat with the legion d'honneur in the buttonhole and a jabot and looked rather like the White Queen. Her companion had blue hair, was much made up, very tailored. They asked for Mrs. Huxley and I was so sure they had come to the wrong house that I made them repeat the name. They insisted they were invited and then murmured the "Duchesse de Clermont-Tonnerre." I had an immediate brainstorm as I had written a lot of the cards for the cocktail party and apparently no one could read the date. (I was not meant to be a private sec.) so they thought it was yesterday!"

KINGHAM, SUNDAY   August 15th [1948]

Dear love, suddenly the sky is all blue and the poplar trees shine and the thatched roof shines and the wheat shines and I shine because I believe I have come to understand. It was not understanding that kept me in such a black sinful state. And I must try to tell you. I'll then keep this a day or so to be sure it is exactly what I mean. I think now I can feel the good in your silence and not what seemed wilfully cruel, because somehow I feel your love again and know that it is here.

Fundamentally we wish the same things, that is each in our way we have an idea of love which is very pure and demanding, asking of it the limit of what it can give as a discipline of the spirit, a way towards growing. We went at it finally at complete opposite ends, hence the conflict. It was never a conflict of sex, curiously enough, at least I believe I am right in this. Sex got mixed up in it because I at least was wholly involved and so inevitably that got involved. But it was almost a conflict of a way of life against another way of life. Do not laugh at me if I say that I think we both believe in austerity (that "greater limitations release deeper powers") that austerity in tenderness and tenderness in austerity which Von Hügel says is the essence of Christianity. But I felt that the limitations of the situation itself were so very great, the limitations of time, your marriage, all the impossibles, that in a way one was given full license within them. The austerity was to be all the rest of the year; the austerity was what was already imposed from without. So I was safe to love you passionately and with all of myself all the time we were together, the little time, because the usual

dangers did not exist, of fervor overspending itself, of over-intensity pro-
voking a violent reaction and so on. This was a great misunderstanding of
the nature of things on my part. I see it now. I could have been helped out
of it if you had been able to bring your tenderness to bear at the moment
when austerity was your deepest need. There is every excuse for you that
you could not and more and more I understand how difficult it was and
more and more humbly I am grateful for what you gave. It was a very great
gift. Just because it was so great and nourishing, I felt the lack of it so terribly and the loss became a real <u>désarroi</u>, a derangement of my whole self.

That in essence seems to me what happened.

In Bremond's <u>Prière et Poésie</u> he says, "Je ne pense pas qu'il y ait un
seul homme assez dépourvu d'imagination pour n'avoir pas éprouvé, au
moins une fois dans sa vie, cette surexcitation de l'intelligence, ce vertige
momentané du coeur et de la pensée que j'apelle état poétique." That is an
exact description of my state of mind <u>all</u> the time I was with you. It was at
the root of all that you called "excessive." You really became poetry to me
and that was your greatest gift. As I tried to tell you once, this has happened
to me before, perhaps twice before, but never where there was any fulfillment. What such a fulfillment might be came as a complete revelation.
Whatever you do in your life you did this for me and I can never never
tell you what it meant. But again just because of the great joy, the not finding it, the wall instead became very terrible. Hence again the excessive and
over intense pain and suffering, which must have seemed quite <u>mad</u>. But
that is because you have never admitted the extent and depth of my joy in
you, the suddenness of it, the unexpectedness of it etc. The poem "Now I
Become Myself" and those very fruitful weeks were the immediate tangible result. I really felt I was a new person. But just as that new person was
being born and beginning to grow, fully alive, powerful, <u>sane</u> (at that time
my life seemed full of meaning and I longed to give all I could to other
people, to work harder than ever and so on), just at that moment the barriers went up. You were frightened by the violence; I was hurt by what
seemed like indifference. From then on, it was a real conflict which we
haven't solved yet.

We are different also in that with me my deepest feelings very quickly <u>act</u>, come to the surface, in words, in physical going-out-toward. I think
it makes a person like you who is all inward, who needs time, who is

reserved (as I alas, am not at all) even feel that a person like me must be superficial, and also that if everything is expressed there is nothing left. I think you were right when you once said that if we had lived together in a different way and over a longer stretch of time a certain current would have been established within which we could each have lived in our own way. As it was we violated each other in spirit without meaning to, not out of too great feeling or too little feeling at all, but out of our <u>natures.</u>

Finally I believe with my whole heart that there is a way back to joy. I meant what I said at the very beginning that I love you with my soul and it doesn't matter about any of the rest—in the long run. You are right about absence and silence. I am not going to write another letter like this. I have just reread your last letter and realize how rich it is, and how blind I have been not to see that. But I was absolutely locked up in non-understanding, couldn't reach you at all. Now if you do not feel like answering this, please do not. It has done me good to be able to write it and to know that you will read it. I am looking forward to DuBos. And I am looking forward to the years ahead in which even long and continual parting will not make any fundamental difference. The love is there. And in the end I feel sure that we shall both be enriched by it.

God bless you, dear Juliette, and be with you.

[ ]

<u>Monday</u>

Just sent off a wire. I'm sorry about that letter, but in a way it had to be written I think—and thrown away—and it was true, but not to <u>find</u> the truth. Let me know what the <u>doctor</u> said about your legs. Is Julian's cold better?

------

désarroi: disordering.
Je ne pense pas . . . : I do not think there is a single man without the imagination to have at least once in his life experienced that exuberant thrill of understanding, that momentary intoxication of heart and mind which I call the poetic state.
"Now I Become Myself": in *The Land of Silence.*
reread your last letter: not extant.

55A OLD CHURCH ST.   Tuesday, Aug. 17th [1948]

[In pencil at top:] Read the end of this first—the beginning is just <u>news</u>.
My Darling, not a real letter but just a sigh of tiredness and relief at your
telegram and to answer various questions which I have never answered. I
didn't see Anthony and the children as I had just three evenings in London
and spent one with Kot, one with K.T. and one with Jane and Annie. But
I shall plan to see them next week I think. It was hard to do anything those
days. I was really ill, but alas now I have given away all the food I brought
what shall I bring them? Perhaps a bottle of wine.

I long for the DuBos (do you remember his sad bafflement with
Edith Wharton in the Lubbock book?) and Basil promised to forward it as
soon as it comes and I shall dive for the pages you mention and any others you find as you proceed. How lovely to be sharing this. I wonder also
about Camille Mayran whom I just missed in Paris and who as you know
is a great friend of Lucile Sumpt's. She lost both her houses in the war, one
in the country and her husband is dying of t.b. Was DuBos a Catholic? She,
of course is, very. I was enormously helped by the Von Hügel letters these
last days and at its best the Catholic mind seems to me much wiser than
the Protestant, wholer and saner and also more gentle, more human. But I
also think it is almost impossible to be a converted Catholic. The strain of
belief is too great and one has to accept too many impossibles. Basil says
that he becomes less and less Christian as time goes on. He teased me very
much because I steeped myself in all this, but it did help. The essential
Christian wisdom is after all a beautiful wisdom and in the end it all comes
back to what one can dig out of oneself, call it God or the soul or whatever it may be, the dying to self, the renunciation and the being reborn.
"Teach us to care and not to care" as Eliot says in <u>Ash Wednesday</u>. I said it
many times and also just two words "Dieu seul." All the love came back
and the meaning and all the bitterness was washed away.

It was so terribly beautiful to wake up and be able to look out with a
rinsed eye at the wheat field in the distance. I went down often to listen to
it, a sound I have never heard before, that little creeping rustling whisper, the
<u>richest</u> sound. This morning the reapers were out to cut it down. Another
joy was a small task of cutting every day all the seeds off of two beds of poppies, so <u>fragile</u> and winged and airy—then deprived of making their fruit,
they go on flowering all summer. I liked making poets of the poppies.

I wonder what you will think of Ella whom you will surely see as she is such a friend of Jo's. I haven't seen her or Don Stewart (her humorist-playwright husband, a very sensitive darling man who has, I think, been twisted out of his true function by Ella's militant politics). Ella is better than her face, I think, very bright and warm and childish, as people are who oversimplify. It was she who came back from Jugoslavia seeing nothing but the good. The congress does look rather far to the Left. I wonder if there will be any honest statement of differences. But every attempt must be made while there's still time, and even if the fruits are only felt much later. Every bridge that can must be built. But how hard it is even for two single human beings to understand each other when national feeling is involved. Basil's sister is an old Empire-builder, convinced that the British were intended by God to rule the world, that it is sheer tragedy for India to be on its own etc. etc. But people have got to learn about freedom the hard painful way. There is no other way, as for children too. We had one fairly hot argument after which I held my barbarian peace, but I have never felt more American. And I thought of Julian and his amazing vision and generosity about such matters when he doesn't get impatient. On the other side of course is the general ignorance in the U.S. of the positive side of British rule, as well as ignorance of our own hideous mishandling of Porto Rico and so on. I piled all this on, put ashes on my head without ceasing, but at the end all I felt was the absolute certitude of superiority on her part, _very_ irritating. It followed on a belligerent taxi-driver who took me to Paddington and shouted at me the whole way (I think he was drunk), "I don't think, I _know_ we're the greatest people on earth." And that all began because I said I was glad to be back in London! What is one to do?

Everyone asks about Balliol. Apparently it has been in the papers. Is it really decided? If Beirut is off till Feb. I expect you will be in Paris until after you come back. The year stretches on. I do hope you can get the week in Dordogne, but also, dear love, the inward peace you need and which I have done so much to take from you when all I meant was the opposite, as we both really know.

5:30

Ruth's [Pitter] fat cheerful niece just brought me your Sunday and Monday letter. How terribly happy I am that you wrote this before my

Kingham letters came. Darling, I tried very hard not to put this awful black time on you, but I couldn't write lying happy letters any longer. It seemed a kind of betrayal to go on and so I had to write little nothings—and hope you would try to reach me. And you did. O bless you, dear love. What a difference this makes. And we shall bless our sorrows and be at peace together. Doesn't it almost seem to you now that we have reached it? I mean the place where we can love and need each other again each in our own way? That is all that matters. A life that has brought me you seems to me almost unbelievably rich. Please do not deny it. I feel you will as you read that sentence. It is true. Do not deny it. Let it in and keep it in your heart. The suffering is nothing now, nothing. On the contrary you have taught me a great deal by it and together as time goes on we shall discover all we learned.

Of course the great joke is that what I want is peace too. And tenderness and being included more than anything else. It was perhaps the lack of those things which made the passion become really terrible and destructive. It need never again get to that point or to any point at all beyond what you feel, if, O darling, you will once let the love in—and out—then there is nothing to fear. And I think there is no guilt in a bad sense, for either of us, only the sad clash of time and temperament, so many outward tensions to match and increase the inward ones. The triumph is that anything good came out of it. Please do not speak of guilt again (unless you want to—of course you must say everything and anything which is in your heart). I do not mean by this that I am pleased with myself or do not often return to my failings, but now only having forgiven myself, and to learn. Please forgive yourself too and think of me not as a person you have hurt but as a person you have opened and enriched and taught things beyond all words, everlasting things. And do not forget either how you managed to do this in spite of all your other life having to go on. And sometimes remember that one of the things you gave me was passionate love when I needed it as plants need water, but when I myself didn't believe it was possible. That was a small miracle. Miracles do not have to happen more than once in a lifetime or be repeated in any sense, that you must know too.

I must try to get for you Bowra's wonderful chapter on Sappho in the Greek poets. People who haven't read it don't know what I meant exactly by the lines, but he makes it so clear that she was always training the girls

she loved for marriage by loving them (and this love in the service of
Aphrodite in whom she believed) so renunciation was always there and had
to be in the end. It was not self-indulgence, hence perhaps the pride and
the absolute honesty of her poems which have been debased by self-indulgent Lesbians like Rene Vivian (who makes me quite sick).

My treasure, do not speak of how I have loved you. It has been so
badly, but as well as I could then. Now I hope in a year or two I shall learn
to do it better and more worthily. And meanwhile how blessed to be able
to write to you like this. The darkness was only that really—though my
whole life seemed to be involved because in a way it is. But not as a
responsibility for you, only for me.

I shall get this to the six post and continue tomorrow. You will be
leaving so soon, forgive me if I write often these next few days.

Sleep well, blessed dear one. And do not say lack of love. It is not true,
not at all. My treasure, my great treasure.

[ ]

K.T.: Katharine Taylor; see footnote to letter of 10 August 1948.

DuBos . . . bafflement . . . Wharton . . . Lubbock book: See footnote to letter of 25 January
1948.

Camille Mayran: Pen name of Marianne Hepp (Mme. Pierre Hepp), French author and
novelist, winner of the Prix du Roman de L'Académie Française for her *Histoire de
Gotton Cornixloo, suivie de L'Oubliée,* and the Prix Femina-Vie-Heureuse for her
novel *Dame en Noir.* Sarton met her at the Huxleys'. Though they saw each other
rarely, they became intimate friends by letter through their respective work; see *May
Sarton: Selected Letters 1916–1954.* Sarton wrote "Joy in Provence" for her; see *A
Private Mythology.*

Lucile Sumpt: See footnote to letter of "Early May 1948."

Ash Wednesday: "Ash Wednesday," one of Eliot's most heartbroken yet inspirational
poems, mirrors his conversion to Anglo-Catholicism; written in 1930, it is a farewell
to his wife, Vivienne. "Because these wings are no longer wings to fly/But merely
vans to beat the air/The air which is now thoroughly small and dry/Smaller and
dryer than the will/Teach us to care and not to care/Teach us to sit still."

Dieu seul: only God.

look out with a rinsed eye: The young Sarton often heard the poet Raymond Limbosch
say, "Il faut rinser l'oeil," a phrase she uses in one of her last poems, "Rinsing the
Eye," in *Coming into Eighty:* "We must rinse the eye, the poet reminds me/ . . . An
explosion of memory has rinsed my eye."

Ella: Ella Winter; see footnote to letter of 11 June 1948.

Every bridge that can must be built: See "Invisible Bridges," a.k.a. "Innumerable Friend," in
The Land of Silence; dealing with "bridges that nations cannot overthrow," it was her
Christmas poem for this year, 1948.

Basil's sister: probably Mrs. Gilder Palmer, his widowed sister who lived in Tyringham but kept house during Sarton's visit to Kingham while Basil's wife, Jay, was in the United States.

hideous mishandling of Porto Rico: In 1928 Puerto Rico had petitioned the United States for autonomy without statehood. Vast unemployment in the 1930s only exacerbated the demand for a redefinition of status, creating a deepening dichotomy between widening support of statehood and an emerging nationalist movement; the result was serious outbreaks of terrorism and the arrest of many leaders.

Balliol: Balliol College at Oxford, which Julian attended after Eton. The matter referred to is unidentified.

your Sunday and Monday letter: not extant.

Bowra's . . . the Greek poets: Greek Lyric Poetry from Alcman to Simonides, 1936, by Sir Cecil Maurice Bowra (1898–1971), English classical scholar; Sappho (b. 612 BC), one of the most famous lyric poets of all time, known as "the tenth muse."

what I meant exactly by the lines: "Only in the extremity of spirit and the flesh/And in renouncing passion did Sappho come to bless"; see "My Sisters, O My Sisters" in *The Lion and the Rose.*

Rene Vivian: Renée Vivien (1877–1909), pen name of Pauline Tarn, militantly feminist Anglo-French poet and novelist who dared to explore her lesbian sexuality only in 1899 when she settled in Paris and became the lover of the American heiress Natalie Barney. Always fascinated by death, she died at thirty-two from drink and starvation.

55A OLD CHURCH ST.

Aug. 18th [1948]

after lunch,

your letter of 16th and 17th just come

My darling, my exhausted bird, how can I thank you for these letters? That of yesterday and the cry today which I had to hear and I bless you from all my heart. All day I have felt so frightfully sleepy, as if I had come at last to the end of the long journey. It is so very good to be here at last. Do you feel it? It will not be terrible your needing me a little, but only good. No more rending and breaking and trying to reach you. Or you to keep me from getting in. Now we stand together in a very simple clear love and can help each other just by being there, and there won't have to be many letters even, just the daily things that happen and this delicate thread of love and imagination about each others' lives which has become a real inward continuity. Is it not so?

And I feel so much about Julian and you now in these next months. It is rather upsetting about the meeting in <u>November</u>, bringing all decisions so close upon him, the planning and all. Will it mean that you can't get away to the Dordogne? It seems to me as I look back on this year of yours that it has been in the deepest sense a part of the harvest of your and Julian's long battle too. I am so glad you let me see his letter. There is the tender shoot of shared responsibility and true regard for each other on the desert now. There is this late lovely greenness. It has come from both of you, but I think that it could come from you is such a proof of the love you have learned, and at what cost, that you must be shining with it all the time. It is a triumph of the spirit, darling. Never forget that when you are in the arid places where you blame yourself.

As far as I am concerned I tried to tell you a little about that in my letter yesterday. Our relationship has been is and will be more than my dearest and perhaps even wildest hopes. It is a great reality.

You must not write any more about it, nor try any more to tell me these things. You have done it once and for all. There won't be that pressure any more. But all the time I felt it must happen once—for your sake as well as mine. Then we could begin to build.

I have no time either. In a minute I go to Kot's, then dinner with the family. Spent the morning at the bank, hair etc. and all I long for now is to work and be quiet. But soon I shall not be able to.

Last night I lay awake a long time, in gladness, thinking of you in a way that I haven't been able to because it always made me cry so terribly, about all the beautiful things you have said and done, the incredible sweetness of it. It all came back like a balm.

Let us promise ourselves now not to go back to any of the failures (which were nobody's fault you know—God has forgiven long ago because where there is true love, all is forgiven and I loved you very much and you loved me and we got lost on the way, that is all). When you feel the slightest pang of self-criticism or remorse, darling, now, please please, immediately think of something else, even say simple words to yourself, like, "It's all right. It's really all right. That is over." I think it helps [now] and then to literally absent yourself. Perhaps in a remembered impersonal landscape like your lake at Neuchâtel. Just in the last five days I have learnt to do it. It is such a saving grace.

Do not be sad about the poem to Jean-Do. You see she helped so much because she always told me that real love would not be destructive but that I must wait a very long time and she told me that she understood how when one loved a person as I love you, "On devient insupportable."

She knows all about how hard it was for you, how difficult. There is <u>no</u> shadow there towards you, so please do not imagine there is. How I wish someday you could see her and talk with her—the point is really that she has always been like me, an impossible <u>lover</u>, loving too much etc. but learning to <u>renounce</u> through loving more not less.

My dear, try to rest now. Not to think about me except when it is gentle and sweet to do so. There <u>is</u> an angel in all this and it is our love. There it is which has suffered so much and now can sleep and wake up in the morning smiling at the new day, thinking by some miracle we happened to live in the same world at nearly the same time.

Do you leave the 22d? I thought to write once more tomorrow morning (I go to R. West's with Ruth for the day) but had not meant to write today. But how good it is to be able to talk again.

And once you leave for Breslau (which will be exciting and good I think) then we shall start on a new étape the good leafy moderate path, full of cool shade and silences and long perspectives.

Here you are. Here I am. And all is well.

Dearest love, until tomorrow

[ ]

Are you sleeping better now? What did the doctor say? It is awful that <u>you</u> have had to go through these last weeks, but we must not think of that. Only go forward in peace. <u>No regrets</u>.

---

your letter of 16th and 17th: not extant.
glad you let me see his letter: not extant.
dinner with the family. The Sartons, having arrived from Belgium, were staying in an apartment on Manchester Street in London.
"On devient insupportable": One becomes <u>unbearable</u>.
on a new étape: on a new stage of the journey.
<u>No regrets</u>: An allusion to the refrain Sarton often quoted from Edith Piaf's famous comeback song, "Non, Je Ne Regrette Rien" ("No, I Regret Nothing").

55A OLD CHURCH ST.   Aug. 19th, Thurs. [1948]

Dear love, first all the news and I'll finish this this afternoon when there may be a letter from you. How lovely this burst of communication and how very good to take up normal life again and not to be so exaggerated any longer! The peace of it.

Well, I am going to see Anthony and his wife tomorrow for tea which will be fun. Today looked like a great stretch of peace and I wanted to go and pay a visit to the Wilton Triptych, but then Amélie Hanbury-Sparrow called. She is my German friend and I am godmother of her adopted twins (adopted after her own adored child was killed by a flying bomb here in England). She brings with her her astonishing German son who held out as a boy against Nazism, alone, and with a terrible Nazi father. His disillusion now has been one of her problems and I am glad to know him. I lunch with them today.

I have kept forgetting to thank you for the news of Grace, for your sweetness to Ellen and all you have done for me there. It is perfectly wonderful that she seems at last to be out of the shadow.

Yesterday I had an amazing letter from George Raut. I felt so upset at my behaviour that night that I wrote him a polite note and sent "The Lady and the Unicorn," imagining that he must surely love the Cluny Tapestries. Now comes this highly exaggerated very charming letter. I am glad to see some people are even more exaggerated than I am (and with less reason!) and I think I shall have to send it to you as proof of this interesting fact! Someday we must go back there together—but first I must answer it. Only Dorothy Osborne's ceremonious pen would be quite worthy.

It is very nice here—nice and easy, except that a horrible fairy called Raymond comes every evening and sits around at Ruth's feet. He plays the clavichord so I try to forgive him his abominable preciosity and Cockney accent (he pronounces chaise longue, chaise lonje, for instance and goes into horrible rhapsodies about birds' nests). I have to leave the room now and then I get quite sick. Ruth's fat niece is here and is making me a most wonderful white lamb hat, you know, just a Russian hat, round with a flat crown, but very becoming and it looks like white Persian lamb if there is such a thing. Three pounds and I shall pay her with dress material when I get back. Wonderful!

In one letter you asked about the story. I finished it in Belgium and sent if off and Mother was sure it would sell. It's a very tender young love story and I quite like it. But Diarmuid says not one of his clients is selling anything and it sounds rather frightening. However I shan't get panic-stricken. As soon as I'm home I'll write some pure American stories (one about our grocer, a fat man with very small hurting feet I am thinking of) and we'll see. I can't for this autumn make any other plan of earning as those things must be done ahead.

Everyone talks about Julian and Balliol. Is it definite? It came out in the papers apparently. Also darling do you know yet when you leave for Breslau?

The night you dreamed that I smiled was the night when everything came clear for me, I think. All that Sunday was a great shining day. What a relief it was.

Darling, I hope my letter of yesterday, written so fast, didn't sound pretentious. Who am I to make suggestions as to what you should say to yourself? But you will understand and I am not going to worry.

Later, before tea

And just in from a four hour conversation with Bob and Amélie. Ce jour est plein de bonheur et de richesse. Ruth's niece, Mary, is dieting to try to get thin and it makes her very sad, so this morning going out to get flowers for Amélie, I got a little bunch of flowers for her, roses and things as a consolation prize and she said so simply, "No one has ever given me flowers before." It made me terribly happy to be the first. I got the Camus Plague for Kot hoping he may like it even if written by a bloody foreigner. He seems in a rather cross mood, though I made him laugh yesterday, but whenever I tried to be serious he argued me down so hotly—and started off in a real fury because a friend had written me c/o S. S. Koteliansky Esq (!). In America it is done like that, but he went on about it for quite five minutes. He is perfectly sure that you will come to England in the middle of Sept. for the British Ass. with Julian. He will be terribly disappointed if you don't, but I am afraid you may have to go to Switzerland. I wonder.

But O darling, what a wonderful boy this German boy is. I wish I could tell you all that he said, it did me so much good. What I suddenly saw freshly was how much we all depend on the unsaid, taken for granted supports in any community—on people's fundamental decency, honesty and so on, the invisible web of protections, of safeties in which we move, held up by faith which we do not even realize is there—but take it away, and the individual is absolutely alone and naked and desperate. The boys he knows, he says, suffer from the fact that they do not see any of the big lines of the future, nor are they supported by living in a more or less stable society in which certain bonds can be counted on. They are like isolated molecules. The organic quality of the community is gone for them. He didn't say exactly that but that is what I felt as he talked. I was very glad because when I asked if that faith could be helped if a faith in Germany itself could come back, he said, "I never think of Germany; I could believe in Western Europe perhaps." And then, "I think every young person today has the duty to support in every way he can every international organization," and then added proudly, "I belong to three." He is about 16, not yet in the University.

What is awful is that the average German boy who believed everything he was told ten years ago, now doubts everything, looks for the snail under every leaf and does not believe that any motive is pure. That is I suppose the inevitable violent reaction, but it is very hard to deal with.

No more now—Love and love

[   ]

Don't try to write often anymore—all is well now!

---

the Wilton Triptych: probably the Wilton Diptych, c.1395, England's finest example of International Gothic; in the National Gallery in London. Authorities disagree as to whether its artist is English, French, or Italian. Richard II's portable altarpiece, it depicts his delivering his kingdom to the Virgin and the Christ Child, who are about to hand it back to him, confirming that Richard ruled with their help and protection.

Ellen: Ellen Paine, Grace Dudley's sister.

George Raut: Friend of the Huxleys, whom Francis Huxley recalls as "exaggerated, charming and generous."

"The Lady and the Unicorn": see The Lion and the Rose.

Dorothy Osborne's ceremonious pen: Sarton was presently reading the letters of Dorothy Osborne. See footnote to letter of 14 August 1948.

you asked about the story: a story she began on 29 July 1948 and completed on 3 August; title uncertain.

Julian and Balliol: circumstances unidentified.

Bob and Amélie: Amélie Hanbury-Sparrow and her older son.

Ce jour est plein de bonheur et de richesse: Today is full of happiness and richness.

average German boy who believed . . . ten years ago, now doubts: While clearly a reference to the entire German culture, this is probably also a reference to the Hitler Youth, mainstay of the Nazi regime, with compulsory membership by 1940. It was a propaganda machine for inculcating the young with Nazi ideology of a new age ruled by racially pure Germans. As the war progressed, its members were ruthlessly exploited.

————————

AT RUTH's [PITTER]   Aug. 25th, 1948

Darling, just back from a rather hectic day at Rebecca West's—but with at the end of it one of those pure gifts, the unexpected peaceful hour of illumination in the empty carriage on the way home through all the loveliness. Ruth and I stretched out in luxury each with a whole seat and a book and I came back to DuBos as to some hidden stream and read a little and looked out and read again. How grateful I am for all your search and the finding and sending. It is a real treasure. Of course all my marks are different from yours (though how beautiful the quotation you sent in your last about introspection and the music of a Bach aria). I can't bear ever to finish it and dole it out page by page, not to go too quickly—p. 104 (end of the long paragraph); p. 123, end of the day, p. 125 (wonderful!) and all he says of Bergson, and Valéry, everywhere. What seems so rare is la justesse du <u>sentir</u>, du sentiment, la valeur du coeur ici justment où l'esprit et le cerveau sont si délicats, précis et distingués. Je crois que dans un critique c'est extrêment rare qu'il n'y ait aucune déformation de caractère. Ici on sent l'homme dans son entier, et que c'est justement cet homme entier qui en fait un critique exceptionel. Un ascetisime fondé jamais sur un refoulement, une negation (comme dans Aldous par ex.) mais au contraire par une idée plus complète de la personnalité entière.

Je ne peux pas te dire comme j'ai eu horreur de la pièce d'Aldous où mon amie allemande-anglaise m'a emmené hier soir. Du point de vue humain Aldous n'est jamais au centre, mais <u>toujours</u> à côté, et jamais plus que quand il parle de choses sensuelles, cette horreur et fascination d'un adolescent pour le "défendu"—une déformation si crue et si visible partout.

Aug. 26

I have a great deal more to say about all this but will wait till I get to Ireland. I'm sending Claudel and a Thurber which made me laugh aloud in the bus to Switzerland. It's a most beautiful washed windy blue day and

I am off to the bank, to my family to say goodbye, to Kot, etc. Yes, I did sell two stories here in England which eased things these last weeks—one for 35 guineas ("The Paris Hat" as a matter of fact) and another ["The Desert"] for 25 guineas which I wrote on the boat going home last year and which never sold in the States. How awful it is all through DuBos, the worrying about money. And dangerous to have to produce too much. Of course he had behind him the accumulated years of reading and thinking, a kind of bank account. But still it is terrible.

I'll try to get Hartley's first for Grace but fear it is out of print. What a charming book it was.

As I look back on these days the most significant moment was going to Battersea and seeing the outdoor sculpture show—there under two immense trees on a small rise pelouse, stand Henry Moore's three figures— what <u>presences</u> they are, composing all the air around them, composing for an instant the world itself as if all were clear and calm now, forever. And how completely shabby and false the pseudo-classic or even purely realistic sculpture looked. Not as Brancusi said more and more like a corpse, but less and less like anything with meaning at all. I dislike Gill very much. It is too soft somehow, almost sentimental, very "lovely." How I wanted to see these things with you. Though my eyes were very open even without you. The Wilkinsons took me there (you remember she wrote me a wonderful letter about the poems). I spent the whole day with them, practising what Basil calls "leaning back" because they are very tiring, both talking at once, interrupting each other, railing at everything in an amused abrupt very living way, but tiring. However I love Winifred when she suddenly says things like, "I hate balanced people!"

I had an awful dream about you and Mary T.

I'm writing this in pieces because I shall forget what I want to say, these last days being a little too full for ease of spirit. I hope I shall be able to get on with a series of poems "Conversations with an Angel" and perhaps a story. I have a funny feeling that Kot and I have reached the end of something and it is sad. I do not feel the slightest real communication with him and am reduced to gossip. How hateful.

Friday

Fulton was there at Kot's yesterday and I was really rather glad, then James [Stephens] launched into such a horrible performance, never stopping showing off from the time he arrived that I left after half an hour.

The Breslau meeting sounds rather awful from the papers here. But perhaps things are happening behind the scenes where the Russians are not forced to put on the old record and play it again and again. I am anxious to hear what Ella thinks of all this. The headline in the <u>Chronicle</u> (not a big one but the head of the note on the meeting) was, "Prof. Huxley scolds the peacemakers." You won't have time to write till you get to Switzerland and I shan't expect it.

A beautiful day again but I am a wreck of fatigue. However a few real working days will set that right. More soon.

With dear love

[   ]

I have found a <u>wonderful</u> book, Buber's <u>Between Man and Man</u>. I'll send it or another copy when I've finished.

P.S. I never said a word about the snaps. I like all the laughing ones best. Do you want them back? They are very good, I think. I wish mine of you were so, but they are unspeakably sad and mad. I have torn them up. Please try to get someone to take a good one.

---

quotation you sent in your last: not extant.

la justesse de sentir . . . . : What seems so rare is accuracy of feeling and perception, the delicate quality of heart and soul together with the intellect, formal and refined. I believe that in criticism it is extremely rare when there is no fragmentation of the whole person—mind and heart. In DuBos one feels he is whole, and it is just such a whole man who makes an exceptional critic. An asceticism never founded on pulling back or on negation (as with Aldous for example) but the contrary, on an idea larger than the personality itself. ¶ I cannot tell you how horrified I was by Aldous's play [*The Gioconda Smile* opened in June at the New Theatre in London for a nine-month run] where my English-German friend [Amélie Hanbury-Sparrow] took me last night. From the human point of view, Aldous is never at the center, rather <u>always</u> to one side, and never more so than when he is speaking of sensual matters. He has an adolescent horror and fascination with the forbidden, a vulgar, obvious exaggeration in everything.

Hartley's first: L[eslie] P[oles] Hartley (1895–1972), English novelist; *The Shrimp and the Anemone,* 1944, the first of his Eustace and Hilda trilogy, was followed by *The Sixth Heaven* in 1946 and *Eustace and Hilda* in 1947. In *The Sketch,* 11 May 1938, L.P. Hartley, in reviewing *The Single Hound,* writes: "*The Single Hound* is a work of art . . . . Miss Sarton has brought together two worlds, the world of sense . . . and the world of the spirit, and reconciled them."

pelouse: lawn.

Henry Moore's three figures: Three Standing Figures (1947–1948), in Darley Dale stone, erect-

ed in Battersea Park (the gift of the Contemporary Art Society); Henry Moore
(1898–1986), English sculptor and graphic artist, known in informed circles as the
leading avant-garde sculptor in England before his reputation grew rapidly after he
won the International Sculpture Prize at the 1948 Venice Biennale.

realistic sculpture . . . Brancusi said . . . like a corpse: "I think of Brancusi," Sarton wrote to
Bill Brown on 20 October 1947, "who said that realistic sculpture made "des
cadavres" and the better it was the more like a cadavre and this also was what drove
him to abstraction."

dislike Gill: Eric Gill (1882–1940), British sculptor, engraver, illustrator, typographer, and
writer, proponent of a romanticized medievalism.

Wilkinsons: Walter and Winfred Wilkinson, Quaker friends of Judith Matlack.

"Conversations with an Angel": not found.

Buber's Between Man and Man: published in 1947, bringing together previously published
works of Martin Buber (1878–1965), Viennese-born philosopher, theologian, and
Zionist, who emphasized the relationship between man and man and between man
and God, rather than between man and State.

ROCKBROOK HOUSE   Aug. 30th, 1948
RATHFARNHAM, CO. DUBLIN

Darling, I am terribly anxious to hear about Breslau. I fear it must have
been a great strain and hard on Julian trying to steer a course through all
the passions. However I must admit that it seemed from the beginning a
very thin chance. I hope it will not all have seemed a waste and that perhaps there were some good <u>unofficial</u> talks. Beatrice said yesterday that she
heard on the radio you were leaving 24 hours early. And now at last you
are with your mother in Switzerland. How happy she must be and perhaps
the weather will be good and you can see your lake really blue. Bill wrote
me that he had lunch and a lovely time with you and Julian, said very
charming things about you which I will spare you.

This is a heavenly place—high up on the green hills back of Dublin,
a large comfortable Georgian house with a sheltered terrace and gardens
at the back and the great view of Dublin and the bay in front. Perfect nat-
uralness of everyone, so good to be in—immense amounts of food and
drink, endless conversations in soft Irish voices. The lord has a strange
bruised face (bruised from the inside) opaque and purplish and carries on
a long monologue in a monotone which is often very witty, but rarely
deals in ideas. Everyone calls him the lord and when B. took me round the
gardens and said, "The lord's work all this," I thought for a moment she

meant the Almighty. Paddy, the older brother was here until yesterday, with his wife and babe. He looks like an aristocratic version of Jimmy Durante, immensely long face, great charm. I have hardly seen Michael yet. He went to a ball Sat. night and played tennis most of yesterday.

I am either falling to pieces or the air here is fearfully relaxing like Montreux. I feel slightly dizzy all the time and so tired it's like an illness. And should be working, but at present it's out of the question. However it's very pleasant here and very kind so I'll just wait and see if I don't feel a bit more alive in a few days.

I copied out for you because I am good for nothing else, a few pps. of Buber's book. The trouble is that these pieces without the context don't really give very much. But they have helped me back into a true relation with myself at last. A great deal has happened to me inwardly in these last weeks which eventually I shall try to write to you.

I am saving DuBos and reading a little at a time. Wish there were a Browning here. I simply have never been able to see that B. was a poet at all. I thought DuBos's analysis of James's brilliant (taste as a substitute almost for morality, his moral sense being actually an aesthetic sense).

Now there is wind and rain. Last evening we drove back to the strange purple lonely Wicklow hills—amazing country.

Darling, I am sorry I am so stupid, but I cannot help it. Try to get some rest at your mother's.

With dearest love
M—

Beatrice: Lady Beatrice (Elvery) Glenavy, wife of Gordon Campbell, Lord Glenavy, governor of the Bank of Ireland; mother of the humorous writer Patrick Campbell and of the novelist Michael Campbell. Irish friend of Koteliansky; she befriended but later turned upon Sarton.

Bill wrote me . . . with you and Julian: In a letter dated 24–25 August 1948, Bill Brown writes: "I'm beginning to see how much you've gone through. I had lunch with Juliette and Julian on Monday—having a talk with Juliette that was unfortunately interrupted by Julian's coming home half way through. She was darling, looked so fresh & blue-eyed, and I think, wanted to talk. She began by saying it was really all her fault for not keeping it at a certain control level—that you had built her up into something she wasn't at all and that she never really could give enough and felt exhausted by the demands. I said obviously it was no one's fault and that you could hardly be expected to act differently, at the time, being so completely involved emotionally. I felt that she loves you very much and will permit herself to enjoy it when it's a little further removed from the last weeks. . . ." In 1997 Brown wrote to this editor, "Juliette I thought wanted me to understand the difficulty of her position which I assumed was wife, mother, non-lesbian, etc. She was reserved, polite,—and beautiful."

Paddy, the older brother: Patrick Campbell, humorist, lived in England.

a few pps. of Buber's book: See Appendix.

Browning: Probably Robert Browning (1812–1889), English poet, never considered profound, particularly known for his "The Ring and the Book." His courtship of and marriage to English poet Elizabeth Barrett Browning (1806–1861) is immortalized in their letters, and in Rudolf Besier's play *The Barretts of Wimpole Street.*

DuBos's analysis of James: analysis by French critic Charles Du Bos (1882–1939) of Henry James (1843–1916), American short story writer, novelist, and critic. Sarton unwittingly spoke of her own work when she wrote of James to Bill Brown in 1946: "It is really all about a sense of values isn't it? And how rare that is in literature or anywhere for that matter."

———

ROCKBROOK HOUSE   Friday, Sept. 4th, 1948
RATHFARNHAM

Darling, your card mailed Monday just got here today. I have been following the Congress news up to your departure. The one thing that seems amazing is that Julian did not expect what happened, but I am sorry it turned into the usual old record put on. I'm sure he did everything possible to build the impossible bridge, and I fear it was an awful strain and extra fatigue. Did you say something about an important council meeting now? Today you are off to Switzerland and will find a letter from me there as I wasn't sure it would catch you in Paris. Letters to and from Ireland take a long time, so if you want to catch the boat, here is the address (it leaves Sat. morning but mail must be in Friday the 10th, as we leave at the crack of dawn): Cabin B45, Tourist Class, Britannic, Cunard White Star, Cobh, Eire, Sept. 10th. On the 8th I go to Bowen's Court, Kildoreerie, Kirk, Co. Cork just for two nights.

I know that Neuchâtel has its own special strains but perhaps anyway you can have early nights and long sleeps and catch up a little. I'm relieved to hear the bloodstream is working, though I didn't realize it had stopped working! I feel almost completely out of touch, which is all right, but it makes it rather difficult to write.

This has been a lovely time. Beatrice is like sunlight alive in a room. The lord reads my poems and plays Beethoven quartets to me and fills me with Irish whiskey and Irish tall tales. I have hardly seen Michael who works like a beaver, plays tennis, goes to parties, etc. We went one night to the Abbey and saw a new rather poor play of Lennox Robinson's with a very amateurish performance. The audience interested me, an audience of large-ankled giggling Irish girls and their followers, a most "popular" audience. Strange to see Yeats looking down at them from the wall. The next night was more fun—though I forgot that we went backstage and stood in the green room where so much history has been played out and Beatrice suddenly sighed in her lilting voice, "Where has all the quality gone?" But the next night we had dinner at Jamme's with lots of wine and drinks with Mrs. Knight, Gordon's sister, a sort of hag of a woman who adores the Irish comedian Jimmy O'Dea and has a perpetual box for his show—where we were bound—then Michael, Beatrice and I. Haggie Knight and I had a great argument about Michael's attitude to Julian (whom he felt inhuman). I was rather angry that M. thought J. should have paid any attention to him. Well, it was fun and I think embittered no one and I was glad of the chance. There is an Irish tendency to laugh at and destroy everything with infinite charm but at times I find it extremely irritating. Michael often does it. And in his own young way, he can be very inhuman.

Then off we went to the box to see a very childish vulgar, thoroughly amusing show interspersed with awful hammy singers who sang Traviata for my delight, and every most sentimental song for the last ten years, backstage to have a drink with Jimmy—then home. A lovely evening. I was very drunk and happy.

It rains all the time and from my window I watch the trees moving and changing every second, the leaves turned back, and beyond purplish hills that come and go in the mist and right in the foreground the square emerald of the terrace decorated at the moment by the collie and an adorable marmalade cat who follows him everywhere and curls up inside his paws.

I'm reading nothing but Irish things, life of Parnell etc. after three weeks of nothing but religion and philosophy—and I am not writing much. I get into awful panics about the immediate future but I expect when I get home I'll think of some wonderful saleable story. At present it is quite hopeless to try. I haven't one idea. A few poems, that's all.

The only sadness is to feel perhaps too aware of the inward separation in this marriage. Gordon never does anything but argue in an icy way every word B. says and under her beautiful smiling impassive calm, it must be corrosive. He is a strange man. At first he terrified me but one can get him to talk well about poetry for instance. Only he is always once removed from human life, I think. And she so warm and so human. She showed me a most beautiful photograph of Kot, the youngest purest face I ever saw. It almost made me cry.

Now darling I must I think tell you something because it is rather on my conscience. Immediately after I had written you that I had said nothing to Kot, he asked me a direct question and I unfortunately answered. I think it made him terribly angry. Nothing was gone into. I just burst into tears and went away and came back and we never spoke of it again. He takes it for granted that it is one more of my literary adventures and <u>all</u> on my side and quite hopeless so I don't think you need to worry. It will certainly never be spoken of again and I feel I am in his mind <u>beyond the pale</u>. This is sad but cannot be helped. And time will mend all. That is what I try to believe. It was unfortunate that I had to be at Kot's during those very bad days (before I went to Basil's). That is a very long time ago and I am a different person now.

I was very glad to see that DuBos (p. 331) has a long passage about loving one's neighbor <u>as oneself</u>, with the latter part emphasized. The one thing that still makes a knot in my mind, darling, is that I seem to have succeeded so little in making you love <u>yourself</u>, and as that was the point (however far I may have gone from it at times into wishing to make you love me) it is sad. I feel now that it is rather like a kaleidoscope; with one shift all would fall into place, nothing would have to be denied, all would be accepted: love, you, me, life itself. And perhaps someday it will.

With very dear love from your old
May

I am nothing. Only the words are real.
Radiance pours out of the nothing I am,
Light from a wound. This does not seem
But is, this rest outside and in time,
In balance and reserve all I am not.
What matter that the heart is chaos
The body become so poor and small

Withered by parting beyond consolation?
I lose all earthly joys for this one joy.

The tree of light shows where the seed grew;
The radiant leaves promise and hope forever,
The poem that surpasses all self-pities
And tells of love, if only to the skies,
But to them says it every day, every hour:
I am nothing but the words of praise endure.

—

Outside the wind tears at the trees;
Dark comes into the room like a stranger
And we are invaded by huge loneliness.
The quiet evening has its special danger;
The shape of the heart fills the empty room.
Outside is wilderness, the terrible hills—
Look out, it is coming to burst open the door,
Burst in on the books, the game of solitaire,
Landscape pursued by a cloud, see, it is here,
Passion and loneliness and all human pain
And these too living presences of wind and rain.
Say to the soul be still in the quiet room,
But what real ghosts come in or do not come?

Aug.–Sept. 1948]

———

Bowen's Court: the Bowen family home in County Cork, completed in 1775 by the third Henry Bowen and left to Elizabeth Bowen upon the death of her father in 1930. Despite its majesty, it was not until 1949, after the success of Bowen's novel *The Heat of the Day,* that she put in plumbing and other amenities. Sarton describes it to Judith Matlack in a letter of September 1948: "This is a huge house with vast resounding halls, the old wall paper peeling off and everything very grand and very shabby and rather <u>cold</u>—no bathrooms, the w.c. is across a large ballroom (from my room) and down three long staircases and one's every step echos—now that Elisabeth's novel is to be a Literary Guild Selection they are hoping to put in bathrooms. Little Colleens appear with jugs of hot water and cups of tea every morning. We eat in a simply vast room which was the front hall, looking out on the really splendid trees and meadows!—one grove of oaks is called "the Lambs Drawing room," sheep grazing everywhere." Dene's Court in Sarton's novel *A Shower of Summer Days* is based on Bowen's Court, of which work Bowen wrote to Sarton in 1952: "I read the book twice and parts again. I hope [it] has made you as happy as it has made me, and I know many others. . . . you have done something so good in this novel, so strong and understanding and delicate."

Abbey . . . Lennox Robinson . . . performance: The Abbey Theatre, a famous Dublin play-
house, opened in 1904 for the production of plays by and about the Irish; the building burned in 1951 and was reopened in 1966. Esmé Stuart Lennox Robinson
(1886–1958) was an Irish actor, critic, manager, prolific dramatist, and anthologist
(*The Golden Treasury of Irish Verse*).

life of Parnell: Charles Stewart Parnell (1846–1891), Irish nationalist leader, tireless agitator
for home rule; referred to frequently throughout the works of James Joyce, for
whom he was a political hero.

I am nothing . . . : In addition to "I am nothing. Only the words are real," unpublished,
and "Outside the wind tears at the trees," which appeared, with changes, as
"Landscape Pursued by a Cloud" in *The Leaves of the Tree*, "Song," as it appears in
The Leaves of the Tree, was also enclosed.

ROCKBROOK HOUSE   [September 1948]

RATHFARNHAM

My angel, it was so wonderful to wake up this morning to a world of sunlight, I went for a walk before breakfast and I think of you and hope your
lake is shining for you. I must be quite mad as I thought last Friday was
the 6th, hence my wire. Letters take so long to get here that I fear you
may not catch the boat, but do not anyway worry. A great peace has
descended on me.

I was delighted to have your letter and to know that you are making
a report on the congress. I passionately wish to hear it. What you say of Ella
Winter reminds me of what R. West said apropos of the Wallace convention. I had asked if they were very anti-British (because of Palestine) and
she said, "They were really more anti-American than anything else." I saw
no report of Ella's speech. (What did you think of her?) The two small clip-
pings are all I have. I left England before the blow-up and here the papers
hardly carry international news except headline news. One has a queer
cut-off feeling as a matter of fact. No one seems to care about the French
crisis, about Burma, about anything. For a little while it is very restful, I
must say. But I should begin to feel very guilty after a month of it. What
surprises me really honestly is that Julian <u>expected</u> anything better. I wish
I had heard the discussion with Laves about making a front of progressive
liberals. I am sick and tired of everyone putting ashes on their heads viz the
Russians. No country has clean hands. And one can understand the reasons
for things without having to make everything black and white. It is all
grays, different shades of gray, different kinds of paint. But I have always felt

the greatest danger in America not to be dollar imperialism etc. but rather the wide-eyed idealists who want such a pure world that they are incapable of moving one difficult inch forward through the jungle. They are the real wreckers and even perhaps war-makers. Well, I shall be eager to hear all you say and think.

Thanks for the clipping about Giorgio. No, Dorothy Hillyer is a dynamo of a woman, divorced, chief editor at Houghton Mifflin. I guess several hearts will be broken by this but I think it may be a good marriage. Every letter I get has a report of it. It seems to be shaking the continents!

I keep thinking about France and what is happening there.

Last night the usual Sunday gang who come to play tennis and stay on to dinner for talk and poker. I went for a long walk by myself because there was a most beautiful and irresistible light everywhere on the hills—then came back to find Erskine Childers and a typical Am. college girl, and Norah McGuinness, the painter, some of Michael's Trinity friends, an actress called Sheila something. I was amazed to find Erskine so little of a person. He was enormously flattering about my poems, but I learned afterward the other poets he admires, all ones I loathe and detest, so I was a little dismayed!

I shall be sorry to leave here. It's been a lovely peaceful time and I am so fond of Beatrice.

My treasure, will you get a little rest? I can't bear to imagine how tired you must be. But try to be very passive for these days. Can you go to bed very early and have breakfast in bed?

I am awfully sleepy and stupid and must pack and try to finish a poem. I'll write from Elisabeth's once more before I sail. Then there will be a fairly long silence as I only arrive the 18th.

I have had a running battle here with Beatrice who out of the warmth of her whole personality and a sort of simplicity and greatness of heart can't see anything but the simplest kind of poetry, is violently anti-Yeats, anti–Edith Sitwell etc. etc. and the same thing for painting and music. They call all modern music "Bartokerie" here. It is absolutely baffling and I get nowhere except to enjoy the argument. Most conversations are monologues anyway I have decided.

No more now.

With dearest love
[   ]

Wallace convention: Henry Agard Wallace; see footnote to letter of 15 April 1945.

the French crisis: Following a brief period of stability, a renewed rise in prices and corre-
sponding demands for higher wages led to the fall of Robert Schuman's government,
despite the unsuccessful attempts of Schuman and André Marie to form a lasting cabinet. At the time of this letter, radical leader Henri Queuille had formed a government with Schuman as foreign minister, and union leadership initiated another wave
of strikes.

Burma: In January 1948, having been proclaimed an independent republic free of any ties
with the British Commonwealth, the new state of Burma embarked on a program
of radical nationalization of resources and industries; at the time of this letter, the two
Communist parties, dissatisfied with their efforts, broke out in rebellion in southern
Burma. In addition, the Karens, rebelling to achieve an autonomous Karen state,
succeeded, together with the Communists, in occupying large parts of southern and
central Burma while the "People's Volunteer Organization" (part of the Anti-Fascist
People's Freedom League's old army) ravaged central Burma.

Laves: Walter Laves (1902—?), educator; replaced Howard E. Wilson (1901–?; deputy
executive secretary for the Preparation Committee of UNESCO, 1946; director of
UNESCO seminar of International Education, summer 1947; first United States rep-
resentative at UNESCO until 1950) as assistant director general at UNESCO.

viz: namely.

clipping about Giorgio: Marquis Giorgio Diaz de Santillana (1902–1974), professor of philosophy and history of science, Harvard University; friend of the Sartons. In September
1948 he married Dorothy Hillyer, who was first married to American poet Robert
Silliman Hillyer (1895–1961); she succeeded Ferris Greenslet as editor in chief at
Houghton Mifflin.

Erskine Childers: probably the son of the Anglo-Irish writer and politician of the same name
who died in 1922.

Sheila: probably Sheila Richards, wife of the actor Denis Johnston.

"Bartokerie": derisive reference to the new, modal harmonies and irregular meter of
Hungarian composer Béla Bartók (1881–1945).

BOWEN'S COURT   Sept. 9th, 1948

Darling love, your wire has just been brought up the great resounding
staircase by the maid. Bless˜you for it. This is a strange and beautiful place
from which to take off for the new world. It's all tremendously grand and
bare, with such great windows through which always the sight of
immense silent trees, not a leaf moving—great green meadows and the
trees—the house itself is gaunt, shabby, vast so everything echoes—anything but cosy but with a most poetic atmosphere so I can imagine how

one could write here and live here. It seems too huge for any intimacy and people wander about like ghosts, diminished into dwarfs by the high ceilings, by the great spaces around them and somehow pathetic and dear in consequence. The only other people are Eddie Sackville West and a cousin of Elisabeth's who used to come here as a child for her holidays and danced in the ballroom just outside my door. I feel now how much this is Elisabeth's real self and real place and it explains a great deal. They are planning to live here all year round soon. One feels extremely detached from the world here in Ireland, that is one of the strange things. It is partly the quality of the light and air, so luminous and ethereal and not quite <u>real</u>—the quality of things seen in a dream. This morning when I woke up and pushed back the curtains the trees were just looming out of a thick white mist. Every now and then hosts of rooks wheel up and circle round the house, hundreds of them. Then there is silence or only the sound of a cart creaking in the distance. I feel the typewriter is an anachronism. One is <u>en plein</u> 19th century still here, as Eddie said last night. Glass-walled bookcases, Victorian and huge shabby carpets and the original wallpaper (paisley in the dining room) peeling off the walls—the only heat open wood fires; no bathroom; one W.C. to get to which I cross the huge expanse of the ballroom, then go down two flights of stairs every step echoing as I go.

Elisabeth darling and warm, smiling her catlike smile—being asked in for drinks by the woman who sells liquor in the village, talking the village talk, knowing everyone by name. Every afternoon at five there is an expedition to a neighbor's for baths. It is all, as you see, strange and delightful.

But part of me swings back to Paris for a last look at you, at the river, at the lights on the ceiling; part of me stays in Belgium in the little chair opposite Jean-Do's; part of me remembers with tender gratefulness the fun at Glenavy's and dear Beatrice with her childlike <u>joie de vivre</u> which nothing in her hellish life has touched or tainted; part of me seems to be here—and a large part looks forward to the great leap back into small human responsibilities, lectures, work etc.

The DuBos has been most precious these last days and weeks, a sort of inner continuity. I look forward to finding Volume II which I sent ahead to the boat.

I wonder how you are. It's a great relief to know that you got to

Neuchâtel as I felt how it weighed on your mind, not seeing your mother and feeling her waiting for you. Now, with this behind you you can enter the last months of UNESCO and all they will bring and demand. Paris will be lovely when you get back. I love this moment, edged in bronze, when the green just begins to turn. Are you finding some peace, my darling? Are you finding your own true joy, impersonal and sweet, in trees, in the lake, in sleep, in long thoughts? I do hope it has been a good week.

I no longer feel your physical presence. How strange time and distance are—and how powerful! And if I could only see you in this state, all would be well. But I'm afraid all my new-found wisdom is only a way of living without you and if you were there I would give up all wisdom for a single glance.

With all my European love. The American kind will be discovered at the other end of this long journey.

[   ]

Eddie Sackville West: Edward Charles Sackville-West (1901–1965), author and music critic; first cousin of Vita Sackville-West. The brook-crossing scene in *A Shower of Summer Days* is based on Elizabeth Bowen and Edward Sackville-West's having walked calmly through a brook while Sarton had to remove her loafers and wade through.
en plein 19th century: in the middle of the nineteenth century.
joie de vivre: exhilaration.

---

139 OXFORD ST.   22 Sept., 1948

Dearest treasure, what a lovely thing it was to find your letter here when I arrived, rather dizzy and queer late Saturday night. It is now Thursday and the balloon of my mind safely fastened and housed and work begun. I did not write at once as I think you will not be back from the Dordogne for some time and no doubt won't have letters forwarded. How I hope it works for Francis and that you have a lovely time, all three in that legendary, or rather mythical part of France. It has always suggested darkness and wildness to me, the pre-history. Is it very beautiful? There are lots of Romanesque churches, aren't there? and I expect Julian will have been taking pictures madly while (I hope) you sat under trees drinking wine and hearing all about the Expedition. I do so hope it was all good and you come back for the last lap restored in spirit. Your letter sounded so well, so alive and back in yourself. It made me very happy. Only it is terrible about your friend and all the operations and the hormones—how hard to accept. One can only say that character transcends circumstances and that is what it is to be human—and yet it is hard to accept pain for others or for one-self. And your little mother who had to be left and wrenched away from with all the guilt of being really glad to go. But at least now you will not have that need to answer her need tugging at your heart and nerves for a few months.

As for me, I am in a rather disturbed state of mind. I suppose just the settling in. Judy, perfect in understanding, perfect peace, so it is not that. And it is not you with your endearing maddening re-iterated "ifs." No, it is in a way a sense of middle age, of having arrived at a peak, at a place where there is real change of point of view, perhaps. I feel immensely dis-satisfied with all I have done. And also very eager to work and very cross to have to write stories. I've finished one in these three days, only to recopy now and send off. But what I need is to write poems, which means the long hours of tough thinking, not personal poems, and I do not see how I am to do it or make the time. It is lovely to be doing cleaning and cook-ing and clothes-washing and ironing again. And this great big steady table on which I can spread papers—and all the books. But the telephone rings, so many people to see and a real horror of conversation. It is so rare that a conversation is creative. I miss Edith Kennedy always so much when I come back to Cambridge, for it used to be coming back to her and she had the gift of creative conversation as I have never known anyone else to have it. Mostly it is two monologues and at the end one has spent a little bit of one's essence, thrown it away, and not communicated anything. I sup-pose really that I feel rather dispersed and wish now to concentrate every-thing, to be silent, to give nothing out at all, but make myself a cocoon and live inside it.

You do not have to change you know. You just have to be yourself to the limit. That is all anyone wants of you. But I can't accept lies like that you are cold and inflexible. That is just rubbish and it is very wicked to say such things. Be cold to me if you must (though of course you are not) but be warm and loving to yourself. It is strange to have an ocean between us.

What the ocean does I think is to take away all <u>sensation</u>. In one sense it is true that I am not there or anywhere near you now, which must be a great relief! But in another sense the distance is a sort of freedom and so we are closer than before. Really your letter was [a] great blessing, darling. It made me feel acutely what a lot of nonsense passion is, how unimportant on some levels and that other things are not nonsense, such as our being able to exchange views about life and the world and write to each other. You see, I am becoming quite middle-aged and wise and an awful old realist. I just want to work now and be left in peace for a long time.

I felt the second volume of DuBos not quite as good as the first and wonder if he re-wrote the first and not the second? I am happy to find that he loves Joubert as I always have, putting him in a special heaven with Mozart and Tchekov. All I think had accepted and hence although of exceptional sensibility also were exceptionally serene. That is so very rare. And so they do not butt their heads against walls but just fly over them.

Now I have got Rivière's <u>Aimée</u> from the library which DuBos speaks of often. I wonder what it is like.

Here the air is full of the poison of the elections where everything but the truth is spoken. But I am relieved that many of my friends who were for Wallace have changed and like me will vote for Norman Thomas, a protest vote of course. But it seems all one can do.

Did Janet [Flanner] ever do a piece on UNESCO? I haven't seen it in the New Yorker yet.

The total result of Breslau seems to be that everyone came with preconceived ideas. Those who were pro-Russian stayed pro-Russian and refused to admit that the Russian contingent had behaved at all badly and just felt it was so good that "differences of opinion could be expressed." It all seems bitterly hopeless. And now the murder of Bernadotte. So much violence is there just underneath, in everyone. And at the same time such a desperate hunger for peace and quiet and to be left alone. Or to take refuge somewhere. It takes courage to be part of a time that is really between worlds where there will be no rest and no end to the struggle and where one must fight in every possible way that the soul be not lost in the struggle. Here coming back I feel it. Nothing but greatness is demanded. And yet who can find greatness in himself and what do we serve great enough to pull it out of us? I think the only question now when one meets a person is (though not to say it), "What do you serve?"

Sometimes I blame myself for these months of intense absorption in myself and in you and then I seem to see that they have made me grow and perhaps be more ready than I was before to look out with steady eyes and try to build and help. I don't know. It is what I hope.

How are you? I am sorry for this letter. My thoughts are with you without intermittence but I have found it difficult to write. I am driving myself hard just now. I must. And the wide margins for letters are gone. But you will understand. Write when you can but do not have it on your mind as a compulsion, only when it is fun do let me know what is happening and what is decided about the big meeting—and anything and everything else.

Now you are here in the middle of my life and it is good.

[   ]

-----

the Expedition: Francis Huxley had led an expedition of young scientists to Gambia to study the problem of hippopotamuses devouring rice planted along rivers there.

gift of creative conversation as I have never known anyone else to have it: Edith Forbes Kennedy (see footnote to letter of 30 October 1937), who worked hard to make ends meet and bring up her three sons, held informal gatherings in her small, shabby Cambridge house. Of her Sarton writes in *A World of Light:* "For her, conversation was as important and as real as any other art. In that sense the atmosphere at 29 Shepard Street resembled one of the eighteenth-century salons in Paris, dominated as each was by a woman of charm and brilliance."

your letter was [a] great blessing, darling: among those that were destroyed.

loves Joubert: Joseph Joubert (1754–1824), French *pensée* writer. To Camille Mayran, 10 February 1963, Sarton writes: "Joubert is one of the two or three people I really want to <u>know</u>, to have as a friend, if there were a Heaven where this might be possible—Joubert and Tchekov."

Aimée: a novel by French novelist Jacques Rivière (1886–1925).

the elections: The 1948 elections had five candidates for president: Harry Truman, Democrat; Thomas Dewey, Republican; Strom Thurmond, States' Rights Democrat; Henry Wallace, Progressive; and Norman Thomas, Socialist.

Norman Thomas: Norman Thomas (1884–1968), American political leader and sociologist. An ordained Presbyterian minister, he eventually resigned his ministerial duties to devote his entire life to writing and speaking for social reform and pacifism. As Socialist Party candidate he ran unsuccessfully for many offices, including the presidency (1928–1948).

The total result of Breslau: Julian and Juliette Huxley had gone to Breslau (now Wroclaw), Poland, on 27 July to attend the conference "Des Intellectuels pour la Paix" ("Intellectuals for Peace").

Bernadotte: Count Folke Bernadotte (1895–1948), Swedish soldier, humanist, and diplomat who was assassinated while serving the United Nations as mediator between the Arabs and Israelis.

I think the only question . . . is . . . "What do you serve?": Serving something greater than
  oneself was at the heart of Sarton's sense of being a poet.

———

139 Oxford St.   Oct. 28th, 1948
Cambridge, Mass.

O darling, I am distressed about the packing and that you leave for good
so soon. It overwhelms me to think of it. But thank heavens you have eked
out four extra days alone to do it in and perhaps Nelly will come and help?
And be there, soothing and kind. Will your address be Pond St. in
December? Or <u>what</u>, said the Akond of Swat? This is the only thing I need
to know sometime, but there is no hurry and I shall expect few if any letters for the next six weeks.

It is very good news that your mother was through the wood by the
time you left. So you have a little peace of mind about her. And I think of
your coming back to no cook etc. Well, it is nearly over and there must be
a certain exhilaration as well as the pains of parting in doing all these last
things very well. There must be a most heart-warming atmosphere around
you just now, everyone being able at last to tell you and Julian what you
have done. I do hope the parties go off well and are fun. It seems rather
grim that you should have a cousin on your hands as well as everything
else. I do not see how you do it. My days which are really empty just fly
away and I never catch up but run after them as if they were autumn leaves.

I'm happy that the weather is gold for you. Here, too, all the lights of
afternoon are so beautiful, deep rose and then turquoise with the leafless
branches against open skies. One forgets how beautiful trees are without
their leaves. I shall be very anxious to hear the report of Julian's trip to
England. Perhaps where you settle will depend on that, though surely you
will have a few months at Pond Street before you move into anything new.
I hope you will.

O dear, I am sorry it is a girl if Anthony's wife is so determined to
have a boy. Will they really try again right away? It is very brave of them
really and I feel tenderly about them and their little family and their
courage and sweetness and dignity. Are things better for Anthony at the
job? He spoke of changes or chances that might turn up in the next few
months and I hope something will.

I am a little frightened about Beirut. I just talked to Giorgio on the phone (haven't seen him since his marriage but am going over on Sat. for a drink. I have always liked Dorothy Hillyer) and he seemed astonished that it would go through as it would seem pro-Arab. Well, perhaps you will pluck the flower from the nettle, danger, and if so it will be a good deed and worth all the fears beforehand. But it does seem an added strain on top of everything else. And Julian having to think ahead to the next thing already, while still in the midst of this.

Next week I go off for ten days, first three days of lectures at a college near N.Y. then down to Savannah Ga. for a reading at the Ga. Poetry Society where I expect to be killed by Southern kindness, but I love the old town and shall be glad to see it again.

Mother has had the first two of the x-rays and is hugely relieved that they don't give her nausea and the pain is not too bad. She is getting weller every day and the relief of having kind efficient help in the house makes an immense difference. The peace when I go over there, the feeling of her being really taken care of, is wonderful. Tomorrow the temporary maid goes and the permanent one arrives so she will be well settled in by the time I leave. But of course she can't use her arm and does have a good deal of pain at night and sleeps badly. All this has made me realize freshly how dear my parents are. And I go about singing their praises to myself all day. But at the same time it has pulled me out of my own life, broken the inner current and I find it hard to get back where I was when I first came home—full of ideas and thoughts and energy of that inward sort which makes all the difference between just living and living deeply. But I expect it will come back soon.

I am sure that the thing with Beatrice will straighten out and that perhaps she writes very fast and doesn't realize how harsh the written word can be, so much harsher than the spoken word. I did fall a little in love with her, as you so perspicaciously suggest on the margin, but it was lovely and peaceful and romantic and not at all physical and I don't think that is at the root of all this battle. But more that because Kot has shut me out she really thinks there is something radically wrong with me and no doubt there is. And there is nothing to be done but be patient and believe in the roots of friendship we planted. I am very fond of her but we will always fight about certain things which I do perhaps take too seriously. I really wince when people call Mozart superficial, for instance, and it is quite silly to care so much. Also she hates modern poetry such as Edith Sitwell, Eliot, calls Yeats superficial and rubbishy etc. And I too have made violent attacks because these things matter far too much to me. And I think she is probably dead right that I take myself, my work, etc. all much too seriously and megalomanically, but I think that is compensation for my total lack of success. It is so hard to go on believing and in order to do it, one persuades oneself that what one does is important. So you see, darling, I am learning from this too and all will be well in the end. Only attacks from friends are much harder to bear and more disturbing than attacks from the world, or its indifference. I do mind very much about Kot.

Enough of all this.

How fine that you had a talk with Maurois about Du Bos. I am rather disappointed in his book on Gide. It is over-written, too many words I feel—and perhaps too much anxiety to prove Gide's essential holiness and to underestimate the conflict in him, to whitewash just a little and I resent that when applied to a real genius. It is not necessary. But of course what shines through all DuBos does is the lovely quality of himself as a person, the intellectual life at its purest and most sensitive and good.

Last night I heard Bowra give a lecture on the Romantic Imagination, quite dull, alas, and a little pompous. Only it is good to feel how he cares about poetry. He spoke of how it heals. And I loved him because he said he was back in Cambridge with "rapturous delight." But very few people not poets can talk about poetry formally without seeming beside the point. That is the real trouble. Love and love, my darling—I am terribly happy when I think of you. Sleep well after these terrific days and don't try to write except a p.c. now and then just so I know you're alive.

[   ]

Nelly: see footnote to letter of Monday [July 1948].

Or what said the Akond of Swat?: "Who, or why, or which, or what,/Is the Akond of Swat?" from The Akond of Swat by Edward Lear.

trees . . . without their leaves: See "The Sacred Wood" in The Land of Silence: "But winter only shows structure more marvelous."

frightened about Beirut: At this time there were repeated alarms from Palestine; the Israeli army occupied the hills north of Beirut and were said to be 120 kilometers from the town; the Lebanese had no army with which to fight.

college near N.Y.: Briarcliffe Junior College, now defunct.

first two of the x-rays: On 8 October 1948, Eleanor Mabel Sarton had been operated on in Boston's Parkway Hospital for breast cancer.

Beatrice: probably referring to Lady Glenavy's letter to Sarton dated 17 September 1948, at the top of which she writes, "This is an awful letter! I think I have turned into Kot," and in which, admitting she does not know what Sarton had said to Kot, writes: "Perhaps it all boils down to this—you mustn't confide about erotic love to old outsiders, they only feel it is ridiculous and disgusting . . . I don't think anything terribly REAL has ever happened to you—I think you are wrapped up in yourself, finding it all terribly interesting & endlessly adventurous & exciting. I think you hardly notice the existence of other people." On 25 September 1948, Glenavy continues: "I'm not a bit angry or infuriated. . . . I think I wanted you to know what Kot felt, why he cast you out, because, really, I wanted you reinstated—It was very bad and clumsy my effort and a great impertinence both to you and Kot. . . . I was trying to tell you that when you talk to old people about your troubles, if they are real great sufferers like Kot, you want to be pretty sure that your troubles are real troubles & not just 'piffle before the wind.'" And she reported that Kot did not want to hear from Sarton again. Despite her protestations that she had wanted Kot to reinstate Sarton, Lady Glenavy's intervention accomplished the opposite; her motives remain questionable. Years later, Sarton's correspondence with Juliette bears this out. The following year, 1949, Marjorie Wells told Sarton it was untrue that he had not wished to see her, and Kot and Sarton spoke immediately by phone. "I was so relieved that I burst into tears afterwards," she wrote her parents. And in June 1951, after three years, Kot and Sarton had tea. She writes to Jean Dominique: "Tu peux t'imaginer, mon hibou, comme ce fait me rend heureuse et soulagée. Je n'ai jamais cru qu'il pourrais jusqu'a la fin fermer la porte sur tout l'amour et la confiance qu'il y avait autrefois entre nous deux." (You can't imagine, my owl, how happy and healing it was. I never believed that he could have ever finally closed the door on all the love and confidence we shared between us.) As Koteliansky lay dying, he asked Marjorie Wells to read and reread Sarton's letters to him.

Maurois . . . his book on Gide: Le Dialogue avec André Gide (Paris: Editions Correa) by André Maurois (pen name of Émile Herzog, 1885–1967), popular French literary and historical biographer, novelist, and essayist.

---

139 OXFORD ST.   Nov. 1st, 1948

Dearest treasure, how I think of you all these days. And somehow or other it is all a parting for me too. I think of your room and the great blue curtains that opened to the moon, and through which once the night I slept there alone a large cat suddenly appeared, rather like the devil. And of the waves of light on the ceiling, and the delicate light wool blankets (those at least will go with you) and the little desk covered with invites from ambassadors and roses. And I think of all the music we listened to in the other room and all the lights over Paris, and the fireworks at 2:00 A.M. and the sunrise once or twice, and the olive-green river. I think of the mantel piece which will never see again the fat cristal candlesticks and the red candles and the Mexican death's head—and of all the leaves which used to come in with you so it was an arbor, pointed pale green beech leaves against the wall and their shadows. And of the little plants in the big window. I think of you looking down at yourself once in the glass table like Narcissus. I think of the dear little birds on my wall. I think of the mornings full of poems and the nights, full of discovery, always full of mystery and love and sometimes terrible journeys, but always the morning again and you there. Never never will there be such a place, such a time again, such a spring. O, how I hate your leaving. How I hate it all to be packed and foreigners to live there (I hope they are haunted).

And Edward Lear said, "All things have suffered change. All is packed. All is empty. All is odious. All is anger. All is sorrow. All is bother."

I do hope Nelly is there to help you, that the news from your mother continues to be good, that Julian got off all right, not too cross and exhausted, that the days at least are golden and you have the sun, and the moon. Is there a moon? I can't remember. I am in bed before it rises.

I go off the day after tomorrow for ten days, first lectures, then five days of real vacance in N.Y., then Savannah for a lecture. I feel terribly dull and uninspired. But I expect talking about poetry will make me feel alive again. I have written to a college to see if I could teach next year. It feels like a prison closing but I can't obviously go on like this for another year. I write without joy and that is fatal. But it will all solve itself in time and I do not really worry very much.

When everything is packed and you are safely off to Beirut, I think you may suddenly feel wonderfully light, with wings on your heels. Enjoy the last weeks—Beirut itself looking down on the Mediterranean must be beautiful. Cast all burdens and responsibilities away and enjoy the final time. And then what a blessing to be home in England, after all. With dear believing love.

[   ]

---

all a parting for me too: The Huxleys were about to leave their Paris apartment for a conference in Beirut, Lebanon, and then go on to Italy.

Lear . . . ". . . All is bother": probably in his letters to Evelyn Baring, edited by Lord Cromer.

vacance: Her New York vacation was spent seeing friends Margaret Foote Hawley, Marion Dorn, Madeleine L'Engle, and Bill Brown and attending a party for the Sitwells at the Gotham Book Mart.

write without joy and that is fatal: she refers to having to turn out short stories in order to survive financially and buy time for poetry; she did this for a short time only.

The letter above is the last of Sarton's extant letters from this period, and the letter with which she had originally intended to close this volume. (There are twelve extant letters from Juliette Huxley to Sarton between 1948 and 1951.) Nearly twenty-seven years passed before correspondence was resumed at the time of Julian's death in February of 1975.

YORK   January 12th [1976]

Dear Juliette,

We are in the middle of a series of snow storms and bitter cold, and I sit bundled up here in my third floor study looking out over a white field and dark gray turbulent ocean that erupts now and then in a white fountain as a big wave hits the rocks. Your letter came today and I think I shall try to answer about Julian now . . . if I lay it aside I may never do it. Besides, I am glad to be in touch, and too tired after shovelling snow, to work.

But first I must say that you inadvertently gave me two or three of the happiest days I have had here . . . when for a little while I imagined that you might be able to get away for the week-end. Of course it was impossible, but it was wonderful to look forward to someone coming here at last who would bring a touch of magic and fill my heart with joy. So many people come, but they want to see me, I don't especially want to see them. The flowers, the beauty all around all came alive for me through your eyes.

About Crucial Conversations you say kind things . . . I know it is not my best book by any means. It seemed awfully hard and dry to me. I was trying to do what a critic-friend said I must do, get away from "the omniscient view," but I felt in a strait jacket the whole time and ended by hating the book. Poor Poppy, I don't expect she is in for an easy time. And from now on I shall write as I wish and not as I am told I must to be in fashion. C.C. was an aberration.

It's wonderful about Francis's and Antony's books . . . I have both but have not yet read Antony. I found F's extremely interesting . . . he has done some difficult things so well. And with grace.

Julian? I lay down with my cat and dog after lunch and thought about your question among the purrs and groans of pleasure on either side of me. What is a man like who writes the "official biography" himself and calls it autobiography? That was the first thing that came to my mind. Lately, in the last ten years I have felt intransigent toward intelligent sensitive people who seem unable ever to <u>look at themselves</u>, who, in fact, do not know themselves, because I believe they are the ones who harm and maim others. Did Julian know himself at all? He can't have. His depressed accusations against himself were as far off the mark as his euphoria. As soon as I came to know Julian well (though I never <u>really</u> did) in a kind of intimacy at least, I began to be aware that he was a flawed character or genius, but I did not know what the flaw was. Perhaps, I wonder now, it was a, (in some way), sick ego. The ego was not robust enough, so to give it temporary satisfactions he permitted himself too much popular stuff. Have you sometimes imagined that the Brain Trust which brought him instant fame turned out to be a dangerous indulgence? His need for romantic love affairs (but this is so very common among human beings) was the need for a flattering mirror which a wife cannot be if she is honest. But even in the middle of all that he was so terribly easily bored, and why was that? He <u>could</u> concentrate . . . I remember good hours we had sketching in Tours when he was not bored and worked at a sketch for an hour or so, completely happy. I remember times when he read Wordsworth aloud to me and then the enjoyment was sustained and real. But so often everything disintegrated into anecdotes (what surer way to short-circuit a conversation than a string of anecdotes? There is nowhere to go except to top one with a better one, or to be silent).

Perhaps the flawed ego was so rapacious because it had not learned what the psychiatrists call "to relate" to other people. Julian did not really <u>listen</u>, or very rarely. And by listening I do not mean, of course, only listening to what is said in words, but capturing another's mood or state of mind or heart. I guess he was not <u>really</u> interested. It must have been hard on the boys as well as on you.

I must say that this is rather niggardly for Julian <u>was</u> very good for and to me when I first knew him when I was 25 and he was 50 . . . he was kind and generous and remarkably understanding about my love for women. He helped me to know that I could have "normal" feelings for a man, and of course I was dazzled by his name and fame and enormously flattered by the affair.

All of this is personal . . . he did achieve a great deal and touched the lives of many many people . . . you must have felt that quite freshly at the memorial service in New York and also through all the letters that poured in after his death.

And <u>together</u> you created a marvelous, life-enhancing atmosphere that none of us will ever forget. Your marriage was a remarkable work of art, <u>your</u> art rather than his, I think. But it was no small achievement in itself. And in the last years he must have known that and honored you for it. But of course the total dependency finally became a prison for each of you, sheer hell.

Now I come to the hard part of this letter. Four years ago I was persuaded to get rid of a lot of my papers, including letters, because of the danger of fire in my little farm house in New Hampshire. I had no idea what a job it would be to sort everything out, and to get an expert estimate, before submitting it all to the Berg Collection at the New York Public Library. But I did so before I moved here, and it was a great relief to get it all taken away. There are 400 letters from Julian and quite a few from you <u>before</u> 1944. I obeyed you and burned long ago everything you wrote me when I came back after the war. Also a few letters from Francis and Antony. The Huxley letters will not be available to scholars for 25 years. But then we'll all be dead except A. and F

Presumably there will be a biography after my death (Carolyn G. Heilbrun of Columbia University is my executor and will do it, I presume, also selected letters) and at that time my love affair with Julian has to come out. I hope this does not make you angry. My letters to Kot and his to me are there. My letters to Jean Dominique and hers to me also. Journals . . . well, a tremendous amount of stuff really. And Berg is a very serious, reliable repository. V. Woolf's Journals are there, as you no doubt know. I might add that Julian's letters to me were most often vivid descriptions of what he was doing, not love letters in the usual sense. I did not re-read them, but I remember.

What I have discovered this past year while writing a book of 12 portraits of great influences on my life (It's much better than Crucial Conversations)—Julian, by the way, is not among them—is that the past is treacherous and one's views of it are changing all the time as one changes oneself. It is for that reason more than any other that documents (such as letters) made at the time of the experience can never be replaced, and are precious if true estimates are ever to be made after one's death.

Well, I feel better to have told you all this. I have kept a carbon because I want to know what I said as I am so forgetful . . . I mean if you answer. I'll tear the carbon up if you wish, after that.

It is dark now and soon I must go down into the present and have a drink and look at the news. It's such a terrible world, Juliette, so beastly in every way. Le comble, the fanatical religious wars in which we shall, perhaps, all perish before the century is out. But violence and hatred everywhere, so why do I look at the news? I suppose because one wants to know.

> *With love, as always,*
> *Your old*
> *M—*

---

answer about Julian now: On 5 January 1976, Juliette closed her letter: "One day, you might tell me what you really think of Julian—not for publication. But only if you feel you want to." On 8 February 1984 she wrote to Sarton: "Many of your letters to me have come alive in my hands—Your thoughts about Julian—our Strange ghost—so penetrating and viable your questing. . . ."

away for the week-end: As Juliette was to have been in New York the previous June for Julian's memorial service, it had seemed a possibility that she might get up to York, Maine.

they want to see me, I don't especially want to see them: In the intervening years, Sarton's work, particularly the publications of *Plant Dreaming Deep* in 1968, *Kinds of Love* in 1970, and *Journal of a Solitude* in 1973, had brought her an enormous readership and hundreds of letters, often with requests for permission to visit from people who felt that through her work they had found their dearest friend.

About Crucial Conversations you say kind things: Sarton's fifteenth novel, published in 1975, deals with Poppy Whitelaw's abandoning her long, stifling marriage; of it Juliette writes: "It has luminous insights & a wonderful fluency. A very unusual, interesting theme: one longs to know what happens in the long end of the explosion."

Francis's and Antony's books: Anthony Huxley had just published *Plant and Planet* and Francis his more esoteric *Way of the Sacred.*

and calls it autobiography: referring to Julian Huxley's *Memories*, begun when he was seventy-nine and published four years later in 1970.

the Brain Trust: During World War II, Julian Huxley, in the role of encyclopedic pundit, was the center piece of the BBC's *Brains Trust* program, somewhat analagous to *Information Please* in the United States.

memorial service in New York: Sir Julian Huxley died on 14 February 1975; on 8 June a Day of Tribute was held for him at the New York Society for Ethical Culture. At eleven that morning, Edward Ericson, Anita Loos, former ambassador Arthur Goldschmidt, and May Sarton, represented in absentia, spoke. At four-thirty in the afternoon, Ashley Miller directed a concert of trumpet and organ music by Viviana, Barber, Widor, Hovhaness, and Torelli, followed at five by more than a dozen eulogies by scientists, philosophers, and writers. The Committee of Sponsors was made up of more than two hundred international scholars and dignitaries. Lady Huxley was guest of honor.

and honored you for it: Some months later while she was working on her memoirs and in response to a similar letter from May, Juliette wrote: "Then I went down and found your letter sitting on the mat and tears were blessed as of deliverance. You wrote perceptive and healing words—which just now act like sweet magic. I am grateful to you for thinking as you did, and for that warm touch of understanding. Sometimes I get lost in the jungle of remembrance, and Julian's demon closes down on me."

my little farm house in New Hampshire: After the death of her father in March 1956 and the sale of the house at Channing Place, Sarton bought an old farmhouse in Nelson, New Hampshire, in June of 1958, into which she moved alone on 1 October of that year. It was there that she wrote some of her best poetry including *A Private Mythology* and *As Does New Hampshire*, as well as *I Knew a Phoenix*, *The Small Room*, *Mrs. Stevens Hears the Mermaids Singing*, *Plant Dreaming Deep*, *The Poet and the Donkey*, *Kinds of Love*, and *Journal of a Solitude*. In 1973 she left Nelson for York, Maine.

expert estimate: Sarton's papers were appraised by Robert F. Metzdorf in 1972.

I obeyed you and burned . . . everything you wrote me . . . after the war: The letters that Juliette requested she burn and that Sarton did burn on 1 December 1948 were primarily Juliette's letters from the summer of 1948.

Heilbrun . . . will do it, I presume: Carolyn G. Heilbrun, distinguished author and critic, was Avalon Foundation Professor in the Humanities at Columbia University before leaving that institution. She has not written a biography, but has devoted chapters or parts of chapters to Sarton in her books *Writing a Woman's Life* (Norton, 1988); *Hamlet's Mother and Other Women* (Columbia University Press, 1990); and *The Last Gift of Time* (Dial Press, 1997).

portraits of great influences: A World of Light.

kept a carbon . . . tear the carbon up: It was unusual for Sarton to keep carbons of letters; see footnote to letter of 11 April 1948.

Le comble: the excess.

YORK   September 26, 1977

Dearest Juliette,

You are a maddening woman, but I love you, and it is a great thing that you are writing to me at all. "Age brings its cloud of distance from a past crowded with manyfold experiences" . . . I'm sure that is true. Pain is no longer acute; joy is no longer as intense as one looks back. No one can re-create the ethos of a love affair long after it is over. But if there is such a cloud etc. then why indulge in recriminations. After forty years can't we love each other in a quietly receptive way, all passion spent? You did love me once, damnit, and at the end we were both suicidal . . . if you have blocked it all out, then you are really blocking out something you valued, blocking the flow and that is a poor idea at any age. I exploit people; I am dangerous; I tried to blackmail you. That, apparently, is how you defend yourself.

First, it did not occur to you that I could have turned the tables. You and Julian exploited me, just as one example . . . but frankly I never thought of it that way. Nor do I wish to. Julian long ago warned me that once your mind was made up you were relentless. And so you were for thirty years or more, and I accepted that. I minded not seeing you twice because I think the second time might have been gentler and more fun . . . I think I deserved more than one hour.

Still, it was lovely to see you and be whizzed home in that dandy car! (What brutes to fine you six pounds when you couldn't have it inside because of workmen.) And the miracle was that you seemed exactly the same . . . looking so young, being so yourself.

Now, maddening woman, you will have to accept that I can't let your assessment of me lie there like a black snake between us. I do not exploit people and I never have. I just can't see that. If you mean in life, that is. Every writer uses his experience in his work (Aldous! D. H. Lawrence! K.M.!) and if that is how you meant it, I may be the sinner that every writer is. I have, however, not been malicious ever in my work. I have not satirized or been clever at the expense of real people. Never.

Dangerous? Perhaps I am because I am very open, I do not keep secrets well or easily, but I did not tell Julian about you and me, although I wanted to and paid a high price for not doing so. In my experience love affairs are almost never able to be kept entirely secret. Someone knows. There are rumors. And more harm is done by the gossip than would have been done by the truth. (Example, everyone knew about Bowen and Charles Richie except, perhaps, Alan Cameron.)

Next day

I should never have begun all this! There remains blackmail. A dirty word and a dirty thing. No one can defend it. But I think you have forgotten the context. If a man murders his wife because she is unfaithful we can forgive him better perhaps than if he did it out of petty rage. That doesn't make murder not a crime, however. You had cut me off. That was brutal, too.

It's because I am open . . . and perhaps dangerous . . . that I am valuable and have been able to help a lot of people through the work. Yesterday someone sent me a copy of one chapter of a book called The Transparent Self (I'll send it along later if I can get copies of the book). It might be of use to you in your autobiog. by the way. Sidney Jourard says, "This is a curious thing about experiencing which we psychologists are just starting to learn. (We are slow in this respect, lagging behind artists.) We are learning that sharing one's authentic experiencing with another person has important effects upon both the discloser and the listener. Many a patient undergoing psychotherapy comes to understand his existence and to assume responsibility for its future course as a consequence of revealing himself fully to another human being—his therapist.

"But by the same token, the person who reads or listens to the hitherto concealed authentic experience of another is enriched by it. To learn of another's experiencing is to broaden and deepen the dimensions of one's own experience. Authentic writing is psychedelic for the reader—it 'turns him on.' In ways that we do not yet fully understand, the disclosed experience of the other person enables us to see things, feel things, imagine things, hope for things that we could never have imagined before we were exposed to the revelations of the discloser. Since we are all similar to one another in basic respects, as well as unique in others, we can understand another's offbeat experiencing if it is fully and effectively disclosed; the vicarious experience that reading or listening provides can shape our essence, change us, just as first hand experience can. Experience seems as transfusable as blood."

And I suppose all this has been written because I am about to send you The House by the Sea. There are several passages about you and Julian. I do not think you will be displeased but you may be.

I have not forgotten that you asked me to tell you why I think your marriage to Julian was a good one . . . "real," I said. That will be for another day, but I'll remember. It's just that I'm sitting in a nest of unanswered letters, with poems trying to get me to stop and get at them . . . and hundreds of bulbs arrived yesterday . . . and lectures loom . . . and I'm just back from a heavenly week with Huldah in the mountains of N.H.. It was the longest time we had had together and I think now a real foundation is being built. I am so happy!

Dear Juliette, laugh at me, that is best . . .

M—

---

all passion spent: "His servants he with new acquist/Of true experience from this great event/With peace and consolation hath dismist,/And calm of mind, all passion spent." From "Samson Agonistes" (1671), by English poet and prose writer John Milton (1608–1674).

minded not seeing you twice: Sarton saw Juliette for tea at four-fifteen on 3 August 1977; Juliette had originally indicated that she would also be free on 5 August; she withheld that visit.

because of the workmen: Juliette had left her car out on the street to accommodate the window cleaners with their ladders.

about Bowen and Charles Richie . . . Alan Cameron: Charles Almon Ritchie (1906?–?), educated in England and Canada, a career diplomat. Model for Robert in Bowen's novel *The Heat of the Day.* Bowen's relationship with him began in 1942; in 1948, the year before *The Heat of the Day* was published, Ritchie married his cousin Sylvia Smellie. Alan Cameron was Elizabeth Bowen's husband.

The Transparent Self: The Transparent Self: Self Disclosure and Well Being, by Sidney M. Jourard (Van Nostrand Reinhold, 1971).

The House by the Sea: The first journal after her much-acclaimed *Journal of a Solitude, The House by the Sea,* published in 1977, reflects the great change of scene, inner and outer, since her move in 1973 from Nelson, New Hampshire, to York, Maine.

Huldah: Huldah Sharpe, Nashville, Tennessee, heiress who had tried to meet Sarton for four years; Sarton had pushed the matter away, somewhat frightened by her wealth. But Sharpe's "perfect example of androgyny" endeared her to Sarton. "For instance," Sarton wrote to Charles Barber, "she designed her own wedding dress and told me 'I wanted to look like a boy cardinal.'" Sharpe belonged to the muses Sarton called the "mal-aimés," the unloved; she was unloved by her mother, her father died when she was nineteen, and she had a tragic marriage. Ned in *Anger* is based on her and she was the muse for the poems in *Halfway to Silence.*

YORK   Oct. 6th, 1977

Dearest Juliette,

I have been thinking and woke up this morning remembering that you told me once that when Julian went off for the first time with a lover he said "you are my bread, she is my wine" or something like that. The strange thing is that when he and I were lovers I felt just the opposite, that you so charming, witty, and adorable were his wine and I was his bread, that with me he came down to earth, to something rather simple (as far as he was concerned anyway) a rest from the tensions and complexities of marriage. When I said that your marriage seemed a good one, I meant that few marriages stay alive as long as yours did. (After he became so old and difficult of course it became a frightful servitude and nightmare, a hostile dependency of a killing kind.) For an outsider you two seemed to enjoy each other so much. So often married partners are bored by each other. That was how I felt in the Zoo days.

Later I became aware of the immense cost to you of a marriage where too often you were forced to become a nurse; I became increasingly aware of Julian's selfishness, of all that he took for granted. Thank goodness that for some years you knew a true and tender love with Alan. But though so dear, you were no equals (at that time anyway). He could never challenge you intellectually as Julian did. Perhaps you could rest with him as Julian did with me (for a far briefer time). But for each of you surely the reality was your marriage.

It was, in my view (limited at best), a good marriage because you were good partners. Julian would never have accomplished what he did without you. You were marvelous in bringing people he needed to him, in creating that intoxicating atmosphere of grace and just plain enjoyment that every-one felt who had the chance to be invited to be with you together at tea or a meal. The trouble is that in any marriage, good or bad, the wife picks up the pieces . . . the wife gets the irritability, the exhaustion following on the fun, the anxiety above all. But that is just where you were so marvelous, the way in which you patiently and lovingly brought Julian back from his breakdowns and I don't mean the real breakdowns even, but the every day breakdown when self-doubt or just fatigue made him so impossible a com-panion. (I had a small dose of that when he was ill in Tours with me.) I think I was good for Julian because I was not deeply in love with him and so I could call on the tenderness and gentleness in me and become, like you, sometimes a nurse. I could never have sustained that role because I was not that committed. But isn't the proof of a good marriage that the two part-ners keep on growing? That you surely did, and in so many monogamous marriages one senses a kind of static plateau where habit has replaced growth.

I knew Julian for a short period in his life. I wonder how much he was willing or able to change later on? Did he keep on growing . . . of course not after he became senile. There the demon took over completely. But before that? Certainly the Unesco job used his full powers in an entirely new way, the breadth and the range could all come into play. And it was an immense task that you each took on there in middle age . . . preceded by a lot of anxiety and depression for each of you, the sheer terror of undertaking that huge job. But again it was a good marriage because you each found the strength and imagination to do it, and to do it so well. There again you were of immense help to Julian.

I feel that it was really you who brought up the children . . . Julian was too self absorbed to be a good father. Yet they have each turned out to be exceptional men, men of real achievement. Isn't one sign of a good marriage the children and what they become? They did have in Julian an immense stimulus to do something in the world. I wonder what they really felt for him . . . I have no idea.

What happened to me, of course, is that the more I saw of you both the more I became aware that you were the great <u>person</u> of the two, and the deeper my allegiance then to you. (Is that irrelevant? In some ways, yes.) You had had a stern childhood . . . I shall never forget that you told me that your mother gave far more love to the girls who lived with you as her charges than to you. This is so excruciating still even to think of I can barely write it down. You had been <u>mal aimée</u> first as a child and later in your marriage. But somehow you did not wither, but grew all the time more understanding, wiser, more discriminating, and always able to encompass "the other." (This was next to impossible for Julian, wasn't it?) So in the end it must be said that it was a good marriage because you flowered and became such a person <u>in spite of</u> . . . I don't know how you did it, except that at the center there was very fine steel. I am not the first to observe that on the whole women are stronger than men. Did Julian resent your strength? Did he feel guilty toward you and about you? I have no idea. And if he did, how did he handle it? Guilt can make people into friends.

I feel rather raw and without a skin today. So I had better stop. The autumn is sad . . . the leaves are falling before they turn. And I must summon myself to revise a horrible lecture.

Love, dear Juliette, and the greatest admiration,

M—

---

tender love with Alan: Alan Best, Canadian natural historian, friend of the Huxleys, sculptor
who taught Juliette rudiments of sculpting; later he became a zoo director.

you had had a stern childhood: Juliette's father had been a young lawyer when his partner
absconded with the contents of the safe; suddenly the family became poor. Instead
of declaring himself bankrupt, he insisted on paying back every cent of his debts;
broken by the ordeal, he died young. Her mother, undaunted, turned the house into
a *pension* and took in young girls from German-Swiss and Russian families to "finish" them and teach them French, running the house—and Juliette's life—with
Calvinistic severity and Swiss frugality.

mal aimée: unloved.

YORK   Jan. 25th, 1978

Dear Juliette

I can see how marmalade might be a rest from all the letters and
papers . . . but oh, I do understand how energy drains away in all the little
grinding tasks.

> "Slowly the poison the whole bloodstream fills.
> It is not the effort nor the failure tires.
> The waste remains, the waste remains and kills."

That Empson villanelle haunted me after I had read your letter. Today we
are expecting a rain storm on top of a historical blizzard a few days ago, so
the mountains of snow will flood everything and it is a dreary prospect (the
blizzard was so beautiful while it lasted), and I am off to fetch Judy, imprisoned in her nursing home, for a couple of days here. One sweet thing that
is happening as a result of House By the Sea is that many of her students,
sometimes from 50 or 60 years ago are writing me . . . and so full of praise.
She was a wonderful teacher. Now she doesn't even remember that she
ever taught! Maybe it is better to forget everything than to remember
everything. Who knows? Her present can be vivid still, but not the future
nor the past.

By the way, I never said or thought "perfect marriage" . . . I sensed a
lot of tension always. I said it was a good marriage, because it was such a
fruitful one in many ways. I expect there are perfect marriages, but I have

never happened to meet one. My feeling is that one of the partners pays an outrageous price in any marriage . . . and it is usually the wife. Did you ever think of leaving Julian? I expect not because whatever his romantic escapades he was so dependent on you. What did come through to me as a young person beholding you and Julian together was an enchanting foam of laughter and teasing, of constant <u>exchange</u> between you. You did, together, create a magical atmosphere. How I admired it!.

About the Memories . . . it seems to me that if you write an autobiography it simply cannot read like an official biography and the second volume of J's did read like that. He didn't need to go into love affairs, but he didn't go into anything in depth (the fight at the zoo for instance) or some of the problems at UNESCO. No sense of what it was to be a father also. Achievements, honors, travels but none of the anxieties or agonies that go into these things. It made dull reading and I'm not the only person who thought so. As usual, the childhood and youth part was much better.

You are engaged in an excruciating work, but I hope you will not cast it aside out of sheer exhaustion. Someone has to try to tell the truth. If only for yourself. But I dread it all for you. As I told you I haven't yet been able to read my mother's letters. I was <u>grateful</u> for the one you sent. That was kind of you.

And Crete sounds grand. Maybe the thing is to get away often in between bouts.

You say you have no resentment which is generous of you but does not quite convince me. I expect you have. It would be natural. I do have resentment that you have to "put down" or denigrate as merely distasteful what happened between you and me. That is not worthy of you, is it? And it is not worthy of me. Something happened that was real for the time you permitted it to have. I sometimes wonder why you allowed it to happen at all. Curiosity perhaps played a part. I loved you before I fell in love with you . . . I suppose through a kind of identification. I felt <u>with you</u>. And I have wanted ever since to be your friend. To enter a clear space. To walk down a field in the evening light toward the sea.

But I realize more and more that for you it is like a thicket and so an impossible hope.

Nevertheless please write now and then. I like to hear about Marmalade, and Crete, and whatever you are doing.

And now I must plunge out into the rainy world.

love from

M—

---

marmalade: reference to Juliette's annual labor of love: making marmalade with Seville
   oranges.
"Slowly the poison . . .": from "Missing Dates" by William Empson (1906–1984), English
   poet and critic.
imprisoned in her nursing home: Judith Matlack was suffering from Alzheimer's disease.
excruciating work . . . tell the truth: Juliette's memoirs, *Leaves of the Tulip Tree,* were not completed and published until 1986.
mother's letters . . . the one you sent: See footnote to letter of 13 August 1937.

YORK   April 27, 1978

Dear Juliette,

I have wanted to write for ages, but have been and still am on a roller
coaster of readings so my suitcase stays more or less packed. Just back today
from Cambridge which suddenly burst into flower the day before yesterday, quite unlike the bleak coast here. Usually the students in colleges are
pretty blasé, so much is coming at them, but last night, much to everyone's
astonishment, the hall was packed to the gills with people sitting on the
floor all around me as well, others standing in the long hall behind the
room, and still others standing outside to look in through the windows. I
got rather rattled, the light was bad (hard for me to see the poems and journals I was reading from), but it was lovely and rewarding just the same.

Your letter filled me with joy. I am so glad you and Morgan are
friends, and of <u>course</u> I understand. He is not disturbing—he is the present
and does not come with clouds and auras around him of the unresolved
and painful. I never thought for a moment that you would or could have
asked me to stay with you. After all, only since Julian's death have we even
been in communication. Before that, for 20 years, you have made it clear
that I was allowed to come to tea because it might give Julian pleasure and
you and I hardly exchanged a word. I was, on the contrary, very grateful
that you were willing to see me, and keep a delighted memory of your driving me back in the little car. That was so kind and unexpected. Maybe I

was of some use after Julian's death because you could ask me questions and I tried to be honest. But it is only human that I minded a little that our friendship (yours and mine) did not appear to have an identity of its own, and finally I decided to be honest with you about that. Maybe it never can. What is cruel, perhaps, is to trivialize someone else's feelings, for what was distasteful to you, had some real value to me and remains quite intense. So really, dear Juliette, please set your mind at rest. I am very fond of you. I do not believe I am a threat. And I don't see that we have to talk about this any longer. (That sounds as though you had done the talking. I mean I shall not refer to it again.)

I loved hearing about you from Morgan. Not indiscretions but he did enjoy you and described you laughing, things like that, and gardening. He might have done two hours work instead of one for you a day . . . what is one hour in a garden? But what the young do not know is what life costs in energy. I often think of how much I took for granted at Morgan's age. It made me exceedingly happy to think of you seeing each other, and now that I know he is staying with you, I am happier. In fact, delighted.

The Tr/Self is so badly written I don't wonder you didn't like it. House By the Sea seems a long time ago . . . my life has changed since then, though perhaps not for the better. At the moment everything seems too much and I would like to be wrapped up like a mummy and entombed for a month.

I do have a week now, with my 66th birthday in it, to be here, though inundated by people. But I hope to get out into the garden—an hour digging about seems to make me feel centered again, instead of dispersed in a million directions. You know how that is.

I'll try to write a real letter before too long. Meanwhile work Morgan a little harder and may the spring be full of flowers.

Ever your old
May

---

roller coaster of readings . . . back today from Cambridge: Within a period of two weeks Sarton had spoken at the University of Maine at Orono; in Bath, Maine; at Clark University in Worcester, Massachusetts; and at Radcliffe College in Cambridge. Of the last she wrote a friend: "200 had to be turned away . . . people stood in the hall and outside the windows to try to hear. The President was amazed. You see the faculty does not know I exist but I am loved by the young and that is beautiful."

glad you and Morgan are friends: Morgan Mead, a young teacher who corresponded with
     Sarton and met her in 1974; in 1977, while he was studying in England, Sarton
     arranged for him to call on Juliette Huxley, who offered him bed, without board, as
     he needed a quiet place to write.
The Tr/Self: The Transparent Self: see footnote to letter of 26 September 1977.
House by the Sea seems a long time ago: The House by the Sea had been published five years
     earlier and brought Sarton the often overwhelming responses of new correspondents
     and visitors.

YORK   Oct. 29th, 1978

Dearest Juliette,

     I write that and fall silent. But I must say a word in answer to your
letter of the 14th before I am swallowed up in a month of lectures and
poetry readings . . . thank you for writing right away when you had finished the book. As I look back on it now I begin to see that it is a kind of
myth-making, the way things perhaps could be and so rarely are when it
comes to dying. I never could bring myself to talk with my mother about
dying, saw there were always flowers, did the practical things, but could not
bear to sit beside her and give her a chance to talk if she wanted to . . . that
has haunted me. Maybe the book will help a person here or there to do
what I did not do.

     One often curses machines . . . but it does seem a miracle that you
have been listening to Aldous's own voice, reading those lectures. How
strange and how moving. Yes, awareness. And surely Aldous's lack of self-
pity was one of the moving things about him . . . did it come because he
had to face serious disability always? The sheer effort of surpassing near
blindness precluded self pity perhaps? You can't waste energy being sorry
for yourself. Too much is at stake. So with Laura in her determination to
get things sorted out before it was too late. I have had a remarkable letter
from a psycho-therapist who has worked for 20 years with patients dying
of cancer. He enclosed two brief papers on his findings . . . and in one some
figures, such as that 62% of his patients suffered from buried anger, being
unable to show or admit anger against a person, not a cause or idea (there
they could be angry) . . . I have always believed that my mother's cancer
came from buried anger against my father, so this was illuminating. 30%
suffered from guilt about a parent. Of course one can't help wondering

whether this is not true of everyone, not only cancer patients! At any rate this therapist is convinced that the search for identity must go on to the very end, and in this he has been able to help the dying. He is requiring my book to be read by all his students and assistants, by the way. I am pleased.

I wonder whether you have resumed your own search for identity, as I expect this is what your autobiography is all about. You asked me about Julian shortly after his death "Who was he?" and now I expect you are asking yourself "Who am I?" So it is rather important that you keep at what must be extremely painful and hard at times.

Now I must go out into a heavenly calm autumn radiance and walk poor Tamas who has been impatient. I'll go on with this later.

I suppose that you grew a lot through Julian but also perhaps that in some ways you were stopped from growing. I wonder whether in a marriage this is not often true. Someone has to submerge his or her ego (for sometimes it is the man who does so) for the sake of the other. What I wonder sometimes is what "spoiled" Julian because I think he was a very spoiled baby person for whom it was difficult if not impossible to encompass another human being's needs at any given moment. And of course that got much worse as he became senile, and the ordinary "controls" were no longer operative. These are the mysteries you are dealing with and I shouldn't enter that territory, I know. But all of this has been woven into my own life in a queer way, so I do think about you both quite a lot . . . and wonder . . .

Oct. 30th

I had to plant two tree peonies that came at last just in time, so never got back to this yesterday. Two white ones, one semi-double, one single . . . I have about seven now here and there, but none has done tremendously well. Only I keep hoping that this time I think Raymond and I found better places, so maybe . . .

I hope your ash survived the assault, and perhaps feels better for the loss of dead limbs.

How splendid about Antony's gold medal, so richly deserved. Whatever your cogitations you must come back to the fact that you and Julian produced two remarkable sons, and that their bringing up was mostly done by you. Morgan said that Francis has found an apartment and settled in, good news.

Things are quite good with me just now. I was thrown into depression this summer by making the mistake of accepting an invitation to be with Huldah and her daughter and grandaughter at their summer place in New Hampshire for two weeks. It was a disaster and should have been foreseen as a possible disaster, but I allowed myself to be tempted because there are two houses. There are marvelous walks around brooks and waterfalls, pellucid lakes to swim in, lovely old mountains, not too high, but I think it was too hard for Huldah to bridge an intimate relationship with her daughter there, (between her and me) and the little girl, six years old. Conflict created in Huldah a kind of frozen anger and I suffered a lot and should have left. But all is serene between us now . . . perhaps after a year and a half we are beginning to accept each other's natures, so different, and not to expect what is not possible. I shall go down to Tennessee to be with her at Thanksgiving for a week between lectures.

I'll feel even better when I can solve the problem of what next to write . . . I feel written out, but I have to write a book a year to live (it's too much, you know) and I do have one vague idea that might work for a short novel using some of what happened this summer, but changed enough to be unrecognizable . . . I would be inside a 20 year old girl. I'm tired of writing about old age! It should be funny and sad, too. But lighthearted.

Dear Juliette, to whom can I write as I can to you, who understands everything so well? You are the one who is aware.

All blessings on your autumn which I am told is beautiful this year in England after the soggy summer.

Love,
May

---

month of lectures and poetry readings: Beginning at Simmons College in Boston, Sarton went on to readings and book-signings in Hartford; at the Haverhill (Massachusetts) Public Library; at MacAllister College in St. Paul, Minnesota; at the Bookshop on the Square in Cleveland, Ohio; and at the Woman's Bookstore in Toronto.
when you had finished the book: A Reckoning.
a kind of myth-making: In *Plant Dreaming Deep* Sarton writes: "We are all myth makers about ourselves, but part of growing up, I suspect, is the shedding of one myth for anoth-

er, as a snake sheds its skin. . . . the romantic style, or stance, falls away, and one emerges from it more naked, more realistic, though no less vulnerable."

face serious disability always: At fourteen, Aldous Huxley began having eye problems which were to plague him all his life; he suffered profound respiratory problems, severe skin disorders, and ultimately cancer.

so with Laura . . . things sorted out: Laura Spelman, protagonist in *A Reckoning*, who, in facing her death and learning to let go, concentrates on what she calls "the real connections."

remarkable letter from a psycho-therapist: The letter came from both Eda and Larry LeShan; Larry is a psychologist who has for many years worked with cancer patients, and is author of *Beyond Technique: Bringing Psychotherapy into the 21st Century;* Eda is an author and playwright whose plays include *The Lobster Reef* and *A Gift of Time.*

what your autobiography is all about: Leaves of the Tulip Tree, see footnote to letter of 25 January 1978.

Raymond: Raymond Philbrook (1913–   ) of Kittery Point, Maine, still lives in the two-hundred-year-old house in which he was born. Growing up, he did whatever work people needed him to do; it was as handyman and gardener that he worked for Sarton. He wrote her a poem which begins: "The roses are hilled and the flower beds covered/By the handyman whom you discovered/Hanging around like a long lost soul/When you took up residence at Wild Knoll."

ash survived the assault: Men removed great dead branches of Juliette's ash tree with a "brutal speedy self-powered saw."

Antony's gold medal: The Horticultural Society awarded Anthony Huxley its gold medal for his book *Gardening.*

Huldah and her daughter and granddaughter: Huldah Sharpe's daughter Leslie, estranged from her Greek husband, and grandaughter Christina spent summers with her in Center Sandwich, New Hampshire.

vague idea that might work for a short novel . . . inside a 20 year old girl: "We Aren't Getting Anywhere," an unpublished novella, opens: "It's awful to be only eighteen. I feel I have nothing to clothe myself in, and writing what has happened may be a way of finding some shelter or whether there is anything in the mess of this summer worth saving." Accompanying the manuscript is a page of "Random thoughts after a hard visit," among which are: "To feed someone well, but give him no chance to participate in the conversation, to give even a very little of what he has in him to give, is to starve him. Resentment and pain are inevitable. The guest feels an outcast," and "Differences of temperament when extreme, may lead to an ethical rift. The ethos itself is involved."

YORK   Jan. 27th, 1979

Dear Juliette,

Here I am at last . . . your marvelous last letter was dated December 3rd, and I must have imagined answers nearly every day since then, but it has been a strange time here, a time of severe depression, for one thing, but

I am emerging and glad to be alive now like a newborn babe, or Jonah just out of the whale.

You were wise to say "expect nothing—and what blooms is a gift of the gods." I had set my heart on things that proved impossible, a real success with A Reckoning (so I could lose the pressure of a book a year which is quite murderous), and a supportive lover with whom I could maybe end my days in amity. Wild dreams of an old goose! A Reckoning was sneered at in the N.Y. Times. I read the review in St. Paul just before reading poems to a huge audience and had cried so much I could hardly see the page. The Times has "wasted" every book of mine for the past 20 years and for a time I simply felt I had been beaten in public one time too often and would not publish again. Angry letters poured in (and to the Times too, but they haven't printed <u>one</u>) but that only made it worse as I saw how widely read it is. Then I learned that it was a real effort to "put me down" and that "they" are out to get women, and that made me feel better, a warrior instead of a worm. I had always told myself to believe they meant well but had happened on a reviewer who didn't like my work by accident. The roulette game of reviews. The book has sold nearly 19,000 but a really good review in the Times might have sent it soaring. Anyway that's over and I am writing a novella and starting a journal again as that is a safe hostage to fortune if all else fails.

I think in time Huldah and I will come to some sort of viable friendship and I cling to that as better than nothing. Il vaut mieux mâcher le malheur que le néant. And that is enough about me.

I am catapulted to the typewriter at last because of all the bad news from England, the bitter weather, so much <u>snow</u> while we have days and days of rain, and of course the horrible chaos of strikes. It is a bad atmosphere to be living in and I worry about you and wonder whether you are working at the autobiog. again? I feel that is the important thing and to hell with going through millions of letters and papers. There should be no "duties" for you now you are queen of the clan, and besides you had enough of duty God knows. I hope you can be ruthless about such things and meditate in peace and write when the spirit moves. Is the secret self meant to be private? you ask that difficult question. What else have we ~~got~~ to give? It seems to me a false sense of privacy to enclose it, as though one were important . . . and no one really is. What might be important is one human being's truth as he sees it after a long life. You are such an extraordinary human being, Juliette . . . what hammered the steel? What fires?

No, Julian never really talked to me about his problems, about the "daimon" side of him, and I never saw it, a cranky spoiled child when he was ill in Tours, but not the fiend he became later on. What I felt was a horrible mutual dependency as though you would claw each other to pieces and at the same time Julian wouldn't let you out of his sight. But that was the end, when he was senile . . . can one judge by that? He did drive himself mercilessly, didn't he?

And you say you might go to Israel in March . . . dangerous my instinct says. Who wants to be blown up by accident? Wouldn't flowers carpet the hills in Greece as well? How lucky I was to go there 16 years ago before the smog . . . that incredible light was still there, and the other day I saw a TV thing and the whole of Athens is blighted and dark now, and the marble stained and black. I couldn't believe it. But away from the city it must still be beautiful . . . but of course you have been there.

Now I have a garden indoors and when I go down in the morning the sun shines through the innumerable red and white petals of cyclamen and azaleas and amaryllis in the plant window . . . such luxury. The flowers and the animals keep me alive. But I am really starving just the same.

This long silence cannot tell you how happy your letter made me when I found it after the long lecture trip . . . such a real blessing.

You, too, may it be a good year full of unexpected revelations, small and big, a good year for your secret self.

Ever your
M—

To add to something on the reverse of the page . . . what hammered the steel? Is there any way to wisdom except through excruciating pain? It is so mysterious . . . do we grow through joy? I am awfully tired of my anger, but I suppose it provides some gas to the old motor. The novella is a transposed version of my traumatic summer . . . in it I am an 18-year-old girl sent to take care of the horrible children.

––––––––

Jonah just out of the whale: See "Jonah" in *A Grain of Mustard Seed.*
sneered at in the N.Y. Times: In "Four Novels: Politics and Family," in the *New York Times Book Review,* 12 November 1978, Lore Dickstein asserted that while Sarton could effectively evoke the private sensibility of one person, "in *A Reckoning,* when sepa-

rate voices and the fabric of their lives are necessary to create a world outside the main character, this kind of interior singularity approaches solipsism."

a real effort to "put me down" and that "they" are out to get women: Sarton was relieved to hear this from Carolyn Heilbrun.

starting a journal . . . a safe hostage to fortune: from "Of Marriage and Single Life," an essay by Francis Bacon (1561–1626), English philosopher, statesman, and essayist: "He that hath wife and children hath given hostages to fortune; for they are impediments to great enterprises, either of virtue or mischief."

Il vaut mieux . . . : Better to chew on misery than on nonexistence.

Is the secret self meant to be private? you ask that difficult question: On 3 December 1978 Juliette had written: "You talk of myth-making writing—how deeply does one seek the myth beneath the stark truth—the truth which really has so many faces. Myth anyway takes a shape—imposes a choice—reincarnates something which could be precious to one's secret self. Yet what of that secret self? Isn't it meant to remain private?"

what hammered the steel? What fires?: possible allusion to "What the Hammer? what the chain?/In what furnace was thy brain?" from "The Tyger" by William Blake (1757–1827), English poet, painter, and mystic.

Greece . . . there 16 years ago: Sarton went around the world on the occasion of her fiftieth birthday, and celebrated the day itself by climbing the Acropolis; see "Birthday on the Acropolis" in *A Private Mythology.*

The novella . . . 18-year-old girl . . . horrible children: See footnote to letter of 29 October 1978.

[YORK]   June 10th [1979]

Dearest Juliette,

I hear you have had frightful weather in England lately and do hope you got away to some place where there was peace and sun. I have one marvelous white tree peony in flower and the light flowing through those petals has given me a lift. These have been crowded days, but happy ones, because the crew (two men and four women) who have been here for a week making a documentary film interview were so sensitive and considerate that I forgot I am fat and old and felt like myself, the secret self that doesn't change much with the years and wakes each morning with hope. I really think the film is going to be quite beautiful, flowing in and out from the walks through the woods and gardening to reading poems.

Just as I thought I could resume an inner life again after months away, it seems, what with one thing and another, I have to go into the hospital for a mastectomy on the 17th. They are letting me give a last reading I had promised on the 15th to raise money for a Shakespeare Theatre in a town north of here. I shall be in the small hospital here in York with the surgeon who did a small operation before (that proved non-malignant) and who is a very humane man. A woman friend of mine is manager of the hospital so it will all be rather homey. I knew I might be in for this before H. and I went to England but I wanted that time so much . . . and just put it out of my mind and enjoyed. The film, too, seemed important. So, with all that back of me, I am ready.

Anyway, I am convinced that cancer is psycho-somatic and I knew last year that something had to "give"—there was just too much anger and pain. Maybe this op. will exorcize the demons. Who knows?

This is not the real letter I had hoped to write, I am trying to clear my desk and simply wanted to send you my loving thoughts. You say I exaggerate, dear Juliette, but how do you know. I mean how does any one really <u>know</u> about another person's feelings?

Ever your old
May

---

a documentary film interview: World of Light: A Portrait of May Sarton, a film by Martha Wheelock and Marita Simpson, Ishtar Films. In addition to Wheelock and Simpson the crew consisted of Felipe Napoles, Liz Van Patten, Barbara Murphy, and John Simpson.

town north of here: Camden, Maine.

surgeon . . . a very humane man: probably Dr. Richard Dow.

woman friend . . . manager of the hospital: Susan Garrett had for years been administrator of York Hospital; her book *Taking Care of Our Own in the Life of a Small Town Hospital* (Dutton, 1994), based on her experiences there, offers insight into how inseparable human interest is from the politics of health care, and what made York Hospital a nurturing environment for Sarton.

H. and I went to England: Huldah Sharpe and Sarton spent eight days together in England traveling to Sark, Guernsey, Jersey, and London.

YORK   Feb. 21, 1980

Dear Juliette

I have been silent as you asked, but I think of you a lot and when I had lunch with Morgan Mead the other day and he said he had written you a long letter in November and had no answer, I suddenly got anxious and wonder if you have been ill.

Dealing with all those letters and papers must have been like an illness. I suppose you are in a kind of purgatory still, and it is not fair. You should be in Fra Angelico's Paradiso, holding hands in a garland of friends dancing on a green sward. Cannot the past be laid to rest, done with, once and for all? "The past is a bucket of ashes," someone said. It is your life now that matters . . . snowdrops in the garden, and the duck able to go out if she is still with you? Being with yourself and not with other people, the dead, I mean, not Francis and Anthony, needless to say.

We have had a strange winter, without snow. I did not know how I missed it till, the other day, we had one and I saw the blue shadows of trees in the afternoon, and the field an ermine field at last, leading down to all the blues of the sea, more blue than ever against the white. I have started a new novel . . . a celebration in fictional form of a dear old friend who died two years ago at 87. I couldn't find the way to do it, but in Klosters, where I had hours alone while Huldah went on huge walks in the snow, and there were no "things that have to be done," it suddenly came to me how to do it. It is an immense relief and joy to be in the uncluttered timeless world of creation again. In the morning I am happy as a lark once I can get started, but by afternoon the doubts creep in and I see how bad it is. Never mind. It progresses . . . and that is the main thing at this point. The momentum begins to be there.

A Reckoning has just come out in England . . . there had been some good reviews in the daily papers so I was able to "take" the bad sneer in the TLS without going into a tailspin. It's only a pity that that is the one that will be read over here. But I guess one does not suffer the same pain twice over. I nearly died of the one over here in the Times two years ago. Now I have become immune.

Jimmy Durante died the other day, the old Jewish comedian with the big nose and childlike charm. Apparently he ended his TV appearances in the late years when he was an old man by saying, "Good night, folks, and goodnight Mrs. Calabash, wherever you are." Some say she was an old school teacher whom he had loved as a boy, but I prefer to believe that she was imaginary. So, good night, dear Juliette, wherever you are.

Your,

M—

Fra Angelico's Paradiso: Fra (Guido di Pietri) Angelico (c. 1400–1455), a Dominican friar known for the blissful serenity of his religious paintings; Vasari wrote that he had the gift of transforming men into angels and saints, "making them so beautiful that they truly seem to be in Paradise."

"The past is a bucket of ashes," someone said: "I speak of new cities and new people./I tell you the past is a bucket of ashes./I tell you yesterday is a wind gone down, a sun dropped in the west./I tell you there is nothing in the world only an ocean of tomorrows, a sky of tomorrows." From "Prairie" (1918) by American poet Carl Sandburg (1878–1967).

have started a new novel . . . celebration . . . of a dear old friend: The Magnificent Spinster, based on Sarton's teacher at Shady Hill and lifelong friend Anne Longfellow Thorp, grandaughter of the poet Longfellow.

Klosters: For Christmas and New Year's, 1979–1980, Sarton went to Klosters, Switzerland, with Huldah and her daughter and granddaughter.

bad sneer in the TLS: Valentine Cunningham in "Sophomoronic Sapphism," *The Times Literary Supplement,* 8 February 1980, praised Sarton's skill at making one feel, as Laura Spelman feels, what it is like to die, but asserts that the lesbian theme—which was neither Sarton's point nor intention—diverted the novel from death.

nearly died of the one over here in the Times two years ago: See footnote to letter of 27 January 1979.

Jimmy Durante: Jimmy (James Francis) Durante (1893–1980), comedian famed for his prominent nose, which he called his "schnozzola," and his raspy voice and fractured English.

P.O. Box 99   February 13th, 1984
York, Maine 03909

Dear Juliette,

Lately I have been thinking of you so much that it seemed shattering to find your blue slip of a letter among all the valentines this morning . . . shattering that pane of glass I have felt stood between us. So that I have not written. I felt, after the business of the letters (mine to Julian) perhaps wrongly, that you really did not want to hear from me, that the Sarton chapter was closed.

Oh, it was so moving to hear from you, at last opening the door to communication between us! And that my letters to you "have come alive in your hands." I assure you that I "do not forget the good moments." They have been very much alive in my mind for forty five years or so. Can you believe it? I mean that so much took place so long ago? And also how time telescopes as one gets older, so a year flashes by in a moment.

I wish I were coming to tea and we could talk. Maybe that will hap-

pen before too long. In mid-November I have to go to Belgium for a celebration at the Univ. of Ghent of my father's centennial. All but one of my
dear old friends in Brussels is dead now, so I shall stay only a couple of days
and I would like, if you are at home, to stop off in London over one night,
and talk a little about nothing and/or everything, on my way home. There
is no hurry about this . . . I just mention it in passing.

And you kindly ask how I am. I'm well these days except for the
inevitable <u>bobos</u> of approaching old age, such as bad arthritis in my knees
which for a time made me wonder if I could stay here because my study
is on the third floor. I forget names—but then I always did! And so much
pours in here in the mail I would be stuffed like a pig with names if I tried
to remember them all. In a month a new journal, <u>At 70</u>, comes out and I'll
send you a copy which will tell you really what goes on here.

At the moment I am in an awful bog over a novel I have been struggling with for over a year. The problem is that I am trying to celebrate an
old friend, and former teacher of mine (in school), Anne Thorp, who died
at 87 ten years or so ago. A long life and full of people. The fact that I am
dealing with a real person although it is a novel (that at least frees me from
exact dates etc) sometimes freezes my imagination completely. But I hope
to finish it by the end of the year.

March 20th I set out on a series of poetry readings that will take me
to the West Coast, and even Montana where I have never been. It is so
moving now, Juliette, that the audiences greet me with so much love
because they have read the books . . . and three times last year they stood
when I came out on stage. I suppose partly because I have survived so long!
But it is heartening since I am still out in the wilderness as far as the literary establishment goes. It doesn't matter now. The Ph.D. theses are beginning on my work (one at Harvard Univ) and I feel it will all happen in
time . . . after I am dead, no doubt.

But being loved and trusted by so many strangers has its daunting side
. . . lately I have been in revolt against being an EAR for so many
unknowns who write to me as a friend. And whom I must try to answer—
at least 50 such letters a week. It creates a permanent state of guilt and
every now and then makes me seriously depressed . . . so it is good to get
away on the lecture circuit.

The other day I woke up thinking about your garden . . . I suppose
there will be snowdrops out any day now? Here we are still wintry, with

melting snow and brown grass all there is to be seen, except for the ocean
... and all its blues and grays, and the great sunrises. My dog and cat are
still with me. We make a very affectionate family and I can hardly wait to
get to bed with one on each side—such purrs and groans of pleasure. Do
you have an animal?

I also wondered whether you had found a solution to not being able
to get TV because of the hospital opposite. I suppose cable TV would do
it ... I do not have that yet as this is such a remote place.

Au fond, I am rather lonely ... Judy died a Christmas ago after years
of not being there, but I took her death hard. There are a few good friends
around here—one comes once a week for dinner, for instance. But on the
whole it is a solitary life, good when I am working well, lonely when I feel
suddenly empty after writing too many letters.

I have now told you, I fear, more than you want to know about penguins! ... but I hope it will invite an answer. How is it to be the matriarch
of such a clan?

All blessings and love, as always

Your old
May

———

coming to tea . . . before too long: Sarton did visit Juliette, beginning a series of regular visits,
once and sometimes twice a year until the end of Juliette's life. On 11 December
1984, after that first reunion, Sarton wrote: "And thanks for you, a bright star in my
heavens still and always."

celebration at the Univ. of Ghent . . . centennial: On this occasion the University of Ghent
founded a chair in George Sarton's name.

all but one . . . friends in Brussels is dead now: Jacqueline Limbosch.

bobos: French, childish term for hurts or wounds.

series of poetry readings: In March and April, Sarton spoke in Lynchburg, Virginia; Asheville
and Waynesville, North Carolina; Bloomington, Indiana; San Francisco and
Valencia, California; Kalispell, Montana; and Seattle, Washington, with appearances
through the months of June, July, and August as well.

50 letters a week . . . creates a permanent state of guilt: See "Guilt" in *Coming into Eighty*.

My dog and cat: Both Bramble, a wild cat she tamed, and Tamas, a Shetland sheepdog she
bought from the Frenches, came with her from Nelson, New Hampshire, in 1973.

Au fond: for the most part.

took her death hard: See "Mourning to Do" in *Letters from Maine*.

more than you want to know about penguins: a favorite expression of George Sarton's.

———

January 27th, Sunday [1985]

Dearest Juliette,

and why not dearest? You are really the only living person who makes a "spark" when I see your handwriting in the mail, and since dead people do not write letters, that makes you rare and treasured. Glad the wine came, though so late. I sent off that large-type journal, Recovering for Dora by air post some time ago, but even by air it all takes ages. It looks a little odd in such large type and has no photographs which is a pity but perhaps you will dip into it before you take it to her.

It is so sad about Dora. But isn't it understandable that she may choose to "opt out"? It sounds like hell to be imprisoned by her legs, and nursing homes, even the best, are prisons. Lucky she who sees you now and then, a reviving presence. I wonder whether she has tried the little radio? I should think music would be a help. When my father had his gall bladder out at seventy, and I brought him home from the hospital, we sat and talked and I asked him what his first experience of a hospital had been like. He answered, so typically, "It was a musical experience."—I had brought him a transistor radio and he listened to classical music for hours. The other side of this charm, and he was charming, was that of course he had round the clock nurses whereas mother did not for her cancer operation. I wonder whether I shall make peace with my father before I die. Still, I have to admit and honor him for it that he taught me a lot about discipline and how to work very hard by example. And I also identify with him because he, like me, was always an outsider. But as a human being in relation to other human beings he did fail in a lot of ways.

For me it is when we meet, so rarely, that there is such turbulence under the surface, so much that I would like to ask or say that I can't, that conflict may obscure the very real pleasure there is in the moment.

It's great that Green Inheritance is out and Antony both glorious and modest. And maybe Francis is home again with all his tales to tell.

The person I miss most these days is myself. I am buried alive under correspondence and in a mild state of psychic revolt. It is a relief to be writing to someone I love for a change.

We too have had bitter cold for weeks and it numbs the mind, but not the fur pelts, Bramble and Tamas, who are exhilarated by it. Tamas is now 91 in dog years but becomes wildly excited still by deer tracks in the woods, and Bramble races up trees with a fat tail while I bumble along behind in sheepskin and boots trying not to fall on the ice. The great joy is the birds—many finches and titmice burbling at the feeder, a few Dureresque red squirrels, blue jays . . . in the extreme cold silence where nothing moves, their wings and constant flying in and out are wonderful to behold.

On Feb. 15th I have to have all my remaining teeth out and new ones put in. It all takes place in one awful day . . . but my dentist who is really brilliant and imaginative assures me they will stay in and that I shall look better rather than worse. I'm glad the decision, which has been pending for months, is finally made. The problem was to find a really good man near here. It's the right time to do it with no public appearances ahead, till September.

Tiger has come and I am saving it to read while I recover.

Regan of course is enough reason for serious depression but if I start on that this letter will go on too long.

Keep warm, dear Juliette, take good care of yourself . . .

With my love, always
Your old
May

---

glad the wine came: Sarton traditionally sent a case of red and a case of white wine to Juliette each Christmas.

large type journal . . . so sad about Dora: Dora Clarke; see footnote to letter of 27 October 1936. The firm which W. W. Norton had used for the large-type editions of Sarton's books went out of business; these large-type books are no longer available. Clarke was at this time no longer able to read well, "curiously floating, lucid but word-tied, placid but like a sponge."

peace with my father before I die: Sarton did write of her father in *At Eighty-Two,* see pp. 299–300. However, she excised some of this section before publication, feeling it not fair should readers, who might not otherwise know what a great man he was, learn the extent of his selfishness as all they knew of him.

meet, so rarely: reference to the annual or semiannual visits Sarton made to London.

Green Inheritance: Anthony Huxley wrote *The Green Inheritance* for the World Wildlife Fund.

in the extreme cold silence where nothing moves: See "The Silence Now" in *The Silence Now:* "In the immense silence where I live alone."

dentist . . . brilliant and imaginative: Maurice Dinnerman, D.D.S.

Tiger: unidentified.

Regan: Ronald Reagan, U.S. president whose policies and mentality Sarton found execrable.

November 17th Sunday [1985]

Dearest Juliette, your letter for the plumber (hideous) welcomed me home
two days ago . . . I am fragmented to the point of hardly remembering my
name . . . the tour this time, though all went very well, was extremely
exhausting because of all the travel, small planes, big planes, interminable
waits in airports and I came home in pieces to meet, as usual, an <u>avalanche</u>
of demands with only four days here and Bramble perhaps having to be
put to sleep tomorrow . . . I drive down to south of Boston on Thursday
to do a book signing luncheon, then next day a dinner of "gays" at which
I am being honored in order to draw a crowd and raise money for AIDS.
But perhaps I can discover who I am by writing you . . . it was such a blessing to find your letter although the news of Alan's son is so <u>grim</u> . . . can
anything be done for leukemia in such an acute stage? One wonders if the
agonizing treatments should be given at all???

I know so well your feelings now your book has gone to be published
. . . "left out so much of my tale, too" . . . so hard to find a balance between
being honest and over-exposing oneself or others. It is familiar to me, God
knows, that struggle for a balance. But the book is bound to be full of
<u>aperçus</u> no one but you could have. It is not a word I use lightly or to flat-
ter. Someday a book of your letters should be published. Meanwhile I am
waiting eagerly for <u>this</u> book.

Reviews of Spinster have been lukewarm. I think it may be a book
that grows on people and a quick reviewer bogs down . . . only one has
noticed that it is rather a feat technically. I have had good letters from writers who see how hard it was to do. But it is true I never get a break and I
should be used to that by now. At any rate the book signings in Cal. were
subway crushes and that is heartening. Also in remote places where they
expected an audience of 50 or so and then 500 turned up, it is wonderful
way off in the boondocks to see that my work has meant something to
such a variety of people of all ages and both sexes. This time a lot of men
spoke to me most feelingly. One, a darling man in San Francisco 80 years
old who said he would not have appreciated my work as much at 70 (!)
and has been giving my books away by the dozen.

Also I get again a sense of what an immense country this is . . . on the East Coast one forgets Idaho! From the small plane I looked down during a marvelous sunset on steep hillsides ploughed and black, for the winter wheat I presume . . . it looked like a huge naked woman's body, something so sensuous, all those valleys and hills and creases and amplitude, I was close to tears as we winged in. In San Francisco I stayed one night in a really marvelous grand hotel, The Stanford Court . . . I basked in it, Godiva chocolates by my bed, wonderful meals sent up, a long hot bath . . . and a huge sold-out audience. And my dress! Can't describe . . . it's black silk jersey with wide padded shoulders (which diminish my tummy) and very wide sleeves which are covered in intricate brilliant designs, brilliant blues, greens, reds in a small pattern or patterns so when I raise my arms to acknowledge applause the sleeves open like brilliant wings. It has a mandarin collar, also in brilliant patterns which remind me of my mother's designs. I have never had a dress that was so commented upon . . . such fun. Mother used to say "clothes are your armor" and this one is very good armor indeed.

I was moved to find Grace Dudley's letter in yours . . . moved that she wrote you so warmly, for she was very shy and reserved. You only met her in the hospital in Paris . . . but she had a radiance. I have a lot of guilt about her, alas—

Yes, it must be upsetting, moving, strange to read Julian's letters . . . the essence maybe that was often obscured by his bad humors and that something pressured in a not good way that my mother caught.

One small adventure—a fan had written me that she lives in a very old house near San Francisco, going back to the early days, her husband descended from Spaniards from Castile. I was curious to see it, rather rare out there. So we went for tea, a friend and I . . . a lovely serene rather Tchekovian house and garden, beautiful trees . . then she suggested we go in after tea and see the house. She warned me there would be some shocks . . . SHOCKS! The whole house is inhabited by dreary sad animal heads her husband has shot. Deer on the walls, a moth eaten polar bear under a table, a raccoon on the stairs, an eagle suspended above, ducks stuffed in the dining room to show how they fall when shot! It was incredible. How could one live in such a morgue?

I must go down now and greet and take out to lunch my former house sitter and friend who is in the middle of radiation for a recurrence of cancer ... her substitute is a huge piece of luck. Edythe never let me pay her so I could never ask for small tasks to be done. Judy, the new one, is younger and was eager to help and I paid her by the hour. She cleaned out the garage where years of gardening tools and stuff had piled up, got it all in order, washed my car, cleaned the ovens in the house, tidied drawers and God knows what else! She did it <u>joyfully</u> which is just plain wonderful.

November is dreary here ... rain all last night, but I can see the ocean from my bed now the leaves are gone ... there are compensations. But after California it does look rather sad, all brown and sad. Nevertheless I prefer New England and the paperwhite narcissus in the house to the roses and zinnias and all the rest of it out there, such a jumble.

When I was in that grand hotel I longed for you to be there and that I could share the poached salmon and fresh raspberry tart with someone so loved ... it is awful that I cannot run in for tea. I give a lot and get so empty but as long as you are there, there is <u>someone</u>, thank God.

Love,

M

P.S. I have ordered some <u>wine</u> for you for Xmas, to be delivered <u>Dec. 20th</u>—Barrett's.

---

your letter for the plumber: Juliette's letter of 1 November 1985 was written while waiting for the plumber to arrive to unclog a blocked kitchen sink; three men did arrive with a pressure machine and expirated the blockage.

tour this time: Her lecture schedule for the fall of 1985 had been particularly heavy, including September appearances in Athol and Boston, Massachusetts; Portland, Maine; the Smithsonian in Washington, D.C.; and St. Vincent's in Pennsylvania; October appearances at Carlow, Penn State, and Bucknell in Pennsylvania; Trinity in Connecticut; Wakefield and Newport, Rhode Island; Concord, New Hampshire, and again in Portland; and this letter was written immediately after appearances in Moscow, Idaho; San Francisco, California; Duluth, Minnesota, and Newark, New Jersey.

perhaps ... put to sleep tomorrow: Bramble was euthanized the following day, 18 November, the same date on which Eleanor Mabel Sarton had died in 1950; she is buried at Wild Knoll, her grave marked by a sculpted relief by Barbara Barton.

book signing luncheon: Robert D. Hale, owner of Westwinds Bookstore in Duxbury, Massachusetts, former president of the American Booksellers Association and author of *The Elm at the Edge of the Earth*, had arranged an author's luncheon and book-signing.

I am being honored: At this event Sarton read her poem "AIDS" (see *The Silence Now*) and was presented with the Human Rights Award. Sponsoring organization unidentified. Possibly Unitarians.

Alan's: the young Alan Best, whose uncle had been Juliette's lover.

now your book has gone to be published: Leaves of the Tulip Tree was published by John Murray
the following year.

aperçus: insights.

Reviews of Spinster . . . lukewarm . . . one noticed . . . feat technically: In "A Tale of Two
Handmaids," Joan L. Slonczewski's review of Margaret Atwood's *The Handmaid's
Tale* and Sarton's *The Magnificent Spinster* in *The Kenyon Review,* Fall 1986, the
reviewer concludes: "Surely there is room for both these visions of the life of
women, the dystopic and the celebratory; the prophetic and the contemplative. In
the end, I count it as evidence for the richness of the contemporary scene in fiction
that it can encompass two writers as different, and as magnificent in their own ways,
as Margaret Atwood and May Sarton." The review which "noticed that it is rather
a feat technically" may be Valerie Miner's "The Light of the Muse," *Women's Review
of Books,* III:3 (December 1985), in which Miner acknowledges Sarton's ability to
successfully maneuver the boundaries of fiction, autobiography, and biography,
"deftly revealing how every story is about author as well as subject. . . . This addition to her 'landscape' is an intricate, yet accessible experiment in form; a testimony
to independence; an enlightening portrayal of old age; a celebration of friendship and
an engrossing story." A full-page ad for *The Magnificent Spinster,* published in the late
fall of 1985, appeared in the *New York Times* on Sunday, 1 December.

good letters from writers . . . how hard it was to do: John Forbes of the Univeristy of Virginia
wrote: "Your primary objective was to recreate Anne in four dimensions—the last
one a dimension of essence or spirit . . . and you did it, you did it!" A writer friend
from Berkeley: "I couldn't put it down. The book grew and grew as Jane did, as the
pages turned, and it left me completely satisfied. You deserve great praise for figur-
ing out an effective way of telling it all. It works perfectly." Another: "Your *Spinster*
is magnificent. I loved the inventive telling of it, marvelous projections of an endear-
ing/wise persona midst multiple personalities that lit up page after page. I was cap-
tivated. Such a warmly human & humanizing experience—transmutations of fact
into fiction . . . a rich & complex tapestry: smooth running threads with no knots,
no tangles in sight."

darling man in San Francisco . . . would not have appreciated my work . . . at 70: Sarton loved
telling the story of David Engelstein (1905–1996), a teacher, Marxist, and voracious
reader who, having once discovered Sarton, shared her with everybody he knew,
and proudly acknowledged he had "turned 60 people onto her work."

So we went for tea, a friend and I . . . Tchekovian house and garden: While giving a seminar at
the Starr King School of Theology in Berkeley, Sarton stayed with Doris and Gerald
Beatty. Together they visited Alysone Delaveaga at her estate, an historical landmark
near Orinda; the animals referred to had been shot by Delaveaga's husband, Ned,
and other members of the family.

house sitter and friend: Edythe Haddaway (1916–1998) accompanied Sarton on her trips to
Europe at this time and shared with her most Christmases and Thanksgivings; Sarton
called her daily at 3:00 P.M. and lunched with her once every week until the week
before her death in 1995.

her substitute: Judy Burrowes.

Feb. 16th, 1986

Dearest Juliette, your letter of 8th and 9th came very fast as a valentine and
sent me soaring instead of crawling into the cardiologist's where I sat for
one hour in a crowd of people. When I finally saw him was too aware of
all the others waiting and almost forgot to tell him about my numb right
foot. I liked him, Petrovich (Polish perhaps). He has cut lanoxin, the only
drug I am taking now, in half. Says it would be dangerous to cut it out
entirely as the heart would race. Decided against an electric shock as it does
work but may last only a few days, so why bother? I felt he was sensible
and took it in, I think, when I told him loudly that I had never been unable
to work for 6 weeks before and <u>had</u> to get well. It was not very encourag-
ing . . . I see him again on the 28th. The side effects of lanoxin, a friend told
me, are known to be apathy and lassitude, so that explains why I am like
the dormouse in Alice.

 Well, it was wonderful to have your letter . . . I meant it when I said
"there is no shadow" about my not being in the book and I am touched
that I ever was. It is far better than that that we are at last, after all the cold
years when you hardly spoke to me, in communication. So please erase that
right away from the granary pile of guilt.

 The paragraph about forgetting milk and eggs and having to go back
again into the snowy cold made me smile for two reasons. One it sounds
exactly like me these days and two, it is pure literature, exactly what V.W.
said to Vita about style in that paragraph you sent. I do have the book, in
fact did a blurb for it in the American hardback edition, in which I said it
was a perfect example of an <u>amitié amoureuse</u>—not primarily passionate
surely . . . Madame de Stael and Madame de Récamier come to mind. And
I was so shocked by Vita's lack of responsibility toward her many lovers that
this restored some of my esteem for her anyway—she cherished Virginia
and there is so much tenderness there. Whereas she thought nothing of
breaking up a marriage and then abandoning the wife a year later! I must
say Virginia took Vita's immediate infidelity with generosity, didn't she? I
must go back now and reread the letters . . . I have by my bed a biog of
Vita all built around gardening, have you seen it? It seems very good, well
written . . . but I am bogged down in a manuscripts [sic] and stuff at the
moment.

 Well, I'm glad you have kept my letters . . . I thought you had burned them long ago! And I would love to have them back someday . . . as soon as I am dead there will be a selected letters. There are lots at the Berg, to Basil de Selincourt, Kot, I can't remember all there are, Julian as you know. I had imagined letters could take the place of a biography. That is what I felt when I read Isak Dinesen's letters—but I was wrong, as I found out when I read the excellent biog by a woman called Thurman.

Have you seen Out of Africa? I saw it yesterday with Nancy, my sec. . . . I had not wanted to go because <u>Out of Africa</u> is one of my favorite books of all time, but really, Juliette, it is an amazingly beautiful film, in spite of handsome Robert Redford who is all wrong of course as Finch-Hatton. It is a pure romantic film of farewell, farewell to Africa as it was, farewell to the farm, to Finch-Hatton, to romantic love perhaps. But what is marvelous is the restraint, the lack of <u>words,</u> and [Meryl] Streep's performance (I have never liked her, too cerebral, but here it works).

Do get that tenant out. I can see that he clings like a limpet to his rock. Oh dear . . . it is worrying.

Another dazzling day here. February is being kind with small snowfalls at night to keep everything clean and white and then cold sunny days. The birds make loud cheeps as though rehearsing for song, an orchestra tuning up. I hear an owl at night (it's mating season for them . . . but why in the frigid cold I wonder?) Deer tracks, raccoon tracks in the snow when I walk Tamas, a short walk each day as we creak and are very old parties now.

I wait for the day when I can write a poem about Bramble, but that takes psychic energy and that's what is turned off at present.

The light stays on now till after five, I mean the sky light, and there are brilliant sunsets. (Behind the house through woods . . . the sun rises right over the sea before my bedroom windows.)

I wish I could waft you here with no travel strain . . . you would like this house, I think. And we would have lobsters and a glass of champagne . . . and talk . . .

Bless you for that saving letter. It did me a lot of good.

Much love as always

M

Feb. 16th, 1986: After the previous letter of 17 November 1985, Sarton went to New York from 4 to 7 December to speak at the Poetry Society of America and the

Riverdale Country School; at home on 28 December, her Christmas tree, which had been standing beside the fireplace, caught fire; the entire library was in flames, which Sarton herself extinguished before the firemen arrived.

Petrovich: Dr. Lawrence J. Petrovich.

heart would race: At this time Sarton was being treated for a fibrillating heart, a condition from which her mother also suffered.

dormouse in Alice: From Céline Limbosch's letter to George Sarton in October 1919 reporting seven-year-old May "dormant comme un loir" [sleeping like a dormouse] to her own allusions to being "well in" to work, references to the dormouse and *Alice's Adventures in Wonderland* frequently recur.

my not being in the book: reference to there being no mention of May in Juliette's 1986 memoir *Leaves of the Tulip Tree*. On 8 February 1986, Juliette wrote: ". . . I am tormented by your brave but not entirely candid remark about my leaving you out of my book. It is a curious mismanagement on my part: an example of my untidy thinking of these last months. I had written you in— and also wanted to quote a letter about Julian—his 'flaw.' I meant to think it over, and put the pages aside; somehow they never got back into the main bulk, and I forgot all about leaving them out until the damn thing got right into print and paging. Jock Murray was adamant—it would mean a whole reprint. How stupid can you be. Of course you are hurt and annoyed—and of course, I am disturbed and regretful. Maybe there will come a way to put that right. One never knows. But please believe me—if you can—it was not my intention. . . . "

V.W. said to Vita about style in the paragraph you sent: from *The Letters of Vita Sackville-West to Virginia Woolf,* edited by DeSalvo and Leaska, which includes excerpts from *The Letters of Virginia Woolf,* Vols. 3, 4, 5, and 6. Juliette had quoted this from Virginia to Vita, London, 16 March 1926: ". . . As for the *mot juste,* you are quite wrong. Style is a very simple matter; it is all rhythm. Once you get that, you can use the wrong words. But on the other hand here am I sitting half the morning, crammed with ideas, and visions, and so on, and can't dislodge them, for lack of the right rhythm. Now this is very profound, what rhythm is, and goes far deeper than words. A sight, an emotion, creates this wave in the mind, long before it makes words to fit it; and in writing (such is my present belief) one has to recapture this, and set this working (which has nothing apparently to do with words) and then, as it breaks and tumbles in the mind, it makes words to fit it: . . . Yes, dearest Vita: I do miss you: I think of you: I have a million things, not so much to say, as to sink into you."

in fact did a blurb: On the jacket of the American edition Sarton is quoted: "These delightful letters give us the seasons of an intimate relationship between two extraordinary women . . . un *amitié amoureuse.* I know of no other comparable except for that between Madame de Staël and Madame Récamier, a century earlier. Here we only glimpse Virginia Woolf but we do come to know Vita Sackville-West in a new light, the light of tenderness, concern, and love for the genius whose muse she became. It is a fascinating record."

amitié amoureuse . . . Madame de Stael . . . Madame Récamier: Madame de Staël-Holstein (born Anne Louise Germaine Necker, 1766–1817), Swiss-French literary critic and belles-lettrist, known for her celebrated salons, her lovers, among them Benjamin Constant, her conflict with Napoleon and subsequent exile from France, as well as her great influence on French Romanticism; her closest and perhaps only woman friend with whom she shared loving admiration was Jeanne-Françoise Julie Adélaïde

Récamier Bernard (1777–1849), leader of French society, also known for her salons and long devotion to Chateaubriand. Epitomizing the essence of what Sarton means by *amitié amoureuse* [loving friendship], de Staël writes in a letter to Récamier: "You have made me experience, dear Juliette, something that is quite new to me: a friendship which fills my imagination and spreads over my life an interest which one other sentiment alone has inspired in me. This year especially there was something angelic about you; that charm which deigned to concentrate on me moved my soul, and I felt cut off from some heavenly influence when you disappeared."

many lovers: Among Vita Sackville-West's lovers were Margaret Voigt, Violet Trefusis, Mary Campbell, Hilda Matheson, Evelyn Irons, Olive Rinder, and Alvide Lees-Milne.

breaking up a marriage . . . abandoning the wife a year later: reference to Violet Trefusis, whose marriage and affair with Vita are chronicled in *Portrait of a Marriage* by Nigel Nicolson.

biog of Vita all built around gardening: Vita's Other World: A Gardening Biography of Vita Sackville-West, by Jane Brown (Viking, 1985).

Basil de Selincourt: Basil de Sélincourt (?–1966), literary critic for the *Observer* in London; lived in Kingham, Oxfordshire; a great supporter of Sarton's early work and long-standing friend.

Isak Dinesen's letters: Isak Dinesen: Letters from Africa 1914–1931, edited by Frans Lasson, translated by Anne Born (University of Chicago Press, 1981). Isak Dinesen, pen name of Baroness Karen Blixen of Rungstedlund (1885–1962), Danish short story writer whose portrait signed by Cecil Beaton, given her by Bill Brown, Sarton kept on her desk in the "cozy room" until her death. Of it she wrote prophetically to Brown in 1969, "It's a supreme photograph. . . . If only we can look like that two days before we die—the transparency, the ineffable smile, the wall so very thin between flesh and ghost." See *Among the Usual Days,* p. 269.

excellent biog . . . Thurman: Isak Dinesen: The Life of a Storyteller, by Judith Thurman (St. Martin's Press, 1982). After reading it, Sarton approached Thurman as a possible biographer for herself; Thurman was not available.

Out of Africa . . . Nancy, my sec: Out of Africa (1985), based on Dinesen's story of her life on a coffee plantation in Kenya around 1914; produced by Sydney Pollack, winner of seven Academy Awards and starring Robert Redford, Meryl Streep, and Klaus Maria Brandauer. Nancy Jahn Hartley, Sarton's secretary and archivist for twelve and a half years, often accompanied her to films.

Finch-Hattan: Denys George Finch Hatton (1887–1931), English officer, trader, and safari leader in Kenya, second son of the thirteenth earl of Winchelsea. Dinesen had a passionate love affair with him; he was killed in a plane crash at Xipingo. Sarton felt Redford's looks did not do justice to Finch Hattan's very British, elusive beauty and thought Charles Dance would have been far better suited for the role.

Do get that tenant out: See footnote to letter of 11 April 1986.

poem about Bramble: See "Wilderness Lost, for Bramble, my cat" in *The Silence Now.*

Bless you for that saving letter: See Appendix for letter of Sunday, 9 February 1986.

YORK   February 27th [1986]

Dearest Juliette, it is too horrifying, un-necessary and heartbreaking about the fire and devastation of Francis's flat—thank goodness at least he is there and was able to come himself and begin to set things to rights if that is possible. But I resent, too, the shock for you in the middle of this devilish winter.

Except for that news your letter was a godsend. I must explain at once because of the typing that I am just home from the hospital where I was taken in an ambulance on the 21st after a mild stroke (left side luckily) in the middle of the night. I called my doctor at 6 A.M. and he met me at the emergency entrance—I am a hilarious compendium of miseries as I also have, it seems, a bleeding ulcer and the heart trouble is no better. It b/ is to laugh [sic]. In the hospital I kept thinking of Kot and his running away in his pajamas. I had two fights, one with my doctor who should have found the ulcer weeks ago, and one with a nurse who would not let me have lovely spring flowers close to me. I won that fight after a "little talk" with the head nurse.

The main thing is to feel so weak and stupid in the head . . . I am more aware than ever before of the sheer psychic energy it takes to write a poem . . . and shall I ever be able to summon it again? But I am lucky that the stroke was slight—the cat scan showed clearly a small triangle of cerebral hemorrhage. And my left hand is not quite itself but soon will be I believe. Friends take turns to spend the night and cook my supper. It is peaceful to be home again. The sea the most wonderful Fra Angelico blue this evening, the field white and gold.

I wonder why Vita was afraid of being poisoned at that dinner.

Please give Francis my warmest sympathy.

And really you cannot imagine how happy your letters make me . . . so write again when you can, but not ever as an obligation. Time stands still here these days.

Of course I wrote quite differently and better to you than to anyone else because I loved you—there is a more elegant way of saying this, but not after a stroke!

Love anyway, now and always,
May

---

fire and devastation of Francis's flat: Juliette had written: "Francis rang up from California Monday morning: his flat had a fire Sunday night—he is coming, arriving today midday. I went to the flat Monday, found it destroyed in one room, & all the other rooms badly damaged—front garden littered with burnt letters & pages of books &

pictures & pathetic scraps of furniture. Cry tears of misery . . . Francis had a tenant who saved much, fire engine came but late as many <u>other</u> fires. Grim."

running away in his pajamas: On 7 June 1947, Koteliansky tried to commit suicide; he was hospitalized and given shock treatment. During his hospitalization he decided he had had enough and simply walked out of the hospital in his pajamas and went home.

cat scan: CAT (computerized axial tomography) scan.

Fra Angelico blue: Fra [Giovanni] Angelico (pseudonym of Guido di Pietro, 1387–1455), Italian religious painter known for his delicacy of color. Sarton used this phrase frequently for a serene, moving shade of blue which never failed to remind her of Angelico.

why Vita was afraid of being poisoned at that dinner: On 15 February 1986, Juliette wrote: "You are so <u>right</u> about St. Spender's journals. And I was <u>so</u> wrong about Vita and Virginia. Their letters become so trivial—Vita's so blatantly 'covering up.' Funnily I remember a big Dinner Party when she was near me, a City Dinner, you know, with Lord Mayor and six courses and speeches and endless toasts—and she was almost in tears about the food which she believed would poison her—Harold [Nicolson] kept trying to reassure her, calling on us to help. People are fussy about their food outside home—"

April 11th, Friday [1986]

Dearest Juliette,

The third packet of letters has come and I do dip in now and then and read here and there, agree that some sad ones should be torn up.

I think perhaps I had to give everything up, ever seeing you again for one, and go down into the dark cave before I could come out into the light. And that seems to have happened at last. I have turned the corner and begun a new journal called After the Stroke. This one will end with my 75th birthday in '87 instead of starting there as I had planned. It is wonderful to have something to hang my life on again . . . it has been lying about in total confusion for so long. It has been years since I have experienced the spring here, day by day, and that is a joy. The salt hay is still on the flower beds (it's cold at night) but treasures are humping up under it and sometimes I take a pile off and release daffodils or tulips, yellow for lack of sun. The grass is beginning to turn green, too, and alleviates the brown everywhere.

It is awful not to see you, so far away and soon to be swallowed into all the doings around your book coming out. But at least there is that to look forward to and I expect you will have copies sometime in May? I have in these last days since "giving up" felt, I must confess, bitterly at times that it took you so long to see that I am not a monster . . . wasted years after Julian died.

The bitterness has to do not only with all that but (will it never end till I die?) the total lack of luck I have had with my work. A great deal _is_ luck. Since Basil de Sélincourt I have never had a critic on my side. The poems are brushed aside as derivative and of no account . . . and _that_ is why I have wanted to give them a chance and see them live as I do when I go on tour now. It has taken 40 years of being beaten first—so the great audiences are not trivial to me—and many writers would have committed suicide long ago—Sylvia Plath did and <u>demanded</u> success, Anne Sexton had success too young and did. . . .

There must be something of value in my books since so many people's lives have been changed by them. And the evidence is there. Oh well, forgive this complaining so unsuitable . . . a sign of convalescence no doubt when one feels cranky and irritable. Old wounds open etc.

How are you? I'm afraid this last cold was too much after the horrible winter . . . but maybe things are moving legally at least, to get the tenant off your back—you mentioned an "affidavit" in your last letter. <u>Are</u> you feeling a little better?

And maybe your garden is bringing you fresh treasures to contemplate—yesterday in the mail came a tiny box with some sprigs of trailing arbutus in flower in it . . . that pungent scent, the waxy pink trumpets—my nose could hardly believe it. In Nelson about now I went out to find it under sodden leaves, beside a nearby lake. It has the signature of New England in it . . . nothing rich or easy, the poor rocky land, the hard climate, and the ways in which people survive here.

The iris reticulata, a very intense dark blue, has come out inside the terrace wall. Every day something big happens. And every morning around eight I take PIERROT, the kitten, out to explore—he rushes around, a fat ball of fluff, his blue eyes black with excitement, his small tail lashing. I suppose he is, after all, the healer Carol[yn Heilbrun] meant him to be. At four A.M. he burrowed his way into my hand and lay there, purring very loudly till five, quite a dear.

I wish you had a duck in your garden again!

I wish you were near enough so I could drop in and take you out to lunch. I wish lots of things that will never happen now.

But love doesn't change.

Your old

May

---

never had a critic on my side: Sarton felt this truth deeply for most of her life. She never had the kind of support Pound gave to H.D., the kind of support Bogan denied her; she never was accepted by the literary establishment. But in the later years a number of prominent critics strongly came forward. Carolyn G. Heilbrun wrote about Sarton in *Writing a Woman's Life* (1988), in *Hamlet's Mother and Other Women* (1990), and in *The Last Gift of Time* (1997). In the first of these, Heilbrun writes: "Thus the publication of *Journal of a Solitude* in 1973 may be acknowledged as the watershed in women's autobiography." Biographer and critic William Drake has a significant chapter on Sarton and Bogan in *The First Wave: Women Poets in America 1915–1945* (1987), and Harvard professor Alexandra Johnson has a chapter on Sarton in her 1997 *The Hidden Writer: Diaries and the Creative Life* which Sarton sadly did not live to see. See also footnote to letter of 3 June 1992 for university press books which did come out before her death and brought her inestimable fulfillment.

Sylvia Plath did . . . Anne Sexton . . . did: Sylvia Plath (1932–1963), brilliant, tormented poet whose marriage in 1956 to poet Ted Hughes provided, for its first six years, a strong union of two dedicated writers; in October 1962 Hughes left for good, and on 11 February 1963, having descended into a deep, clinical depression, she gassed herself in front of her two children. In the thirty-five years since her suicide Plath has become a heroine and martyr of the feminist movement. Anne Sexton (1928–1974), *née* Harvey, married in 1947, began writing poetry in 1957. The birth of her first daughter helped trigger a series of mental breakdowns and suicide attempts that would pattern the rest of her life. In a 1957 workshop with Robert Lowell, Sexton met Sylvia Plath. In her Pulitzer Prize–winning volume *Live or Die* (1967), "Wanting to Die" is addressed to the dead Plath; in it she reproaches Plath for having gone alone "into the death I wanted so badly and so long." Sexton claimed suicides are a special people; "We talked of death," she wrote of Plath, "and this was life for us." At a candlelit dinner in a restaurant in Cambridge in August 1974, Anne Sexton appointed her twenty-one-year-old daughter, whom she had earlier sexually abused, as her literary executor; less than two months later, on 4 October, she killed herself.

things moving legally . . . tenant . . . affidavit: Lady Huxley had rented an attic room to a quiet tenant, Bill Humphreys, for some ten years; ultimately he refused to leave 31 Pond Street largely because his rent was low. Juliette was obliged to take him to court, resulting in a prolonged affair. At the time of this letter he had feigned illness and was in hospital, and no final court order could be made.

PIERROT, the kitten: the Himalayan kitten which Carolyn Heilbrun gave to Sarton after Bramble's death and delivered personally from New York; for more see pp. 79–82 in *The Last Gift of Time* by Carolyn G. Heilbrun (Dial Press, 1997).

YORK   Saturday Aug. 8th, 1987

Dearest Juliette,

I am just back from a week away on the Cape where I rested between walking poor Grizzle about every hour as she could not be let out without a leash (as she is in this safe haven) and somehow will <u>not</u> do her business on a leash. Never again.

There I finally read my letters to you, those you so kindly sent ages ago. I felt that I did not want to read them, that it would be too painful. What Beatrice Glenavy did was psychologically speaking as though she had torn out one of my eyes or cut off my right hand. You may not remember that you said at the time to me, "Do not try to explain. It will only make matters worse." She succeeded in what she needed to do which was to destroy my friendship with Kot . . . I do not think she cared a hoot whether it would affect you and me or not. You might reread my poem Giant in the Garden (p. 150 in Collected Poems).

But I am glad I made myself read the letters. The effect has been astonishing. For on every page what they show is true love, love that entered into and at least tried to share the other person's life and needs. For years I have felt only guilt about you, that I had asked too much, that I have always been a bad lover though a good friend. I now know that is not true and feel a kind of liberation. I can look on that person who truly loved you with love and understanding. I can now take <u>myself</u> into myself as I did you quite often. I feel redeemed. So thank God you did not destroy those letters as you so well might have.

As for publication—how very generous of you to suggest the possibility. I think the problem is that the quality of this relationship on all sides was the strange fact that I had been Julian's lover before the war. It was a triangle in which all three behaved in exemplary ways. That would be its value as ten years of falling deeply in love and coming through to friendship. It might be possible to cut all references to Julian except those to do with his marriage and his and my friendship after the war. I think however that in the end after we are all dead the truth should be known. I presume you did destroy the letters at the time of Glenavy's behavior. How I hate the Irish who would gladly betray their own mother if it made a good story.

As usual when I have gone away for a week it takes a while to feel at home. Pierrot was in raptures as he had missed Grizzle and me terribly and never came near the family who were here, except to be fed. Last night he even jumped up on the bed and lay beside me for an hour or so . . . he has not done that since Grizzle came. Absurd to be as anxious as I was all those days about him. Partly he is so white that at night he is in danger from any predator.

We are having a real drought, the corn drying on the stalks so the farmers are suffering. My bed of annuals is a disaster area, the cosmos only about a foot high. I began watering as soon as I got home.

Tons of stuff I have to answer here, but I wanted to write you first and while I was feeling so blest. It has been an extraordinary friendship, Juliette . . . and especially that it got mended in the end.

I am grateful all over again for everything, including your always putting your finger on the weakness in a poem.

There were, while I think of it, two things not letters from me. One was a note about Kot's cousin . . . he came here and we had a long talk and he saw all Kot's letters to me which are at the Berg with mine to him. So I don't think I'll send that letter you marked. I think the book is out but I'm not sure. The other was a short extremely painful letter from you to Julian, begging him for peace. Did you put it there on purpose? It must have been before the war when he and I were lovers. Shall I send it back or leave it there? These letters will go to the Berg in October. Before that I'll have Nancy [Hartley] put them all through the copier so I can still think about publishing someday and they will be here.

I am enjoying the house because for little Sarton and her family who were here last week, I had to tidy up untold messes and drawers. I am the worst housekeeper in the world I'm afraid. But now I can enjoy the order and the peace of it. Sarton, named for me, because her parents used to read my poems to each other before their marriage, is now seven. She came with a little friend. They dashed down every morning and gathered mussels and had mussels for breakfast, which is a big treat, though mussels for breakfast is not my idea of a good breakfast. The best was to hear that her parents, both social workers, did have some peaceful times alone. I know they needed that. It is the second year I have left them the house and I hope it may become a tradition, "the summer place" of joys.

I put so much away to tidy that now I can't find anything! Oh dear, what an old fool I have become.

Dearest Juliette a heart full of love from your old

May

Awful typing—sorry

---

week away on the Cape: Sarton's friend Irene Morgan (d. 1995), who spent winters in New Mexico, had a summer home in Harwich, Massachusetts.

poor Grizzle: Tamas had died on 5 November 1986. On 6 May 1987 Sarton brought home a recalcitrant short-haired wirehaired dachshund puppy she named Grizzle; finally proving too much for Sarton, in 1989 Grizzle went to live with Janice Oberacher, whose dachshund, Fonzi, Sarton had given her years before.

destroy my friendship with Kot: On 26 October 1948, Sarton had written to Beatrice Glenavy: "At the root of this is of course Kot. And that is what makes me think it in some ways hopeless. I believe that Kot is a genius, but I do not think he is a Christian. I would therefore not myself shut out people whom he has shut out—any more than I would ever refuse to read the mss. of a young person out of fear that I might have to tell the truth and hurt them. It is not pleasant to run that risk but I think it part of being human. Kot will not read Michael [Campbell]'s stories for instance because he is afraid he will not like them. What I miss I suppose is something which the Bible calls charity. I do not believe most people are black or white but that most people are gray—and have too many obvious faults myself to sit in judgement with such ferocity. I think Kot is pure and that is so rare a thing that it amounts to genius. But I do not think he is good which is something else."

Giant in the Garden: "Giant in the Garden" first appeared in *The Land of Silence*. Sarton's page reference is to the 1973 edition, *Collected Poems (1930–1973)*, and not the later *Collected Poems (1930–1993)*.

the truth should be known: In January 1976, after the silence of twenty-seven years and having just learned from Sarton that she had given her correspondence with Julian to the Berg Collection, not to be made available to scholars for twenty-five years, Juliette writes: "And of course there will be a day of revelations. That can't be helped, and so you did what was obvious in disposing of his letters as you did. During his life I have tried to keep the Image to protect him as best I could. Francis thought it a pity, and a diminution of the truth. So, if in 25 years' time, a curious new image surfaces, he, in any case, will not resent it. Nor will Anthony for that matter. I am glad there is this time lapse, anyway. I suppose Viola has also sold her letters—maybe with less discretion. I don't even know if she is still alive." Viola is Viola Ilma Ali Youssuff, who, according to an article in the *New York Evening Journal* of 14 December 1932, was the granddaughter of a Quaker missionary who married into the Abyssinian royal line. Juliette refers to her as "Sandra" in Ch. 9 of *Leaves of the Tulip Tree* in an episode in the early 1930s when Julian met her on the boat going to Egypt, declared to Juliette his intention of pursuing her (when she followed in the next boat to go on safari with him), went to the United States to be with her, and nearly did not return. "What Julian really wanted," Juliette writes, "was not just a passing affair with a pretty girl, but a definite freedom from the conventional bonds of marriage." Viola had not sold her letters at the time of Juliette's letter of 1976; she paid Juliette a visit some time after that, seeking her permission to publish them, and Juliette refused to give it.

family who were here: Stephan and Dorothy Molnar and their daughter, Sarton Molnar-Fenton.

Kot's cousin: Koteliansky's nephew, Martin Packman, had been writing a biography of Kot since 1984.

short extremely painful letter from you to Julian, begging him for peace: Undated, on "The Zoological Society, Regent's Park N.W.8" letterhead, Juliette wrote: "Middle of the night Thursday, Oh Julian—I can't make sense of things anymore—& I am a bit lost & sad—It seems strange and sad & stupid that this should come upon us now—nay, not come upon us—by us almost—Us—we were getting on fine; we were happy—We <u>knew</u> we were—& now—oh God Julian—this is too idiotic. Here am I tossing my insights—listening to your voice and rereading your letters—ah misery—<u>Must</u> I be <u>made</u> miserable so you may be happy? Why couldn't you both leave me alone—~~& not~~ Your selfishness can be so cruel—so cruel your eagerness to thank me for saying 'It's your affair'—when you know so well nothing I could say would alter your wish—& your decision—oh Julian—how I hate all this—my heart growing more restless and vulnerable when I so fondly thought it never would again—my mind digging up the ghosts—& then reenacting things I never wanted to think of again—What is the good of hiding my fears <u>decently</u> when you make your happiness so blatant—And there we are again—you see—my sweet—[indecipherable] & we shall get into tangles of words & actions which God only knows how we shall untangle. I want peace—oh Julian—Peace—Give me back my peace—Give me hope of peace—Be strong now. Take my fears upon you as you said you would. Take my unrest and my vulnerable heart and give me peace—It is for you to give me peace—now—a peace which cannot grow out of words & explanations & promises—for such <u>destroy</u> it—Find the way—For all my little store of wisdom is drained away, & I have rebellion—Julian—Your wife."

peace of it: Having once made order of them, Sarton labeled all the drawers and cupboards in the kitchen; the labels remained in place until her death.

[YORK]   [June 3, 1992]

Dearest Juliette, Oh my love,

What bliss to find a word from you on this June morning when all the lilacs are in their glory and the damp air full of their scent! I still dream of flying over perhaps in the autumn but my life has suddenly become miraculously full and I am still not well, though better thanks to Dr. Ferida Kahnjani. She was massaging my head yesterday and said suddenly: "May, I can feel how much is happening in your head!" It made me laugh because she is right. God is giving me a little canter at the end, I think.

I say "Oh my love" because at last Norton is going to reissue the

Collected Poems to add in the three books not in the first one published 20 years ago, so I am having to re-read it all to catch the typos and in a few cases change a word or take a poem out. I have not looked at my poems for two years since I was not able to read them to audiences when I did have to to choose what to read each time. I have been transported into all stages of my adult life in this process and so moved by the poems I wrote for you, I can't tell you. You decided long ago you wanted none of that. You pretend it was madness but you can't destroy such a reality. It is there in the Poems. Please read them some day. In the Collected poems which I presume you have? If you do not have these, tell me. I'll have them copied for you.

> The Lady and the Unicorn
> Question
> Perspective
> "O Saisons! O Châteaux!"
> Song Without Music
> These Images Remain, 9 sonnets

Later Giant in the Garden which disposes of Lady Glenavy rather rightly—

> A willful giant looming in the garden
> May like a mad dog one day go berserk
> (Have you not heard the lewd and murderous bark?).

She managed to separate us for 20 years, but nothing can separate us now because we are so old, I expect. I find it marvelous that because I am 80 I can say a lot of things now and intend to live a while longer to do so.

But the great miracle, Juliette, is that poems come . . . it is because I do it in bed at night. Up here at my desk it is "ought" . . . and piles of stuff I should answer. I have no peace. But at last I can listen to music again which was not possible for five years after the stroke—I simply wept from frustration. . . .

Please suddenly try to write once in a while . . . I know the effort is immense but this is the _idea_ of writing . . . forget about doing it and just think aloud some day. Today I am playing Chausson's Chanson de l'Amour et de La Mer with Janet Baker . . . wow! It would make a walrus sing.

This weekend a conference in Portland to celebrate my 80th—36 papers will be read by scholars from all over the country—Many, thank God, about the poems <u>at last</u>. Books come out on my work etc. I now have 17 honorary doctorates—It is all happening too late as all I want <u>now</u> is <u>not fame</u>, but to look at flowers and live a little and to see you again. <u>Yes!</u>

———

Dr. Ferida Kahnjani: Dr. Ferida Khanjani, holistic chiropractor in York, Maine, who treated Sarton for one year with macrobiotic diet and massage.

a little canter at the end: reference to Maxine Kumin's contribution to Sarton's eightieth-birthday festschrift, *Forward into the Past,* titled "A Little Finishing Canter for May Sarton," at the end of which Kumin quotes Oliver Wendell Holmes on the occasion of his ninetieth birthday: "The riders in a race," he said, "do not stop short when they reach the goal. There is a little finishing canter. . . ."

add in the three books not in the one . . 20 years ago: Unlike *Collected Poems, 1930–1973,* the new *Collected Poems, 1930–1993* includes *Halfway to Silence* (1980); *Letters from Maine* (1984); and *The Silence Now* (1988). *Coming into Eighty,* Sarton's final volume of poetry and winner of the Levinson Prize, was published in 1994.

what to read each time: It had been two years since Sarton was well enough to appear publicly for poetry readings. When preparing such readings, Sarton would each time go through her poetry again to make her selections. She had not had occasion to do that for two years: but now, proofreading the manuscript for *Collected Poems, 1930–1993* she once again, after two years, revisited her poetry.

do it in bed at night: Pierrot, the Himalayan cat, had the habit of meowing in the middle of the night to be let out, and again several hours later beneath Sarton's window to be let in. Having made her way downstairs with eyes half closed to let him out, Sarton would be wide awake; it was then, in the silent house, that lines would run through her head. She made notes on a pad beside her bed, and worked on them the following day. It was in this way that most of the poems in *Coming into Eighty* were written; its dedication reads: "To Pierrot, The Muse Mews."

I simply wept from frustration: From early childhood when Sarton was taken to the Boston Symphony concerts given at Harvard six times a year and exposed continually to her father's vast collection of recordings, music deeply affected her; listening to it came to be inextricably connected to writing poetry. In the last years, hearing music when she was not able to write poetry caused profound despair.

Chausson . . . Janet Baker: The intensely dreamlike, melancholic *Poème de l'Amour et de la Mer,* the fruit of a painful gestation extending from 1882 to 1890, is the greatest and most ambitious vocal work of French composer Ernest Chausson (1855–1899), student of Massenet and Franck. Dame Janet Baker (1933–), English mezzo-soprano, one of the most intelligent of contemporary singers, was equally impressive in opera, Lieder, and English and French song as well as oratorio. She retired from the opera stage in 1982.

make a walrus sing: This is the end of a typewritten page. What follows is written by hand at the top of this page. There is no signature; possibly a second page is missing.

conference in Portland to celebrate my 80th: A three-day national conference, "May Sarton at 80: A Celebration of Her Life and Work," conceived and executed by Bradford

Dudley Daziel (1946–1994), was held at Westbrook College 11–13 June 1992. Twenty-two of the papers presented were selected by Constance Hunting and published as *A Celebration for May Sarton* (Puckerbrush Press, 1994).

Books come out on my work: Conversations with May Sarton, ed. Earl G. Ingersoll (University Press of Mississippi, 1991); *That Great Sanity: Critical Essays on May Sarton*, ed. Susan Swartzlander and Marilyn Mumford (University of Michigan Press, 1992); *A House of Gathering: Poets on May Sarton's Poetry*, ed. Marilyn Kallet (University of Tennessee Press, 1993).

17 honorary doctorates: Sarton received her eighteenth from the University of New England in Biddeford, Maine, on 13 May 1995, two months before her death.

[YORK]   June 8th [1992]

Dearest Juliette,

I forgot something I wanted to say and had been going to write you when your darling life giving note came two or three days ago, to wit: When I was looking for a tie to go with a white shirt with a thin red line woven in it, I found the silk tie with elegant points you made for me, rich vermilion and french blue. Perfect. It will deck my throat when I read the new poems to what sounds as though it will be a huge audience at that conference celebrating this old turtle on Saturday . . . 3 days of essays on my work. Can you believe it? I shall only be able to attend on the last day. I wish Kot could be there.

I got so excited and scared last night I couldn't sleep and horrible Pierrot woke me to go out, so I climbed the stairs again to bed, only to hear furious mewing downstairs a half hour later! I now think I have to get a cat door for the winter anyway.

I left out above that the silk tie is about 55 years old and still beautiful. Think of it as a metaphor. I loved you and was shut out for years but love stayed fresh and that seems so wonderful now I am 80. Thank you for your love. It is life giving <u>now</u>.

I am trying to write a poem using the image of a hummingbird in the road, crushed by a car, to answer something you felt, that my love was not real because later there were so many others. You made it brief, not I. But anyway, reality can be brief, like that hummingbird's flash of a life . . . no one had felt able to run over the corpse I noticed as I went by it 3 times that day in my car.

I am driven, trying to get the collected poems proof-read for typos in the old edition. Just imagine, the new edition for my 81st birthday will be I suppose about 500 pages. Will it sink like a huge dying whale?

Much too quick—I <u>must get to work!</u>

[   ]
Huge hug

---

only . . . attend on the last day: It was necessary for Sarton to conserve her strength; on the third and final day, Sarton attended this editor's reading from the soon-to-be-published *May Sarton: Among the Usual Days,* read her new poems to a standing-room-only audience, introduced her biographer Margot Peters, attended the final plenary speech by Sandra Gilbert, and hosted a lunch with Gilbert, Peters, Carolyn Heilbrun, and this editor.

wish Kot could be there: referring to Koteliansky's great belief in her work, and how proud he would have been.

a poem using the image of a hummingbird . . . crushed by a car: There was such a poem, which alas has eluded this editor's sleuthing.

new edition . . . will be I suppose about 500 pages: Collected Poems 1930–1993, published in May 1993, is 542 pages.

Huge hug: During the interval between this letter and the next, Sarton wrote to Bill Brown: "Tomorrow Juliette will be 97 and I shall get up at six to phone her—but it is so sad not to be able to see her again. I simply can't travel. . . . Monday, 6:15 AM: I just called Juliette, instantly responsive 'Love, love, love!' but can't remember whether a case of wine I sent had come, or who is there housekeeping—I can't help crying. So I'm so glad you are there, dearest Bill, who knew her and the long love this has been—and is—"

[YORK]   June 21 [1992]

Dearest Juliette,

We have just talked, your voice sounding so young and adorable, mine cracked and old. Never mind, I am happier than anyone could imagine . . . after 50 years of struggle and so much neglect as writer it is all coming out at last like a game of solitaire . . . I feel so loved, Juliette, unbelievable. The conference at Westbrook College. 3 days of essays on various aspects of Sarton was attended by men and women from 32 states, including Alaska, and from Nova Scotia and another Canadian province. 36 papers were read. I stayed away till the third day when I had promised to read poems with the help of the mike . . . the best thing about the conference was, I believe from what I hear, that all these people could meet each other, all with an immediate bond in their love of Sarton's work. So it became all at once a small community and communion. Of course I was terrified. I had sent Susan to hear the first two days and she would report all the enthusiasm and the terrifying build-up to my walking out on a stage for the first time in two years and unable to trust my voice . . . I managed all right for 45 minutes, reading almost all new poems, all those I sent you. I am writing poems and playing music again these days. "I'm on a roll" is the slang of all this and it is quite a roll for an old lady to be on.

The final speech, one of three keynote addresses was by a famous woman critic called Sandra A. Gilbert who launched into a real ovation for my poems . . . comparing to Rilke, Yeats (in speaking of their influence) so generously . . . setting me in a high place as a forerunner (instead of saying as another woman critic said, "derivative and uninteresting"). I really could not believe my ears. And later when I took her and Susan and my biographer, Margot Peters, out to lunch Gilbert kept saying, "I am so honored to meet you." I am now quite fond of Margot. She will do a good sensitive unsentimental biog I think . . . and although I dreaded our meetings at first I now look forward to being forced to look at my history in a rather cool, impersonal and sometimes humorous way. Detachment is the key, of course. Her publishers gave her a huge advance, I gather, but it is in the contract that she have access to everything but that <u>nothing</u> be published while I'm alive.

But better than all this glory is the warmth and faith with which The Women's Press will bring out in one volume my last three books of poems. It was my idea since lyric poets who go on into their old age are rare. From <u>Halfway to Silence</u> on I was 65 and over. So I'll come to see you (Maggie has agreed to come to take care of me) around October 10th for 8 or 9 days and then again in early April perhaps for longer to do some poetry readings, interviews etc. The Women's Press brings out ENDGAME in January, so there will be two books to promote.

D'un côté, tu peux imaginer, toi qui imagine tout avec génie, il y une personne au fond de moi qui voudrait regarder les fleurs, écouter les oiseaux, entendre les long soupirs de la mer, sans bouger, et surtout sans gloire . . . et qui détests cette ambitieuse petit fille qui a tant espérer la gloire et qui l'a maintenant. Quand même, pour le moment, je suis très très heureuse . . . tu le vois dans cette photo assez extraordinaire qui a paru dans un journal—

Oh how wonderful October will be!

So much love,
M—

---

like a game of solitaire: See "A Fortune" in *Coming into Eighty:* "Can you believe it?/Now I am eighty/The long game of solitaire/Has ended/Exactly as he said/It must."

I had sent Susan: Susan Sherman, editor of this volume, lived with Sarton during weekends, academic breaks, and summers.

unable to trust my voice: During the months and weeks preceding this conference, because one vocal cord had atrophied, Sarton took voice lessons; she performed exercises with intense discipline and was able to strengthen her voice.

am writing poems: The poems Sarton read at the conference, and the poems she was writing at this time, appear in *Coming into Eighty.*

Sandra A. Gilbert: (1936–), poet, teacher, critic known for works including *Madwoman in the Attic: The Woman Writer and the Nineteenth-Century Literary Imagination* (1979) and *No Man's Land: The Place for the Woman Writer in the Twentieth Century,* published in three volumes.

derivative and uninteresting: In the *Massachusetts Review,* Vol. 8, Summer 1967, in "Recent American Poetry" Helen Vendler wrote: "May Sarton is a derivative poet, and she lives in a rarefied self-regarding aloofness. There is no surprise in her poetry; it deals in almost all the clichés of literate verse."

took Susan . . . Peters, out to lunch: Carolyn G. Heilbrun, Sarton's literary executor, was also in attendance.

fond of Margot . . . unsentimental biog I think: Although Sarton wanted to believe what she says here, she came to change this view of Peters. On 14 March 1992 she wrote Peters: "I cannot talk with you after these two meetings until you have read the work. The reason is that once you have read it you won't have to ask most questions and you will not make superficial and troubling mistakes in the remarks you make and the questions you do ask." On 11 July 1992 she wrote Carolyn Heilbrun: "At present it looks to me as though I had to have . . . a biographer who will not attack me as grossly unfair because I gave Susan permission long before Margot was even in the picture. Susan is willing to be thrown to the wolves for my sake. I am not willing to do so." On 3 September 1992 she wrote to Bill Brown: "Of course you are right to refuse to answer questions about me when Margot has our correspondence to read . . . In some ways I wish I had never agreed to the biography." In the 21 February 1994 entry of *At Eighty-Two* which Peters requested she delete, Sarton had written: "I felt I tried at least to feel that I could trust her, and now I do not feel that I can." Sarton had been entirely honest with her biographer and expected honesty; it was matters of tone, sensitivity, taste, and judgment that increasingly troubled Sarton about Peters.

Maggie: Margaret Vaughan, friend who accompanied Sarton on her final trips to Europe after Edythe Haddaway no longer could do so. In 1987 Sarton wrote "The Skilled Man, for Bill Vaughan," in *The Silence Now*; William Loring Vaughan, Margaret Vaughan's husband, died in 1988.

D'un côté . . . : In one way, you can understand—you who understand with such genius—that deep inside me there is a person who wants only to look at the flowers, listen to the birds, hear the long sighs of the sea, without moving, and above all, without fame . . . a person who detests the ambitious little girl who so much wanted the fame she now has. All the same, for the moment I am very very happy—you can see that in this rather extraordinary photo which appeared in a newspaper. [Said photo appears in this volume dubbed "The bliss of old age."]

[YORK]   August 15, 1994

Dearest Juliette,

How wonderfully good and blessed it was to hear your voice the other day and to sense that you are well. It made me decide with Maggie Vaughan's help to come over in early November. She goes to Italy in October. We would stay a week or ten days but—oh, how wonderful!

I am rather a wreck since the stroke I had at Easter, and since then an illness with a lot of pain which a covey of doctors have been unable to diagnose. Months of this have been a drain and I have little or no energy and walk with difficulty. Also, I cannot type since the stroke and that means I cannot work. You can imagine what a frustrated life it is!

Susan Sherman is here for the summer and is typing this for me. My hand is illegible as you know. But now hope rises, and the thought of seeing you lifts depression away and sets me on a new course. Maybe I shall even get to write the Christmas poem which I have started and must be written in August.

I hear you've had a very hot summer. So have we but today is a marvelous, brilliant, clear day, clear air, sparkling ocean and hoping to see you soon.

Always with my love,
M—

---

the Christmas poem: Sarton completed "After the War" before the end of August; it was printed by William B. Ewert in December 1994.

Juliette Huxley died on 28 September 1994.
May Sarton died on 16 July 1995.

A p p e n d i x

Working Drafts of Introductions by May Sarton
Letters and Parts of Letters from Juliette Huxley
Unpublished Poems and Original French Letters

WORKING DRAFTS OF INTRODUCTIONS BY MAY SARTON

Sarton made various handwritten and typed attempts at introductions to the original version of this book, ending with the letter of 1 Nov. 1948. She had suffered her first stroke in December 1985; the grave illness of 1990–91 described in Endgame *further affected her typing, her handwriting, and her memory for dates. Some of these drafts, barely legible, attest to the continued and preeminent importance that Juliette Huxley, and this final testament of May's love for her, retained to the end.*

Draft One—1989

Many of these letters were written fifty years ago and the last of them forty one years ago. When Juliette Huxley sent them back to me a few years ago, saying "do with them what you wish" and suggesting that they were certainly publishable, I was committed to other endeavors and did not even read them until early this year, 1989. But when I finally took the folder from the file and plunged in I was quite surprised and delighted. I cannot write letters like these now. And perhaps never wrote as well to anyone else. For this <u>amitié amoureuse</u> as the French call a loving friendship . . . and how much better their phrase is than ours!—called out of me the best I had to give. And then there was time! Time to read, and time to sit in parks in London or cafés in Paris, and write poems. And there was Juliette to write to, Juliette with her gentle teasing, her wit, her always enlivening criticism of my poems, and her glamorous life as Julian Huxley's wife. By a strange chance I met him first; we were fellow guests at the Charles Singers' in Cornwall, Charlie a colleague of my father's and Julian down in Cornwall to see whether it would be possible to grow eucalyptus there, enough to provide for Koala bears at the Zoo, for he was then Secretary of the London Zoo and its country adjunct, Whipsnade. I fell into the Huxley ambience like a duck into ~~a heavenly pond and if~~ heavenly water. I fell in love ~~it was being in love~~ with a marriage, with those fabulous lunches where I might sit beside T.S. Eliot or Kenneth Clark, at that time head of the National Gallery, with the family picnics on the way to a week-end at Whipsnade. And above all I fell in love with the constant flow of teasing and sharing between Julian and Juliette which made them seem the ideal couple and theirs an ideal marriage. As I came to know them better and observe it all with the peeled eye of a lover I began to see that this "ideal" marriage was not ideal, but the creation chiefly of Juliette and that she had married a brilliant, charming, idealistic gregarious man ~~whose wavering ego had to be~~ who was unstable, full of self doubt, and a raging egotist. She had to be as present with sustenance, compassion and tender care as a nurse with a perpetual invalid. It is here perhaps that the quality of our friendship becomes clear, and is present in the letters I wrote to her. When I went back and read them after all those years what struck me was that they were not as insistent and demanding of her attention as I had feared, but rather prove what women can do and be for each other. It would be hard to imagine such letters written by a man either to a man friend or a woman friend.

I was growing up and growing out of my romantic ideas as time went on, and much that I learned about marriage through the Huxleys, and the "family life" I had always envied, brought me to the certainty that marriage was not for me, ~~But~~ Juliette, the "small blue flame" stayed with me even when circumstances and a serious misunderstanding forced her to withdraw and to shut me out for over thirty years. I was still invited to tea when I was in London. But the "real connection" had been broken or buried. I witnessed Julian's radical decline and ~~Juliette's increasing~~ neurotic dependency on Juliette and her long brave struggle to keep them afloat. ~~But~~ I was not confided in and there were no letters to reread and to treasure. But that long painful gap in our intercourse was not after all to be the end.

After Julian's death Juliette wrote me occasionally, sometimes about the disposal of papers since my letters to Julian went to the Berg Collection at the N.Y. Public Library, but these letters then were polite and distant. The change was gradual, but when she began to work seriously at her autobiography, The Leaves of the Tulip Tree, she began to tell me all her fears and doubts and to feel the affinity that writers ~~have~~ share in the always painful struggle to tell the truth and to come to terms with it.

[Incomplete]

———

T.S. Eliot: See footnote to letter of 23 November 1941.
Kenneth Clark: Kenneth Mackenzie, Lord Clark of Saltwood (1903–1983), English art historian, leading scholar of the Italian Renaissance, known for his popular BBC television series and book *Civilization* (1969), *The Nude: A Study in Ideal Form* (1956), *An Introduction to Rembrandt* (1978), and two works of autobiography.

———

Draft Two—1989

A Loving Friendship does not define such an intimate exchange as these letters represent. The French, "une amitié amoureuse" comes closer to the truth. Some years ago Juliette Huxley (Lady Huxley, widow of Sir Julian Huxley) sent me two packets of letters I had written her and said she thought they should be published. I was astonished and delighted and when I finally read them myself, going back 50 years to 1936 for the earliest ones, I felt I was ~~reliving~~ plunged into the past when I was twenty five to thirty or so and it all came back as ~~very real~~ fresh, only yesterday. We do not write letters these days. These days people talk into cassettes or use the telephone.

As I read and lived those years again, I realized that the charm of letter writing is that it is an exchange between two lives, in this case a poet twenty five years old and the extraordinarily charming and original wife of a famous man sixteen years older than her correspondent. Julian was Secretary of the London and Whipsnade Zoos, and went on after the war to become the first Secretary General of Unesco in Paris.

Juliette is now 92 and I am 77. Is it time now to take a look at what our lives were like fifty to forty years ago?

The letters speak for themselves. I am not at this point about to explain circumstances, the story behind the letters. It is not biography that is involved but rather the way in which two women see and help each other. In this sense it is timeless.

I must add that there are two gaps—Aug 38 to May 39 and July 46 to July 47. It is possible that Juliette leading an extremely full life, simply did not keep my letters during those two gaps. Then a far more serious interruption in our friendship took place and between November 48 and

[Incomplete]

Draft Three
February 15, 1995

I have just reread these letters written 40 years ago. Now, at 82, I can see memory and inspiration as my friend. I have had many lovers, many friends since I was 25 and met Juliette Huxley, but none has so nourished the poet and the lover as she did, the incomparable one. How mysterious any such love affair is! How must we have made the link unbreakable, even after 20 years of silence? And what instigated such an intense break, and why? The longer we shared a true communion, how dare to break it as she did, and why?

There had been one passionate week in Paris when Julian, Secretary General of Unesco, was away. One week in 50 years! One had to sustain such intense feeling over 50 years. I find it somewhat inexplicable, especially as during the long silence we each had a full and rich life. Today I have come to see what motivated Juliette. It was, I now feel certain, that in 1946 she extricated herself from a different act of affection she had shared with a man. I am a woman and this raised all sorts of new questions. What happened at Lady Glenavy's made me look unreliable, indiscreet and dangerous. Beatrice succeeded in alienating Kot from me. When Julian died, Juliette was punctilious about sending her letters to me to the Berg Collection, my archive there. When she broke off with me, she asked me to burn her letters. I did destroy those written at the time of the parting but kept those written from 1946 on.

It was not a sudden act nor an elan to open up again our communion by means of letters. She had decided to write her autobiography and wrote me of her struggles and anxieties about that. It is maybe given that no one's autobiography is entirely true for many people are still alive. Juliette was determined to be honest. I feel sure that she, for instance, combined two lovers into one as both were alive. I am not mentioned in the autobiography, and I can see why.

[Incomplete]

---

with a man: Possibly Alan Best; there were others, unidentified.

Lady Glenavy's: See footnote to letters of 21 July 1947 and 24 April 1948.

The Berg Collection: The Henry W. and Albert A. Berg Collection of English and American Literature at the New York Public Library. The Berg brothers were doctors of long standing at New York's Mount Sinai Hospital. In 1940 Dr. Albert Berg established the Berg Collection in his brother's memory. The initial gift included first editions of Donne, Keats, Blake, Wordsworth, and Dickens. Today the collection has grown to include letters and manuscripts of Virginia Woolf, D. H. Lawrence, Eliot, Auden, and May Sarton as well as personal items and furniture, transforming it into a complete literary archive. Its holdings are equaled by only four other institutions—the Houghton Library at Harvard, the Beinecke Library at Yale, the Humanities Research Center at the University of Texas at Austin, and the Huntington Library in San Marino, California.

Draft Four, undated

The Silence, 1946–1976

The last letter I wrote Juliette in 1946 followed on an excruciatingly painful parting. Earlier letters from her showed a growing discomfort within the relationship which had been rich and fruitful for ten years. Her reason for this apparently complete break, she told me and I refer to it in a stunned letter, was that we were in temperament too different altogether, that we could not connect. Yet her letters as well as mine published here suggest rather a real communion, a sharing of our very different lives, and a growing intimacy. Perhaps she had persuaded herself that she was telling the truth. But the truth was, I feel sure, that she could not cope with the guilt our brief love affair had caused her. For her to pretend it had never happened was the result of a time of great stress when she said she was mad and hardly responsible for what had happened. She certainly kept her promise to herself to have done with me as a friend. During those years of limbo I did see her casually when I was invited to come to Pond Street in Hampstead to have tea with Julian. About once a year when I was in London after the war, I saw her briefly, but she did not join us for tea. Julian told me that Juliette was adamant as she had made up her mind, as it reminded her—[Incomplete]

As I remember all this I find it amazing that when Juliette insisted on a separation, presumably permanent, I was not angry or resentful, and I wonder why? Everything in this extraordinary love affair has its mystery— how did I manage to accept brutal rejection without bitterness. Partly because I knew who I was and no one at that point in my life could have persuaded me that I was an impossible person to befriend and to love. I suppose I realized that what she did hurt Juliette, perhaps even more than it did me, for she did violence to herself and rejected something spontaneous and real that she had experienced. The past cannot be destroyed and one pays a high price for trying to do so.

When we separated we were both involved in a dramatic period in our lives. The UNESCO years in Paris had been rich in meeting with intellectual Paris and many trips connected with the organization. I think they were good traveling companions.

I was on a [race?] too, producing novels, books of poetry and memoirs and beginning to be in demand in the colleges to read poems. I taught for three years at Wellesley College.

But I remember everything about the ten years we had shared, and tried to glean whatever I could about her life in the lovely house on Pond St. she and Julian bought after they came back from Paris. I knew that Julian had had more than one severe depression and had been treated with shock treatment from which he painfully climbed out only to lose his grip again. The image comes to me because it seemed so much like a rock climber reaching the top almost, and then slipping. I thought I could imagine Juliette's life as his nurse and housekeeper but the last time I saw them together was shocking. I could hardly take [it] in. Juliette looked like an exhausted servant and it was soon clear that she was a prisoner to Julian's selfish self pitying demands. As soon as I was seated beside him in the garden he shouted, "Juliette, where are you?" as she came in with our tea. She was like a bird caught in a net. The horror for me was to see this and not be able to do anything at all to help.

Juliette was tough and determined, even to wheeling Julian in his wheel chair to the very steep hill on Pond St as it converged with a street that led to Hampstead Heath where she could wheel Julian to a bench to watch the grebes he loved so much.

"My involvement with Julian's depressions was total." She had fought for him in so many ways as though she were fighting to keep him alive, interested, if possible well. And then one day, February 14, 1975, Julian's face came on the TV and I knew of course what that meant. I was intoxicated by the relief for Juliette free at last, and cabled her at once to invite her to come and rest here. She did answer to tell me she was coming over to see Matthew Huxley, Aldous's son. But I stayed in an intoxi-

~~cated state of hope~~ Everything had changed in those silent years but not ~~our~~ love.

It took a year after Julian's death for a miracle to happen and it did not occur to me that it would. In the first year after Julian's death Juliette was overwhelmed and overworked by sorting the huge mass of [ ] in his files. My letters to Julian turned up and by my wish she turned them over to the Berg Collection at the New York Public Library where his letters to me had been given. After the last serious breakdown when Julian was at a loose end Juliette had suggested that he write his autobiography. This he did while he still had the energy and was not confined to a wheel chair after the stroke.

Julian wrote his autobiography to keep himself occupied.

Juliette wrote hers to find out who she was and to try to understand her long difficult marriage to Julian.

[Incomplete]

---

her letters . . . published here: It was Sarton's wish, to which Juliette Huxley agreed, that certain of Juliette's letters, chosen by Sarton, would be included in this volume; they, together with a few others added by this editor, appear in the Appendix.

Following are six handwritten fragments of drafts and parts of prefaces, of which two holographs are reproduced in this volume. These fragments are undated, but at least some seem to have been written on 15 February 1995, five months and one day before Sarton's death. It was not possible to determine an order or connection among the six. Indecipherable passages are indicated with brackets.

Fragment One—draft for "Draft Three," above

I have just reread these letters written, most of them, 40 years ago— Now I am 82 I ~~can see as my friend memory and imagination~~. That I have had many lovers, many friends since I was 25 and met Juliette Huxley, but ~~never~~ none has so nourished the Poet and the lover as she did, the incomparable one— How mysterious any such love affair is! How much it [ ] the link unbreakable even after 20 years silence—and what instigated such an intense break and why—The longer/We had shared a true communion. How dare she break it as she did? And why?

There had been one passionate week in Paris when Julian/Dir

General of Unesco/was away—one week in fifty years! One had to sustain such intense feeling over 50 years! I find it somewhat inexplicable—especially as during the long silence we each had a full and rich life—

Fragment Two

In '48 she told me that we had to part. We were both gone over to grief and pain, "suicidal" Juliette said once about this period—

This silence she imposed lasted for twenty years. During that time we both lived very rich lives—Juliette began to carve remarkable sculptures from marble—I wrote several novels, had several love affairs which later [?] led to three books of poems—But we did not break the silence, not for 20 years!

Why finally in 1976 did she decide to break it? After Julian's death there were endless letters and papers to be organized and sent to his archive in Texas or to the Berg where her letters are to me. In the course of her grueling "tidying up" Juliette came upon a bundle of my letters to her, those published here, and read them as though for the first time. She was moved and sent them back to me suggesting that they should someday be published—that was in '76.

––––––––––

his archive in Texas: Woodson Research Center, Rice University, Houston.

––––––––––

Fragment Three

How rare a love to last for 56 years—as mine for Juliette did. The letters go to Nov 1, 1948—telling about two very different lives—and then there is a long silence until 1974, the silence Juliette desired and which I always knew in my heart would end—We met in 1936 when I was 24. and then major work, novels, journals and poems were written between 1946 and 1976 when love ~~was~~ flowered again and Juliette, after Julian died, felt free at last to admit to herself that she loved and "always would."

After all the pain of our separation—"we were both suicidal" she said once—The pure joy of the last years will always be for me a miracle—It was, it seems to me, the gradual unfolding of a true love, and perhaps it was partly because there was time, all the years she was herself [silent?].

Fragment Four

[ ] I had one love affair with someone else—But I [ ] jealousy did not exist, perhaps because the [other?] relationship was founded on the impossible—

Juliette was married to Julian Huxley and that in itself was a full time job—it included many travels to Africa where they covered miles and miles, to Roumania, to South Africa—They had two sons. It was a full life that included several male lovers—

And I was creating a life around poetry and poetry readings and that took me all over the country—

The 20 years included my father's death and my buying an old farmhouse in Nelson, N.H. and my writing there Plant Dreaming Deep and the Journal of a Solitude. It included a 3-year stint teaching creative writing at Wellesley College—

So what was missing for 20 years? That is for me the mystery I struggle to understand—

Fragment Five

~~But~~ The meetings were very different from her letters which communicated the vision of old age that [spoke?] to me poignantly— She was in her nineties and I [ ] my lot similar.

There was no shadow when we talked and laughed about forgetting things and tasted the moment to the full—

Years after all [was? our?] [ ] a week—and lasted 56 years—That was the moment of course—

And that happened because in an [impetuous?] way we needed to share our lives—we needed each other—and the faithful love did not fail—

Fragment Six

It was a great pleasure/for them/and involved a lot of wit and laughter. And I enjoyed it but it never occured to me that as soon as I left—I would be done in in the same way—especially as Beatrice knew that Kot and I had become intimate friends after the war.

So I told Kot I had flirted with her, knowing he would tell Juliette, as indeed he did—and I suffered blame from all sides— Perhaps Juliette was glad of an excuse to break off with me— There was no relenting—and I remembered that Julian had once told me, "When Juliette makes up her mind, she's adamant."

But her decision which must have been very painful stemmed from a powerful sense of guilt she had suffered ever since we had been lovers in Paris [ ] days—and had a magical week of true love, passionate love—When she broke off with me it was to tell herself that that week (the one in 56 years!) was a disaster

LETTERS AND PARTS OF LETTERS FROM JULIETTE HUXLEY

Sarton intended a group of Juliette's letters to her to accompany her own to Juliette; see Draft Four of her introduction, "The Silence, 1946–1976." I have added several selections to her choices.

31 POND STREET NW 3   March 12, 1975

My dear May,

Thank you for your understanding letter—all you say and do not say. And for the cable, yes, thank god—and yet how hard it was when it really comes, the naked sword with no escape.

The boys have been wonderful—they took everything off my shoulders and accomplished the terrible things that have to be done. The ceremony at Golders Green was all their idea—Ecclesiastes "There is a time to be born and a time to die . . ." a piece from Wordsworth Ode to Immortality, two poems from the Captive Shrew, and the end, the Ecclesiasticus—"Now is the time to praise famous men . . ." Lord Holford began by saying a few words—and the organ played some Bach. Both boys read their parts simply and firmly. It made it all bearable. We took Julian home to Compton to the family grave last week—he sleeps there with his parents and brothers, Trev and Aldous. I hope he finds his peace, at last. Restless voyager.

Who—who—really—was he?

Juliette

And for the cable: Sarton had written and cabled in response to Julian's death on 14 February 1975.

Lord Holford: Probably William Holford, with whom Julian Huxley sat on various groups and committees on higher education and planning.

[Undated]

Dearest May,

I tried in vain to put these letters in some order. It is beyond my power. Beside, many have no date—just the name of a day. So I send this first batch, hoping you will manage to disentangle them, and moreover that you will bravely deal with them as you see fit. It is perhaps unnecessary to keep the sadnesses we all incur unless they become purely documentary . . . . I hesitate therefore to send them, but trust your wisdom.

31 Pond Street NW 3   January 19th, '76

Dear May,

Thank you for your letter. There is much in it to ponder and little to disagree with. As you wisely kept a carbon, there is no need for me to repeat your points. Or to discuss them. I am grateful that you wrote frankly and sincerely—in a way, it is a help to me, confirming much of my thoughts and releasing many personal tangles.

It is also deeply interesting to relate Julian to his "tribe." Aldous was also a Huxley, marked with a similar if not absolute flaw. It would be a delicate dissection to contemplate the Huxleyness they were born with. One wonders, too, about Trev, of whom Julian never spoke, yet wrote in his Memories the reason why, why Philip Thody takes up his book on Aldous with a truly surgical thrust.

As to our marriage having been what you kindly call a remarkable work of art, I think one might truly say that every marriage which survives is a work of art.

I was rather glad than sorry that Julian kept all his romances out of the Memories. Maybe you regretted it personally. And of course, there will be a day of revelations. That can't be helped, and so you did what was obvious in disposing of his letters as you did. During his life, I have tried to keep the Image—to protect him as best I could. Francis thought it a pity, and a diminution of the truth. So if in 25 years' time, a curious new image surfaces, he, in any case, will not resent it. Nor will Anthony for that matter. I am glad there is this time lapse, anyway. I suppose Viola has also sold her letters—maybe with less discretion. I don't even know if she is still alive.

And now I wonder if your own letters to Julian, most of which are somewhere in files, should not also join J's at the Berg Library. It will take me some time to gather them, as the work of sorting J's papers began and had to be given up as too much of a job. But it can be done, given enough time. Please let me know.

. . .

I am now trying to forget what was left of Julian in the last years of his life—almost all—and recover the good.

Best wishes,
Juliette

———————

Julian never spoke: In 1914, Trevenen Huxley, named for the Huxleys' distant cousins the
　　Trevelyans, had a breakdown, escaped from the same nursing home to which Julian
　　had just returned for a "rest-cure," and hanged himself in the nearby woods.
in his Memories: Julian Huxley's autobiography, published in the United States in 1970.
I suppose Viola: See footnote to letter of 8 August 1987.

———————

July 14th, 1976

My dear May

. . .

Do go on remembering things about Julian. Yes, he had this charm, a curious unusual intellectual charm. I am just reading a book about Mrs. Humphry Ward which he read in 1973 and heavily annotated. One can almost hear him, saying Pshaw in the margin. Only his writing was already crimped and shrunk, and so difficult to decipher. You don't need to regret what you said about him—there was truth in it, and interesting points. I wish I had asked him more questions: for instance when he replied to my saying, in the last months of his life, that he had a demon inside him, destroying us both. He said "of course I have a demon, had one since I was 4." I suppose we most of us have some sort of demon—but his was a major one.

. . .

I hope you keep well.
Greetings
Juliette

———

Mrs. Humphry Ward: Mrs. Humphry Ward (Mary Augustus Arnold, 1851–1920), granddaughter of Thomas Arnold; aunt of Julian Huxley; prolific, popular novelist and
playwright, considered sentimental and frivolous and held in contempt by Virginia
Woolf and others.

———

September 29th '76

Dear May,

> The time has come the walrus said,
> To talk of many things.

I am sorry I haven't yet answered your letter or thanked you for sending me "THE WORLD OF LIGHT"—in which I found all your gift for
perceptive understanding and writing. It is a fine piece of work, must have
been very difficult so often, as feelings are tangled up and often uninhibit-
ed. I mostly enjoyed your Father and Mother. But I too find it difficult to
overcome some of my mixed feelings towards you in writing about your
book. You see, what happened between us in Paris left its mark on me—
and the last thing I want is to harp back on the final disaster of our relationship. That it was a disaster is not in doubt—for when you threatened
to "tell all to Julian" I really felt betrayed in so absolutely unexpected a way.
It is a great pity that the memory of this remains so clear in my mind—as
I have always felt so much admiration for your courage and your great
gifts. And let me add that of course, should you now wonder, I have of
course forgiven everything. And understand how you must have been
yourself in a sort of no-man's land, where it was impossible to realize reasonably what was happening. But there is memory which I cannot get rid
of.

. . .

All best wishes and again thank you for a fine book.
Juliette

———

To talk of many things: From "The Walrus and the Carpenter" in *Through the Looking Glass*
by Lewis Carroll.

November 25th, 1976

Dear May,

Your letter of Oct. 31 was waiting for me on my return from $2^{1}/_{2}$ weeks in Kenya, at the invitation of Unesco to celebrate their 30th anniversary when Julian was the 1st D.G. A very generous invitation, which allowed me to take a companion (at my older age, they no doubt felt it unsafe to let me loose in Africa by myself). I took a delightful cousin by marriage—Chloe Tickel, who had never been to Africa and loved it as much as I. So we both came back with stars in our eyes—but alas, cold beastly weather after the delicious (if droughty) summer in Kenya. Our high point was seeing a BONGO, licking salt at the Ark Lodge in Aberdares Forest Park, and looking fantastically beautiful, with dazzling white legs and mask over black markings. I would have chosen off-white for better camouflage, but maybe there is a good reason which he chose that sparkling attire. They have vertical stripes over a blond pelt, the stripes also white and ears like petals, mostly white. One just could not resist that utter beauty.

Thank you for your letter. I am sorry you had that horrid review in the NY Times. I guess some jealous person arranged it all. Aldous never read HIS reviews, and some of course were pretty horrid. He felt they couldn't matter less, the book was done, and he was quit of it. But it is a difficult position to make for oneself, after all, one writes for a public. It must be a compensatory comfort to hear that your friends appreciate the book so highly.

I enjoyed seeing Evie so much. She has a great "finesse" and apprehension. Of course her life is very full, and the last book about the Himalayas was a triumph, I thought, of the inner eye.

The remark you allude to in your postscript was in a letter to me, sometime after the episode which had its comic side. The letter is possibly here, but I haven't dug it out. I don't remember what made you write it. Anyway, let us not mention it, it is part of a curious past, bits of which are best forgotten. I didn't invent it, even though you can't remember it, because it shook me profoundly.

Julian was curiously present in Africa. I felt myself looking at it, feeling it, for him mostly.

Sybille is busy with the executrix's duties over Eda Lord's death. She is deeply unhappy, as one always is after such a dear relationship. It will be a long time till she recovers, a long journey into unsuspected jungles. And I don't think one can do it anyhow but alone. I have not really emerged from mine—Julian is still possessive and imprinted. It could not be otherwise.

Happy Christmas—somehow. I don't send cards anymore, but wishes go forth.

Juliette

---

the NY Times: In the 3 October 1976 *New York Times Book Review* Pearl Kazin Bell wrote a brutal review of *A World of Light*. "She is Alfred Kazin's sister," Sarton wrote Charles Barber on 13 October, "and asked for the book in order to put me down. It really is a dirty business." See footnote to letter of 26 November 1945.
seeing Evie: Evelyn Ames (1908–1990), American poet, memoirist, novelist, and naturalist.
in your postscript: Not extant.
Eda Lord's death: Sybille Bedford (1911–), Anglo-German novelist, travel writer, and biographer, particularly known for her two-volume biography of Aldous Huxley. Eda Lord had been her longtime companion.

October 12th '77

I woke this morning with lead in the heart and tears in the eyes—it happens, quite often—though sometimes it is a cup and full of peace. Until the post comes, at about 8, and I go down to make toast and coffee for my tray, I read Julian's Essays of a Humanist on the front page of which he wrote: Juliette, with gratitude for forty five years of forbearance, stimulus and love. Spring 1964. More than ten years ago. Then I went down—and found your letter sitting on the mat . . . and tears were blessed as of deliverance. You wrote perceptive and healing words—which just now act like sweet magic. I am grateful to you for thinking as you did, and for that warm touch of understanding. Sometimes I get lost in the jungle of remembrance, and Julian's demon closes down on me. I know that trying to write this autobiography, I am biting much more than I can ever hope to chew. Yet somehow I can't leave off—for if I do for a few days, I am driven back to it. It will never be published in my lifetime of course nor even for many years after. Maybe never. But that is another story.

It has been a lovely, soft, gentle day—I took my tray out in the garden and watched the nasturtium climbing so hopefully, radiantly among the roses. Then I walked upon the haunted Heath, where every step reminds me of holding his arm as he stumbled so slowly along. There is a young grebe, his symbolic bird, growing more beautiful every day. The leaves here too are beginning to fall, before they turn. No, Julian never really grew up—and survived himself so cruelly. He was happiest at Unesco, where his wings were really stretched to their fullness. It was a strange time in our lives—and of course, he <u>did</u> grow then, into the polymath fulfillment which was his pattern. Using that brilliant brain like an acrobatic turn, yet fruitfully—for he did, after all, create I.U.C.N. You know, May, he never got any recognition for his many contributions to so many important problems, and I know it embittered his last years. Tormented and tormenting.

But enough. My deep thanks for that wonderful letter—for saying so much which means more than you can imagine. Even the mal-aimée . . . That does, perhaps, explain a lot of my hedgehogness. . . .

I am so glad you are happy. Let your joys have all abiding.

Love—
Juliette

---

never published in my lifetime: Leaves of the Tulip Tree was published in London in 1986 by John Murray, Ltd., eight years before Juliette's death.

I.U.C.N.: Julian created the International Union for Conservation of Nature which attracted the great powers to intervene in the conflict between man and nature; it was the precursor of the World Wildlife Fund and the Charles Darwin Foundation for the Galapagos Isles.

Jan 17th '78

. . .

I want to say that I have no resentment—towards you, or Julian, or any of the many women "friends" of his life. It happened—and I expect would have happened with any other wife of Julian, had she stayed the course. I did, for a time, feel, as I wrote, denuded and impoverished. Late in the day. I am now more detached from that long ago person I may have been. She is dead anyway. I don't quite know who is left, staring at the mountain of papers, letters, manuscripts, photographs—and staggering as small pieces come away to be sorted and valued. I have help, and don't complain really, but I wish I could see the end of this long excavation, of my effort at Memories—and all. The strange mythology of our marriage, which to your eyes looked perfect, could not be eroded by the equally strange acrobatics involved. Someone else should write my part in it. And, after all is said and done, are such marriages not common practise—ordinary as ditch water, only different in our case because Julian was that curious dimorphous person, a great mind with an adolescent romantic heart, forever chasing the rainbow.

There is so much I didn't know—for instance that he told you he would never see you again etc. One piece of the puzzle—your stepping into that perfect marriage which you saw—falls into place. I also know that, had it not been you, it would have been another. He was lucky, for you were, and are, so highly gifted and articulate....

Oct 14th '78

My dear May,

Early this week, your book arrived—and I have just finished reading it. After many a day dies the swan. You have attempted the most difficult task, the deciphering of an ancient palimpsest inherited by generations of seekers, of demanders and questioners. And found one sort of answer, followed one set of stepping stones across that infinite stream, of life into death. You have confronted

" . . . the angel who could speak God's name—
The bush that burned and still was not consumed."

It was strangely brave of you—I see you holding that crucible and sifting through memories, through the deep pain of the death of loved ones, through the mysteries and terrible realities. Tenderly unwinding the spool which leads to "the alabaster chamber." It was indeed terribly brave of you—and perhaps you demand of your readers the same courage, the same detachment, perhaps the same unexplored shadowy theme which can never be the same problem for more than very few—too complex and infinite. It is good that Ella came, at midnight. It is the grain of gold within the crucible.

---

your book arrived: A Reckoning.

After many a day dies the swan: "And after many a summer dies the swan," from *Tithonus* by Alfred Lord Tennyson, the line Aldous Huxley used as the title of his 1939 novel on the theme of immortality and time.

"burned and still was not consumed": "Behold, the bush burned with the fire, and the bush was not consumed," Exodus 3:2.

Ella: Possibly Ella Winter; see footnote to letter of 12 August 1947.

April 21st, '79

Dear May

. . . I am putting your letters to me aside, and will return them to you. There are quite a few, and I don't want to send them by mail.

Like some old vintages, one's past has to mature, to lose the bitter knowledge and turn it into a sense of grace. It does not come in a day . . . but the signs are there.

May 2, 1979

My dear May,

I have just finished sorting out your letters to me—so they are ready for you when you come. But I should very much like to know WHEN you are coming, as I don't want to be away, though it is possible I shall take a trip abroad sometime in May. So please, don't wait to let me know. I have been cooped up here too long I feel, with this horrendous winter, still at it, too—we had flurries of snow an hour ago. And the wind is icy cold, and blows through the house at every crack.

I would also like to ask your promise that, should you use the letters for publication in any way—you would not reveal my name. They are of course your copyright, and I give them back to you—with some regret, I must say—yet feeling that it is best. Rereading some—not all, as I could not bear it—I am left with disquietude—a sense of a past which now too avidly encroaches on the present. Julian's letters to me also disturb me deeply—yet I must decide what to do with them—and with all the oth-

ers. Such a decision is hard to make—and I change its direction constantly. I wish HE had left some instruction—some sign. . . .

June 8th, '79

Dear May,

Your letter arrived only a few days ago—how slow our mails are getting. I had certainly not realized, when you told me about the Berg, that
my letters had also gone there. As you say, the early ones. And it was a bit
of a shock. Just getting to my age means getting detached from so much of
the past, and the thought that I would as it were survive in those long forgotten letters, rather upset me. In so many ways, it would be better to dis-
appear absolutely. But of course, that is impossible, especially as I have now
four great-grandchildren. Lucinda has just produced a miniature infant, a
boy, so her Philippa has a little brother, and a problem of accepting the
intrusion. Isn't life difficult. . . .

Anyway, there is nothing to be done about it now, I had destroyed
most of yours—after Paris. And will burn the others. So far, have not con-
tacted the Berg about yours to Julian, but will, when I work up the energy. The weather has been implacably depressing, and left me with no urge
to action, an almost total inertia. Except when I go to the garden, full of
surprises and still deep joys, but also weeds galore. I garden to a standstill,
which is foolish.

July 14th '79

. . .

Jemima has grown snow-white feathers she preens meticulously. She
quacks when I leave her, but makes delicious contented gruntlets when I sit
down, and she at my feet. I don't KNOW what I shall do with her—
winter will be impossible anyway, she isn't house-trained and must stay outside. But she is quite adorable, but little trouble. Alan's nephew, also Alan Best,
is attentive and brings hay, food, and lately cod-liver oil to oil her—because
she can't lay eggs without lubrication, he tells me. She beaks it all down
without a qualm. Perhaps being a duck-sitter has its compensations. . . .

Jemima: Juliette's pet duck, given to her by Alan Best's nephew, also Alan Best, to live in the garden at Pond Street and brighten Juliette's life.

20th 12 1979

. . .

It hasn't been possible for me to write to you—because I went through your letters to Julian before handing them on to the librarian, Bertram Rota, who is engaged in the discussion with Berg, such as valuation etc. For reasons I cannot really understand, I suffered a lot of posthumous shock, which I haven't got over yet. I cannot explain, nor go further into what is after all a natural reaction, and definitely feel that silence is best in the circumstances. I feel sure you will agree with me.

I feel sure also that you will understand it is after all a most personal matter—to do with me alone, and I want to ask you to leave things alone for the time being, anyway. In time, no doubt, I shall disentangle the knots and tangles I have got myself into.

March 6th, '80

Dear May,

I find your letter difficult to answer. Anyway thank you both for your silence and for it. No, I am not ill, but neither can I say I am well. It is a long winter, and one feels between too many worlds. Many good friends are ill or dying around one, just now, John Skeaping, who taught me carving. Stephen Spender has been over two months in hospital, across the road, with both legs in plaster, having torn tendons in both. A very painful and tiresome affair.

The past, as you know as well as I, cannot be done with, "once and for all." It is what makes one now. For better for worse.

So let this be a time of non-allegiance, both wishing the other well, and time passing. Please give my regards to Morgan—I will try and write him later.

John Skeaping: Fifty years earlier, Juliette had studied sculpture at the Central School with John Skeaping, a well-known British painter and sculptor.

Stephen Spender: See footnote to letter of 2 April 1939.

Morgan: Morgan Mead, a young teacher who had written Sarton and met her in 1974; when Mead later went to London to study, Sarton arranged for him to meet Juliette, in whose house he lived for several months.

———

Feb 8/84

Dear May,

. . .

Many of your letters to me have come alive in my hands— Your thoughts about Julian—our strange ghost—so penetrating & viable, your questing.

"Where is the life we've lost in living?"

But there are too many questions unasked—& not to be asked.

If you can do so, send a word or two.

My good & warm wishes to you, my dear. Let us not forget the good moments & count them blessed.

POND STREET   Jan. 20th '85

My dear May

Your book, The Reckoning, arrived yesterday, for Dora. So I spent the afternoon and most of the evening re-reading it—comfortably in big print. I had read it before, but my brittle memory had forgotten most of it. Re-read with the nostalgia of things past-yet oh so much still alive:

> Espérez-vous que la postérité
> Doive mes vers pour tout jamais vous lire?
> Espérez-vous que l'oeuvre d'une lyre
> Puisse acquerir telle immortalité?
>   Joachim du Bellay

. . . Your book [*House by the Sea*] brought me close to your Maine living, day by day. You were then 66—am I right? and would be now 74. A long way to 88, my age. How to compare? One cannot get within, but much resurges. The need for aloneness—the need for friends, the self-hood dwelling, still seeking its fulfillment—yet knowing it not, still feeding on reflected star-light from great minds long dead, with hope of guidance through one's labyrinth. Your book sparks off so much—the search avidly feeds. And will continue—unanswered.

Last night I slept two hours—then woke to a nightmare now forgotten—and for an hour felt lost: a book, a book—as some king called for horse. The Oxford Book of French Verse—that was my need—and I reread much DuBellay—Ronsard singing of love. But it is DuBellay who grips, who plumbs depths and finds the words. And his spelling adds, French becomes an adventure into form, like sculpture into image. Take heart, my dear, your work too will outlive your days, and your seeking bring more light.

––––––––––

called for horse: "A horse! a horse! my kingdom for a horse!" Shakespeare's *Richard III,* Act V, Sc. 4.

DuBellay: Joachim Du Bellay (1522–1560), French poet, companion of Ronsard, next to whom he was the most famous member of the Pléiade.

Ronsard: Pierre de Ronsard (1524–1585), French poet particularly known for his *Odes* and *Amours,* sensual love poems which celebrate rustic pleasures and evoke his native countryside.

––––––––––

22nd 6. '85

. . .

Your mother's letter shakes me. What she says about Julian is true of his euphoric times—when he truly was burning the candle at both ends, not himself IN himself, but reaching out—as she says—possessed by his deamon, insensitive, hurtful, full steam ahead and nowhere to go. . . . But how superficial was it? Was it his true self,—or half-self: or was it the possession of that well-known deamon-daimon which he acknowledged fully? Then in between, moments of otherness—perfect when we traveled, alone in foreign lands. Unforgettable. Returned to his desk, insatiable and all the rest—then the breakdowns, nullifying the other self—digging down deep to bury the identity—to be destroyed by self-doubts and self accusations. Really, he was a strange tormented man, and tormenting too. Is he at peace now? Or still reaching out with flaming sword to reach some other sphere? It is a disturbing thought.

Your mother was a delicate intuitive. And I am happy about her lines on me. And pleased that I was, in her eyes, "tender and dear with J." I often wonder about that. In the end, I was detached, and often remorseful about it. It took me years to get over it, as much as I can. Her words are a comfort now. Thank you for sending the letter. It helps, in a way, to get the right angle, for I often wondered where I was in all this strange destiny. . . .

_____

Your mother's letter shakes me: At this time Sarton was reading her mother's letters as she prepared and edited some of them for *Letters to May,* published the following year by the Puckerbrush Press. On 8 June 1985 she wrote to Juliette: "I'll enclose a letter of my mother's . . . wondering whether to send it or not, but what she said about Julian interested me (though it is not kind) and you will recognize its perceptiveness. And be glad, too, I hope that she felt so drawn to you. Throw it away when you have read it."

_____

Oct 2nd 1985

. . .

Maybe Aldous was part of J's insecurity—but not of his curious imbalance. I can't find that clue. I am not at all convinced I could have been "his delight." He needed me—of course; and that is some fulfillment. Maybe neither he nor Aldous had much understanding of the heart. But read Aldous's LETTERS—such a generous sharing of interests, so varied and so fertile. Maybe not too much heart—if one knew what that really is—But enough.

. . .

_____

Aldous's LETTERS: Letters of Aldous Huxley, ed. Grover Smith (Chatto & Windus, 1968; Harper & Row, 1969).

_____

[Undated; after October 1985]

. . .

Arthur Hailey on the radio, Desert Island Disk-ing. He is said to have sold several million copies of each of his books. So he plays us Brahms and maudlin songs, and in between warbles stale gossip. Oh yes, I am in a bad mood. A bit like a caged animal, no lion but some moist-eyed little furry mammal, huddling for warmth. . . .

And in between taking up that female torso I gave Francis years ago, and which the fire damaged slightly. I find new shape growing under files and carvers, and new delight in improving (?) a curve, a sinew. How could Genesis not even mention that God enjoyed carving his Eve out of a rib of Adam? Surely it was a perfect creation—the purest joy even God could know. And everything in that Creation week was perfect in its manner—and he never rejoiced in his genius. . . .

. . .

———

Arthur Hailey: English-born Canadian novelist (1920–) whose best-selling novels focus on the airplane industry in *Airport*, the auto industry in *Wheels*, the banking industry in *The Moneychangers*, and at the time of this letter, the pharmaceutical industry in *Strong Medicine*.

———

Sunday, 9th Feb. '86

One day nearer spring. It is nearly one o'clock, I am in dressing gown and plan to return to bed—but been reading more Letters to Virginia and Vita: compulsive reading. Yet not tearing flamboyant flags from skies British or Persian. One goes on expecting. Must copy, later, a pregnant passage. But what I want to say is that YOUR letters could beat many of these. I am going to tidy them up and sort them out—some day soon, when my books are back in shelves and roof is behaving itself. (IF EVER.) And send them to you. Why shouldn't you make a book of your letters? Think of it. They'll be written—so no effort—only notes to clear background, and let them fly. You have of course many more correspondents with many more fine letters. Gather them in—and DO a book. Please. I find V. and V's letters thrilling because so alive with the fugitive moment—the flame still warms the heart? anyway the mind. Vita's heart is vocal but faithless.

> "Lay thy sleepy head, my love,
> Human, upon my faithless arm." Auden

One is conscious of two candid friends, wrestling words of their truth.

Maybe you have read it all, and maybe don't think as I feel. No matter. YOUR letters are there to cull, and they are gold treasures.

. . .

Virginia and Vita: The Letters of Vita Sackville-West to Virginia Woolf, ed. Louise DeSalvo and Mitchell A. Leaska (1985).
Auden: Verse 11 in Part VIII of "Song for St. Cecilia's Day" in *The Collected Poetry of W. H. Auden* (1945).
V. and V's letters: Sarton had blurbed the American edition: "These delightful letters give us the seasons of an intimate relationship between two extraordinary women . . . an *amitié amoureuse*. I know of no other comparable except for that between Madame de Staël and Madame Récamier, a century earlier. Here we only glimpse Virginia Woolf but we do come to know Vita Sackville-West in a new light, the light of tenderness, concern, and love for the genius whose muse she became. It is a fascinating record."

[Undated, just after the fire, February 1986]

. . .

Yes, I kept your letters, and started to sort them when the fire calamity overtook me. They can wait—as you said. They must wait. Re-reading yours to Julian—curiously impersonal in a way—yet warm in affection-love. I wonder what his were like. The Berg must be bursting with confessions—cries for help—and all the symphonies of love, "while thou art pouring forth thy soul abroad in such an ecstasy."

. . .

And here now is a glimmer of sun, timid and vanishing in snow clouds. Time for lunch—which is the bits and left-overs in the fridg. And tarragon salata. And maybe a glass of sherry to bite the soul into a short flame of life. LIFE. Think that we have it—for whatever it means to you and me. A piece of paper with hieroglyphs to convey our bond of deep companionship in the land of exploration—mind and heart and whatever contains soul . . . No, letters never tell the whole story. But they have a short-hand power of reality of the moment, impulsive and true. The whole story is a forest "où la main de l'homme n'a jamais mis les pieds" if you remember that immortal film whose name I have forgotten . . . I wonder how common our forests are. oh man all too human.

Flurries of snow, icy cold, a feeling of impotence in face of winter. Don't wait too long for psychic energy. Start your poem about Bramble.

––––––––––

"such an ecstasy": From "Ode to a Nightingale" by John Keats.
"où la main de l'homme . . . : where man's hand has never set foot. Unidentified.

––––––––––

This is as far as Sarton got in selecting letters, partly because the project had been set aside, and partly because she was too ill to think of choosing any from the years that followed.

––––––––––

March 17th '86

. . .

I have been looking through your letters, prior to making a package—or two or three, there are so many, and send them safely to you. It is too difficult for me now to put them in order—some have no date, just a name of the week . . . and I regret I just cannot manage it. My silly old brain can't keep up the effort. And re-reading the letters is in itself difficult—and cannot be done at a stretch. But they will arrive in due time, and I don't know what you will do with them—nor mind really. They are YOURS anyway—and I only hope you will not regret re-reading them, and return to those troubled days when we were both in a different jungle. Trying to understand—failing to read the writing on the wall . . . I don't really remember enough—for I was, as I told you before, going through a dark tunnel most of the time. So take them easily, don't brood on them, but maybe find in your letters a few precious lines, cris du coeur—but now so distant that they must not hurt anymore.

. . .

––––––––––

cris du coeur: heartfelt cries.

––––––––––

Aug. 3rd 88

Dearest May,

... Sad about your tiresome weather, but more about <u>your</u> feeling so unwell—which is all <u>wrong</u>, & your garden rejecting its "power of life"— yet only <u>momentarily</u>—Let rain fall and feed the waiting seeds—& it'll blossom. I know for <u>sure</u> how good your help is to those friends in your ambience who drink from your well & rejoice. The novel is demanding & fiercely so, but you will <u>do it</u>, and achieve your aim. Keep going in spite of difficulties, the mastering of which creates its crown. I do truly believe in <u>you</u>, your gift & your purpose. Think of that "considerable body of read- ers" you have, who can only reward you by being fed with your <u>hard working</u> inspiration. And what of your being there for the friends in need, & your shining help in their lonely quest. Go ahead & be at peace—at PEACE—So be it, dearest May, <u>& accept it.</u>

I wish I could help somehow. Grieve to be so old. Over 91—too old really to clutter up the place, but helpless so much accept.

Dear love to you & wishes & blessings

———

The novel: The Education of Harriet Hatfield.

———

Sept. 20 [1989]

Dearest May,

. . .

Such lovely news about your book & publisher's eagerness to publish. Oh so many congrats thereto—& golden wishes for further leaping progress. What by the way is homophobic? Can't find it in my small Oxford Dict. And if I may say so, a choice public of 25,000 is not despica- ble!—Don't forget best sellerdom is a vulgar achievement allowed to cheap & uncritical readers— . . . I seem to be a survivor, hanging on a cliff— Thinks of dying in a cloudy future, yet also "for whom the bell tolls." It's probably lucky one can't tell—not for sure.

Darling May, here endeth my letter for I have nothing to say except send all love and gratefulness.

It is wonderful to know you.

Juliette

————

"for whom the bell tolls": From "Devotions upon Emergent Occasions #6" (1624), by John Donne (1572–1631), English metaphysical poet; dean of St. Paul's cathedral and possibly the most influential preacher in England.

————

Sunday, November 24th, '91

Dearest May—

I have so much to thank you for, yesterday's two cases of delicious wines, & yesterday a lovely letter sent Nov. 17th—News of your being able to write lovely poems again is superb. I am <u>rejoicing</u>. And even more, your getting rid of <u>that depleting</u> pain & so I can now really look forward to <u>seeing</u> <u>you</u> in March—Of course it is quite a few <u>months</u>—& winter is between. Not a favorite season, alas, with ô (10' to 4PM here) <u>ô</u> <u>oh</u> <u>ô</u> & <u>just</u> <u>the</u> <u>phone</u> <u>rings</u> & the <u>miracle happens</u> of <u>your voice</u> at the end of magic lines, your voice, & your <u>promises of coming</u>. ô I <u>can't believe</u> it but it must be <u>true</u>.—Talk of <u>telepathy</u>—so powerful a <u>proof</u> should be <u>stamped in history</u>—I am <u>shaken</u> to my <u>very bones</u>—***Please take note—& <u>tell me your</u> feeling.

I am still breathless—& <u>incredulous</u> because meeting with a <u>miracle</u> shakes one like <u>nothing</u> on <u>earth</u>—as of course it is not <u>of the earth</u>—But one <u>must</u> believe it <u>can</u> happen, it <u>does</u> happen. Even if only once in a lifetime—What was <u>your</u> time? I know you are writing <u>now</u>, I can almost <u>see</u> you doing it—maybe even <u>same words</u>—nothing else matters just now.

A cup of tea brought by Hannah welcome. My mother's supreme antidote to <u>all</u> stress or emotion, <u>cups of tea</u>—How right she was—

There is nothing else to say—I must digest all this strange feast, slowly & deeply—& look forward to <u>your</u> letter as I know <u>you</u> are writing just <u>now</u>—

I will end here for I could only <u>repeat</u> myself if I wrote on—oh strange world of thought—could one but cultivate this wilderness—!

love, love, love
Juliette

UNPUBLISHED POEMS AND ORIGINAL FRENCH LETTERS

Enclosed in letter of 27 October 1936

Apologia

I have wanted to follow the young men
Pasting the words of Lenin and Marx
On their banners,
The young men marching
In beautiful arrogance
Down the streets of your cities.
I have wanted to join an army,
To worship among the many, to be lost.
I deeply long to be the first upon the barricade,
To die a splendid death
(Life is more difficult)
I would be lost among the many,
I would also be the first upon the barricade.
But I shall never be one of you.
I shall stand apart, outside,
Ignorant, sceptic,
For I am also someone else.
I do not walk briskly along
Observing the decay of the middle class,
Putting a red feather in my cap
And waiting for the festival.
On the contrary,
I linger at shop windows
Acquisitive (Donne at two and six)—
I am sharply confronted
With the beauty of a man's eyes
Reflected in the window,
Myself and the man,
The infinite possibilities of us—
I am swayed with satisfaction
By a woman's ankles
(Nowhere else, nowhere the bone so exquisite)—
I go down the street buying Japanese flowers
That open in glass.
I am wholly filled with contentment.
Prophecy concerns me not.

The spring is sufficient,
The unexpected meeting is sufficient.

It is only here
With Donne in my lap,
The gas-fire burning,
The tea tinkling on the stairs
That I cannot enjoy
That I am forced to listen
(How unwillingly)
To the undertone that accompanies
Each pleasure as I taste it—
Abyssinia is in it,
And Belgium,
And men making drawings on the pavements,
Selling pencils,
Playing violins,
The ear cannot annihilate this question.
Is it possible that Marx has solved it.
Why then do we stand on street-corners
Predicting war?
They say there is this positive exit.
Why do we not take it?

It is to man we look.
We believe in man.
It is man who stirs us on.
We believe the kernel to be still good,
The pure in heart more than a phrase—
I have known one.
But I have seen too many
Confused and amorous,
Lost in one human madness or another.
Where is the concentrated one?
Where is the standard-bearer?

O rise up, you who lie in the mud
Whose bodies are still unrotted
(Fifty dug up this year, identified)
Turn the horror full, the blast upon us,
Come back, come back to us.
Point at the brilliant bomb that hangs in the sky
While we hold arguments of peace

And wait for a horrible death—
O rise up, shattered arms and legs,
Save us, shattered hands,
Though you have failed once,
Though you have died once.
Come back to us, man we have destroyed!

The cry is to you too, the living,
The pure in heart,
The single-minded man,
The burning heart.
Young man at the factory gate,
Girl with your lover,
You who are not tainted yet,
On whom there is no blight of death,
Rise up!

And though I stand apart a little longer,
Ignorant, sceptic,
Though I shall scout you a little longer,
Yet I am aware
Of man's probable annihilation,
Of his possible survival—
I sleep in a house divided against itself,
And I cannot live with you,

But I could die for you.

———————

Apologia: Although written in 1936, this poem has interesting connections with "To the Living," written in 1946. See *The Lion and the Rose.*

———————

Enclosed in letter of 5 and 7 December 1936

Invocation

Mute, mute melancholy
Shroud, shut away melancholy
Play not shrilly on it,
Pluck from this instrument
The unquiet discord.
Hush, hush, melancholy—

The muffled string now
Speak alone of snow,
Of people lost in wilderness
To whom death comes by sleep,
By snow, secret and slow.
Shroud, shroud melancholy
The heart too like a sword,
The screaming word.

Dec. 1936

At This Time

At this time when so many things die proudly
And death is flaunted before your living face,
When riders in pink coats herald it loudly
Blowing their horns, giving the fleet fox chase—

Almost for a moment you might catch your breath
Thinking that passion and this stubborn grief
Might burn its way at last to a final death—
Forgetting it is the root and not the leaf.

This love knows all the seasons. It contains
The emerald violence of the early leaves,
Long sultriness, followed by passionate rains,
As well as silence and the winter shroud it weaves.

And though at this changing time you almost would
Have wished it were a fox and brought to bay at last
Or a leaf and blown to death, yet deep in your blood
Like a tree it attains its stature, the roots fast.

[Oct. 1934]

Out of the Torn Sky

Out of the torn sky
Thrashed through with lightning,
Shaken with thunder,
The rain has come,
The rain is falling around us
Enclosing the house and the room and September,
Resolving the elemental anguish
To certain notes played over,
Half-listened to—

To certain notes in a pattern,
To certain continual sounds
That do not alter,
For love that came once like thunder
Striking us unaware
Now falls like rain upon us,
Now checks the wild warm tears,
Resolves the abandoned grief
To certain notes played over.
And we know now. We know,
We are well aware
What soft doom encloses the house and the room and September,
And must stay suspended there—
While we stay suspended here.

[Aug. 1936]

The Diviner

What other way is there than love
To touch, to go down deeper
Than the muffled mouth,
To go behind the golden screen of eyes
To meet you?
What other way than love
For I am shaken with the need of knowing
Where your heart beats,
The measure of the blood in the wrist flowing—
I am drawn by what seems necessity
To find out your center
As men may utterly desire to creep back to the womb.
Their faces are carved helmets
Yet locked under the fine bone
In each this living hunger stands
Like a diviner
His whole weight struggling
Against the torrents underground.

[1934?]

From letter of 30 October 1937

Do you for an instant think these words
Are more than wisdom's effort to conceal

Beneath the crashing sounds of falling swords
The heart's intention, adamant as steel?
Or that the silence following that alarm
Is not more dangerous than the former noise?
I am disarmed: Noblesse oblige, disarm!
This elegance of swords, these childish toys
Are love's protection and its camouflage,
Deeper than any kiss lies its excess,
Banished, it will appear like a mirage,
Silence can only point its countlessness.
To force this kind of peace is your affair
But can you break the heart which is the snare?

First letter of 13 January 1938 in its original French

Il neige—cette neige qui semble ouvrir un silence dans l'âme. Tout dans la chambre semble <u>violent</u> de couleur—le vert, le bleu, le jaune—c'est comme une fête enfermé dans un voile, dans une tente de neige. Il n'y a qu'une chose qui j'ai éperdument envie de faire—c'est mettre mes bottes et traverser le monde pour te voir. Tout à coup depuis des semaines tu es devenue encore un de ces êtres à qui j'écris à travers les océans—penses que tu es à un lieu d'ici et que j'attends <u>un mot</u> qui ne vient pas est inconcevable. Je te mets dans la lune—je te regards de loin—je t'aime en pierrot. Et, mon Dieu, j'ai soif de cette <u>vieillesse</u> qui vient si lentment. C'est vrai qu'on est malade de jeunesse. Peut-être faudrait-il s'enfermer dans une bibliothéque, tout apprendre, tout <u>savoir</u> et ne rien <u>sentir</u>—et ne commencer à vivre qu'à trente ans!

Enfin—fais un signe à travers l'espace. Est-ce que tout n'est pas possible? Même peut-être la <u>sagesse</u>? Je me le demande—

M—

Second letter of 13 January 1938 in its original French

This [drawing] is my hat and waistcoat of ocelot that I <u>adore.</u>

Petite flamme—je t'écris sur cet hideux papier parce qu'il présente une surface immense où je pourrai lancer toutes mes pensées—mon amour—ma tendresse (pourvu qu'il ne se met à brûler!) D'abord, mon "boy," tu es jeune <u>et</u> sage (quel miracle). Comment fais-tu pour être <u>si</u> jeune et <u>si</u> sage à la fois. Puis j'irai par la neige acheter demain du déséspoir d'opale. Il a neigé toute la nuit—nous sommes toutes les deux dans un monde blanc, impossible, un monde voilé, magique—nous marchons sur deux pouces d'irréalité—nos pieds ne touchent pas <u>la terre.</u> Ici, après des houles et des vagues de neige pendant toute la nuit, elle tombe doucement comme une promesse—de temps en temps les arbres bougent d'un centimètre et laissent tomber des <u>édredons</u> silencieux.

J'aimerai que tu me vois un jour dans cette chambre qui est ma coquille où je me retire, où je fais entrer mes petites cornes sensibles d'escargot, où je travaille. <u>La gloire?</u> mais ma chérie, ne vois-tu pas que cette gloire imaginaire remplace seulement un bonheur réel— unc joie humaine—dans des moments jeunes et farouches et désespérés je me dis "Je suis née pour aimer malheureusement et pour <u>immortaliser</u> ce malheur!" C'est une armure, un <u>panache</u>—et voilà tout.

> Glory is that bright tragic thing,
> That for an instant
> Means Dominion,
> Warms some poor name
> That never felt the Sun,
> Gently replacing
> In oblivion—

Je t'envie cet attachment vrai, et profond, <u>créateur</u> qui te lie à tes enfants. Je pense à Anthony et tout ce qu'il doit souffrir avec une espèce d'angoisse—et comme c'est difficile de ne pas <u>toucher</u> la blessure si on est mère. Mais il y a la grande joie que tu entres dans le coeur même de la vie avec tes enfants. Tout a sa saison et son heure. Ah mon Dieu, je sais qu'on est toujours en péril, que vivre à son plus simple (et les enfants sont la vie a son <u>moins</u> simple) est tout de même parvenir à marcher sur les flots—un acte de foi, d'amour, d'espoir sans cesse à renouveler, récréer en soi-même. Mais toi (ne le doutes <u>jamais</u>) tu as une génie pour marcher sur les flots— et tu <u>es</u> en toi—même cet amour et cet espoir. Quand j'avais lu ta lettre j'ai dû un peu plurer. Et puis j'ai travaillé—

J'écris un roman avec <u>tous</u> des personnages imaginaires, étranges (tu seras contente de cela!) mais c'est écrire avec son moelle—je dois tant penser avant d'écrire.

Edith est rentrée dans la vie quotidienne mais elle est encore fatiguée—je sens, <u>divine</u> plutôt qu'elle a peu des émotions—qu'elle veut rentrer dans le dur mais <u>absolu</u> patron d'une vie de travail pour ses enfants, et de milles amitiés sans une qui soit intense, perçante, qui touche <u>terri-</u>

blement au coeur. Tout cela sans explications, sans <u>clarté</u>. Je veux dire que
je <u>comprends</u> tout à fait, mais j'aimerai qu'elle me le dise gentiment au lieu
de s'enfermer dans un silence cruel. Un jour peut-être nous en parlerons.
Malheureusement, moi je ne change pas! C'est deux mois ont été une
longue transition dans un vide. Mais j'en sors.

Une chose qui me fait sortir ce sont ces poèmes de Jeanne Plateau—
une vieille fille peintre—amie (par lettres seulement) de Jean Dominique,
qui a vécu une vie triste, presque toujours malade et dont est <u>surgi</u> cette
fontaine de poésie pure. Je vais t'en copier.

Je pense avec un <u>serrement</u> de coeur à te revoir—le 1er avril. No t'en-
ferme pas, toi. Je sais que c'est plus facile d'avoir le coeur ouvert avec un
océan qui dissout les problèmes. M'enfin—je t'aime tant. Et, ma chérie, je
tâcherai d'être sage aussi, de t'aimer si doucement que même Alan ne s'en
doutera pas—et seulement toi, tu le sauras.

Voilà le soleil! Je vais sortir faire "un homme de neige" avec les enfants
les voisins. Je t'embrasse

M—

<u>Le livre parait en Angleterre le 10 mars,</u> soit gentil pour le pauvre Marc
solitaire—

————

Glory is that bright tragic thing: #1660 in *The Complete Poems of Emily Dickinson.*
J'écris un roman: "Fire in a Mirror," unpublished.
Jeanne Plateau: Poésie (Les Imprimés du Limbourg, 1938), published posthumously. Sarton
    received news of Plateau's death from Jean Dominique while she was at Whipsnade
    for the Coronation Day party in May 1937.
les enfants les voisins: Binks, Sally, and Elizabeth Barrett.
le pauvre Marc solitaire: The autobiographical protagonist in *The Single Hound.*

————

Referred to in footnote for letter dated 1 February 1942

These Have No Dirge

These have no dirge. For these no holy word is spoken.
They dig their own graves, and fall, shot in the back:
Today the boy we loved, the flier, is reported missing.

We think of him under the ~~African~~ foreign sky, his life taken,
Of the fierce clean death, the final ringing shock:
But these are frozen in freight-cars, gassed and beaten.

The heart burns for the jews, the bitterly forsaken.
Our tears burn on the African sand and the harsh rock.
The boy many loved is dead and the whole world trembles.

Today the whole world aches and our hearts are shaken
But not for him who fought for us and will not come back:
(In Warsaw children go stark mad in the Ghetto streets)

For his was a chosen, a willed act, and clearly undertaken,
And his death carries no image of torture and wrack,
But we are haunted by the screams of a whole people.

The whole world trembles but the rage is not spoken.
Hearts burn. Tears fall. But the burning act alone can speak.
What are we doing? What are we doing, impotent and haunted?

January 1943

The Martyrs

These are the ones of simplest strength, of purest love,
Born to be fathers walking through the evening orchard,
The rooted meditative men who would invent and build
A life natural and clear above all others:
These would have come into their ripeness like green trees.

But in the hothouse of oppression, blossoming is all,
The quick and violent flare that marks the place
Where lies the living germ (trees are cut down).
These are the ones who go from flower to seed
In the one gesture, marvelously potent, of their dying.

Wherever the oppressor stalks there is this blossoming,
He walks upon the seeds of liberation, on the strength of trees,
And where the martry's blood is spilled, the forests of the future
Are planted, and await the season when they can bear
The fruits of freedom, its seeds fall sweetly through the air.

Also called "Dedication," 1942

These Have No Dirge: Written in January 1943. To Rollo Walter Brown she writes on 1
March 1943: "We had sad news, that the boy for whom 'Navigator' [Edmund

Kennedy] was written is reported missing in Tunisia. It came, that news, the day the Jewish Congress printed its really fearful report on what is happening to the Jews in Europe—5,000,000 will have been liquidated in six months time. Putting these two elements side by side I ached all over. The poem came from them."

———————

From letter dated probably 21 July 1947

Song

The crust of bread,
The grain of wood,
A smooth flat stone,
Grass under wind,
So would love be
If love were kind
And not alone;
Simple and good
And safe in bed
Reasonably.

Now it is mad
Complex and wild,
In constant danger;
It has no name,
Changeling of grief
And licked by flame.
I love a stranger,
Mother and child:
When she is sad
I lose belief.

When she is gay
I leap to truth;
I grow and learn;
Beside her love
Love in my hand
Does simply move
Nor strain, nor burn:
All becomes myth
I am all day
Grass under wind.
                July 19th, '47

To go with letter of 18 May 1948, "The first swan poem I wrote."

The Swans

I think this was a dream and yet we saw
The stone bridge and the still canal
And I remember how laburnum threw
A gold rain on the waters very well.
After all, what we saw may have been true.

There in a rocky angle, the two swans
On a small platform as if upon a stage
In all that watery world, the rooted ones,
And face to face, a snowy double image,
Stood in suspense among the ruined stones.

Then as we watched the ritual play began,
Their wings arched and each shivered once
Then gravely bowed their necks and swan to swan
Lifted their heavy bodies in the dance
As if their long necks flowed upon the silence.

They drew their figures strictly on the air
As if, like skates on ice, their beaks must draw
A perfect circle and what was written there
Repeated endlessly with concentrated awe
Until the tension was too great to bear.

In one ecstatic motion, straight and pure,
The weaving necks were lifted and each now
Stretched to the sky as if he could endure
The little space between them better so.
God, how they trembled! How immaculate they were!

Who would not pray, looking on such a scene
To be alive, passionate, part of the dance,
And fiercely yielding up all that is human,
Become a part of natural delight for once?
Lovers, take on the grave image of the swan.

———

The Swans: This poem appeared in *The Leaves of the Tree* in a slightly different form.

———

Enclosed with letter of 18 May 1948

"Now I Become Myself," which appears in The Land of Silence, *was enclosed, with the following differences from the published version:*

"Or love sleep in the walled city" . . .
"Is my hand and the shadow of the word . . ."
"Grows in me who become the song"

Letter of 11 June 1948 in original French

VOUVRAY   le 11 juin, 1948

Toujours et partout. Main sur Moi. Forêt à genoux. Source qui donne soif—où es tu? Et que fais-tu, petite flamme bleue et si lointaine? Est-ce que tu vois la même lune en crescent avec une planète très brillante à ses côtés qui ne peut être que Vénus? Et sur quelle cité inconnue de moi, au dessus de quelles tours, de quelle église—ou sur quelle grand place vide et pleine d'absence? Pendant deux jours par angoisse j'ai cessé de fumer. Il me semblait que tout dans ma vie était un gâchi, dépens fou, extravagance sans place secrète, et qu'il fallait m'enfermer et me taire. Mais voilà, hier après une journée de cours à Tours avec la Grace <u>chancelente</u>, tout à coup la poésie est revenue. J'ai recomencé à fumer comme un vieux Turque. Les oiseaux chantent dans mes bois—rien de très beau, un petit gémissement mais il me semble revivre. Après des journées un peu difficiles—si tu étais ici nous ririons. Grace est vraiment malade, la pauvre. Elle ne sait à peu près <u>rien</u> digérer et à l'air d'une tête de mort. Avec cela d'un courage parfait que j'admire. Car cela doit être horriblement décourageant—état qui dure depuis un an. Nous avons vu un médecin mais les drogues empirent les choses—il faudra le revoir. J'ai dit que nous ririons et c'est un peu étrange de suivre cette phrase par la maladie de la pauvre G. mais comme elle est malade elle devient aussi vague et peu dessinée qu'un nuage, oublie de commander les repas, devient absorber à un point maniaque par "les choses," peur que je vais verser du café sur mon drap de lit, ou faire une tache de vin sur la nappe etc. etc. au point que je deviens de plus en plus nerveuse et vais sans doute casser toute la vaisselle par sympathie pour <u>ses</u> peurs! Et puis ce n'est pas ma maison et je n'ose rien commander alors tout est très mal ordonné. Enfin, j'ai fini une nouvelle pas trop mal. Quand j'é-touffe dans le jardin et les murs clos je m'en vais dans la campagne regarder les coquelicots rouges—et les grands champs de blés transis par le vent. J'aime ma chambre, mes livres, la petite table, les fleurs qui en font un autel—et je ne comprends vraiment pas pourquoi je suis si triste, affreusement, et d'où vient-elle cette tristesse dont je n'ai nullement envie, et qui m'assomme à la fin?

J'attends les nouvelles du Maréchal Tito et de ton chapeau de roses. Ella Winter (l'amie de Jo Davidson) est revenue éblouie de la Jugoslavie. Entre autre choses du Maréchale lui-même—dont elle a parlé comme d'un Dieu charmant et puissant et mâle. Elle a dit qu'il n'y avait pas de "neurotics" dans ce pays. Je ne vois pas de charme dans un pays si dépourvu, je dois dire.

Maréchal Tito: Yugoslavian leader Tito's hostility to the Soviet Union culminated on 28 June 1948 with the Cominform expelling Yugoslavia from membership; three weeks later in July the Yugoslavian Communist Party gave him a vote of confidence, and the party was purged of Cominform supporters.

Ella Winter: English writer, author of *And Not to Yield*; divorced from Lincoln Steffens, married Donald Ogden Stewart, one of the Hollywood Ten, friend of Sarton and Muriel Rukeyser.

Jo Davidson: Sculptor, friend of the Huxleys who lived at Bécheron in Tours and sculpted most of the famous people of his time. His bronze bust of Julian was eventually acquired by UNESCO.

Enclosed with letter of 30 August 1948: passages from Martin Buber's Between Man and Man.

I have not the possibility of judging Luther, who refused fellowship with Zwingli in Marburg, or Calvin who furthered the death of Servetus. For Luther and Calvin believe that the Word of God has so descended among men that it can be clearly known and must therefore be exclusively advocated. I do not believe that; the Word of God crosses my vision like a falling star to whose fire the meteorite will bear witness without making it light up for me, and I myself can only bear witness to the light but not produce the stone and say "This is it." But this difference of faith is by no means to be understood merely as a subjective one. It is not based on the fact that we who live today are weak in faith, and it will remain even if our faith is ever so much strengthened. The situation of the world itself, in the most serious sense, more precisely the relation between God and man, has changed. And this change is certainly not comprehended in its essence by our thinking only of the darkening, so familiar to us, of the supreme light, only of the night or our being, empty of revelation. It is the night of an expectation—not of a vague hope, but of an expectation. We expect a theophany of which we know nothing but the place, and the place is called community. In the public catacombs of this expectation there is no single God's Word which can be clearly known and advocated, but the words delivered are clarified for us in our human situation of being turned to one another. There is no obedience to the coming one without loyalty to his creature. To have experienced this is our way.

Each of us is encased in an armour whose task is to ward off signs. Signs happen to us without respite, living means being addressed, we would need only to present ourselves and to perceive But the risk is too dangerous for us, the soundless thunderings seem to threaten us with annihilation, and from Generation to generation we perfect the defence apparatus. All our knowledge assures us, "Be calm, everything happens as it must happen, but nothing is directed at you, you are not meant; it is just 'the world', you can experience it as you like, but whatever you make of it in yourself proceeds from you alone, nothing is required of you, you are not addressed, all is quiet."

Each of us is encased in an armour which we soon, out of familiarity, no longer notice. There are only moments which penetrate it and stir the soul to sensibility. And when such a moment has imposed itself on us and we then take notice and ask ourselves, 'Has anything particular taken place? Was it not of the kind I meet every day?' then we may replay to ourselves, "Nothing particular, indeed, it is like this every day, only we are not there every day."

"In order to come to God," says Kierkegaard about his renunciation of Regina Olsen, "I had to remove the object." That is sublimely to misunderstand God. Creation is not a hurdle on the road to God, it is the road itself. We are created along with one another and directed to a life with one another. Creatures are placed in my way so that I, their fellow creature, by means of them and with them find the way to God. A God reached by

their exclusion would not be the God of all lives in whom all life is fulfilled. God wants us to come to him by means of the Reginas he has created and not by renunciation of them. If we remove the object, then—we
have removed the object altogether. Without an object, artificially producing the object from the abundance of the human spirit and calling it God,
this love has its being in the void.

God indeed is not the cosmos, but far less is he Being minus cosmos.
He is not to be found by subtraction and not to be loved by reduction.

[ ]

Acknowledgments

My gratitude to May Sarton for her ineffable *oeuvre*, for her love and trust which are with me always, and for this life's work she has bequeathed to me with all its leavening joy and responsibility.

To Polly Thayer Starr whose wisdom and poetry light my way, whose understanding intensifies all the intensities. She, whose own vision is failing, enables me to see the fur on the bee, and points the way to *Einblick*.

To Bill Brown whose love and understanding of May enrich my work; whose love of poetry enlarges my life, and who teaches me, constantly, that the past, when honored and understood, is the greater part of the present.

To Mary-Leigh Smart and Beverly Hallam, for their unfailing support and friendship, and for keeping the doors to memory open.

To Adelaide Cherbonnier, whose friendship and restorative laughter brought comfort and affirmation to May, for generously passing on to me, as if a legacy, that same supportive friendship.

To Richard Henry, for friendship and lucid listening, perception, and patience; and for the beauty of his service for May, a shining memorial.

To Carolyn G. Heilbrun, Rosemary Matson, Nanette de Meusey, and Mary Morain for their imaginative support of this work.

To Doris Beatty, Charlotte Heimann, Elizabeth Knies, Jacqueline Limbosch, Charyl Morales, Edith Royce Schade, Michael Sirmons, Lina Taylor, and Martha Wheelock for helping with so many of the infinite details which otherwise would have been insurmountable.

To Edythe Haddaway, *in memoriam*, May's best "pal," whose faithful friendship, risibility, and legion kindnesses were an irreplaceable part of May's life for twenty years—for her impeccable editing and tireless support of this work, and for the integrity of her never-to-be-again friendship shared with me.

To Rodney Phillips, who, while honoring all the great traditions at the Berg, is making imaginative and invaluable innovations—for his life-saving help; to Philip Milito, who has now served four curators, for his equanimity and dependability throughout; and always to Steve Crook, in whose hands the careful cataloguing of May's papers resides.

To Patty Aleandri, Ruthie Buccini, Rosemary Capaldo, Carol Bassett, Jana Mencio, Sharon Schoeller, and Nancy Yablonsky for their invaluable gift of peace of mind.

To Karen and Will Balliett, for their brilliant friendship and support.

To Lenora P. Blouin for her monumental and seminal contribution to Sarton scholarship, present and future; her *May Sarton: A Bibliography* (Scarecrow Press, 1978), a revised and expanded version of which will be published in 1999, has been and is indispensable to me, as is her friendship.

To Shoji Masuzawa, for being there at all hours to navigate me through the exasperating problems that threaten to derail hours or years of work, and for meeting whatever challenges arise. His availability, expertise, and composure are increasingly invaluable.

To Francis Huxley, for his generosity in permitting me to use his mother's letters, for going back to the difficult past and writing his illuminating foreword, for family photographs, and for being there to answer questions from the mundane to the sublime; his cooperation, help, and contributions have made this volume infinitely richer.

To Philip Lyman, *in memoriam,* who continued to produce—as he had for forty years—every unfindable or arcane title I needed when I needed it; who brought to our long friendship his own scholarship and love of sleuthing, and understood, as few do, its joys and inexorable demands. He made himself indispensable in myriad ways. This volume is the richer for his caring, his knowledge, and his judgment. I am the richer for his gentle kindness.

And to Nancy Jahn Hartley, for whom no acknowledgment has been sufficient. Her work for twelve and a half years as May's secretary and archivist has provided a bedrock of accuracy and order for curators and scholars; her work on the original manuscript of these letters—and her moderating wisdom concerning them—made all the difference in what I was able to go on to do; her availability, at all hours, her remembering what no one else could remember, her pointing the way, her professional skills and hunches, her humor and compassion, her unwavering friendship, have all made her the *sine qua non* of this life's work on May's letters. As part of her dedication to Nancy in *Endgame,* May wrote: "... devoted friend of the work." Devoted in life, as in death; to Nancy Hartley, my deep abiding thanks for the generosity of that devotion.

Index

Abbey Theatre, Dublin, 275, 278
"Abschied, Der" (Sarton), 145
ACLU (American Civil Liberties Union), 76,
    177–78, 179, 189
Adams, Henry, 178, 180
"After Teaching" (Sarton), 223
"After the War" (Sarton), 341
"AIDS" (Sarton), 321
Aiken, Conrad and Mary, 42
"Airman's Mother" (Sarton), 106
Aldington, Richard, 62, 64
"All the Children Have Hello to Say" (Sarton),
    139–40, 141
"Aloysha and His Horse" (Sarton), 219, 220
American Civil Liberties Union (ACLU), 76,
    177–78, 179, 189
American Journal, The (Sarton), 95
Ames, Evelyn, 356, 357
A. M. Heath Ltd., 249, 250
Among the Usual Days, see May Sarton: Among the
    Usual Days
Andersen, Hans Christian, 59
Anderson, Clinton P., 140
Andres, Henry, 206
Anger (Sarton), 298
"Answer" (Sarton), 64
"Apologia" (Sarton), 38, 371–73
Apprentice Theatre, 42
Aragon, Louis, 124, 125
Armengaud, Marie, 93–94, 95
As Does New Hampshire (Sarton), 295
"Ash Wednesday" (Eliot), 259, 262
Askew, Constance, 64
Asquith, Herbert, 13
"Astounding Air, The" (Sarton), 181
At Eighty-Two (Sarton), 318, 340
Atlantic Monthly, 93, 95
"At Muzot" (Sarton), 70, 237
"At This Time" (Sarton), 41, 374
Atwood, Margaret, 322
Auden, W. H., 44, 85, 86, 125, 137–38, 141, 366,
    367
Austria, 51–55, 88, 90
Avril, Jane, 37, 38

Bacon, Francis, 311
Bacon, Martha, 187
Baillot, Marie Juliette, *see* Huxley, Lady Juliette
Baillot, Mélanie Ortlieb (Juliette's mother), 148,
    155, 157, 182, 187, 207, 272, 282,
    283, 286, 290, 300, 301

Baker, Janet, 336
Baldensperger, Fernand, 62, 64
Baltus, Georges, 48, 216, 222, 223, 245, 246, 248
Balzac, Honoré de, 184, 185
Baranovitch family, 208
Baring, Evelyn, 125
Barnes, Djuna, 174
Barrett children, 67, 193
Barrie, Sir James Matthew, 74, 76
Barsaq, 62, 64
Bartók, Béla, 279, 280
Barton, Barbara, 321
Beatty, Doris and Gerald, 322
"Because What I Want Most is Permanence"
    (Sarton), 121
Bedford, Sybille, 357
"Belgian Horse, The" (Sarton), 217–18, 219
Belgium:
    MS in, 40, 52, 54, 55–56, 68, 77, 79–80, 148,
        152–57, 206, 207, 212–25, 244–49,
        281, 315
    in MS's writings, 129
    and World War II, 85, 86
Bell, Pearl Kazin, 357
Bell, Vanessa, 13, 99
Benét, William Rose, 186, 187, 189, 190
Benson, Theodora, 75
Berg brothers, 347
Berg Collection, MS archive in, 21, 53, 208, 293,
    324, 332, 333, 344, 346, 347, 349,
    354, 361, 362, 367
Bergner, Elisabeth, 76
Bergson, Henri, 233, 234, 269
Bernhardt, Sarah, 17
Berry, Walter Van Rensselaer, 193, 194
Bertin, Célia, 156
Best, Alan, 59, 60–61, 118, 142, 144, 157, 299,
    301
    nephew of, 322, 361
    suspicion and jealousy of, 61, 62, 180
Better Tomorrow, A (film), 127
Between Man and Man (Buber), 271, 272, 383–85
Between the Acts (Woolf), 99
Betz, Maurice, 71
Bille, Sabine Corinna, 214
"Binding the Dragon" (Sarton), 83
"Birthday on the Acropolis" (Sarton), 311
Black Lamb and Grey Falcon (West), 109, 111, 206
Blake, William, 81, 83, 311
"Bliss" (Sarton), 58
Blixen, Baroness Karen (Dinesen), 324, 326